DEFINING CRIMES

Defining Crimes

Essays on the Special Part of the Criminal Law

Edited by

R A Duff and Stuart P Green

OXFORD
UNIVERSITY PRESS

OXFORD
UNIVERSITY PRESS

Great Clarendon Street, Oxford OX2 6DP

Oxford University Press is a department of the University of Oxford.
It furthers the University's objective of excellence in research, scholarship,
and education by publishing worldwide in

Oxford New York

Auckland Cape Town Dar es Salaam Hong Kong Karachi
Kuala Lumpur Madrid Melbourne Mexico City Nairobi
New Delhi Shanghai Taipei Toronto

With offices in

Argentina Austria Brazil Chile Czech Republic France Greece
Guatemala Hungary Italy Japan Poland Portugal Singapore
South Korea Switzerland Thailand Turkey Ukraine Vietnam

Oxford is a registered trade mark of Oxford University Press
in the UK and in certain other countries

Published in the United States
by Oxford University Press Inc., New York

First published 2005

British Library Cataloguing in Publication Data

Data available

Library of Congress Cataloging in Publication Data

Defining crimes : essays on the special part of the criminal law / edited by
R. A. Duff and Stuart P. Green.
p. cm. – (Oxford monographs on criminal law and criminal justice)
Includes index.
ISBN 0–19–926922–X (hardback : alk. paper)
1. Criminal law–Great Britain. 2. Criminal law. I. Duff, Antony.
II. Green, Stuart P. III. Series.
KD7950.D44 2005
345—dc22 2005013751

Typeset by Newgen Imaging Systems (P) Ltd., Chennai, India
Printed in Great Britain
on acid-free paper by
Biddles Ltd., King's Lynn

ISBN 0–19–926922–X 978–0–19–926922–8

1 3 5 7 9 10 8 6 4 2

General Editor's Introduction

In this innovative volume, Antony Duff and Stuart Green bring together a set of new essays addressing the 'special part' of the criminal law. There has been longstanding scholarly interest in certain types of offences, such as homicide, sexual offences, and property crimes, but theoretical writings on the criminal law have tended to focus on the 'general part', that is, doctrines applicable across the range of offences—such as the fault requirements, defences to crime, complicity, and so forth. Yet as soon as such examples are mentioned, questions of definition become obvious. Is omissions liability, or inchoate criminal liability, properly a matter for the general part or the special part? Are there any general principles that should determine whether or not certain conduct should be criminalized? Are there general principles to indicate which wrongs should be left to private parties to pursue and which wrongs should properly be the business of the criminal law? These and many related questions have often been assumed to be largely a matter of political contingency, whereas the essays in this volume demonstrate that there are several points of principle on which philosophers of the criminal law can make illuminating contributions. Some of those concern the proper boundaries of the criminal law, and others concern the way in which the criminal law should classify and label the types of conduct that it penalizes. These essays explore the issues of principle in the context of a range of different crimes, and the editors' introduction explains just why the special part of the criminal law warrants the more searching examination that this volume provides.

Andrew Ashworth

Preface

Earlier versions of the papers in this collection were presented and discussed at a workshop at the Paul M Hebert Law Center, Louisiana State University, in March 2004, sponsored by the Pugh Institute for Justice. Grateful thanks are due to the Institute, to the Law Center, and to Chancellor John Costonis for their generous financial support and hospitality, to Robert Rose for indexing, and to Jennifer Moses.

Thanks are due to the contributors, not only for their papers, but also for their patience and co-operation during the protracted editorial process. Each paper received a detailed commentary at the workshop, and we are extremely grateful to the commentators for their work, which both stimulated discussion during the workshop and provided helpful critiques for the authors. For reasons of space we were not, regrettably, able to include commentaries in this volume, but we can at least list the commentators by name—John Baker, Phil Bates, Vera Bergelson, Tony Dillof, Marcelo Ferrante, Kimberly Ferzan, Kevin McMunigal, Penelope Pether, Ken Simons, and Leo Zaibert.

February 2005
RAD
SPG

Contents

Table of Cases

Table of Legislation

Australia

England and Wales

Germany

Israel

Pakistan

New Zealand

United States

International Law

List of Contributors

Markus Dirk Dubber is Professor of Law and Director of the Buffalo Criminal Law Center, State University of New York, Buffalo

R A Duff is Professor of Philosophy, University of Stirling

Claire Finkelstein is Professor of Law, University of Pennsylvania

Stuart P Green is Professor of Law, Louisiana State University

Jeremy Horder is Fellow and Tutor in Law, Worcester College, Reader in Criminal Law, University of Oxford, and a Law Commissioner for England and Wales

Kyron Huigens is Professor of Law, Benjamin N Cardozo School of Law

Douglas Husak is Professor of Philosophy, Rutgers University

A P Simester is Professor of Legal Philosophy, University of Nottingham

G R Sullivan is Professor of Law, University of Durham

Victor Tadros is Lecturer in Law, University of Edinburgh

1

Introduction: The Special Part and its Problems

R A Duff and Stuart P Green

Philosophers and theorists of criminal law have often focused on the 'general part' of the criminal law (the part containing supposedly general doctrines, rules, and definitions) rather than its 'special part' (the part containing the definitions of particular offences). One could speculate about the reasons for this. Perhaps they saw it as being the primary task of philosophy, whether analytical or normative, to explicate general principles, or to identify general features of the criminal law—principles and features that could apply not just across a particular system of criminal law, but across all legal systems. That would certainly have led them to focus on the general rather than on the special part, and to illustrate their accounts, as they have tended to do, with examples of particular offences (such as murder and rape) that one would expect to find in every legal system. Or perhaps they thought that the definitions of particular offences were too parochial, too dependent on the contingencies of particular times and places, to be a fit subject for the kind of universality to which philosophy aspires.[1]

Whatever its underlying reasons, such neglect of the special part has been unfortunate. Nothing in the criminal law is likely to be more universal than the recognition of certain core offences such as murder, rape, and theft. It is also difficult to imagine a general part that was not in some way analytically dependent on the special part. The point is not that the general part is not also foundational; even a system of criminal law that drew no explicit distinction between a 'general' and a 'special' part would have at least an implicit general part. Rather, the point is that if we theorize about the criminal law by focusing exclusively on the general part, or on only a few supposedly paradigmatic offences, we will lose sight of much of the

[1] See N Lacey, 'Contingency, Coherence and Conceptualism: Reflections on the Encounter between "Critique" and "the Philosophy of the Criminal Law" ', in R A Duff (ed.), *Philosophy and the Criminal Law: Principle and Critique* (Cambridge: Cambridge University Press, 1998), 9.

complexity and variety of criminal law that a more comprehensive account would capture.

Happily, the last decade has seen something of a renewal of philosophical interest in the special part and its distinctive problems; indeed, some of the most interesting recent work in the philosophy of criminal law has been on special part issues. This volume is intended to contribute to that renewal, and to demonstrate the philosophical indispensability of the special part to any adequate analytical or normative study of criminal law. In this Introduction, we will sketch some of the central issues that the special part raises, and connect them to the papers collected in this volume. Those issues are of two general kinds: one concerns the scope of the special part—what it should contain; the other concerns the way in which the offences that it contains should be defined and structured.

1. The Scope of the Special Part

The question of what the special part should contain raises two distinct sets of issues: the distinction between the special part and the general part, and the scope of the criminal law.

'General Part' v 'Special Part'

There is no clear or agreed upon account of the distinction between the 'general part' and the 'special part', or of just which aspects of the criminal law properly belong to each part;[2] nor do we think that much is to be gained by attempting to work out a precise, sharp distinction.

For a start, we can assume that the special part contains, at a minimum, the definitions of specific criminal offences. This, of course, leaves a host of questions about what else is contained in the special part, what the general part consists of, whether the special and general parts together exhaust the whole of the criminal law, and the extent to which the two parts are mutually exclusive.

Consider the doctrine of provocation. If one surveys a range of criminal codes, one sees that the doctrine almost invariably appears in what is

[2] See J Horder, 'The Classification of Crimes and the Special Part of the Criminal Law', in this volume, § 2; also Lacey, n. 1 above; M S Moore, *Placing Blame: A Theory of Criminal Law* (Oxford: Oxford University Press, 1998), 30–5; J Gardner, 'On the General Part of the Criminal Law', in Duff, n. 1 above, 205; V Tadros, 'The System of Criminal Law' (2002) 22 *Legal Studies* 448. A further question worth noting concerns the distinction between the general part and the broader political morality to which arguments about what doctrines or rules the general part should contain will appeal: to put the matter very crudely, legal positivists will be inclined to draw fairly tight boundaries around what is to count as part of the (general part of the) criminal law, while anti-positivists will want to include, or to make essential reference to, some critical moral principles as part of the law.

designated as the 'special part', and specifically as part of the definitions relating to homicide. The typical formulation is as follows: a homicide that would otherwise be murder is mitigated to voluntary manslaughter if the defendant acted under provocation that caused him to lose self-control and 'was enough to make a reasonable man do as he did'; or if he acted 'under the influence of extreme mental or emotional disturbance for which there [was] reasonable explanation or excuse'.[3] The question is whether the fact of such placement in criminal codes means that provocation is properly thought of as belonging to the special part.

While it is true that, in English and American criminal law, the doctrine of provocation applies only to homicide, there is a good argument that, as a conceptual matter, it should nevertheless be viewed as belonging to the general part. The fact is that there is nothing intrinsic to the doctrine of provocation that makes it applicable only to homicide: in principle, it could be applied to most, if not all, offences (even if it would require a vivid imagination to conjure up situations in which the commission of some offences could be ascribed to provocation). Under this approach, the fact that the doctrine is applied, in practice, only to homicide is not determinative of its place in the criminal law. What matters is whether the doctrine is in principle capable of general application. Thus, we might say that those criminal law principles that are theoretically capable of general application are part of the general part, and those that are not are part of the special part.

Conversely, there are some criminal law principles and concepts that are typically codified in the general part, but which might more properly be conceptualized as part of the special part. Think of attempt, which is usually defined in general terms: that is, the law defines it as an offence to attempt to commit any offence,[4] and provides general definitions of the fault and conduct elements of attempts. Now if we should have such a law, it belongs to the general part in that it embodies the doctrine, not essentially tied to any specific offence, that it is criminal to attempt what it is criminal to do. But perhaps we should not have any such general law: perhaps we should instead decide separately for each specific offence whether, how far, and by what criteria criminal liability should extend beyond the commission of the substantive mischief with which the offence is concerned.[5] In that case, the locus of the doctrine of attempt would shift from the general part to the special part.

[3] Homicide Act 1957, s. 3; Model Penal Code, s. 210.3(1)(b).

[4] Or any offence of a suitably serious or non-trivial type: so English law criminalizes only attempts to commit indictable offences (Criminal Attempts Act 1981, s. 1(4)), while the Model Penal Code criminalizes only attempted crimes, not attempted violations (ss. 1.04, 5.01(1)).

[5] See P R Glazebrook, 'Should We Have a Law of Attempted Crimes?' (1969) 85 *Law Quarterly Review* 28; for some further complications, see Horder, this volume.

Some of these controversies about the proper scope and content of the general part (about how substantive, and how general and authoritative, it should be) will concern us later, since they obviously bear on the ways in which the special part can define specific offences: before that, however, we must discuss some issues that arise more directly from the special part.

The Criminalization Question—Underlying Principles

Before we can ask how specific offences should be defined, we must have some idea of what should count as an offence at all: what kinds of 'conduct'[6] should be criminalized? Or to move back a step, what kinds of criterion, principle or value should guide decisions about criminalization? Slightly more precisely, what kinds of consideration should bear on what is logically the initial decision whether a certain kind of conduct is *in principle* criminalizable; and what kinds of consideration should then bear on the further decision that it would (or would not) be right to criminalize it all things considered.[7]

Two familiar principles, or slogans, have formed the focus of much discussion of the first (the 'in principle') question: the Harm Principle and Legal Moralism. The former takes harm and its prevention to be the primary concern of the criminal law; the latter takes wrongdoing or immorality, and its punishment or prevention, to be its primary concern.

So what should count as 'harm' for purposes of the criminal law? Is a Feinbergian analysis in terms of setbacks to interests adequate? Should we refine it so that harm requires some relatively lasting setback, or a setback to a subset of interests, such as 'welfare' interests?[8] When, if ever, is the risk of harm, rather than actual harm, sufficient to justify criminal sanctions? What room is there for ideas of harm not only to individuals, but also to groups, communities, and the state?[9] Is harm to self (as opposed to harm to others)

[6] We use here the broader term 'conduct' rather than the narrower term 'act', since it unequivocally covers omissions or failures to control what one could control. But to talk of 'conduct' still presupposes that as a matter of general doctrine or principle the law should not criminalize mere thoughts, or conditions or states of affairs that cannot be portrayed as (flowing from) conduct; see further D Husak, 'Does Criminal Liability Require an Act?', in Duff, n. 1 above, 60.

[7] See e.g. J Schonscheck, *On Criminalization: An Essay in the Philosophy of the Criminal Law* (Dordrecht: Kluwer, 1994), distinguishing three successive 'filters' through which decisions to criminalize should pass; A J Ashworth, *Principles of Criminal Law* (4th ed., Oxford: Oxford University Press, 2003), chs. 2–3, on the range of 'principles and policies' that should bear on decisions about criminalization.

[8] See J Feinberg, *Harm to Others* (New York: Oxford University Press, 1984), chs. 1–3; J Kleinig, 'Crime and the Concept of Harm' (1978) 15 *American Philosophical Quarterly* 32; A von Hirsch and N Jareborg, 'Gauging Criminal Harm: A Living-Standard Analysis' (1991) 11 *Oxford Journal of Legal Studies* 1.

[9] See M D Dubber, 'Policing Possession: The War on Crime and the End of Criminal Law' (2001) 91 *Journal of Criminal Law and Criminology* 829 (also *Victims in the War on Crime*

the kind of harm with which the criminal law is properly concerned? Are there cases in which the causing of something other than harm—such as 'offence'—will justify criminal penalties?[10]

A second set of questions concerns the substance and scope of legal moralism. Under such an approach, what kinds of immorality, or wrongdoing, should be the concern of the criminal law? Should the criminal law be concerned with moral vice, or at least with 'the grosser forms of vice';[11] or only with moral wrong*doing*, however that should be understood?[12] Must wrongs be wrongs *against* some person, or should the criminal law also be concerned with wrongs that are in some respect 'free-floating'?[13]

A third question concerns the relationship between harms and wrongs. To what extent are the two concepts intertwined? At least many wrongs clearly consist at least in part of harms, but are there harms that consist at least in part of wrongs?[14] There are certainly 'pure' harms, which involve no wrong (harms that flow purely from natural causes, for instance); but are there 'pure' wrongs, which involve no harm?

Criminalization Principles Applied

We also need to inquire into the force that such principles are to have. For example, should the principles be exclusive, holding that harm and *only* harm, or wrongdoing and *only* wrongdoing, provide adequate grounds for criminalization?[15] Or should we instead see them as specifying grounds, but

(New York: NYU Press, 2002), Part I), and 'The Possession Paradigm: The Special Part and the Police Power Model of the Criminal Process', in this volume, on what he sees as the shift from a (legal) concern with harm to individual victims to a ('policing') concern with disobedience to the state.

[10] See J Feinberg, *Offense to Others* (New York: Oxford University Press, 1985); A P Simester and A von Hirsch (eds.), *Incivilities: Regulating Offensive Behaviour* (Oxford: Hart Publishing, 2005).

[11] J F Stephen, *Liberty, Equality, Fraternity* (ed. White; Cambridge: Cambridge University Press, 1967 [1873]), 152; but note that Stephen is talking about why 'acts' are 'forbidden and subjected to punishment'. For an ambitious contemporary 'virtue theory' of criminal liability, see K Huigens, 'Virtue and Inculpation' (1995) 108 *Harvard Law Review* 1423; 'Homicide in Aretaic Terms' (2002) 6 *Buffalo Criminal Law Review* 97; and 'Is Strict Liability Rape Defensible?', in this volume.

[12] See Moore, n. 2 above, 23–45; also *Act and Crime: The Philosophy of Action and its Implications for Criminal Law* (Oxford: Oxford University Press, 1993), 46–59. But see Husak, n. 6 above, on the problems involved in trying to specify an 'act requirement'.

[13] See J Feinberg, *Harmless Wrongdoing* (New York: Oxford University Press, 1988).

[14] See Feinberg, n. 8 above, 65–70; R A Duff, 'Harms and Wrongs' (2001) 5 *Buffalo Criminal Law Review* 13.

[15] Mill's Harm Principle, in its canonical formulation, is of this kind: 'the only purpose for which power can be rightfully exercised over any member of a civilized community, against his will, is to prevent harm to others' (J S Mill, *On Liberty* (London, 1859), ch. 1, para. 9). Moore suggests an analogous version of Legal Moralism: in order to serve its proper function of doing 'retributive justice, criminal law must punish all and only those who are morally culpable in the

not necessarily the only possible grounds, for criminalization?[16] Or should we see them simply as specifying necessary conditions of criminalization—as declaring that we may not criminalize conduct that is not harmful, or that is not wrongful?[17] Can we combine them, so that the law should criminalize if, or only if, both the harm criterion and the wrongfulness criterion are satisfied?[18]

Another subject of inquiry concerns the way in which harmfulness or wrongfulness can ground criminalization. As both Mill and Feinberg present their harm principles, it is the *prevention* of harm (to others)[19] that provides a good reason for criminalization, which on its face would allow the criminalization of conduct that does not itself cause harm, or perhaps even create a risk of harm, if this would help to prevent other kinds of harm-causing conduct, or to avert harm that might otherwise ensue. It is not hard to think of relevant examples: if one thinks that failures to prevent harm should not always or necessarily be said to cause the harms that ensue,[20] then Good Samaritan statutes that criminalize failures to avert serious harm when one could do so easily and without significant cost or risk to oneself must be seen as criminalizing conduct that is not itself harmful, in order to prevent harm;[21] and certain kinds of *malum prohibitum* offence seem to criminalize conduct that is not or need not be harmful itself, in order to prevent some kind of harm.[22] Alternatively, we could read the Harm Principle as allowing the criminalization only of conduct that itself causes, or threatens to cause, harm. (A version of Legal Moralism might also figure here, as a constraint according to which we would criminalize only conduct that is wrongful in virtue of the fact that it causes or creates a risk of harm.)

doing of some morally wrongful action' (n. 2 above, 35). It turns out later (in ch. 18) that a proper concern for liberty will on balance preclude the criminalization of many kinds of morally wrongful action, including at least most of those that liberals would not want to criminalize.

16 This is how Feinberg portrays his Harm Principle, 'It is always a good reason in support of penal legislation that it would probably be effective in preventing . . . harm to persons other than the actor' (n. 8 above, 26); he later accepts a separate 'Offense Principle', according to which the prevention of 'serious offense' to others is always a good reason for criminalization, even though such offence does not constitute harm: Feinberg, n. 10 above.

17 Compare Husak's application of 'the wrongfulness constraint' (D Husak, '*Malum Prohibitum* and Retributivism', in this volume); see also his 'Limitations on Criminalization and the General Part of the Criminal Law', in S Shute and A P Simester (eds.), *Criminal Law Theory: Doctrines of the General Part* (Oxford: Oxford University Press, 2002), 13, especially at 24–8.

18 See S P Green, 'What's Wrong with Bribery', in this volume. This is how Feinberg develops his Harm Principle: the 'harm' that the criminal law can legitimately aim to prevent is *wrongful* harm; see Feinberg, n. 8 above, 31–6.

19 A further set of issues of course concerns harms to self; we cannot pursue these here.

20 One can believe this without holding, as Moore does (n. 12 above, at 267–78) that omissions are *never* causes.

21 See e.g. the statutes from Rhode Island and Wisconsin (R. I. Gen. Laws § 11–56–1; Wis. Stat. Ann. § 940.34(1)–(2), quoted in P H Robinson, *Fundamentals of Criminal Law* (2nd ed., Boston: Little Brown, 1995), 424–5; also Feinberg, n. 8 above, ch. 4.

22 See Dubber, in this volume, and R A Duff, 'Criminalizing Endangerment', in this volume.

This would be analogous to the way in which both Feinberg and Moore understand Legal Moralism: the principle is not that the prevention of wrongdoing constitutes a good reason to criminalize conduct; it is rather the wrongfulness of the conduct itself that gives us reason to criminalize it.[23]

The answer to this question can make a crucial difference to the relevant principle's scope. This is especially important in relation to the Harm Principle. At its narrowest, the Harm Principle would sanction the criminalization only of conduct that actually causes harm: but unless we count the risk of harm as itself a harm,[24] that would preclude the criminalization of conduct that creates a danger of harm without actually causing any substantive harm—which is surely too strict a constraint.[25] If we read the Harm Principle as sanctioning the criminalization of conduct that causes or might cause harm; and if we add, either as an aspect of the relevant notion of harm or as a separate constraint, that the conduct must be wrongful; then we allow for a more extensive criminal law—though how extensive it is will depend partly on what we build into the idea of 'cause'. It is clear, in any event, that our existing laws criminalize kinds of conduct that are not in themselves likely to cause harm at least in any substantive or direct way.[26]

Part of what is at stake here is the category of *mala prohibita*. There are two things that make such offences potentially problematic. The first is that they involve no obvious wrong or vice other than the arguably trivial one of disobedience to law. The second is that they typically involve less serious harms than we are used to seeing in the criminal law, or at least harms that are more causally remote from the commission of the offence. The result, under either the Harm Principle or the Principle of Legal Moralism, is likely to be doubt about the extent to which the creation of such offences can be justified.[27]

There is at least a danger that the Harm Principle will either be implausibly restrictive, if it sanctions the criminalization only of conduct that directly causes or threatens harm; or too vague (or too disturbingly

[23] See the quotation from Moore in n. 15 above; Feinberg, n. 8 above, 27. Note, however, that at the end of the fourth volume of *The Moral Limits of the Criminal Law*, Feinberg reverts to a 'prevention' mode of specification for Legal Moralism: 'it is always a good reason in support of criminalization that it prevents... harmless immoralities' (Feinberg, n. 13 above, 324) (emphasis omitted).

[24] See C Finkelstein, 'Is Risk a Harm?' (2003) 151 *University of Pennsylvania Law Review* 963, for an argument to this effect.

[25] See Duff, in this volume.

[26] See B E Harcourt, 'The Collapse of the Harm Principle' (1999) 90 *Journal of Criminal Law and Criminology* 109; see also, in this volume, Dubber, on possession offences; and Duff, on endangerment offences.

[27] Husak, in this volume, directly addresses this problem, in part through a critique of S P Green, 'Why It's a Crime to Tear the Tag Off a Mattress: Overcriminalization and the Moral Content of Regulatory Offenses' (1997) 46 *Emory Law Journal* 1533; and R A Duff, 'Crime, Prohibition, and Punishment' (2002) 19 *Journal of Applied Philosophy* 97; see also Dubber, and Duff, in this volume.

broad) if it sanctions the criminalization of any conduct that might contribute to the occurrence of harm, or whose criminalization would help prevent harm. The question then is whether we can find either a more precise formulation of the principle (one, for instance, that says more about the kind, or the degree, or the proximity, of the harm that must be caused or risked), or suitable further principles that would control its application, to give it a plausible substantive role in decisions about criminalization.

There is a similar problem of apparent over-breadth for Legal Moralism: is it plausible to suggest that we should, in principle, criminalize every kind of 'morally wrongful action', so that the criminal law can punish 'all . . . those who are morally culpable in the doing of such actions'?[28] Suppose that I break an important promise, or tell a serious lie, to a friend: in such a case, I would have breached a duty to keep promises, or to tell the truth, or to maintain my loyalties. My action would clearly wrong my friend, perhaps seriously. We can even assume that my action would cause my friend some serious harm (say, serious emotional injury). Nevertheless, even if the wrongs and the harms suffered by my friend were more serious than many of those that are regularly criminalized, we would still be unlikely to recommend criminalization.

The idea that crimes involve 'public' wrongs seems relevant here, if we can make substantive and plausible sense of it—not the idea that once conduct has been criminalized, it becomes a 'public' wrong in that it can be dealt with by a public system of criminal justice, but the idea that what justifies criminalizing it is that it constitutes a 'public' rather than a merely 'private' wrong: my betrayal of my friend, seriously and harmfully wrong though it is, is still a private matter between me and her (and perhaps other friends of hers and mine). But we would need then to ask what 'public' means in this context. In particular, does a wrong count as 'public' only if and because it wrongs or harms 'the public', as distinct from identifiable individuals (in which case the worry is that the criminal wrongfulness of, e.g., a rapist's action is detached from its moral wrongfulness as an attack on a particular victim)? Or should we rather say that a wrong counts as 'public' if it is of a kind that properly concerns 'the public', the community as a whole (in the case of criminal law, the relevant community is the polity), rather than just those directly affected by it (in which case it begins to look as if the 'public' character of the wrong is an implication, rather than a ground, of its criminalization)?[29]

The idea of crime as a public wrong does at least serve to focus our attention on a central issue about criminalization: when, and why, we should look to the criminal law rather than, or in addition, to civil law or

[28] Moore, n. 2 above, 35; but see n. 15 above.

[29] See further S E Marshall and R A Duff, 'Criminalization and Sharing Wrongs' (1998) 11 *Canadian Journal of Law and Jurisprudence* 7.

other non-criminal modes of regulation, to deal with conduct that does properly concern the law or the polity. Many matters, including some kinds of wrong and some kinds of harm, are of course properly left as purely private matters, to be sorted out informally by those directly involved; perhaps the first decision on the path to criminalization is then that a particular type of conduct is not in that sense a *purely* private matter. But we must then decide whether it is a matter for civil law (the key features of which are that the case is brought and controlled by a plaintiff, not by the polity, and that if the case goes against the defendant the outcome will be an award of damages, or a requirement to fulfil his commitments, rather than punishment as such); or for some non-criminal mode of regulation that might use 'penalties' to try to secure conformity to the regulations;[30] or for the criminal law.

Criminal convictions condemn the convicted person. Criminal punishments are not merely neutral techniques of prevention or deterrence; they express condemnation or censure.[31] We can plausibly argue, therefore, that the idea of wrongdoing, and the particular conception of 'public' involved in the idea of crime as a public wrong, must be central to a decision that criminalization is an appropriate way forward. To put it crudely and over-simply, civil law and non-criminal modes of regulation are primarily concerned with the prevention of harm and with compensation, as well as with spreading the costs of such harms and prevention, whereas criminal law is concerned with the definition and condemnation of wrongs. The truth in 'Legal Moralism' is thus that the wrongfulness of the conduct that is to be criminalized is crucial to the justification of its criminalization: but legal moralists go astray if they claim that we have reason to criminalize any and every kind of wrongdoing, since only 'public' wrongs are even in principle apt for criminalization. The task then is to make clearer sense of the idea of a public wrong, and to try to determine what else must be true of a public wrong if it is to be in principle apt for criminalization. Must it, for instance, either cause harm or be in some other suitable way related to the prospect of harm—and if so, what kinds of harm are relevant? In different ways, the

[30] On 'penalties' as distinct from 'punishments', and as lacking the condemnatory meaning of punishment, see J Feinberg, 'The Expressive Function of Punishment', in his *Doing and Deserving* (Princeton, N J: Princeton University Press, 1970), 95. On non-criminal regulation, see, e.g., D M Kahan, 'Gentle Nudges vs. Hard Shoves: Solving the Sticky Norms Problem' (2000) 67 *University of Chicago Law Review* 607, 609. This possibility is especially germane to the regulation of corporate activities: see D Nelken, 'White-Collar Crime', in M Maguire et al. (eds.), *Oxford Handbook of Criminology* (2nd ed., Oxford: Oxford University Press, 1997), 891, at 911–21, and further references cited there.

[31] One can see condemnation or censure as in this way a defining feature of criminal law without taking the communication of that censure to be central to the justifying purpose of criminal law or punishment, as some theorists do (see, e.g., A von Hirsch, Censure and Sanctions, Oxford: Oxford University Press, 1993; R A Duff, *Punishment, Communication, and Community* (New York: Oxford University Press, 2001)): see also Feinberg, n. 30 above.

papers in this volume by Dubber, Duff, Green, Husak, and Simester and Sullivan all contribute to this question. Dubber, Duff, and Husak discuss relatively general issues about the scope of the criminal law in relation, for instance, to offences of possession and endangerment, and to the large category of '*mala prohibita*'. Green, and Simester and Sullivan, discuss the kinds of wrong that are involved in particular kinds of offence (bribery; theft and other property offences), in part to show why they are kinds of wrong that properly count as 'public', i.e. as in principle apt for criminalization.

We must turn now from questions about the scope of the special part to questions about the way in which its content, its specific offence definitions, should be structured.

2. Defining and Classifying Offences

There are two related general questions about the way in which the special part should define particular offences. One concerns the style or mode of offence definition, and of classification; the other concerns the extent to which substantive general principles (which figure as doctrines of the general part) can or should govern the definitions of particular offences.

Modes of Offence Definition I—The Descriptivist Approach

We can distinguish two quite different approaches to offence definition. While it is unlikely that a system of criminal law could embody either type in its ideal form, the contrast between them brings out some important questions about the proper aims of the criminal law, and about the tones or voice in which it should address the citizens.

One ideal type we can call descriptivism. The guiding thought here is that the criminal law, insofar as it is addressed to citizens, must aim to lay down clear 'rules of conduct' for them that will tell them precisely what they must or must not do, on pain of punishment if they break the rules. To achieve this combination of clarity and certainty in the rules of conduct,[32] the rules should, as far as is possible, specify the proscribed or prescribed types of conduct in purely descriptive terms, to minimize the extent to which citizens have to call upon their own normative standards and understandings to interpret and apply the law. For we cannot assume that citizens will share enough in the way of values and normative understandings to ensure

[32] Clarity and certainty are two often touted advantages of a codified criminal law, and two obvious desiderata for the criminal law (the third being consistency): see, e.g., Law Commission No 143, *Codification of the Criminal Law* (London: HMSO, 1985), paras. 1.3–9. We still need to ask, however, what should constitute clarity and certainty—and whether there are other, possibly conflicting, desiderata.

consistency in their interpretations of the law, or certainty and clarity in the predictions that they will want to make about the conduct of others or about the responses of the courts; nor can we assume that they will have the kinds of moral commitment that would securely lead them to refrain from wrongdoing.

Something like this ideal was clearly held by many advocates of the Model Penal Code,[33] and is implicit in Paul Robinson's draft Code of Conduct.[34] It rests on (or is made more plausible if we accept) both a distinction between 'facts' and 'values', and a certain kind of separation between law and morality.

As for facts and values, this ideal would at least be rendered more plausible if we could intelligibly aspire to a complete and purely descriptive specification of the content of moral norms: if, that is, any moral norm could in principle be analysed down into a purely descriptive specification of a type of conduct, and a normative operator ('right' or 'wrong', 'ought' or 'ought not') that is attached to that specification.[35] We could then believe that the criminal law is grounded in, and seeks to apply to citizens' conduct, moral norms, while also arguing that it should provide purely descriptive specifications of proscribed and prescribed conduct: for those specifications could aim to reproduce the content of the moral norms that the criminal law embodies.[36]

As for law and morality, the suggestion is not that the criminal law is not or need not be grounded in morality, or should not respect at least a negative version of Legal Moralism (i.e. a principle that only wrongful conduct should be criminalized); it is, rather, that the criminal law should eschew moral language and moral concepts in its offence definitions—in order to serve the aims of clarity and certainty. It should be a criminal law whose content is intelligible to, and whose rules are applicable by, those with

[33] For a good, because extreme, example, see R L Gainer, 'The Culpability Provisions of the Model Penal Code' (1988) 19 *Rutgers Law Journal* 575.

[34] P H Robinson, *Structure and Function in Criminal Law* (Oxford: Oxford University Press, 1997); his Draft Code of Criminal Conduct is at 211–20. We cannot here discuss the separation that Robinson and others urge between a Code of Conduct addressed to the citizens, to tell them what they must or must not do, and a Code of Adjudication that is addressed to the courts, telling them how to deal with breaches of the Code of Conduct: see M Dan-Cohen, 'Decision Rules and Conduct Rules: On Acoustic Separation in Criminal Law' (1984) 97 *Harvard Law Review* 625, on which see R Singer, 'On Classism and Dissonance in the Criminal Law: A Reply to Professor Dan-Cohen' (1986) 77 *Journal of Criminal Law and Criminology* 69. Although Robinson favours separating the two codes, he does not favour the kind of 'acoustic separation' that Dan-Cohen ties to such a separation.

[35] On the fact/value distinction in moral philosophy, see R Crisp, 'Fact/Value Distinction', in E Craig (ed.), *Routledge Encyclopedia of Philosophy* (London: Routledge, 1998); at http://www.rep.routledge.com/article/L130; one of the most influential modern versions is R M Hare, *The Language of Morals* (Oxford: Oxford University Press, 1952).

[36] For a sophisticated argument that a descriptive criminal law can still track judgements of moral blameworthiness, see A C Michaels, '"Rationales" of Criminal Law Then and Now: For a Judgmental Descriptivism' (2000) 100 *Columbia Law Review* 54.

diverse or with no moral values of their own; and, we might add, it must be such as to give even an amoral person with neither moral concern nor moral understanding motivating reason to obey the law (namely, the fear of punishment).[37]

Such an ideal type fits happily, if not inevitably, with a Feinbergian view of the structure of criminal wrongdoing. On Feinberg's account of the Harm Principle and of the idea of harm as it figures in that principle, the idea of a 'harmed condition' is conceptually 'fundamental': we 'can hope to analyze the idea of harm (harmed condition) without mentioning' how such harm was caused.[38] It follows that we can hope to identify the kinds of harm that properly concern the criminal law, qua harms, without reference to any notion of wrong or of wrongdoing, since such reference would involve 'mentioning causally contributory actions'. Of course, to determine which harms should concern the law, we must bring in judgements of wrongfulness, since only those that are caused by wrongful actions should be criminal;[39] but our initial identification of the harm, as a 'harmed condition', requires no such judgements. In defining crimes, we might thus take as our ideal paradigm a definition that specifies the harm (the harmed condition) in virtue of its causal contribution to which the conduct that is to be criminalized is wrongful, and then defines as criminal any conduct that makes a suitable causal contribution to the occurrence of that harm. Robinson's Code of Conduct thus replaces the often complex sets of offences of homicide and wounding that we find in many legal systems with one simple clause: 'You may not cause bodily injury or death to another person.'[40]

We would of course need to add an account of what could justify causing such harm, which we could most simply do by providing a general account of justifications for all offences—as Robinson does in ss. 52–67 of the Code of Conduct. We might also want to criminalize attempts to cause such harm, or conduct that creates a serious risk of such harm, which we could again do by making general provision for such inchoate or secondary liability—as Robinson does in ss. 49–51 of his Code of Conduct.[41] And we would need to add specifications of the fault required for liability, as well as of any

[37] Cf. O W Holmes, 'The Path of the Law' (1897) 10 *Harvard Law Review* 457, at 459: 'If you want to know the law and nothing else, you must look at it as a bad man, who cares only for the material consequences which such knowledge enables him to predict, not as a good one, who finds his reasons for conduct, whether inside the law or outside of it, in the vaguer sanctions of conscience.'

[38] Feinberg, n. 8 above, 31.

[39] See n. 17 above.

[40] Robinson, n. 34 above, 213 (s. 3 of the Code of Conduct); see also the English draft Offences Against the Person Bill, ss. 1–2 (*Reforming the Offences Against the Person Act 1861* (London: Home Office, 1998).

[41] Note, however, that s. 51 retreats from a pure descriptivism, by prohibiting the creation of 'a *substantial and unjustified* risk of causing a result made criminal by this Code' (emphasis added).

excuses that can be claimed—though for Robinson these are matters for the courts, and thus for the Code of Adjudication rather than for the Code of Conduct.

We should note the tones in which, on this account, the criminal law addresses citizens. It speaks to them in the language of prescriptions and prohibitions, of what they 'may' or 'may not' do (or, in the case of omission crimes, what they 'must' do); it defines behavioural rules that they are to obey. Nothing within the law expressly indicates *why* they should obey it, and given its descriptive character it would present itself in the same tones whether what it prohibited was conduct that was also, extra-legally, morally wrong, or conduct that was extra- or pre-legally neutral. If we ask why we should obey its prohibitions or prescriptions (bearing in mind that to obey a prohibition is to do more than act in a way that conforms to it; it involves acting *because* that is how I am ordered to act), the answer will then need to refer either to the law's authority or to its power: obey because it is the law, or obey because otherwise you will be punished. Under the kind of descriptive ideal sketched here, the law, we could say, speaks to citizens in the voice of the sovereign other: sovereign, in that it claims the power or authority to exact obedience from them; other, in that it does not appeal to values or goals that they supposedly share with each other or with the sovereign, but only of what *it* requires *them* to do.

Modes of Offence Definition II—The Moralistic Approach

The other ideal type of offence definition looks not for descriptive purity, but for moral adequacy. It aims not merely to make clear what conduct is prohibited or permitted, but to declare to citizens what count as public wrongs that require a public condemnatory response; not to detach the criminal law's offence definitions from the moral norms that must underpin them, but precisely to give those moral norms, insofar as they should be given force by the criminal law as public norms, adequate expression in the law. Advocates of this type of offence definition do of course take such desiderata as clarity, certainty, and consistency seriously: but they will insist that *what* must be made clear is the wrong that underpins each offence, and that what can count as clarity, certainty, and consistency in such moral matters is not the same as what counts as clarity, certainty, and consistency in factual matters.

On this view, we should not try to separate 'fact' from 'value', or the criminal law from morality, in the ways that the descriptivist view tries to do. Advocates of such a view are likely to deny that we can separate fact from value in that way: not that *no* separation is possible—we could of course produce purely descriptive specifications of situations, and of conduct at least insofar as it consists in bodily movements and their causal effects (it would be harder, if not impossible, to describe recognizable *actions*); but that we cannot analyse moral norms out into a purely descriptive specification of conduct, to which the operator 'right' or 'wrong' can then be added, since no such descriptive specification could capture the content of the norm. Rather, the articulation of moral norms requires an extensive set of 'thick' ethical concepts—concepts that 'seem to express a union of fact and value',[42] since they describe the world, including human actions, in terms of substantive and specific ethical values. Criminal law also, on this view, needs a stock of 'thick' concepts, which will at least be closely related, if not identical, to thick extra-legal ethical concepts: for that is how it can characterize criminal wrongs *as* wrongs. On this view, we should therefore look for an ethically rich criminal law, which speaks to the citizens not of descriptively specified types of conduct that they must or must not engage in, but of wrongs that they must not commit—or more precisely, insofar as the wrongs of which it speaks are already recognizable pre-legally as wrongs, of wrongs that they will be called to answer and to be punished for if they do commit them.

From this point of view it is not necessarily a defect in the special part if, for instance, it uses the concept of dishonesty in defining theft and cognate offences;[43] or if it defines one kind of murder as homicide that 'is committed recklessly under circumstances manifesting extreme indifference to the value of human life'.[44] Indeed, reliance on such ethical concepts would be regarded as a strength. The criminal law should define a category of public wrongs in terms that enable the citizens to recognize them as wrongs, which means that it must define them in richly normative terms that are at least closely connected to those that structure the citizens' pre- or extra-legal moral thought.

Such an approach must of course presuppose that there exists a sufficiently rich, widely shared and understood set of norms and values outside the law on which it can draw, and by reference to which citizens can interpret and apply the law; and that presupposition has come under familiar kinds of attack from various quarters.[45] From this point of view,

[42] B Williams, *Ethics and the Limits of Philosophy* (London: Fontana, 1985), 129; see ch. 8 more generally on thick ethical concepts and their significance.

[43] Theft Act 1968, s. 1. But see A P Simester and G R Sullivan, 'On the Nature and Rationale of Property Offences', in this volume, at nn. 17–23.

[44] Model Penal Code s. 210.2(1)(b); see also the Scots law notion of 'wicked recklessness' (G H Gordon, *The Criminal Law of Scotland*, 3rd ed. (M G A Christie, vol. II Edinburgh: W Green, 2001), 295–310; California Penal Code § 188 (under the murder statute, a killer acts with implied malice 'when the circumstances attending the killing show an abandoned and malignant heart'). See also K Huigens, 'Homicide in Aretaic Terms' (2002) 6 *Buffalo Criminal Law Review* 9. The idea of 'extreme indifference' or 'wicked recklessness' also clearly bears on the doctrine of felony murder, discussed by Claire Finkelstein in 'Merger and Felony Murder', in this volume.

[45] For very different kinds of attack along these lines, see, e.g., A MacIntyre, *After Virtue* (2nd ed., London: Duckworth, 1985); A W Norrie, *Crime, Reason and History*

however, the absence of a sufficient set of shared values (a sharing that need involve neither universality nor identity, and that may consist in shared procedural norms as well as or in partial place of shared substantive norms of conduct) marks the absence of the possibility of a legitimate or just system of criminal law—as something distinct from the exercise of bare power.

This conception of offence definition can be most plausibly interpreted as embodying a quite different conception of the relationship between the law and the citizens, and of the tones in which the law should address us. The law now claims to speak as our law, as the common law of the polity that embodies our values as citizens; not in the voice of the sovereign other, but in what claims to be our collective voice declaring our own values to ourselves.[46]

To follow this approach through would involve attending not just to the range of harms caused by various forms of criminal conduct, but also to the wrongs that they involve. It would require us to analyse and classify existing crimes in terms that, and seek modes of definition that, as far as is possible and consistent with other norms of legislation, capture the relevant wrongs. One crucial issue will be how far the law should seek to discriminate different wrongs, since whatever force there is to the principle of fair labelling,[47] and to the demand that matters relevant to sentencing should be proved at the trial, there must clearly be limits to how fine-grained our offence definitions should be.

A number of recent works in criminal law theory exemplify versions of this approach,[48] as do several of the papers in this volume. For example, Victor Tadros, in his piece, argues that, although some of the harms associated with domestic abuse may be similar to the harms associated with other assault-type crimes, a fuller account would recognize the distinctive, even unique, effects such abuse has on its victims' sense of self-worth. Antony Duff rests a crucial distinction between attacks and endangerments on a distinction between the kinds of wrongs that such acts, respectively,

(London: Weidenfeld & Nicolson, 1993); H Bianchi, *Justice as Sanctuary: Toward a New System of Crime Control* (Bloomington: Indiana University Press, 1994); J Waldron, *Law and Disagreement* (Oxford: Oxford University Press, 1999).

[46] See further Duff, n. 31 above, 56–68. Dubber's critical discussion of the 'Police Power Model' of law, in this volume, is also clearly relevant here.

[47] See Ashworth, n. 7 above, 89–92.

[48] See, e.g., S Shute and J Horder, 'Thieving and Deceiving: What is the Difference?' (1993) 56 *Modern Law Review* 548; J Gardner, 'Rationality and the Rule of Law in Offences Against the Person' (1994) 53 *Cambridge Law Journal* 502; J Horder, 'Rethinking Non-Fatal Offences against the Person' (1994) 14 *Oxford Journal of Legal Studies* 335; J Gardner and S Shute, 'The Wrongness of Rape', in J Horder (ed.), *Oxford Essays in Jurisprudence* (4th series; Oxford: Oxford University Press, 2000), 193; A L Bogg and J Stanton-Ife, 'Protecting the Vulnerable: Legality, Harm and Theft' (2003) 23 *Legal Studies* 402; S P Green, 'Cheating' (2004) 23 *Law and Philosophy* 137; S P Green, 'Lying, Misleading, and Falsely Denying: How Moral Concepts Inform the Law of Perjury, Fraud, and False Statements' (2001) 53 *Hastings Law Journal* 137.

entail—that attacks involve being guided by wrong reasons, whereas endangerments involve not being guided by right reasons. Jeremy Horder draws a similar distinction between crimes in which the offender is 'active', and those in which the offender is 'passive', in relation to the relevant harm, and uses it to reconceptualize the unclear and controversial distinction between crimes of 'specific' and crimes of 'general' intent. Andrew Simester and Bob Sullivan discuss both the wrong of theft (and why it should be a matter for the criminal rather than the civil law), and the distinctive wrongs involved in other types of property offence. Stuart Green offers an analysis of the distinctive wrongs involved in offences of bribery, in terms of the idea of a duty of loyalty that is breached.

Another issue concerns the question whether new or newly significant forms of criminal activity should be dealt with through already existing legal prohibitions, or whether instead new offences should be created to deal with the problem. For Tadros again, speaking in the context of domestic abuse, there is an important symbolic role that creation of a new offence might play, one which marks out the failure of an earlier legal regime to recognize such behaviour as significantly wrong. On the other hand, by bypassing already existing offences to deal with new problems, we risk losing out on the range of associations that such offences will have previously engendered.

A final issue concerns so-called *mala prohibita*, which seem to involve the creation of purely legal wrongs rather than the definition of pre-existing moral wrongs: how can these be explained and justified on this approach? Douglas Husak's paper directly tackles this question: he argues that if we accept the 'wrongfulness constraint', that only morally wrongful conduct should be criminal, it becomes extremely difficult to justify the creation of *mala prohibita*.

Classifying Crimes

Whatever mode of offence definition we use, we must deal with two classificatory issues. First, as we saw in the previous two sections, we are engaging in a form of classification when we decide what kinds of conduct shall constitute a given offence.[49] Secondly, we engage in another sort of classification when we decide how various groups of offences should be categorized. For example, we might want to know whether a particular offence is a felony or misdemeanour, an offence against the person or one against property, or an inchoate offence or a consummated one. Such matters of classification can have important consequences in relation to

[49] The task here is to identify the 'elements' that go to constitute one or another offence. For example, we must decide whether 'murder' should include only intentional killings or also accidental deaths caused during the commission of certain enumerated felonies or in the course of highly dangerous, 'implied malice' kinds of behaviour. The question of felony murder is addressed by Finkelstein, in this volume.

sentencing, in connection with evidentiary or jurisdictional rulings, in determining the applicability of certain defences, and elsewhere.[50]

Traditionally, our codes have classified crimes in terms of the harms they cause or the kinds of victims they affect, as in the case of Model Penal Code classifications such as 'offences involving danger to the person', 'offences against the family', and so forth.[51] But we can also imagine circumstances in which we might consider the possibility of classifying offences in terms of, say, the kinds of wrongfulness they entail (e.g. grouping together offences that require some form of deception), or the kinds of mens rea they require or do not require (e.g. grouping together all of the strict liability offences). Alternatively, we might also wish to distinguish offences within each group by reference either to the precise sub-category of harm involved (so within the group of offences involving bodily injury we will distinguish homicide from wounding, and perhaps serious from less serious types of wounding), or to the causal contribution the conduct makes to the occurrence of the relevant harm (so we will distinguish actually and directly causing harm from creating an unconsummated risk of it, and from other modes of facilitation or encouragement).

General Principles and Particular Wrongs

On some conceptions of the general part, it should contain doctrines, rules, and principles that quite tightly constrain the special part's offence definitions. This is particularly true of what Gardner labels as the 'supervisory' and the 'definitional' general part. The supervisory general part 'contains guiding principles for the creation, interpretation, and application of new criminal laws', while the definitional general part 'specif[ies] how crimes (and defences to crime) are to be defined. [It] provide[s] the detailed linguistic and conceptual apparatus of the law.'[52] A key question about both aspects of the general part concerns their scope: how rich, and how general, should they be?

Consider, for instance, just a few examples drawn from two familiar actual or proposed criminal codes, the Model Penal Code and the English Law Commission's Draft Code, which display a relatively ambitious conception of the general part's scope and authority. The Model Penal Code includes a qualified version of the act requirement (which we can express, in

[50] In this volume, for example, Huigens explores the consequences of categorizing statutory rape as a strict liability crime; and Simester and Sullivan address the significance of the category of 'property' offences. See also S P Green, 'Prototype Theory and the Classification of Offenses in a Revised Model Penal Code: A General Approach to the Special Part' (2000) 4 *Buffalo Criminal Law Review* 301; S P Green, 'Deceit and the Classification of Crimes: Federal Rule of Evidence 609(a)(2) and the Origins of *Crimen Falsi*' (2000) 90 *Journal of Criminal Law & Criminology* 1087.

[51] See, e.g., Model Penal Code, Part II.

[52] Gardner, n. 2 above, 208.

its most general form, by the slogan *mens non facit reum nisi actus sit reus*): 'A person is not guilty of an offence unless his liability is based on conduct that includes a voluntary act or the omission to perform an act of which he is physically capable'.[53] The English Draft Code is more cautious:

> For the purposes of an offence which consists wholly or in part of an omission, state of affairs or occurrence, references in this Act to an 'act' shall, where the context permits, be read as including references to the omission, state of affairs or occurrence by reason of which a person may be guilty of the offence.[54]

The English clause is, as the Law Commission makes clear, 'an interpretation clause': it does not constrain the substantive content of the law or the possible bases of liability, but simply requires users of the Code to interpret 'act' in these broad, not to say all-embracing, terms.[55] By contrast, the Model Penal Code provision does seem to constrain the possible content of the law, the possible bases of liability, by requiring liability to be based on a 'voluntary act' or 'omission'. Such a provision is of course controversial, both as to its meaning and as to its plausibility: it is not clear either what should count as an 'act', or whether such a requirement can be plausibly interpreted in a way that renders it non-vacuous.[56] The question it raises for our purposes is whether the special part's definitions of specific offences should be constrained by a general requirement, or even a strong presumption, that every offence should be defined to include a 'voluntary act' or 'omission'. Markus Dubber's paper in this volume clearly bears on this question, since the expansion of 'possession' offences, and the expansive meaning given to the idea of 'possession', put great pressure on any substantial act requirement; and insofar as we find that expansion worrying, we can see one significant merit to an extensive general part whose substantive or 'supervisory' doctrines constrain the special part.

The 'act requirement' is primarily a supervisory doctrine, though it also has a definitional element insofar as the general part tries to define what should count as a 'voluntary act'.[57] By contrast, the definitions of fault elements that both our sample codes provide are, initially, no more than definitional rules; but they can easily become substantive supervisory doctrines.

Each code defines a collection of fault terms: 'purposely', 'knowingly', 'recklessly', and 'negligently' in s. 2.02(2) of the Model Penal Code; 'knowingly', 'intentionally', 'recklessly' in s. 18 of the English Draft Code.[58]

[53] Model Penal Code s. 2.01(1).

[54] Law Commission No 177, *A Criminal Code for England and Wales* (London: HMSO, 1989), vol. 1, Draft Criminal Code Bill, s. 16.

[55] Law Commission, n. 54 above, vol. 2, para. 7.7.

[56] See Husak, n. 6 above; A P Simester, 'On the So-called Requirement for Voluntary Action' (1998) 1 *Buffalo Criminal Law Review* 403.

[57] See Model Penal Code, s. 2.01(2).

[58] An earlier Draft Code had defined an additional four terms—'purposely', 'heedlessly', 'negligently', and 'carelessly' (Law Commission No. 143, n. 32 above, Draft Criminal Code,

Such definitions already exert a modest constraint on the special part insofar as they require these terms to carry the specified meanings whenever they are used: legislators or common law interpreters cannot give 'intentionally' or 'recklessly' a different meaning in the context of different offences. (This might reflect a misguided belief that non-ambiguous terms must always admit of such general definitions, misguided because it ignores the Wittgensteinian idea of family resemblances; or a concern that to allow courts or legislators to give different contents to the terms in different contexts would be confusing.) They exert a more significant constraint if it is also declared that one of these types of fault is a universally or presumptively necessary condition of liability, so that each offence must be defined (explicitly or implicitly) as requiring at least that kind and degree of fault;[59] and they exert even more significant constraints if it is also declared or assumed that the fault element of each offence must be specified in terms of these concepts as thus defined.

Provisions of this kind raise a further set of questions about the special part, and about the extent to which its offence definitions should conform to the kind of general structure that the more ambitious doctrines discussed in the previous paragraph require. We might at least strongly suspect that the 'descriptivist' approach to offence definition sketched earlier in this section would favour a limited set of (descriptively defined) fault concepts, in terms of which the fault element of each offence would be specified; while the wrong-based approach would reject such constraints, and allow room for a richer set of thick fault concepts, many of which might be peculiar to particular offences.

The papers in this volume that most directly bear on these questions are Jeremy Horder's, Kyron Huigens's, and Claire Finkelstein's. Horder argues that while a strictly 'subjectivist' approach to the criminal law would require even voluntary intoxication to be in principle relevant as evidence in support of a denial of mens rea for any offence that requires intention, knowledge or recklessness, attention to the distinction that he draws between crimes of activity and crimes of passivity in relation to the relevant harm enables us to make better sense of the doctrine that voluntary intoxication cannot support a denial of mens rea for offences of 'general' or 'basic' intent. Huigens goes even further in this direction, arguing that a defendant accused of rape can be said to be at 'fault' in the way that the criminal law requires even

s. 22). In the end, however, the Commission found that 'none of them has proved to be required for the definitions of offences proposed for inclusion in the Code' at that stage (Law Commission No 177, n. 54 above, vol. 2, para. 8.7).

[59] See Model Penal Code s. 2.02, requiring at least negligence as the minimal culpability for any offence, and recklessness when the offence definition does not specify a culpability requirement (s. 2.05 makes some very limited provision for absolute liability); English Draft Code s. 22, specifying recklessness as the minimally required fault element for all offences (and as to each element of the offence), but with the all-purpose get-out clause 'unless otherwise provided'.

if he neither knows nor suspects that the victim does not consent, given the existence of independent rape law 'elements' (as he terms them) such as minority, non-consent, threat, force, and victim incapacity. Finally, Finkelstein addresses the seeming illogic and ad hoc-ness of the traditional merger rule of the felony-murder doctrine, under which liability is barred where the predicate felony is not independent of the homicide. The key to making sense of such a rule is to think of the predicate felony as constituting a wrongdoing separate and distinct from the wrongdoing associated with the killing itself—a situation that occurs where, she says, following the principles of action theory, the act in virtue of which the defendant satisfies the elements of the putative predicate felony cannot properly be redescribed in terms of the resulting death.

2

The Classification of Crimes and the Special Part of the Criminal Law

Jeremy Horder*

1. Mental States and 'Activity' Conditions: A Summary of the Argument

Classification of diverse, but related, phenomena is intended to advance knowledge and is in some sense a basic intellectual tool, or mode, of human thought. In the criminal law, sound classification may act (*inter alia*) as a heuristic guide to what is, morally speaking, at stake in the crimes classified in a given way. Crimes fall to be classified in different ways, ways that will give salience to different kinds of moral distinction between them.[1] Accordingly, the classification may be morally contentious. For example, burglary was formerly classified exclusively as a property crime in English law.[2] This was simply because the crime always commences with the proprietary wrong of 'entry as a trespasser'. This classification is, however, in a way just a matter of convenience, a way of bringing all instances of burglary under one statutory umbrella. There is at least as strong a moral case, based on a 'fair labelling' argument,[3] for classifying the crime according to the criminal intention with which a defendant enters as a trespasser; and, at least in one instance, entry as a trespasser with intent to commit a sexual offence, that is how the crime is now classified.[4] The classification with which I will be concerned here is the well-known and well-established

* I am especially grateful for the painstaking work done on previous drafts of this paper by Antony Duff and Andrew Simester, and for the thought-provoking comments of Ken Simons, which have (I hope) saved me from some embarrassing errors.

[1] *Mala prohibita* as against *mala in se*, property crimes as against violent offences, inchoate crimes as against completed crimes; and so forth.

[2] Theft Act (England and Wales) 1968, s. 9.

[3] Ashworth's term (originally he used the term 'representative labelling', which is in some ways more accurate): see Andrew Ashworth, 'The Elasticity of *Mens Rea*', in Colin Tapper (ed.), *Crime, Proof and Punishment* (London: Butterworths, 1981), 45.

[4] Sexual Offences Act 2003, s. 63.

classification of crimes as either ones of 'general' (or basic) intent, or ones of 'specific' intent.

In law, the main function of this distinction is to provide the theoretical basis for differentiating between crimes—those of specific intent—where evidence of voluntary intoxication is (if relevant) admissible to show that a defendant lacked the mental element, and crimes—those of general, or basic, intent—where such evidence is (even if relevant) inadmissible for this purpose.[5] As we will see (and as the phraseology implies), the general–specific intent distinction has traditionally been understood as a distinction between kinds of mental element. Broadly speaking, recklessness or negligence (and cognate terms) are cast as the basic or general forms of 'intent', whereas intention alone is what is meant by 'specific intent'.[6] In essence, my claim will be that whilst this understanding has proved workable enough, it has theoretical flaws and may hence lead to confusion in practice. It needs to be remodelled in a more sophisticated way. The distinction needs to be recast as a distinction between crimes that hinges primarily on whether the wrong underlying the crime presupposes that the defendant is 'active', or is 'passive', in producing the prohibited outcome.

First, there are crimes whose sole or, at least, central manifestation is when the defendant succeeds in bringing about the relevant result as he or she intends (or tries to do this). In such crimes, the success (or the attempt to be successful) constitutes the underlying wrong, Secondly, there are crimes whose focal case is one in which, whether in the course of positive acts or through inactivity, the defendant *fails* (more or less culpably) *to prevent* a relevant result he or she was duty bound to avoid. Here, the simple bringing about of that result, in these circumstances, amounts to the commission of the underlying wrong. When the distinction is recast in this way, it is primarily with respect to the role that the defendant's (in)activity plays in constituting or bringing about the wrong that crimes are to be classified, in order to determine (assuming one is set to do this) whether evidence of voluntary intoxication should be admissible to deny the mental element.

[5] See U.S. Model Penal Code, Art 2, s. 2.08(2); Crimes Act (NSW) 1900, s. 428D; Australian Criminal Code Act 1995, s. 8.2(2); Pakistan Criminal Code 1860, s. 86. On the attempts to dispense with the distinction in common law jurisdictions, see Stephen Gough, 'Surviving Without *Majewski*?' [2000] *Crim LR* 719. The distinction may also (a closely related point) mark the distinction between crimes—those of specific intent—where an honest mistake of fact as to the absence of a definitional element of the crime need not be reasonable, and crimes—those of general intent—in which such a mistake must be both honest and reasonable, if it is to acquit: *People v Mayberry* 542 P 2d 1337 (Cal. 1975); Ind. Code Ann. 35-41-3-7 (West 1998), discussed in Joshua Dressler, *Understanding Criminal Law* (3rd ed., New York: Lexis, 2001), at 155–6.

[6] Burglary, for example, is a crime of 'specific intent', in so far as it requires that the defendant enter as a trespasser *with the (specific) intention of* committing a particular crime or range of crimes. So, evidence of voluntary intoxication is admissible to raise a doubt whether, when the defendant knowingly entered as a trespasser, he or she had the specified criminal intent.

Classification would no longer hinge on the nature of the mental element, as such, in those crimes, in the way that the basic-specific intent distinction makes it hinge.

The nature of the change that I have in mind is set out in § 4 and § 5, where a fourfold distinction is drawn between, on the one hand, (a) crimes of 'specific' intent, (b) crimes of 'specific' *mens rea*, and (c) crimes of 'ulterior' intent, the three kinds that exemplify or are parasitic upon the 'trying' account of wrongdoing, and, on the other hand, 'general intent' crimes, the kind that exemplify the 'duty failure' account of wrongdoing. Before explaining these distinctions fully, however, in § 2 I will explain why the classification of crimes is a special part concern, before going on in § 3 to provide the background to the main discussion through an examination of the traditional understanding of the general-specific intent distinction.

2. Classifying Crimes: A General Part, or a Special Part Concern?

The classification of crimes is a special part concern, rather than a general part concern, in that it constitutes one dimension of the theory of the special part of the criminal law. On the one hand, the *theory* of the special part of criminal law divides into a normative theory of criminalisation (a theory explaining which wrongs should, and which should not, be crimes), and a theory of the classification of criminal wrongs.[7] The special part itself is concerned simply with the nature of individual criminal wrongs. So, being classificatory issues, whether rape involves a wrong more akin to an invasion of property than to the infliction of physical injury,[8] whether being 'addicted to the use of narcotics' is a pure status offence or an offence involving prohibited conduct,[9] and whether murder is a crime of 'specific intent', are all matters for the theory of the special part of the criminal law. By way of contrast, an argument over the meaning of 'sexual intercourse' can be confined to the meaning that notion should have within the law of sexual offences; and when the argument has that character, the issue is a purely special part issue. For, important and difficult

[7] Classificatory theories, in so far as they are normative, are only indirectly normative, in that, as I have just indicated, their main purpose is to sharpen our moral—and hence legal—grasp of the wrongs in question, whatever normative consequences, if any, this sharpening up process may have. I shall not be concerned here with the normative aspect—focused on the harm principle—of the theory of the special part.

[8] On which, see Stephen Shute and John Gardner, 'The Wrongness of Rape', in Jeremy Horder (ed.), *Oxford Essays in Jurisprudence* (4th series, Oxford: Oxford University Press, 2000), 193.

[9] See *Robinson v California* 370 US 660 (1962). See also *Powell v Texas* 392 US 514 (1968); *R v Larsonneur* (1933) 24 Cr. App. Rep. 74.

though the argument may be, no issue bearing on the classification of crimes is at stake.

On the other hand, the general part of the criminal law is constituted by doctrines (insanity; necessity; provocation; *actus non facit reum nisi mens sit rea*; and so forth) applicable to some section of, or to all of, the special part of the criminal law. Its focal concern is with the meaning that those individual doctrines should have, when they have an application ('should there be an objective test in provocation cases?'; 'should the definition of insanity be wide enough to cover emotional disorders?'; and so forth). By way of contrast, the *theory* of the general part of criminal law divides (like the theory of the special part) into two: a theory of the classification of criminal law doctrines, and a normative theory of which doctrines should be applicable within the criminal law, and if applicable, how widely applicable. The classificatory aspect is concerned, for example, with whether (if ever) duress can justify rather than merely excuse conduct, and with whether diminished capacity is best understood as a denial of responsibility or as an excuse.[10] The normative aspect is concerned with whether, for example, criminal liability should ever be wholly strict, with whether duress should be a defence to murder, with whether voluntary conduct should be a pre-requisite of criminal liability, with whether poverty or deprivation should in itself be an excuse; and so on.[11]

The general and special part of the criminal law, and the theory of the general part, can (although they need not) be treated as in some sense uniquely the preserve of criminal lawyers and criminal law theorists.[12] Whilst, for example, assault is a tort as well as a crime, and whilst insanity has civil law implications as well as criminal law ones, there can always be an argument that when criminal conviction is in issue, special meanings should be given to the meanings of 'assault' and 'insanity' within the criminal law that might be inappropriate (usually, meaning inappropriately narrow) within the civil law. By way of contrast, the theory of the special part of the criminal law does not seem to be uniquely a concern of criminal lawyers. The classification (as opposed to definition) of wrongs is unlikely to differ when those wrongs are being treated as tortious rather than as criminal wrongs.

[10] See, e.g., John Gardner, 'The Gist of Excuses' (1998) 1 *Buffalo Criminal LR* 575.

[11] There are, for example, very obviously distinctions between different kinds of doctrines that might be applied within the criminal law, such as those concerned with responsibility *per se* (like insanity), excusatory doctrines (like duress), doctrines connected to a concern for fair labelling, such as *actus non facit reum nisi mens sit rea*, and so forth.

[12] I ought to add that the general and special parts of the criminal law, as I have defined them, do not exhaust the concerns of the criminal lawyer. There are also what might be called 'threshold questions', such as the jurisdictional extent of the criminal law. I should add that the two sides to the theory of the general part can, of course, be interrelated. For example, whether duress is best seen as an excuse or as a justification (the classificatory issue), might affect our views on how widely, if at all, it is appropriate to permit the defence to be pleaded (the normative issue).

Of those who have written about the distinction between the general and the special part of the criminal law, closest to the view I espouse is that of Gardner:

> The special part supplies the details of particular criminal offences and arranges them into families. The general part, meanwhile, is made up of doctrines that cross the boundaries between (some or all of) these different families of criminal offences.[13]

Gardner separates out 'the details of particular criminal offences', from their arrangement 'into families', a distinction that obviously maps on to my distinction between the special part itself, and the aspect of the theory of special part that is concerned with classifying offences. He does not, as such, distinguish between different aspects of the general part of the criminal law itself—what he calls 'doctrines that cross the boundaries between (some or all of) . . . criminal offences'—and what I call the theory of the general part, concerned either with the classification of such doctrines, or with the question whether particular doctrines should or should not have an application to some or all criminal offences. In place of this, he has a threefold, essentially classificatory distinction, between the 'auxiliary', 'supervisory', and 'definitional' dimensions to or aspects of the general part of the criminal law. For Gardner, the supervisory general part of the criminal law contains mandatory, permissive or advisory (as the case may be) 'guiding principles for the creation, interpretation, and application of new criminal laws',[14] such as *actus non facit reum nisi mens sit rea*. The definitional general part of the criminal law is concerned with 'doctrines that specify how crimes (and defences to crime) are to be defined. They provide the linguistic and conceptual apparatus of the law'.[15] The definitional part is thus concerned with whether, for example, mental elements such as intention and recklessness should bear the same meaning wherever they play a role in the construction of criminal wrongs. If they should, then they have become part of the definitional general part, and can hence become an example of the way in which (at a more abstract level) the law gives effect, if that is what it purports to do, to the maxim—derived from the supervisory general part—*actus non facit reum nisi mens sit rea*.

So far, I hope that there seems to be a good deal that is complementary about the way Gardner divides the general part of the criminal law into sections, and the way I do so.[16] For Gardner, also to be included in the general part of the criminal law is the 'auxiliary' part of the criminal law, 'the automatic or semi-automatic creation of various parasitic modes of criminal liability . . . those dealing with inchoate forms of liability, and those

[13] John Gardner, 'On the General Part of the Criminal Law', in R A Duff (ed.), *Philosophy and the Criminal Law: Principle and Critique* (Cambridge: Cambridge University Press, 1998), 205.

[14] *Ibid.*, at 208. [15] *Ibid.*

[16] What Gardner shows is that criminal law doctrines can themselves be classified, according to the kind of work they are meant to do within the criminal law.

dealing with secondary participation in crime'.[17] This seems right, but there is arguably an over-simplification, one that takes us to the heart of my concerns in this essay, notwithstanding the helpfulness of thinking of these species of liability as—in terms of the harm principle—'auxiliary'. Details marking out the individual character of the wrong to which the inchoate or participatory forms of liability relate, may make it right to think of the individual inchoate offence or mode of participation as an aspect of the special rather than the general part.[18] Let me focus on inchoate forms of liability. To begin with, certainly, the question whether the creation of inchoate forms of liability (or, for that matter, of modes of secondary participation) should be automatic or semi-automatic is a question for what I am calling the normative dimension to the theory of the general part of the criminal law: the part concerned with doctrine-applicability questions. Secondly, the question of what word or phrase is best suited to capture the essence of the *actus reus* of an attempt, whatever the crime being attempted—'dangerous proximity',[19] say, or 'more than merely preparatory act',[20] and so forth—is an issue straightforwardly for the general part itself. For, it is a question about the meaning(s) to be given to doctrines—what Gardner called the 'definitional' general part—that it has already been decided should have an application more or less generally.[21] Thirdly, however, when it comes to the mental element—the particular intention—required for attempts, we have an ingredient of the inchoate offence that firmly connects it with the special part of the criminal law. Surely, for example, when it comes to the question whether a defendant who is guilty of attempted rape is a 'sex offender', the fact that he or she is guilty of an *attempt* to commit rape, rather than of rape itself, and thus that he or she offends against the auxiliary rather than against the special part (in Gardner's terms) of the criminal law, should not affect our judgement that a positive answer to the question is appropriate? Considered in terms of the mental element, attempted rape can be regarded as just one member of a family of what are, broadly speaking, sexual offences (such as assault with intent to rape, burglary with intent to rape, and plain sexual assault).

This, admittedly brief, discussion of how different aspects of a crime or doctrine can be considered as general or as special part concerns, depending on their nature, sets the stage for discussion of the law's approach to evidence of intoxication, and hence of the significance of the distinction it commonly employs between crimes of general and crimes of specific intent, to shape that approach. The question whether evidence of (voluntary)

[17] Gardner, above, n. 13, at 207.

[18] A point noted by Gardner himself: see above, n. 13, at 207.

[19] *Hyde v United States* 225 US 347 (1912), at 388.

[20] Criminal Attempts Act (England and Wales) 1981, s. 1.

[21] So a requirement that a criminal attempt involve nothing less that a direct—purposive—intent to commit the crime is also a general part requirement.

intoxication should in principle, either generally or only in some cases, be admissible to bolster a denial of *mens rea*, and the question whether 'being intoxicated' should be regarded as in some circumstances an excuse in its own right,[22] are questions stemming from a concern with the normative dimension to the theory of the general part of the criminal law (the part concerned with doctrine-applicability questions). By way of contrast, for example, the legal definition of an 'intoxicant',[23] the precise nature of the distinction between voluntary and involuntary intoxication,[24] and the effects intoxication is deemed in law to have on the mind and body,[25] are straightforward general part concerns. Like the idea of 'proximity' in the law governing attempts, they are doctrines meant to have some consistency of meaning across all of the crimes to which—in virtue of answering the questions set for us, in that regard, by the normative dimension to the theory of the general part—it has been decided that they should apply.

Now, when it comes to the relevance of (theory of) special part issues to the legal significance of intoxication evidence, there is more than one approach that the law could take. It could simply permit the admissibility of such evidence to turn solely on its relevance to the presence or absence of the particular mental element (if any) at stake in individual crimes. This would be, obviously, to allow the character of the special part itself to determine admissibility. Ostensibly (although not, as we will see, in fact), such an approach is encouraged by the Model Penal Code, and in particular by its well-known insistence that someone is not to be convicted of a criminal offence unless, 'he acted purposely, knowingly, recklessly, or negligently, as the law may require, with respect to each material element of the offence'.[26] On this approach, intoxication, even if voluntary, would clearly be relevant and hence admissible as evidence bolstering a denial that a defendant acted 'purposely, knowingly [or] recklessly', when a criminal offence was in part defined by one of those mental elements. For, all of them involve—loosely speaking—subjective states of mind, such as a specific intention or foresight, that evidence of intoxication might persuade a court that D did not act on or with, at the material time. By way of contrast, intoxication would not be relevant to any crime that could be committed through negligence, because one of the effects intoxication is deemed (as a general part matter) to have, is the tendency to make one more careless and incompetent:[27] the very element

[22] On which, see G R Sullivan, 'Making Excuses', in A P Simester and A T H Smith (eds.), *Harm and Culpability* (Oxford: Oxford University Press 1996), at 131–52. This possibility is not further considered here.

[23] *People v Low*, 732 P 2nd 622 (Colo. 1987); Law Commission for England and Wales, *Legislating the Criminal Code: Intoxication and Criminal Liability*, Law Com No. 229 (1995), para. 8.

[24] *City of Minneapolis v Altimus*, 238 NW 2nd 851 (1976); *R v Eatch* [1980] *Crim LR* 650.

[25] *Montana v Egelhoff* (1996) 518 US 37, at 49.

[26] Model Penal Code, § 2.02.

[27] See Dressler, above, n. 5, at 319; Stephen Gough, 'Intoxication and Criminal Liability: The Law Commission's Proposed Reforms' (1996) 112 *Law Quarterly Review* 335.

of culpability that the prosecution is seeking to prove.[28] On this approach, thus, one permits the applicability of intoxication doctrines to be more or less wholly dictated by the character—subjective or objective—of mental elements within the special part itself.

This approach, a key part of the 'subjectivist' agenda within criminal law theory,[29] is not, however, the approach taken in (I believe) the vast majority of common law, or former common law, jurisdictions. Whilst there is, of course, much variety in these approaches, central to almost all of them is a distinction drawn from the classificatory dimension to the theory of the special part of criminal law, the distinction between crimes of general and crimes of specific intent. It is this distinction that commonly determines when evidence of (voluntary) intoxication will be admissible to deny the mental element in crimes. I will be seeking to defend a more sophisticated version of it here, in pursuit of a deeper understanding of how crimes can be classified.

3. General and Specific Intent: Refining the Traditional Approach

Most legal systems have rules specifically designed to restrict at least to some extent the use of evidence of intoxication to bolster a denial of culpability (broadly construed). This is because, by way of contrast with, say, tiredness, people frequently *intentionally* become intoxicated, despite knowing that intoxication has effects—impaired motor control and judgement, inattentiveness, short-temperedness, increased aggressiveness—associated with making one more likely to commit crimes in some circumstances.[30] When people do this they are thus knowingly responsible for bringing about the very conditions on which they now seek to rely in defence; and, save in very limited circumstances not relevant here,[31] that is something the law

[28] The prosecution must, of course, show that the defendant was negligent with regard to bringing about some particular consequence—such as death, injury, or damage—but it is hard to see how evidence of intoxication could assist a defendant to show that he was not negligent in that regard.

[29] See Sanford H Kadish, 'Fifty Years of Criminal Law: An Opinionated Review' (1999) 87 *California LR* 943, at 955; Glanville Williams, *Criminal Law: The General Part* (2nd ed., London: Stevens, 1961), 178–83. See also A P Simester and G R Sullivan, *Criminal Law: Theory and Doctrine* (2nd ed., Oxford: Hart Publishing, 2003), ch. 17.

[30] See *Montana v Egelhoff* (1996) 518 US 37, at 49; Gough, above n. 27, at 335.

[31] For instance, even if one is the cause of one's own insanity one can still plead insanity. In some instances, it may also be that one can plead a justificatory defence, such as necessity, even if one was the cause of the conditions of necessity. So, even if it is my loud yodelling that starts a landslide, I may still be justified in breaking into your mountain hut to seek refuge: see further, Alan Brudner, 'A Theory of Necessity' (1987) 7 *Oxford Journal of Legal Studies* 339. On the position where self-defence is concerned, see Andrew Ashworth, 'Self-Defence and the Right to Life' (1975) *Cambridge LJ* 272.

commonly regards as undermining the moral and legal basis of a defence.[32] It is one thing, though, to say that it is no *defence*, as such, to be intoxicated, or to say that evidence of intoxication cannot bolster a 'confession-and-avoidance' plea of duress or provocation. It is, or would appear to be, another thing to say that evidence of intoxication (whether or not voluntary) cannot be adduced to constitute or bolster a claim that the mental element required for conviction of the *crime itself* in question was or may have been absent. Surely, it might be said, if any one of the essential ingredients of the crime itself is absent, the defendant must be acquitted because the crime has not taken place, and it cannot matter why that ingredient is absent. This is the subjectivist line of argument, outlined at the end of § 2, the argument that most common law jurisdictions reject (in whole or in part). What do those jurisdictions have, by way of doctrine, in its stead? In England and Wales, it has been the judge-made distinction between basic (or general) and specific intent, a distinction designed to place restrictions on the admissibility of self-induced intoxication as evidence that the defendant lacked the mental element for the crime.[33] That distinction has also found its way—with that same design in mind—into a number of criminal codes in current or former common law jurisdictions. So, for example, the Australian Federal Criminal Code Act 1995, s. 8.2(1) says that 'evidence of self-induced intoxication cannot be considered in determining whether a fault element of *basic intent* existed' (my emphasis), and similar provisions have been enacted in some individual Australian States.[34]

It has been claimed that the US Model Penal Code 'discarded' the common law distinction between basic or general intent and specific intent;[35] but that is true only if one takes this distinction to be a distinctly old-fashioned one marking a boundary between crimes requiring proof of nothing more than 'wickedness', in some general and ill-defined sense, as the *mens rea*—these being the basic or general intent crimes—and crimes requiring a more 'specific' mental element, such as intention, dishonesty,

[32] One cannot, for example, plead duress, if the threatener was a member of the violent gang one had oneself voluntarily joined, in full knowledge of the gang's activities: *R v Sharp* [1987] QB 853.

[33] See *R v Cruse* (1838) 8 C & P 541; *R v Doherty* (1887) 16 Cox CC 306, 307, as approved in *DPP v Beard* [1920] AC 479, as interpreted in *DPP v Majewski* [1977] AC 443.

[34] See, e.g., Crimes Act (NSW) 1990, s. 428D: 'in determining whether a person had the *mens rea* for an offence other than an offence of specific intent, evidence that a person was intoxicated at the time of the relevant conduct: (a) if the intoxication was self-induced—cannot be taken into account.' The Australian law is illuminatingly discussed by Gough, above, n. 5, at 720–6. See also the harsher provision in s. 86 of the Pakistan Criminal Code of 1860: 'In cases where an act done is not an offence unless done with a particular knowledge or intent, a person who does the act in a state of intoxication shall be liable to be dealt with as if he had the same knowledge as he would have had if he had not been intoxicated, unless the thing which intoxicated him was administered without his knowledge or against his will.'

[35] Dressler, above, n. 5, at 138.

recklessness, and so forth.[36] In fact, the Model Penal Code does rely on, even though it does not clearly articulate, a distinction between basic and specific intent. The reliance is clear when, in § 2.02(2)c, the Code says that in cases where the defendant is voluntarily intoxicated, he or she can be regarded as acting *recklessly*—even if he or she was not consciously aware at the time of the risk of doing the harm in question—if the risk of which he or she was unaware is one of which he or she would have been aware, if sober. The American Law Institute commentary on this clause rationalises it by saying that 'it is not unfair to postulate a general equivalence between risks created by the conduct of the drunken actor and the risks created by his conduct in becoming drunk'.[37] This notion of 'equivalence' (also relied on in a minority of English cases)[38] seems controversial, since like is not necessarily being compared with like. If the charge is, say, driving without due care and attention, then perhaps such equivalence exists. At least for the purposes of criminal conviction, though, there scarcely seems to be compelling analogical force in a comparison between, for example, the risks created by becoming intoxicated, and the risk, on a theft charge, that the defendant will put goods-for-sale into his or her own bag rather than into an authorised shopping basket. In fact, neither the Australian Federal Criminal Code nor (at least on most views) English law,[39] place reliance on the 'equivalence' argument. They simply rule evidence of self-induced intoxication to be inadmissible as part of a defendant's case that he or she lacked the mental element in crimes of basic intent, perhaps in something like the same way that one might (more generally) rule purely self-serving, previous out-of-court statements to be inadmissible, when tendered in support of a defendant's plea. Be that as it may, the important point to note about the Model Penal Code explanation is that, by way of contrast with the position where recklessness can be proved, it is not supposed that there is an 'equivalence'—in point of provable mental element—between, say, forming a particular intention and becoming drunk, or between acting dishonestly and becoming drunk. So, through a contrast between crimes that may be committed recklessly (or, *a fortiori*, through gross negligence) and crimes where a more 'specific' mental element is required, the Model Penal Code continues to employ the basic-specific intent distinction. That brings me to the precise nature of the distinction between crimes of basic and of specific intent.

[36] High-level judicial disapproval of the use of 'wickedness', without more, as an explanation of the mental element in crime can be found in English cases from at least the beginning of the eighteenth century: see the judgment of Holt CJ, in *R v Mawgridge* [1707] Kel 119.

[37] American Law Institute, Comment to § 2.08, 359. Broadly speaking, this is much the same rationalisation as that given by Lord Elwyn-Jones in *DPP v Majewski* [1977] AC 443.

[38] See, e.g., *DPP v Majewski* [1977] AC 443.

[39] *R v Woods* (1981) 74 Cr App Rep 312. See also *DPP v Majewski* [1977] AC 443, where majority support can be found for this view, despite support also being given for the 'equivalence' view in some of their Lordship's speeches.

It has sometimes proved tempting for legislators, courts, and commentators to understand the distinction between basic and specific intent in terms of a distinction between a *mens rea* extending only 'as far as' the *actus reus* (basic intent crimes), or as far as the conduct element thereof, and *mens rea* 'going beyond' that *actus reus* (specific intent crimes).[40] In the latter case, the crimes are also known—for obvious reasons—as crimes of 'ulterior' intent (a kind of crime further discussed in § 4).[41] Although intelligible enough on its face, this (minority) view is not an attractive way of thinking about the distinction, in general, because—in the intoxication context, at least—it detaches the distinction from its key rationale, namely that of indicating the crimes respecting which evidence of self-induced intoxication may, or may not, be employed as evidence showing that the defendant lacked the mental element. As has been pointed out often enough, murder is on almost everyone's list of crimes of specific intent, in that evidence of voluntary intoxication may be used to show that the defendant lacked the intent to kill (where that is required for a murder conviction),[42] but the *mens rea* clearly does not go beyond the *actus reus*, and so murder is not a crime of *ulterior* intent.[43] Conversely, and contrary to Smith and Hogan's claim that, 'where an ulterior intent is required, it is obvious that recklessness is not enough',[44] there are crimes where the mental element goes beyond the *actus reus*, but where evidence of self-induced intoxication is none the less inadmissible as a means of seeking to deny the mental element, because the mental element in question is recklessness. If the defendant is charged with the offence in England and Wales, contrary to s. 1(2) of the Criminal Damage Act 1971, of recklessly destroying or damaging property, being reckless as to whether life is endangered thereby, he or she is charged with a crime of ulterior 'intent' (more accurately, of course, a crime of ulterior *mens rea*); but the ulterior element of *mens rea* being *recklessness*, it has long been clear that a defendant cannot seek to deny that ulterior mental state by claiming that he or she was too (voluntarily) drunk to notice the potentially life-endangering consequences of his or her reckless and damaging or destructive actions.[45] As the U.S. Model Penal Code clearly implies, and as English law (putting aside some wrinkles) has come to accept, the distinction between crimes of general or basic and of specific intent does not lie here. It lies in a distinction of some kind between, on the one hand, crimes that may be committed through

[40] See H Perkins, 'A Rationale of *Mens Rea*' (1939) 52 *Harvard LR* 905, at 924. Dressler, above, n. 5, at 136; *DPP v Majewski* [1977] AC 443; *People v Hood* (Cal 1969) 462 P. 2nd 370, at 378; Australian Criminal Code Act 1995, s. 8.2(2).

[41] For more detailed examination, see Jeremy Horder, 'Crimes of Ulterior Intent', in Simester and Smith, above, n. 22, 153.

[42] *R v Sheehan and Moore* [1975] 1 WLR 739; *State v Ludlow* 883 P. 2nd 1144 (Kan 1994).

[43] See, e.g., Sir J. C. Smith and Brian Hogan, *Criminal Law* (10th ed., London: Butterworths, 2002), at 243.

[44] *Ibid.*, at 88.

[45] See *MPC v Caldwell* [1982] AC 341.

recklessness or negligence (or through analogous forms of *mens rea*, such as a want of due care and attention), and on the other hand, crimes that may only be committed with an in some sense more 'specific' mental element, such as intention or dishonesty. In § 4 below, I will try to do something to draw out this distinction in a way that enables us to avoid Smith and Hogan's gloomy view that:

> The only safe conclusion seems to be that 'crime requiring specific intent' means a crime where evidence of voluntary intoxication negativing *mens rea* is a defence; and the designation of crimes as requiring, or not requiring, specific intent is based on no principle but on policy. In order to know how a crime should be classified for this purpose we can look only to the decisions of the courts.[46]

4. *Mens Rea* and Wronging Successfully (or Trying to)

Let me start afresh. We now know that it is common to distinguish between crimes that are, in whole or in part,[47] ones of general or of specific intent by reference to whether the crime in question may be committed by recklessness (or negligence), in which case it is one of general or basic intent,[48] or whether nothing less than proof of an intention to bring about the forbidden consequence will suffice as proof of the mental element, in which case it is one of specific intent.[49] This way of drawing the distinction has come in for criticism, in that, for example, (i) whilst murder is treated as a crime of 'specific' intent, it can be satisfied by proof of foresight of virtual certainty (although in English law such foresight is sometimes treated as the same thing as an intention),[50] and (ii) whilst, in English law, handling stolen goods does not require an intention that the goods be (or knowledge that they are) stolen—a belief that the goods are stolen will suffice—handling stolen goods is, in the relevant sense, a crime of specific intent,[51] in that evidence of voluntary intoxication may be adduced by the defendant to support the credibility of a claim that he or she gave no thought to whether

[46] Smith and Hogan, above, n. 43, at 243.

[47] A crime such as rape is traditionally thought of as a crime involving both specific and general intent elements, in that whilst there must be a specific intent to have intercourse, there need be only recklessness—or, as in English law, negligence—as to whether or not the intercourse intentionally engaged in was consensual. See further, Kyron Huigens, 'Is Strict Liability Rape Defensible?', in this volume.

[48] See *MPC v Caldwell* [1982] AC 341, and the summary of English law in Simester and Sullivan, above, n. 29, at 562, '[C]rimes of basic intent are crimes where intention or *recklessness* will suffice for conviction (their emphasis).' See also *People v Register* (NY 1983) 457 NE 2nd 704, and the claim by Dressler, above, n. 5, at 324, 'In modern language, self-induced intoxication typically constitutes reckless conduct.'

[49] *DPP v Majewski* [1977] AC 443.

[50] See Simester and Sullivan, above, n. 29, at 561–2.

[51] *R v Durante* [1972] 3 All ER 962, interpreting s. 22 of the Theft Act (England and Wales) 1968.

or not the goods were stolen when they were handled.[52] I will explore the reasons why these examples have proven difficult below.

None the less, the distinction needs to be recast, rather than abandoned, as it contains an important classificatory insight. It should be regarded as reflecting, albeit in a distorted way, a distinction between crimes where the focal case of wrongdoing is the defendant's *active* engagement in bringing about (or trying to bring about) some consequence, and crimes where the focal case of wrongdoing is the defendant's (culpable) *passivity*, his or her failure to do enough to prevent an outcome. So, broadly speaking, 'specific intent' crimes are those where the focal case of the wrong is the case of being successful (or trying to be), in bringing about the forbidden consequence. 'General intent' crimes, by way of contrast, are those where the wrong consists in more-or-less culpably bringing that consequence about, whatever else one was trying to do at the time. It is the latter kind of crime that may be committed by advertent or inadvertent carelessness. This modified view, whilst a step forwards, is still over-simplified. For it suggests that if and in so far as murder can be committed when killing did not constitute success for the killer, as when he or she knew the victim's death was a certain consequence of something else he or she was trying to do (say, setting fire to an inhabited dwelling at night, in order not to kill but to claim on insurance at some later point), then murder will be a crime of general rather than of specific intent. Further refinement of the general-specific intent distinction will avoid this uncomfortable classification, but that is to anticipate.

The distinction between a defendant's passivity and activity, where his or her doing wrong is concerned—the distinction between bringing about an outcome *simpliciter* and bringing it about successfully (or trying to)—is obviously an important distinction, morally speaking, when it comes to questions of credit and blame for conduct. I deserve credit for saving you from drowning if, in throwing a plank in your direction, I intended it to provide a means of floatation: here, saving you constitutes success for me. It would, though, be odd to give me the same (or, perhaps, any) credit if, not knowing you were there, I just happened to throw the plank in your direction, when I was jettisoning it because it was surplus to my requirements; and it would be even odder—wrong, indeed—to give me credit for saving you if, when I threw the plank, I intended it to kill you, but as luck would have it, from your perspective, it ended up being the means of your salvation. Very broadly speaking, we should concentrate our focus, in point of creditworthiness, on cases where I succeed in some worthwhile objective, or on cases where, even though I failed to achieve such an objective, I did at least make a meaningful effort to succeed.[53] Contrariwise, thus, what about

[52] *R v Grange* [1974] 1 All ER 928; *R v Griffiths* (1974) 60 Cr App Rep 14.

[53] For general discussion, see Gardner, above n. 13; R A Duff, *Intention, Agency and Criminal Liability* (Oxford: Blackwell, 1990). Clearly, a host of issues that cannot be dealt with here arise out of the claim. Is the credit due the same, if I put the same effort in, whether or not

the person who successfully does wrong (or tries to)? Is such a person thereby necessarily shown up in a worse moral light than the person who wrongs another accidentally, or who unjustifiably risks such a wrong, when the accident or risk-posing was the perpetrator's fault?

Here, we must take care. The issue cannot be the straightforward one of how 'much' blame reckless wrongdoers or risk-posers must accept, as compared with those who successfully do wrong (or try to). The two kinds of case are largely incommensurable. So, for example, it may be fruitless to try to establish whether some (or all) mercy-killers are more, or less, to blame for killing than some (or all) drunken and reckless drivers who kill, since like is not being compared with like. Each kind of killer offends against a different, albeit related, norm, the former by acting for the wrong reasons and the latter by failing to act for the right (or for permissible) reasons. The mercy-killer offends against reasons not to succeed in killing, reasons one offends against if one acts on them specifically. The reckless driver-killer offends against reasons not to kill, or to bring about any other unwarranted injury or damage, simply because those consequences are unjustified set-backs to others' interests, reasons one offends against if one fails *to conform to* them (where it is my conformity with the reason that counts, not the reason—explanation—for that conformity, which could be pure chance).[54]

When I offend against reasons not to succeed (or to try to), the 'fault' element is obviously bound up intrinsically with the identification of what I have done, as an offence against those reasons. For, unless the commission of the wrong constitutes success for me, I would not have offended against those (kinds of) reasons. An offence may be wholly confined, in the circumstances in which it may be committed, to a norm based on such a reason: a reason not to (try to) succeed in committing a wrong. It is these crimes that are the clearest cases of crimes of 'specific intent'. Consider a criminal attempt. Without an intention to commit the crime embedded in a trying, we cannot begin to make sense of the *actus reus* of an attempt, of the idea of a more than merely 'preparatory' or 'proximate' act. Few completed offences, however, are wholly confined in the circumstances in which they

I succeed? Do half-hearted attempts deserve any credit? Does an effortless success deserve more credit than a hard-working but failed attempt? If I save the world from nuclear disaster by accidentally tripping someone who is about the press the fatal button, thus thwarting him, surely I deserve a small element of credit? And so forth.

[54] In my examples, then, the commensurable comparison is, on the one hand, between mercy-killers, and other killers for whom killing amounts to a success; and, on the other hand, between reckless driver-killers and others who kill accidentally but through negligence or recklessness. In drawing the distinction in this way, I rely on the account of reasons to succeed, and reasons not to fail ('period'), provided by Gardner, above, n. 13. I am not confident that I have used the distinction with the precision that he does, but with luck that may not matter in the present context. The distinction is, of course, one familiar to legal theorists as distinguishing legal reasons as they apply to citizens (reasons to conform to those reasons), and legal reasons as they apply to officials of the system, and judges in particular (reasons to act on those reasons): see H L A Hart, *The Concept of Law* (Oxford: Oxford University Press, 1961), at 114–17.

may be committed to instances in which wrongdoing constitutes a success. Completed offences are almost always offences that may also be committed by advertent or inadvertent carelessness, in some form. However, for some completed offences—like murder, for example—the case in which the wrongful outcome constitutes success for the defendant is still *the central or focal case*, even though the offence may, exceptionally, extend beyond such instantiations; whereas, for some completed offences—like rape, for example—the case of bringing about the prohibited outcome intentionally is by no means the central or focal case. These differences will be addressed more specifically in § 5, where the former kind of completed offences will be designated crimes of specific *mens rea*, to distinguish them both from crimes of specific intent, pure and simple, as well as from crimes of general intent.

Putting this refinement on one side, for the moment, what we can now say is that the distinction between crimes of specific and of general intent marks a contrast between crimes—those of specific intent—where the fault element in successfully wronging another is intrinsic to, or the central case of, the norm or reason against which the defendant acts, and crimes where the fault element, if any, is a product of wholly *ascriptive* rather than normative considerations. For Joseph Raz:

> [N]ormative theory is primarily concerned with establishing what people ought to do . . . Who ought to realise which values and how is the main problem of normative theory. Its most important concepts are ought, reasons for action, rules, duties, and rights . . . The theory of ascription is concerned with the conditions in which blame or guilt can be ascribed to people . . . It is the job of normative theory to determine whose responsibility it is to realise this or that value . . . The theory of ascription deals with the ascription of blame and praise to people who fulfilled or failed to fulfil their responsibilities. It presupposes that we have a normative theory and studies the normative consequences of failure to conform to the requirements of normative theory.[55]

When a defendant offends against a reason not to succeed in wronging (or against a reason not to try to), when he or she is 'active' with regard to the wrongdoing, the success is partly constitutive of the normative failure involved: the defendant specifically ought not to have been (or sought to be) successful in doing what was done. Now, because, as Raz indicates at the end of the passage, ascriptive theory presupposes normative theory, this means that the purely ascriptive considerations bearing on such a case will *not* include the intention with which the act was undertaken. For sure, if, say, someone attempts to kill another, they can and should be blamed for trying to kill; but then, the ascription of blame is a 'supervenient' property. It flows simply from the nature of the normative failure involved in the

[55] Joseph Raz, *Practical Reason and Norms* (2nd ed., Princeton: Princeton University Press, 1990), at 11–12.

attempt to succeed, and is not the product of further judgemental considerations.[56]

By way of contrast, now consider the case in which a defendant offended against a reason not bring about some unjustified consequence *simpliciter*: when he or she—whatever else he or she was doing—was passive with regard to the wrongdoing. A straightforward failure to *conform* (whatever the reason for failure may be) is then the normative issue, and purely ascriptive considerations will therefore include the fault element, if any, in the offence. If, without justification, I destroy your garden shed, then I have failed to conform my conduct to the reasons there are to avoid such outcomes in acting, period: *that is* my normative failure. If the law then withholds criminal liability on the grounds, say, that the destruction was the product of an unanticipated accident (a petrol can I had forgotten I had exploded into flames, and the flames spread to your shed, for example), it does so for the ascriptive reason that I am not sufficiently to blame to warrant criminal conviction.[57] *Mutatis mutandis*, a requirement, in point of blame, that I have foreseen or been aware of the risk of damage or destruction, if criminal conviction is to be warranted when the norm has been breached, is a substantive, additional (ascriptive) requirement. It is not merely a property of my conduct that supervenes or flows naturally from the nature of my normative failure.

This, admittedly complex, analysis helps us to give a simple answer to the question with which we began: why should voluntary intoxication be evidence admissible to bolster a denial by the defendant that he or she possessed the requisite mental element, in crimes of genuinely specific intent? The answer is that, where such crimes are in issue, the particular intent with which the defendant acts is not just a 'definitional element' (a weasel phrase, if ever there was one): it is intrinsic to the normative logic of the prohibition. So, to convict of the crime in the absence (for whatever reason, including voluntary intoxication) of the intent would be normatively self-defeating.[58] Things may be otherwise, where the crime's key normative

[56] A purely ascriptive consideration in such a case, involving further judgemental considerations, might be, on the debit side, that the defendant premeditated the attempt, or, on the credit side, that the attempt was itself mistakenly believed to be in response to an imminent threat of death.

[57] The contrast here reflects one between a duty to succeed in avoiding causing unjustified loss, period, and a duty to try to avoid causing unjustified loss, as explained by John Gardner, 'Obligations and Outcomes in the Law of Torts', in Peter Cane and John Gardner (eds.), *Relating to Responsibility: Essays in Honour of Tony Honoré on his 80th Birthday* (Oxford: Hart Publishing, 2001) 116, at 120. See also Gardner, above, n. 13.

[58] In resisting this view, in *Montana v Egelhoff* 518 US 37 (1996), Justice Scalia voiced the opinion that, 'disallowing consideration of voluntary intoxication . . . comports with and implements society's moral perception that one who has voluntarily impaired his own faculties should be responsible for the consequences' (*ibid.*, at 49–50). The weakness in this view, in so far as it is meant to apply to crimes of specific intent, is that where 'the consequences' themselves have not ensued unless the defendant acted with a particular intention, it is hard to see how it could make sense to ask whether he or she is responsible for them because he or she was voluntarily intoxicated when the harm was done.

failure is a failure to conform conduct to (broadly) outcome-focused reasons, reasons not to kill, injure, damage, or speed, etc., rather than the very different kind of normative failure, examined so far, that involves positively, successfully bringing about wrongdoing, or trying to. It is to the 'failure-to-conform' cases of normative failure, where the focal case is the defendant's passivity with regard to the wrongdoing, that I now turn. As we will see, these are the crimes appropriately called crimes of general intent.

5. Culpable Advertence, General Intent, and Specific *Mens Rea* Crimes

Most completed crimes can be committed through advertent carelessness, even crimes traditionally thought of as ones of specific intent, like murder or theft. What has misled judges and theorists into treating murder and theft, in particular, as crimes of specific *intent* is that to be convicted of one of these crimes on the basis of advertent carelessness, that advertent carelessness must manifest itself in a certain (narrowly defined) way. There are, of course, reasons not to kill intentionally, and reasons not to try to kill; but few (former) common law jurisdictions confine the scope of murder, or its broad equivalent, to cases in which a defendant offends against such reasons. So, murder itself is not a pure case of specific intent. Murder cases include instances in which a defendant has killed whilst intending or attempting to do something else, yet in circumstances where not only was the risk of killing unjustified, but the defendant foresaw death or serious injury as virtually certain, or manifested extreme recklessness or indifference towards the occurrence of death. In the latter cases, as M. Cathleen Kaveny has argued, it is not the villain's *intention* that condemns him or her, so much as the terrible moral (ascriptive) light in which what he foresaw as the almost certain result of his plans shows him:

> his gross disregard for the human lives foreseeably ended as a certain side-effect of his decision seems, in fact, aptly described both with the Scottish term 'wicked recklessness' and with the broad but more specific *moral* terms 'homicidal' and 'murderous'.[59]

Murder cases can, albeit rarely, be ones in which the defendant is condemned for a (normative) failure to *conform* to reasons not to cause death unjustifiably. This can only happen, though, when, to use Weinrib's apt phrase, 'the actor "as good as" tried or intended to kill his victim'.[60] In such

[59] M. Cathleen Kaveny, 'Inferring Intention from Foresight' (2004) 120 *Law Quarterly Review* 81, at 86 (my emphasis).

[60] Lloyd Weinrib, 'Homicide: Legal Aspects', in Sanford H Kadish (ed.), (1983) 2 *Encyclopaedia of Criminal Justice*, at 859, cited by Dressler, above, n. 5, 513. See also Samuel H Pillsbury, 'Crimes of Indifference' (1996) 49 *Rutgers LR* 105.

cases, conviction rests on a finding that death was foreseen as virtually certain to occur, or on the jury's ascriptive judgment that there was 'extreme' or 'wicked' recklessness in killing,[61] or that the killing stemmed from 'an abandoned and malignant heart'.[62] In these latter cases, then, the defendant is convicted on the basis of advertent carelessness, but *only* where its manifestation takes a special, morally heinous form, tantamount to—albeit distinct from—an actual attempt to kill.[63] Such crimes are what can be called crimes of specific *mens rea*.

We can now see why murder falls into the limited category of crimes that may be committed through advertent carelessness respecting which it is morally imperative, as subjectivists insist, that evidence of intoxication—whether or not voluntary—is permitted to bolster a denial of *mens rea*. In theory, an act—say, hitting someone hard on the head with a blunt instrument—might be found to manifest extreme indifference or wicked recklessness with regard to causing death, even when it is accepted that the defendant's intoxication meant that he or she did not appreciate the extent of the harm that might be done to the victim. Employing the inadmissibility account of the rule excluding evidence of voluntary intoxication,[64] it might in theory be possible to say of such a case that the defendant would undoubtedly have been aware that death or serious bodily injury was virtually certain to occur, had he or she been sober. It might be possible to say, thus, that his or her failure to advert to that virtual certainty is morally and legally irrelevant, given the voluntariness of the intoxication (a point considered further below). In many jurisdictions it has seemed wrong, however, to permit juries to consider these possibilities, and hence to convict in the absence of actual awareness on the defendant's part of (a certain degree of) risk that death or serious injury may result. Considerations of fair labelling require that no one be convicted of murder in the absence of such awareness.[65] In this respect, however, murder (like theft) may be one of only a small number of exceptional cases, cases of specific *mens rea*, amongst the large number of *mala in se* where one wrongs the victim simply by failing to conform to the reasons not unjustifiably to do the harm. In the other cases of

[61] As in Scotland: see Lord Goff, 'The Mental Element in Murder' (1988) 104 *Law Quarterly Review* 30.

[62] Cal. Penal Code, 188 (West 1999).

[63] See the sophisticated analysis of such cases in A P Simester, 'Why Distinguish Intention from Foresight?', in Simester and Smith, above, n. 22, 71.

[64] See text at n. 34 above.

[65] See *DPP v Beard* [1920] AC 479, and Dressler, above, n. 5, at 326–7. The same argument obtains in theft cases, where, even if a defendant would certainly have foreseen it as virtually certain, had he or she been sober, that his or her action would permanently deprive another of their property, it seems wrong—for fair labelling reasons—to convict of theft in the absence of actual awareness that this would be the virtually certain result. That theft may be committed through advertent carelessness, in English law, is confirmed by the qualifications made to the definition of the requirement for an intention permanently to deprive, by s. 6 of the Theft Act 1968.

this kind, most legislatures and courts have treated the crimes in question—manslaughter, rape, wounding, criminal damage, and so forth—as ones in which, when they are committed through advertent carelessness, it is perfectly (morally, and hence legally) permissible to refuse to admit evidence of voluntary intoxication as a means of bolstering a denial that the *mens* was *rea*. In these cases, proof of advertent carelessness *simpliciter* will suffice as proof of *mens rea*, and when that is true, the subjectivist argument against the inadmissibility of intoxication evidence to show that carelessness was inadvertent has seemed much weaker. Consider a case in which a defendant says, for example, 'when I subjected the victim to non-consensual sexual intercourse, the problem was that I was too drunk to notice whether or not there was consent; but, the brute fact that I did not notice the absence of consent is the reason you must acquit'. In such instances, it has not seemed to courts in many jurisdictions that fair labelling considerations demand assent to this subjectivist contention.[66] Why?

The answer seems to lie in the fact that the central or focal case of the wrong in crimes of specific *mens rea*, like murder and theft, is still the case of 'active' wrongdoing, the case in which the defendant offends against the reasons not to succeed in killing (or trying to kill), or to succeed in appropriating property without consent, even if those crimes extend somewhat beyond such instances. The instances in which there can be a conviction for murder or for theft, where the defendant offends against reasons respectively not to kill or to appropriate property without consent *simpliciter*—instances of failure to conform to the reasons, period, are the peripheral or exceptional instances. They are only included with the scope of the crime because of the high degree of moral fault involved ('wicked recklessness' etc.), where the defendant can be said to have 'as good as' wronged the victim successfully. That being so, it would be misleading to have a different set of ascriptive rules, such as different rules governing the admissibility of intoxication evidence, applicable to the latter—the exceptional—instances, that are not applicable to the former. For that would be to drive too great a wedge between what are meant to be, morally and legally speaking, cases fit for almost identical treatment, in that they are all, or all 'as good as', the active case of successfully wronging.

By way of contrast, it is true by definition of at least some manslaughter cases, and also true of (say) rape, criminal damage, and wounding cases, that the instance in which the wrong is done intentionally is not, morally speaking, a 'central' case even if it is a bad case. To be sure, someone who is, say, satisfied with nothing less than non-consensual intercourse is worthy of the utmost condemnation; but so is the person who, knowing the victim might not be consenting, regards that matter as having no practical

[66] For the rejection of this contention in English law, prior to the enactment of the Sexual Offences Act 2003, see *R v Woods* (1981) 74 Cr. App. Rep. 312.

significance, as compared with his desire for sex on any terms.[67] In such instances, whilst there is still an obvious difference between the case of intentional wrongdoing and reckless wrongdoing, it is much less clear than it is in murder or theft cases that this difference should fundamentally affect the way that, morally speaking, we characterise the wrong. That is what makes such crimes ones of general or basic intent. Even in crimes where wronging the victim successfully is not the central case, fair labelling considerations may still dictate that one should not suffer criminal conviction respecting one's failure to conform to the relevant reasons without fault. None the less, the very fact that one's failure occurs irrespective of fault means that, in the absence of the kind of special—'central case'—considerations that dictate an exclusive focus on particularly heinous manifestations of advertent carelessness (as in murder and theft cases), the absence of advertence to the risk of such a failure need be given no special ascriptive significance, ahead of other ascription-relevant reasons for that failure, such as voluntary intoxication.[68] Where general intent crimes are in issue, there is, if you will, a moral—and hence, legal—permission to give the absence of advertence special ascriptive significance, for fair labelling purposes, but no moral imperative that this course be taken.

6. Completing the Picture: Crimes of Ulterior Intent

We have now replaced the old specific–general intent distinction with a distinction between crimes of *specific intent*, constituted by cases in which the defendant succeeds in doing wrong (or tries to), as he intends, crimes of *specific mens rea*, where successfully wronging is the central instance of the wrong, if not the only instance, and crimes of *general or basic intent*, where the central case of the wrong is a culpable failure to prevent something happening that one was duty bound to prevent, even if one can commit the wrong intentionally. For the sake of completeness, I should add a fourth category, crimes of *ulterior intent*.[69] All criminal codes include important

[67] On this point, in relation to rape cases, see Jeremy Horder, 'Gross Negligence and Criminal Liability (1997) 47 *University of Toronto LJ* 495; Mayo Moran, *Rethinking the Reasonable Person* (Oxford: Oxford University Press, 2003).

[68] Especially when one bears in mind that one can restrict the possibility that convictions can be obtained in such circumstances, to cases in which the defendant would undoubtedly have appreciated the risk, had he or she been sober. For the Model Penal Code's endorsement of this approach, see text following n. 46 above. See also Home Office (England and Wales), *Violence: Reforming the Offences Against the Person Act 1861* (1998), Draft Bill clause 19, '[A] person who was voluntarily intoxicated at any material time must be treated—(a) as having been aware of any risk of which he would have been aware had he not been intoxicated; and (b) as having known or believed in any circumstances which he would have known or believed in had he not been intoxicated.'

[69] See further, Paul Robinson's classification of some crimes as crimes of 'future conduct intention': Paul Robinson, 'Should the Law Abandon the *Actus Reus-Mens Rea* Distinction?', in Stephen Shute, John Gardner and Jeremy Horder (eds.), *Action and Value in Criminal Law* (Oxford: Oxford University Press, 1993).

examples of crimes—precursor offences—in which, whilst the defendant may not have reached the point at which he or she can be said to have tried to commit the offence, crucial to the conviction will still be a finding that he or she *intended* to commit the crime. Two examples are provided by the offences, in English law, of having anything in one's custody intending without lawful excuse to use it to commit criminal damage, and of being in possession of a firearm with intent by means thereof to endanger life.[70] These cases are really parasitic on the cases, like attempt, in which the reason not to try to commit the wrong is the reason against which the defendant offends, when committing the offence. They are hence, albeit more remotely, parasitic on the case of successfully doing wrong. I say 'parasitic', because whilst intention is just as central to the wrong, it comes in a different form. The intention is closer to the 'thought' or 'bare' form that is normally contrasted with intention-in-action, in a way well explained by Gardner and Jung:

> Bare intentions are personal normative tools using which we change the structure of our future reasons for action. They are new second-order reasons which we evolve for ourselves, which operate to exclude certain existing operative and auxiliary reasons from our future practical thinking unless and until the emergence of further reasons necessitates their reconsideration. Bare intentions work to isolate interim conclusions in extended practical thinking... But it makes no sense to think of *intention in action* as having exclusionary force. By the time one acts with a certain intention, it is too late to do any excluding of considerations. The deed is done.[71]

In one sense, of course, the defendant's intention in cases of ulterior intent is not wholly confined to the realm of thought, because the possession of the firearm, say, is evidence of the intention 'in action'. Hence, Gardner and Jung's claim that 'bare or future intention plays no role in the principles of *mens rea*'.[72] However, the ulterior intent is manifested in an action—the possession—that is obviously not itself meant to bring about the crime in the way the defendant intends. In such cases, therefore, defendants are partly condemned in the light of their 'second order reasons . . . interim conclusions in extended practical thinking', to use Gardner and Jung's language. Be that as it may, cases of ulterior intent will clearly also be cases in which evidence that defendants lacked the future intention due to voluntary intoxication cannot, morally intelligibly, be ruled inadmissible. For these are cases parasitic on the normative failure constituted by successfully wronging. So, the intention with which they acted is, as in attempt cases, a crucial aspect of the norm against which they offend, and no mere matter of ascribing blame for something (else) wrong done.

[70] Offences, respectively, contrary to s. 1 of the Criminal Law Act 1977, s. 3 of the Criminal Damage Act 1971, and s. 16 of the Firearms Act 1968.

[71] John Gardner and Heike Jung, 'Making Sense of Mens Rea: Antony Duff's Account' (1991) 11 *Oxford Journal of Legal Studies* 559, at 567 (their emphasis).

[72] *Ibid.*

7. Conclusion

In a Consultation Paper in 1993,[73] the Law Commission for England and Wales adopted Smith and Hogan's view[74] that there was no thread of principle linking the courts' decisions to categorise crimes as ones of basic or of specific intent. The Commission hence advocated abandoning the distinction. In the Law Commission's then view, evidence of voluntary intoxication should be permitted to bolster a denial of the mental element in all crimes, even ones of basic intent. This subjectivist change was designed to facilitate more complete acquittals in cases of intoxication, but it came with a 'sop' to defenders of a more objectivist approach. The Commission also recommended the creation of an offence of 'dangerous intoxication'.[75] A defendant stood to be convicted of this offence in cases where he or she had become 'deliberately intoxicated to a substantial extent', and had then caused one of certain listed harms, even if he or she was acting in a state of automatism at the time. This wildly exaggerated contrast between a basis for acquittal dictated by wholly subjectivist thinking, and a basis for conviction founded on a wholly unyielding 'objectivism', was, in the Law Commission's later words, 'rejected outright with cogent and persuasive reasons'.[76] So, in their final Report, the distinction between general or basic intent, and specific intent, was restored. In particular, in the draft Bill (clause 1):

> (2) If the person's intoxication was voluntary and the allegation is in substance an allegation that at the material time he
> (a) acted intentionally with respect to a particular result,
> (b) had a particular purpose in acting in a particular way,
> (c) had any particular knowledge or belief, or
> (d) acted fraudulently or dishonestly,
>
> evidence of his intoxication may be taken into account in determining whether the allegation has been proved.

I do not say that this sensible proposal reflects exactly the theoretical distinctions I have claimed underlie the distinction between general or basic and specific intent; but the Law Commission's change of mind seems in some measure to justify the claim made at the start of the essay that there are some classifications which, morally speaking, we cannot do without.

[73] Law Commission for England and Wales, *Intoxication and Criminal Liability*, Consultation Paper No. 127 (1993).
[74] See text above, n. 46.
[75] Law Commission, above, n. 73, at para. 6.31.
[76] Law Commission for England and Wales, *Legislating the Criminal Code: Intoxication and Criminal Liability*, Law Com. No. 229, at para. 1.26.

3

Criminalizing Endangerment

R A Duff *

1. Attacks and Endangerments

Some crimes (types or tokens) consist in attacks on legally protected interests. If I shoot at you, intending to injure you; or start a fire, intending to damage your property; or lie to you, intending to obtain money from you: I attack your interests in physical integrity, in property, in not being harmfully deceived—attacks against which the criminal law protects you. If my attack is successfully consummated, I am (absent a further defence) guilty of wounding with intent, of arson, or of obtaining by deception.[1] If my attack is unconsummated, I am guilty of attempting to commit one of those crimes; attempts are attacks that fail.[2]

Other crime types or tokens consist in endangering rather than attacking legally protected interests. If, without intending harm, I act in a way that I realise might injure you, or damage your property, I endanger your physical security or property; if, without intending to deceive, I tell you that a certain bank is financially secure, realising that my statement might be false and might induce you to open an account with that bank, I endanger your interest in having accurate financial information to act upon. The criminal law protects these interests against such endangerments. If the endangerment is consummated—you are injured, your property is damaged, or my

* Grateful thanks are due to the Leverhulme Trust, for the Research Fellowship during which I wrote this paper; to participants in the Baton Rouge Workshop, and in seminars at Ohio State University and the University of Stirling, at which I tried out earlier drafts; and to Marcelo Ferrante, Stuart Green, Jeremy Horder, Ken Simons and Leo Zaibert for detailed written comments. They will recognise their influence in what follows; they will also recognise that the remaining errors and confusions are all mine.

[1] See, respectively, Offences Against the Person Act 1861, s. 18; Criminal Damage Act 1971, s. 1; Theft Act 1968, s. 15. Since wounding with intent requires an intention to injure, this crime type consists in an attack. Since arson does not require an intention to damage, that crime type does not consist in an attack; but since such an intention is sufficient *mens rea* for the offence, some tokens consist in attacks. Obtaining by deception requires an 'intention of permanently depriving' the victim, and most tokens of this crime type will indeed be attacks; but given the extended definition of that 'intention' in s. 6, and the fact that 'deception' need only be 'reckless', the crime type does not consist in an attack.

[2] See Criminal Attempts Act 1981, s. 1(1); R A Duff, *Criminal Attempts* (Oxford: Oxford University Press, 1996), 221–8, 363–74.

statement is false—I might be guilty of wounding, of criminal damage, or of fraudulent inducement to make a deposit.[3] If the endangerment is not consummated, I might or might not be guilty of an offence, since English and American law have no general offence of unconsummated endangerment analogous to that of unconsummated attack. The Model Penal Code (s. 211.2) could convict me of 'reckless endangerment' if I risked causing you serious physical injury, but English law could convict me only if I endangered you in one of the specific ways that are criminalized.[4] Neither system criminalizes endangering property as such, although I could be guilty if I endangered it by, for instance, causing an explosion or starting a fire.[5] In neither system is it normally criminal to make a statement that I realise might be false, unless it actually is false or misleading.[6]

My primary interest is in the ways in which endangerment is, or should be, criminalized. However, we must first attend (in § 2) to the distinction between attacks and endangerments, as two distinct types of criminal wrong, before turning (in § 3) to the structure and scope of endangerment offences.

2. Distinguishing Attacks from Endangerments

An attack is an action or omission that is intended to harm some value or interest. I can attack your body by trying to injure you; your tangible property by trying to steal or damage it; your reputation by slandering you; your intellectual property by plagiarising your work. Attacks need not, however, be directed against particular people: they can be indiscriminate, aimed at whoever happens to be in their way; they can be aimed at institutions or practices, or even at more abstract values, as when we call propaganda an attack on truth.

Both harm-intending *mens* and harm-threatening *actus* are necessary for an attack. Firing a gun might endanger *V*, but it attacks *V* only if it is intended to harm *V*. To form an intention to harm *V*, however, or to make preparations to actualise that intention, is not yet to attack *V*: the attacker must progress beyond the 'merely preparatory', to be 'in the process of

[3] Offences Against the Person Act 1861, s. 20; Criminal Damage Act 1971, s. 1; Banking Act 1987, s. 35. I can endanger another inadvertently and non-culpably (see at n. 12 below); in these cases, however, only the endangerer who is at least reckless commits an offence.

[4] See, e.g., Road Traffic Act 1988, s. 2; and below, at n. 60–3.

[5] Explosive Substances Act 1883, s. 2; Model Penal Code s. 220.1(2).

[6] But a sworn witness who makes a true material statement that she does not believe to be true commits perjury under English law: Perjury Act 1911. American law is similarly worded (see Model Penal Code s. 241.1(1); 18 USC 1621), but case law requires falsity: see S P Green, 'Lying, Misleading, and Falsely Denying: How Moral Concepts Inform the Law of Perjury, Fraud, and False Statements' (2001) 53 *Hastings Law Journal* 157, at 176; *Commentary* to Model Penal Code s. 241.1, at 94.

committing' the attack;[7] and his actions must engage appropriately with the world.[8]

A certain hostility towards its object is intrinsic to an attack. It need not be motivated by hatred: a contract killer or a fraudster might feel no such animus towards their victims. But their actions manifest a practical hostility towards the interests or people they attack, in that those actions are aimed against those people and their interests;[9] their intentional structure is determined by the harm that they are to cause. One who intends what would normally count as harm might deny that her action is in this sense hostile: someone who commits voluntary euthanasia might argue that her action manifests the compassion that motivates it; someone engaged in consensual sado-masochism might claim that his actions display the mutual respect, and concern for each other's pleasure, that structure this sexual encounter. What such people deny, however, is that their actions constitute attacks, because they deny that what they intend constitutes harm (just as a surgeon would deny that the amputation she carries out constitutes an attack, since it is intended to benefit rather than to harm the patient). There is of course room for disagreement in such cases, and others would insist that such actions still constitute wrongful attacks: in the case of euthanasia, on the person killed (taking the right to life to be inalienable) or on the more abstract value of life; in the case of sado-masochism, on the person's 'real' interests, or on some value that the person embodies.[10] But this would be to argue that what these agents intend does constitute harm, and that their actions do manifest practical hostility towards the interests or values against which they are now seen as directed. Such examples show, not that attacks are not by definition hostile actions that are intended to do harm, but that there can be normative disagreement about what counts as an attack.

Attacks typically endanger their objects: in attacking *V*, I create a risk that she will suffer the harm I am trying to do her. But I can endanger *V* without attacking her, and our concern here is with endangerments that do not constitute attacks: 'endangerment' will hereafter mean 'endangerment that is not an attack'. Our concern is also with endangerment as something that human agents do. Many dangers, including some arising from human beings, involve no human agency. There is a danger that visitors to my

[7] Criminal Attempts Act 1981 s. 1(1), *Gullefer* [1990] 1 WLR 1063, on 'attempt', marking the fact that in ordinary discourse attempts are attacks (the Model Penal Code (s. 5.01) stretches the idea of attempt further, to include any 'substantial step' towards the crime); see Duff, n. 2 above, at 53–61, 385–97. This is not to imply that we should never criminalize 'merely preparatory' conduct: see at nn. 87–8 below.

[8] S M Uniacke, *Permissible Killing: The Self-defence Justification of Homicide* (Cambridge: Cambridge University Press, 1994), at 162, note 7; Duff, n. 2 above, at 219–33, 380–3.

[9] Compare *DPP v Smith* [1961] AC 290, at 327 (Lord Kilmuir); *Hyam* [1975] AC 55, at 79 (Lord Hailsham): a murderous action must be 'aimed at' someone.

[10] Compare, notoriously, *Brown* [1994] 1 AC 212; appealed (unsuccessfully) as *Laskey et al. v UK* (1997) 24 EHRR 39.

sickbed will catch my infectious disease, but I am not endangering them, unless I am failing to do something that I should do to protect them—such as isolating myself. If I am a kind of person who is likely to commit crimes of violence, I might be called dangerous, and risk-fearing governments might look for ways of controlling or incapacitating me:[11] but I endanger others only if and when I begin to actualise my dangerous disposition in violent action.

I endanger another if by act or omission I create a significant risk that he will suffer harm (a risk is 'significant' if it provides a reason against acting as I do, or for taking precautions in acting thus). If the risk is not actualised, I merely endanger him; if it is actualised, I endanger him and harm him. I endanger him whether or not I realise, or could reasonably be expected to realise, the risk that I create: whilst *mens rea* is necessary for an attack, endangerment need involve only an *actus reus*—an act or omission that actually creates a suitable risk. Criminal liability for endangerment can therefore be strict: I can be guilty of an endangerment offence even if I did not (and could not reasonably have been expected to) realise the risk I created.[12] But if criminal liability should depend on fault, and we ask what species of fault could justly make an agent criminally liable for the danger she creates, we will naturally think not of an intention to do harm, but of recklessness as the paradigm of fault, and of indifference (rather than hostility) to the threatened interests as the practical attitude that culpable endangerment displays. Someone who culpably endangers others does not thereby display an active hostility towards them; but in her willingness to take the risk of harming them, and her failure to take adequate precautions against doing so (or even to notice the risk she is creating), she shows that she does not care as she should for their interests.

Given this distinction between attack and endangerment, we can see how they constitute two distinct types of criminal wrong, with different internal structures. One consists in an attack on some legally protected interest—an action structured by the intention to harm that interest, displaying practical hostility towards it. The other consists in a failure of proper concern. I fail to take proper steps to avoid, or even to notice, the danger that my conduct creates, and thus take the risk that I will cause harm to others: but that harm is not the object of my action; rather, it is a side-effect that I fail to care about as I should. If I attack someone, the nonoccurrence of the harm that I intend marks the failure of my action—that is why the action displays hostility to its victim. If I merely endanger them, however, the nonoccurrence of the

[11] On the 'risk society', and the threats it poses to justice, see B Hudson, *Justice in the Risk Society* (London: Sage, 2003).

[12] E.g. Water Resources Act 1991, s. 85(1) (causing 'poisonous' matter 'to enter any controlled water'); *R v Milford Haven Port Authority* [2000] 2 Cr. App. Rep. (S) 423. It might, however, be hard to decide whether a defendant 'caused' the pollution without attending to fault: see *Alphacell Ltd. v Woodward* [1972] AC 824.

prospective harm does not mark the failure of my action: it might even be a source of relief for me—whereas one who intends harm cannot, without forswearing that intention, be relieved at his failure to cause it.[13]

The difference in moral character between the kind of wrong I do to one whose interests I attack, and the kind of wrong I do to one whose interests I culpably endanger, lies in part in the difference between being guided by wrong reasons and not being guided by right reasons. If I wrongfully attack you, the harm that I intend figures in my reasons for acting as I do: I act thus because I believe that by doing so I will harm you—though that is not a reason by which I should be guided. If I culpably endanger you, by contrast, my reasons for acting as I do may be perfectly legitimate; what goes wrong is that I am not guided by the reason against acting thus (the reason for refraining from the action, or for taking precautions) that the risk of harm to you provides.

This difference in moral character is, however, concealed by some familiar approaches to understanding criminal wrongdoing. It is concealed most thoroughly if we combine a simple understanding of the Harm Principle with a 'choice' model of criminal fault. On Feinberg's version of the Harm Principle, we begin (analytically) with some identifiable harm, such as injury to the person or damage to property; we then identify some human action as the cause of that harm, which gives us an *actus reus*.[14] This 'conduct-cause-harm' model does not yet give us a conception of criminal fault, but one might naturally approach that issue by asking about the conditions given which the action's agent should be held criminally liable for the harm for which she is causally responsible—which is also to ask, if we think that criminal liability should track culpable moral responsibility, about the conditions given which she is culpably morally responsible for that harm. A tempting answer, especially for those who find their intellectual home in a liberal neo-Kantianism, is that responsibility and culpability must depend on

[13] This distinction clearly has quite a lot in common with that drawn by Jeremy Horder between 'crimes where the focal case of wrongdoing is the defendant's *active* engagement in bringing about (or trying to bring about) some consequence, and crimes where the focal case of wrongdoing is the defendant's (culpable) *passivity*, his or her failure to do enough to prevent an outcome' ('The Classification of Crimes and the Special Part of the Criminal Law', this volume, at 33); I cannot discuss the differences between us here. It is also close in spirit to K W Simons, 'Rethinking Mental States' (1992) 72 *Boston University Law Review* 463 (see also 'Does Punishment for "Culpable Indifference" Simply Punish for "Bad Character"?' (2002) 6 *Buffalo Criminal Law Review* 219, at 313–15; for critique, see K K Ferzan, 'Don't Abandon the Model Penal Code Yet! Thinking Through Simons's *Rethinking*' (2002) 6 *Buffalo Criminal Law Review* 185). Contrast L Alexander, 'Insufficient Concern: A Unified Conception of Criminal Culpability' (2000) 88 *California Law Review* 931 (on which see J Dressler, 'Does One Mens Rea Fit All? Thoughts on Alexander's Unified Conception of Criminal Culpability' (2000) 88 *California Law Review* 955).

[14] J Feinberg, *Harm to Others* (New York: Oxford University Press, 1984), chs. 1–3; see also P H Robinson, *Structure and Function in Criminal Law* (Oxford: Oxford University Press, 1997), on which see R A Duff, 'Rule-Violations and Wrongdoings', in S Shute and A P Simester (eds.), *Criminal Law Theory: Doctrines of the General Part* (Oxford: Oxford University Press, 2002), 47.

choice: I am responsible for the harms I choose to cause, and culpable if I have no justification or excuse for that choice. From this perspective, intention and recklessness (defined as conscious risk-taking) exemplify the same type of fault, since both consist in the choice to cause or to risk causing harm: the only difference is that intention is a more serious fault, since the merely reckless agent does not choose actually to cause harm. Negligence is then either not a species of 'fault' at all, since it involves no culpable choice; or a lesser type of fault, consisting in a failure to make choices (the choice to attend, or to take care) that one could and should have made.[15]

This model of criminal liability has been variously criticised. One criticism concerns the concept of harm, and whether we can—as Feinberg insists—always identify the harms that are to ground liability independently of the wrongful actions that generate them.[16] Another focuses on the austere typology of wrongs that the 'conduct-cause-harm' model implies: it identifies and categorises wrongs primarily by reference to the interests that they harm, and the extent of the agent's culpable responsibility for those harms—whereas, critics argue, an adequate account of the kinds of wrong that properly concern the criminal law must draw on a richer, 'thicker', set of ethical-legal concepts that reflect not just the causation of harm, but the way, the context, and the spirit in which harm is done.[17] A third kind of objection focuses on choice as the supposedly essential determinant of criminal liability: quite apart from the question of whether 'choice' can be so defined that it suffices for criminal liability (whether we can specify a conception of 'free' choice that will be sensitive to all the defences that the law should recognise), it is objected that choice is not necessary for liability—that we must look as well or instead to the attitudes or dispositions that are revealed both in agents' choices and in their unchosen responses.[18]

[15] See, e.g., H L A Hart, *Punishment and Responsibility* (Oxford: Oxford University Press, 1968); A J Ashworth, 'Belief, Intent and Criminal Liability', in J Eekelaar and J Bell (eds.), *Oxford Essays in Jurisprudence* (3rd Series, Oxford: Oxford University Press, 1987), 1; J Dressler, 'Reflections on Excusing Wrongdoers' (1988) 19 *Rutgers Law Journal* 671; M S Moore, *Placing Blame: A Theory of Criminal Law* (Oxford: Oxford University Press, 1997), ch. 13; K K Ferzan, 'Opaque Recklessness' (2001) 91 *Journal of Criminal Law and Criminology* 597. (I realise that in this paragraph I have constructed a composite figure which each of those cited here might reject; but oversimplified though that figure is, it reveals some central strands in contemporary theorising.)

[16] See R A Duff, 'Harms and Wrongs' (2001) 5 *Buffalo Criminal Law Review* 13.

[17] See, e.g., J Horder, 'Rethinking Non-Fatal Offences against the Person' (1994) 14 *Oxford Journal of Legal Studies* 335; J Gardner, 'Rationality and the Rule of Law in Offences Against the Person' (1994) 53 *Cambridge Law Journal* 502; S Shute and J Horder, 'Thieving and Deceiving: What is the Difference?' (1993) 56 *Modern Law Review* 548. On 'thick' ethical concepts, see B Williams, *Ethics and the Limits of Philosophy* (London: Fontana, 1985), ch. 8.

[18] See, e.g., R A Duff, *Intention, Agency and Criminal Liability* (Oxford: Blackwell, 1990), ch. 7; K Huigens, 'Virtue and Inculpation' (1995) 108 *Harvard Law Review* 1423; V F Nourse, 'Hearts and Minds: Understanding the New Culpability' (2002) 6 *Buffalo Criminal Law Review* 361; K W Simons, 'Culpability and Retributive Theory: The Problem of Criminal Negligence' (1994) 5 *Journal of Contemporary Legal Issues* 365, and n. 13 above.

I will not rehearse these objections, or possible responses to them, here. Instead, I want to note, first, that the moral difference between attacks and endangerments is also less visible if we focus not on choice, but on the dispositions or character traits that lie behind and inform choice and action; and second, that the abstraction and conceptual thinness of the 'conduct-cause-harm' model of criminal wrongdoing might be more apt for endangerment offences than for attacks.

As to the first point, compare an agent who attacks another's property not from malice, but simply as a means to a further end, with one who consciously takes an unreasonable risk of damaging another's property in the course of his intended enterprise: one cuts down his neighbour's tree because it blocks his view; the other aims to burn his own trees, but realises that the fire might spread to his neighbour's tree. Each, we might think, displays the same vice or defect of character—a willingness to damage others' property in pursuit of his own ends, a serious indifference to others' rights and interests; and we might then think that each commits the same kind of wrong. If, however, we attend to the intentional structure of their actions, and the practical attitudes manifested in (part-constituted by) those actions, we can see that the actions constitute different types of wrong. One is structured by the intention to damage another's property; it is oriented towards and guided by the wrong that that intention involves. The other is not thus structured by or oriented towards wrong.[19] The argument that there is a significant moral difference between attacks and endangerments thus depends on the argument that criminal liability should be grounded in the character of our actions.[20]

As to the second point, one objection to a 'conduct-cause-harm' model for attacks is that by separating the harm from the conduct that causes it, it hinders a recognition of the way in which the character of the harm is partly determined by the meaning of the harming action as an attack. The distinctive harm suffered by the victim of theft, for instance, is not just that he loses property, a loss that could equally be caused by natural mischance: it is that his property is stolen—that the thief violates his interests and rights. Once we thus focus on the wrong, on the harm qua wrongful, we see the importance of the thick ethical concepts that characterise different kinds of wrongful attack—characterisations that are unavailable on the 'conduct-cause-harm' model.[21] In the case of endangerments, however, that separation might not be so distorting, since the agent's action is not structured by

[19] See T Nagel, 'The Limits of Objectivity', in S McMurrin (ed.), *The Tanner Lectures on Human Values I* (Cambridge: Cambridge University Press, 1980), 75, at 131–5. I comment at nn. 32–3 below on cases in which the agent foresees harm as a certain, not merely a likely, side-effect.

[20] See Duff, n. 2 above, ch. 11; and 'Action, the Act Requirement, and Criminal Liability', in J Hyman and H C Steward (eds.), *Agency and Action* (Cambridge: Cambridge University Press, 2004).

[21] See nn. 16–17 above.

an intention to harm. What is wrong with action that endangers another's life or property is, we might say, precisely that it is liable to cause harm—harm that we can identify independently of the action that causes it. If I am injured or my property is damaged, not by an attack, but by another's culpably dangerous conduct, I am still wronged; but the harm I suffer does not now seem different in character from the harm I would suffer if I was injured or my property was damaged by natural causes. In criminalizing attacks, we might say, we are criminalizing harmful wrongs—wrongs that do or threaten a relevant kind of harm; endangerment offences, by contrast, criminalize wrongful harms—harm-causing or harm-threatening conduct that is wrongful because it is potentially harmful.

The tasks of definition and categorisation might therefore be simpler for endangerment offences than they are for offences that consist in attacks. We must attend to the likelihood, nature and seriousness of the harm that is caused or threatened, to the worth of the conduct that creates the danger—all these bear on the wrongfulness of the conduct; we must attend to whether the agent was or should have been aware of the risk, which bears on her culpability: but we need not attend to the other kinds of factor, such as the context in which, the intention with which, or the means by which the harm was done, that bear on the moral character of an attack.

To distinguish attacks from endangerments as different types of criminal wrong is not yet to claim that this distinction is either exhaustive or exclusive—that every crime type or token can be classed unequivocally either as an attack or as an endangerment. It is tempting to think that the distinction should be exhaustive—that we should criminalize only what either attacks or endangers some protected interest; but this might be a trivial truth, if we identify a public interest in the criminalization of any conduct that we see good reason to criminalize. As for exclusivity, existing offence definitions often capture both attacks and endangerments: I am guilty of criminal damage if I damage another's property either purposely or recklessly,[22] and of simple assault if I cause bodily injury either purposely or recklessly.[23] I comment later on whether this is consistent with recognising attacks and endangerments as different types of wrong,[24] but we must first turn briefly to a different question, that of how sharply attacks and endangerments can be distinguished. Two issues are worth noting.[25]

[22] Criminal Damage Act 1971, s. 1(1); Model Penal Code s. 220.3.

[23] Model Penal Code, s. 211.1(1); Offences Against the Person Act 1861, s. 20.

[24] See at nn. 53–8 below.

[25] A third issue, which I cannot pursue in detail here, concerns the scope of the intention that an attack requires: that it surely need not encompass every aspect of the action that is essential to its character as an attack. Rape is an attack on its victim's sexual interests and integrity. Rape, and attempted rape, require an intention to sexually penetrate the victim, but neither requires intention (or knowledge) as to her lack of consent, although if she consented the action would not constitute an attack; in English law it is enough that the rapist does not reasonably believe that the victim consents (Sexual Offences Act 2003 s. 1(1)(c)). The criminal law here

Intended Endangerment

An agent might intend, not to cause substantive harm, but to create (or to expose another to) a risk of harm: I set fire to the house of my rival in love, knowing he is inside, intending thereby to frighten him into leaving town by exposing him to a risk of death or serious injury. I attack his property, since I intend to damage it; but surely I also attack him, even if I do not intend to injure him and will be relieved if he escapes without injury.[26] The same is true if I force you into a 'game' of Russian roulette; or if I try to see how close I can swing my golf club to your precious vase without actually hitting it, when the risk of hitting your vase is part of the point of the exercise.[27] (The last example shows that the agent who intends to create a risk need not do so in order to create fear.)

Such intended endangerments should count as attacks. One way to support this claim is to argue that the risk of harm is itself a harm, so that one who intends to endanger intends to do harm. Such an argument has some plausibility: we have an interest in being safe—in being securely free of the risk of substantive harm; that interest is set back when I am endangered, even if no substantive harm ensues.[28] However, first, we should distinguish such harm from the kinds of substantive harm on which it is parasitic—perhaps by calling it a 'secondary' harm:[29] the risk of injury is 'secondary' to the 'primary' harm of actual injury in that I have an interest in not being exposed to such risk only because I have an interest in not being injured. Secondly, we anyway do not need to count risks as harms in order to count intended endangerments as attacks. We need only note that intended endangerments share the crucial features of attacks: they are aimed against those whom the agent intends to endanger; they are intended to threaten, if not to harm, their victims' interests; they manifest hostility rather than mere indifference. I will therefore take endangerments, as distinct from attacks, to consist in the creation of risk without any intention to cause either the relevant substantive harm or the risk of it.

follows the contours of the extra-legal concept of attack: but how do we determine just what must be intended if an action is to constitute an attack? I have proposed a solution to the analogous question in the law of attempts elsewhere (n. 2 above, at 5–29): the 'intent to commit an offence' required for an attempt is an intention such that the agent would commit the relevant offence in carrying it out. That solution should also help with attacks, but I cannot pursue its application here.

[26] Compare *Hyam* [1975] AC 55; Lord Hailsham held such an intention to be sufficient *mens rea* for murder.

[27] Compare *Chief Constable of Avon and Somerset v Shimmen* (1987) 84 Cr. App. Rep. 7; and see generally J Horder, 'Varieties of Intention, Criminal Attempts and Endangerment' (1994) 14 *Legal Studies* 335, at 341–4.

[28] See C Finkelstein, 'Is Risk a Harm?' (2003) 151 *University of Pennsylvania Law Review* 963. Finkelstein is right to argue that we can see risk as a harm, but she relies too heavily on the argument that we must do so if punishment for endangerment is to be consistent with the Harm Principle (at 987–9): for the Harm Principle, in either its Millian or its Feinbergian version, permits the criminalization of conduct that causes *or threatens to cause* harm.

[29] H Gross, *A Theory of Criminal Justice* (New York: Oxford University Press, 1979), 124–5.

(There are also offences that consist in acting in ways that cause or might cause fear, but need not involve the creation of actual risk. If I threaten to kill you, intending you to fear that I will carry out the threat, I commit an offence, even if I do not intend to carry it out and there is no risk that I will.[30] If I use 'threatening, abusive or insulting words' within the hearing of someone who is 'likely to be caused harassment, alarm or distress thereby', I might be guilty of an offence.[31] Such offences constitute attacks, if they are intended to cause fear; if they are not intended to cause fear, they constitute endangerments.)

'Oblique' Intention

The intention to harm that attacks require is what is often called 'direct' intention; so-called 'oblique' intention, the foresight that my action will cause harm as a side-effect, is not enough. One who acts with or despite such foresight of harm does not manifest the kind of hostility that an attack involves. She rather manifests her utter indifference to the harm she expects to cause: she might wish or hope that the harm would not ensue, but she is practically indifferent to it, in that its prospect makes no difference to her action. Rather than treating foresight of harm as a species of intention, as the terminology of 'oblique intention' suggests, we should treat it (absent a justification) as the limiting case of recklessness; someone who acts with such foresight commits an extreme type of endangerment.

In classing 'oblique intention' with recklessness, rather than with 'direct' intention, I set myself against many theorists, and what might be becoming the authoritative definition of intention in English criminal law.[32] I am claiming not just that we can analytically distinguish confident foresight from 'direct' intention (which is uncontroversial), but that that distinction marks a significant moral difference—a difference not necessarily in degree of culpability or responsibility, but in moral kind. I will not try to defend that claim here,[33] but the distinction I draw between attacks and endangerments clearly depends on it.

The rest of this paper will focus on endangerments as distinct from attacks, and on the question of how we should criminalize various types of endangerment.

[30] Offences Against the Person Act 1861, s. 16; see also Criminal Damage Act 1971, s. 2.

[31] Public Order Act 1986, s. 5 (and ss. 3–4); and compare assault, an act by which I intentionally or recklessly cause *V* to apprehend immediate personal violence (see J C Smith and B Hogan, *Criminal Law* (10th ed., J C Smith. London: Butterworths, 2002), 411).

[32] See I Kugler, *Direct and Oblique Intention in the Criminal Law* (Aldershot: Ashgate, 2002) for a survey of the debate; on English law, see A J Ashworth, *Principles of Criminal Law* (4th ed., Oxford: Oxford University Press, 2003), at 173–80.

[33] But see Nagel, n. 19 above; Duff, n. 2 above, at 363–74; A P Simester, 'Why Distinguish Intention from Foresight?', in A P Simester and A T H Smith (eds.), *Harm and Culpability* (Oxford: Oxford University Press, 1996), 71.

3. Criminalizing Endangerment

If we ask why we should criminalize endangerment at all, an initial answer seems easy. We owe it to each other not merely not to attack each other, but to take reasonable care that we do not harm each other in the course of our activities. However uncertain the scope or stringency of our responsibilities to help others avoid harms from other sources might be, and however uncertain we might be about just what care we should take not to cause harm ourselves, we cannot deny that we have some responsibility to try to avoid causing harm by what we do. Sometimes harm is unavoidable; sometimes we cause it justifiably, either because it is not a harm that in the particular context we have reason to avoid causing, or because the reason we have to avoid causing it is outweighed by better reasons in favour of acting as we do. But the fact that a contemplated action might well injure others' interests is, normally, a good reason against undertaking that action, or for taking precautions against the prospective harm; and it often provides a conclusive reason against the action. If we act, without justification, in a way that we realise might harm others, when that prospective harm provides a conclusive reason against acting thus, we do wrong; we do wrong *to* those whom we thus endanger. The wrong consists not merely in creating a risk of harm, but in creating an unreasonable or unjustified risk of harm—a risk whose unexcused creation manifests our lack of proper concern for the interests of those we endanger.[34]

To say that one who creates an unjustified risk of harm does wrong is not yet to say that her conduct should be criminalized: to show that it should even in principle be criminalized,[35] we would need to show that it is a matter that should concern the law at all, rather than being a purely private matter to be dealt with by those involved; and that it should be a matter for the criminal law, rather than for the civil law (as a dispute between the endangerer and the endangered) or for a regulatory regime applying its own, noncriminal rules and penalties.[36] This would involve showing that the conduct in question is

[34] I focus here on endangering others, and cannot discuss offences that involve endangering the agent rather than others (see, e.g., Road Traffic Act 1988, ss. 14, 16, on seat belts and crash helmets). I also focus on individual rather than corporate activities, although the latter are the source of many of the most serious dangers that concern the criminal law: since our ideas of responsible agency are grounded in our conception of individual agency, an account of how dangerous conduct should be criminalized must begin with dangerous conduct by individuals.

[35] I.e. that it passes the first of the 'filters' that Schonscheck identifies: see J Schonsheck, *On Criminalization* (Dordrecht: Kluwer, 1994), at 63–83.

[36] The latter possibility is especially relevant to corporate activities. However, while regulatory agencies often seek to secure compliance without direct recourse to criminal prosecution (see K Hawkins, *Law as a Last Resort: Prosecution Decision-Making in a Regulatory Agency* (Oxford: Oxford University Press, 2002)), they usually operate under the aegis of and in ultimate reliance on a criminal law that defines endangerment offences for which individuals or corporations can be convicted and punished.

not just (potentially) harmful, but wrong, and that the wrong is a 'public' wrong that merits recognition and condemnation by the polity: that it is public either materially, in that it threatens harm to the collective rather than to identifiable individuals, or symbolically, in that it is a kind of wrong to individuals that should concern their fellow-citizens collectively.[37]

I take it that many types of endangerment do constitute public wrongs in this sense, but I cannot pursue that issue in detail here. Nor can I pursue the question of what kind of fault is appropriate for endangerment offences, though I suggested that recklessness is the paradigm fault in endangerment: the practical indifference that the reckless agent shows exemplifies the wrongfulness of endangerment.[38] This is not to say that recklessness should be the requisite fault for all endangerment offences—which would be to condemn the many existing offences that require only negligence, or that make liability to some degree strict: but I cannot pursue here the questions of when, if ever, negligence is an adequate basis for criminal liability, or when, if ever, liability can properly be strict.[39] I want to focus instead on the different ways in which we can criminalize endangerment.

We can distinguish three general modes of criminalization.[40] One identifies as a 'public' wrong, meriting authoritative condemnation by the criminal law, conduct that is already wrongful; another gives a more precise specification of a wrong whose scope is pre-legally controversial or unclear; the third criminalizes conduct that was not wrongful prior to its legal regulation, but that, once legally regulated, becomes wrongful in virtue of the way it hinders the ends that the regulation serves. Dangerous driving exemplifies the first mode, as a *malum in se*. The offence of allowing a dog bred for fighting 'to be in a public place without being muzzled or kept on a lead' exemplifies the second mode:[41] owners of such dogs have some pre-legal responsibility to take precautions against the harm that they might cause, but people disagree

[37] On these aspects of criminalization, see S E Marshall and R A Duff, 'Sharing Wrongs' (1998) 11 *Canadian Journal of Law and Jurisprudence* 7; R A Duff, *Punishment, Communication, and Community* (New York: Oxford University Press, 2001), 60–4.

[38] I leave aside here the question of whether recklessness always requires awareness of the risk one is taking: see n. 18 above. However, the argument that recklessness can be constituted by the very failure to notice a risk, when that failure manifests the appropriate indifference, is strongest when the risk is integral to an attack, as when a violent assailant displays 'extreme indifference to the value of human life' (Model Penal Code, s. 210.2(b)) in his very failure to advert to the obvious risk that he will kill his victim—see *Miller and Denovan* (1960; G H Gordon, *The Criminal Law of Scotland* (3rd ed., M G A Christie, Edinburgh: W Green, 2000–2001), vol. II, at 303–7), *Parr v H. M. Advocate* 1991 SLT 208; or when the actualisation of the risk turns an action into an attack, as when a man is convinced, without good reason, that a woman on whom he forces sexual penetration consents to it—see *Morgan* [1976] AC 182, *Cogan and Leak* [1976] QB 217. Perhaps recklessness in pure endangerment offences always requires conscious risk-taking: but I cannot pursue this possibility here.

[39] See A P Simester (ed.), *Appraising Strict Liability* (Oxford: Oxford University Press, 2005).

[40] See Duff, n. 37 above, at 56–66, 'Crime, Prohibition and Punishment' (2002) 19 *Journal of Applied Philosophy* 97.

[41] Dangerous Dogs Act 1991, s. 1(2)(d).

about its precise scope; the law provides a clear determination of that responsibility. The offence of having a firearm without a certificate exemplifies the third mode:[42] without a legal regulation requiring certification, it could not be wrong to possess a firearm without a certificate; but if the creation of such an offence is justified, it is because the regulation helps to prevent harms of relevant kinds; breaches of the regulation are therefore wrongful because they threaten to undermine that harm-preventive goal.[43]

We can clarify these different modes of criminalization, and the problems of principle that they sometimes present, by drawing some more systematic distinctions between different kinds of endangerment offence, and examining some of the issues that those distinctions raise.[44]

Consummate v Nonconsummate Offences

Endangerment offences are *consummate* if their commission requires the actualisation of the relevant risk, the occurrence of the relevant harm; wounding and criminal damage, when committed recklessly, are examples.[45] They are *nonconsummate* when they are defined 'in the inchoate mode', and do not require the actualisation of the risk; reckless endangerment and dangerous driving are examples.[46] Two structural questions arise here.

First, the law sometimes distinguishes consummate from nonconsummate endangerment offences: homicide from reckless endangerment, or causing death by dangerous driving from dangerous driving.[47] Sometimes, however, it criminalizes only the consummate offence, as with criminal damage;[48] sometimes it criminalizes only the nonconsummate offence, as with perjury—a sworn witness who makes a material statement that she does not believe to be true commits perjury whether or not her statement is false, or believed.[49] I will discuss shortly the question of whether we should have a general offence of nonconsummate endangerment, analogous to that of attempt: the question here is why the law should sometimes distinguish consummate from nonconsummate forms, and sometimes not. The main reason to distinguish them lies in the argument that 'resulting harm' makes a significant difference to the character and seriousness of the wrong

[42] Firearms Act 1968, ss. 1–2. [43] See further at n. 67–81 below.

[44] Several of these distinctions are usefully analysed in D Husak, 'The Nature and Justifiability of Nonconsummate Offenses' (1995) 37 *Arizona Law Review* 151.

[45] Offences Against the Person Act 1861, s. 20; Criminal Damage Act 1971, s. 1(1).

[46] Model Penal Code s. 211.2; Road Traffic Act 1988, s. 2. See further A J Ashworth, 'Defining Criminal Offences Without Harm', in P Smith (ed.), *Criminal Law: Essays in Honour of J C Smith* (London: Butterworths, 1987), 7.

[47] Model Penal Code ss. 210, 211.2; Road Traffic Act 1988 s. 1–2.

[48] See at n. 5 above.

[49] Perjury Act 1911, s. 1; for other examples, see Ashworth, n. 46 above. The example of perjury reminds us that it might not always be clear just what the threatened harm is: is it that the statement is false; or that it is false and believed; or that it is false and believed, and leads to an incorrect or unjust decision?

committed: one who causes the harm that she recklessly risks causing commits a wrong different from, and more serious than, one who fortunately does not cause the harm; she has something more to repent and to answer for. I will not rehearse that argument here,[50] but if resulting harm is thus significant, we must question the practice of defining some offences in the inchoate mode: should not the law mark that significance by distinguishing consummate from nonconsummate versions of all offences?

One answer might be that the resulting harm is not always that significant: for instance that the essential wrong involved in perjury lies not so much in its possible effects (the court being misled) as in the contempt for the law that the perjurer displays. This answer seems implausible for perjury (if my recklessness as to the truth of my evidence leads to an unjust verdict, I have surely committed a greater wrong than if I am disbelieved), and for 'result crimes' generally: if a crime's wrongfulness does not significantly depend on any further consequences of the offender's conduct, it is a 'conduct crime', not a result crime defined in the inchoate mode.[51] A more plausible answer is that definition in the inchoate mode makes it easier to prove guilt when it might be hard to prove that a defendant's conduct did cause the relevant harm:[52] but this would suggest at most that both consummate and nonconsummate versions of the offence should be available, not that they should not be distinguished. I return shortly to the question of how broad the range of nonconsummate offences should be, but the argument so far suggests that when we have good reason to criminalize nonconsummate as well as consummate endangerment offences, we also have good reason to distinguish them.

The second question is: if attacks and endangerments are distinct types of wrong, should the law not define them as distinct types of offence? Sometimes it does so: wounding with intent is distinguished from wounding (which can be committed recklessly) in English law;[53] murder requires an intention at least to cause serious bodily injury, and one who causes death through mere recklessness is guilty only of manslaughter.[54] But often it does

[50] See Duff, n. 2 above, ch. 12; D Z Phillips, 'How Lucky Can You Get?', in D Z Phillips and P Winch (eds.), *Wittgenstein: Attention to Particulars* (London: Macmillan, 1989), 165.

[51] On 'result' and 'conduct' crimes, see Gordon, n. 38 above, vol. I, at 59. Rape is a conduct crime (*pace* Smith and Hogan, n. 31 above, at 30–1), since although it can have devastatingly harmful consequences for its victim, its essential wrongfulness lies in the very act of rape: it is therefore so defined that its commission does not require proof of the occurrence of such further harmful consequences; but we should not say that it is defined 'in the inchoate mode'.

[52] See Ashworth, n. 46 above, at 17–18, for some salutary scepticism about this answer.

[53] Offences Against the Person Act 1861, ss. 18, 20; see the draft Offences Against the Person Bill, ss. 1–2 (*Reforming the Offences Against the Person Act 1861* (London: Home Office, 1998)).

[54] See Smith and Hogan, n. 31 above, at 359–61 (although English law seems to count certain foresight as intention; see at n. 32 above). Even when the *mens rea* of murder is defined in terms of 'recklessness', as with 'wicked recklessness' in Scots law, it is arguable that the recklessness that is to make a killer guilty of murder must be displayed in the course of an attack on another person: see Gordon, n. 38 above, vol. II, at 295–310, and compare Model Penal Code s. 210.2(1)(b).

not: *D* commits the same offence of criminal damage whether she damages *V*'s property deliberately or only recklessly;[55] the same offence of assault whether she injures V deliberately or recklessly.[56] Of course there are limits to the extent to which the law's definitions of offences should reflect significant moral distinctions, but it should in principle reflect a categorial difference such as that between attacks and endangerments, both to advance 'fair labelling',[57] and to ensure that matters that bear significantly on sentencing (as the difference between deliberate and merely reckless actions surely should bear) are properly proved in court. This might cause problems if the prosecution can prove that *D* recognised a risk of the relevant harm, but is not sure that it can prove intention: but they could be remedied by counting the endangerment form of the offence as an 'included' offence in relation to the attack form.[58]

General v Specific Offences

We can focus now on nonconsummate endangerment offences, since these raise the main questions that concern us here.

Such offences can be more or less *general* or *specific*, as to the interest that is threatened, or as to the way in which it is threatened. Robinson proposes a general offence of 'act[ing] in a way that creates a substantial and unjustified risk of causing a result made criminal by this Code': an offence that specifies neither a particular kind of threatened harm nor a particular mode of conduct.[59] Existing offences are more specific in one or more ways: as to the type of (usually serious) harm that is threatened;[60] or as to the (usually especially dangerous) activity that creates the risk;[61] or as to the agent (someone with special responsibilities) who creates the risk;[62] or as to the (usually especially vulnerable) potential victims.[63]

[55] Criminal Damage Act 1971, s. 1(1); Model Penal Code s. 220.3.

[56] Model Penal Code s. 211.1(1); see also Smith and Hogan, n. 31 above, at 411–19, on assault and battery; and the draft Offences Against the Person Bill (n. 53 above), s. 3, defining a single offence of 'intentionally or recklessly caus[ing] injury'.

[57] See Ashworth, n. 32 above, at 89–92.

[58] See Criminal Law Act 1967, s. 6(3); Model Penal Code, s. 1.07(4).

[59] Robinson, n. 14 above, at 218; s. 51 of his Draft Code of Conduct. The offence requires at least recklessness as to the risk: see p. 225, s. 200 of the Draft Code of Adjudication.

[60] See, e.g., Model Penal Code, s. 211.2—'conduct which places or may place another person in danger of death or serious bodily injury'; the Scottish offence of 'causing danger to the lieges by culpable recklessness' (Gordon, n. 38 above, vol. II, at 427–30); and Australian Model Criminal Code, ss. 5.1.25–6 (D Lanham, 'Danger Down Under', [1999] *Criminal Law Review* 960, at 965–7).

[61] E.g. Road Traffic Act 1988, ss. 2, 4, 12, 22, 40; Explosive Substances Act 1883, s. 2 (causing explosions that are 'likely to endanger life or to cause serious injury to person or property'); Dangerous Dogs Act, s. 3, criminalizing those in charge of dogs that are 'dangerously out of control in a public place' (and defining danger in terms of injury to the person); Food Safety Act 1990, s. 8 (selling food that 'fails to comply with food safety requirements').

[62] E.g. Health and Safety at Work etc. Act 1974 (employers); Merchant Shipping Act 1995, ss. 58, 98, 100 (masters, seamen, ship-owners).

[63] E.g. Children and Young Persons Act 1933, ss. 1, 11; Mental Health Act 1983, s. 127. See generally, K J M Smith, 'Liability for Endangerment: English Ad Hoc Pragmatism and

The obvious question is: why should we not operate with a wholly general endangerment offence like that proposed by Robinson, analogous to the law of attempts?[64] Why should we instead maintain this incomplete kaleidoscope of specific offences?

A retributivist argument in favour a general offence is that even if the nonoccurrence of the harm makes a significant difference to the character of the endangerer's conduct, one who culpably risks causing a kind of harm that would make her criminally liable if it ensued still commits a wrong, of a kind that in principle merits public condemnation. A consequentialist argument is that such an offence would provide a more effective deterrent against dangerous conduct, and so against actually harmful conduct. A related argument is that absent such a general offence, legislators are prone to try to fill perceived gaps in the law with often ill-drafted new specific offences, to criminalize kinds of conduct that come to be seen as worryingly dangerous.

On the other hand, from the point of view of penal desert, we must ask whether the kind of wrong involved in nonconsummate endangerment is always serious enough to merit the coercive attentions of the criminal law, and the various costs that criminalization involves.[65] This question gains force if, as I have argued elsewhere, the nonoccurrence of a prospective harm makes a more significance difference to the moral character of the action in the case of endangerment than it does in the case of attack:[66] whilst a failed attack is structured by the harm it is intended to do, a luckily harmless act of endangerment is further removed from the harm that it might have caused, but did not cause; the former is still intrinsically or essentially harmful, whilst the latter is only potentially harmful. As for efficient deterrence, we should note that such a general offence would no doubt be enforced even more selectively than are our existing endangerment laws, given both the likely concentration of resources on what are perceived as the more serious kinds of harm, and the extent to which endangerment is often only noticed when it actually causes harm. Given the familiar dangers involved in allowing officials too extensive a discretion in selecting which cases to investigate or prosecute, we might see good reason to limit that discretion by criminalizing only the more serious kinds of endangerment: those that are more serious in virtue either of the kind of risk that they create, or of the fact that they actually cause the threatened harm—which is

American Innovation' [1983] *Criminal Law Review* 127; and, for further examples, P R Glazebrook, *Blackstone's Statutes on Criminal Law* (13th ed., Oxford: Oxford University Press, 2003), 77–137.

[64] See Criminal Attempts Act 1981, s. 1; Model Penal Code, s. 5.0 (neither offence is entirely general: English law criminalizes only attempted indictable (not summary) offences; the Model Penal Code criminalizes only attempted crimes, not attempted violations). I leave aside here the issue of how we should specify the conduct element of such an offence.

[65] On which see D Husak, 'Why Punish the Deserving?' (1992) 26 *Nous* 447.

[66] See Duff, n. 2 above, at 363–6.

what our existing laws effectively do. Such considerations do not tell us just how general or specific, in which ways, our endangerment laws should be, and do not rule out a 'reckless endangerment' offence as general as that defined by s. 211.1 of the Model Penal Code: they do suggest, however, that we have reason not to embrace a wholly general offence of the kind proposed by Robinson.

Explicit v Implicit Offences

Endangerment offences are *explicit* when their commission requires the actual creation of the relevant risk—a risk specified in the offence definition; they are *implicit* if their definition does not specify the relevant risk (the risk that grounds their criminalization), so that they can be committed without creating the risk.[67] Dangerous driving and 'reckless endangerment' are explicit endangerment offences. Driving 'with alcohol concentration above prescribed limit', speeding, pretending to be a legally recognised doctor, are implicit endangerment offences:[68] although the conduct that they criminalize is criminalized because it is liable to lead to kinds of harm that concern the criminal law, no explicit reference to such harms appears in these offence definitions. Conviction for an explicit endangerment offence requires proof that the defendant created a risk of harm of the relevant kind; no such proof is required for an implicit endangerment offence, nor would proof that the defendant did *not* create such a risk—for instance that this driver's competence was not impaired by consuming an amount of alcohol that put her over the limit—save her from conviction.[69]

Explicit endangerment offences typically declare 'standards', whereas implicit offences lay down 'rules'.[70] To convict a person of an offence of explicit endangerment, the court will have to find not just that he created a significant risk of harm that constituted *a* reason against acting as he did, but that, for instance, the risk was 'substantial and unjustifiable',[71] or that his conduct fell 'far below what would be expected of a competent and careful' agent, and would have been seen as obviously dangerous by such an agent.[72] Such determinations will require attention not merely to the

[67] See Husak, n. 44 above, at 168–9, on 'complex' and 'simple' nonconsummate offences.

[68] See respectively Road Traffic Act 1988, s. 5; Road Traffic Regulation Act 1984, ss. 81–9; Medical Act 1983, s. 49.

[69] The 'explicit'/'implicit' distinction drawn here depends on identifying the kind of harm with which each offence is primarily concerned: where there is uncertainty or disagreement about what the harm is, there might therefore also be uncertainty or disagreement about whether the offence is one of explicit or of implicit endangerment.

[70] See P J Schlag, 'Rules and Standards' (1985) 33 *UCLA Law Review* 379.

[71] Model Penal Code, s. 2.02(2)(c), defining recklessness; see s. 211.2.

[72] Road Traffic Act 1988, s. 2A, on the meaning of 'dangerous driving'. See also Robinson's Draft Code of Adjudication, s. 113: 'creating a prohibited risk' (s. 51 of the Code of Conduct; at n. 59 above) requires 'a gross deviation from the standard of conduct of a law-abiding person': Robinson, n. 14 above, at 224.

seriousness and likelihood of the threatened harm, and to the value of the activity that creates the risk, but to the context of that activity and to the responsibilities (to take care or precautions) that can plausibly be assigned to the defendant and to others.[73]

The merit of criminalizing endangerment through offences of explicit endangerment is that—if the law is properly applied—we criminalize only those who actually endanger others in ways that deserve condemnation.[74] The drawback is that, unless we can rely on some quite specific shared understandings of what counts as an 'unreasonable risk', and of what kinds of care people should take, in a range of contexts, the standards that courts have to apply will not be the polity's shared standards, but the individual standards of each court and its members—which generates the familiar defects of uncertainty in the law's content, and unpredictability and inconsistency in its application. This drawback grounds one reason in favour of offences of implicit endangerment, as a brief look at some familiar road traffic offences will illustrate.

English law defines explicit endangerment offences of driving when unfit through drink or drugs, and of dangerous driving; and implicit endangerment offences of driving with more than a specified concentration of alcohol in one's blood, and of exceeding the specified speed limit.[75] The implicit offences lay down rules that are intended to capture part of the content of the standards declared in the explicit offences. An obvious attraction of such implicit offences for prosecutors is that they make proof of legal guilt easier; but that does not speak to their justice.[76] Another, wider attraction is that they promote certainty and consistency: citizens can know what they may or may not do;[77] courts can apply the law with greater consistency. Such

[73] Cases involving the risk of HIV transmission through sexual intercourse exemplify the issues here (see Model Criminal Code Officers Committee, *Non Fatal Offences Against the Person* (Canberra: Attorney General's Department, 1998; http://www.aic.gov.au), at 75–87; Lanham, n. 60 above). The risk is statistically low, perhaps 1 in 2,000: so does criminalization mark a familiar kind of moral panic, or a judgement based both on the seriousness of the harm and on the breach of trust? But to talk of a breach of trust presupposes a particular view of the parties' responsibilities in sexual activity—a view that might be arguable in some contexts.

[74] Perhaps not all those who commit explicit endangerment offences actually endanger others: the reckless driver who rounds a blind corner on the wrong side of the road might reasonably deny that he has endangered anyone, if there was in fact no one there. But his conduct is still criminally dangerous, given the real (and unjustified) risk of someone being there. It is cases like this that justify the Model Penal Code's definition (s. 211.2) of 'reckless endangerment' as 'conduct which places or may place' others in danger, and that show why 'or may place' is not, *pace* Lanham (n. 60 above) pleonastic.

[75] Road Traffic Act 1988 ss. 2–5; Road Traffic Regulation Act 1984, ss. 81–9.

[76] See Ashworth, n. 32 above, at 85–6.

[77] It might be hard to identify the point at which another drink would put me over the limit: but the law conveys the message that drinking *any* alcohol before driving is risky ('Don't drink and drive'), which opens the way to the 'thin ice' principle; once we start to drink we are on thin ice, and 'can hardly expect to find a sign which will denote the precise spot where [we] will fall in' (*Knuller* [1973] AC 435, at 463 (Lord Morris); see Ashworth, n. 32 above, at 74–5).

offences will, however, capture some drivers whose conduct is not in fact appropriately dangerous: a driver whose capacity and willingness to drive safely are not impaired by an amount of alcohol that puts him over the legal limit still commits an offence if he drives after drinking that much, though he does not thereby create the increased risk of harm that justifies this drink-driving law; so too for a driver whose skills and car are such that she can drive as safely at speeds well over the legal limit as others can at speeds within the limit.[78] Can it be fair to demand that such people obey these laws, and just to convict them if they do not?

Such people might still be acting dangerously: if they believe that they are driving safely, but cannot rightly claim to *know* that they are safe after drinking that much or at that speed, we might say that in driving as they do they take an unreasonable risk that their belief is false. The point is not just that human beings are fallible. It is rather that there are particular reasons for mistrusting drivers' judgements on such matters: we are notoriously prone to exaggerate our driving skills; and someone who is in a hurry, or who has already had a drink, is not well placed to decide whether he can drive safely at that speed, or after another drink. We can thus see some implicit endangerment offences as specifying precautions that everyone should take against causing or risking harm, in contexts in which we should not trust our own case-by-case judgements about how to act safely: given the risks involved in the activity concerned, given our proneness to misjudgement, we should follow relatively simple rules ('Don't drink and drive'; 'Don't exceed the speed limit'), rather than allowing ourselves to decide on each occasion how fast to drive or how much to drink before driving.[79] The law demands not just that we drive safely, but that we *ensure* that we do so;[80] such implicit endangerment offences declare that part of what we must do to ensure safety is to obey these restrictions.

Surely, however, there are people who *know* that they can safely break such rules: drivers who *know* that they can drive safely although over the legal limit as to their speed or alcohol intake. Can we argue that they nonetheless ought to obey such laws; or must we admit that they should in justice be exempt, and that to convict them is to sacrifice their rights for the sake of the greater social good that flows from not allowing such public exceptions to the law? We might appeal to two considerations. First, we owe it to each other not merely to *ensure* that we act safely, but to *assure* each other that we are doing so, in a social world in which we lack the personal knowledge of others that could give us that assurance; we provide

[78] Hence the common complaint that rules, if they are not under-inclusive, are over-inclusive.

[79] This argument embodies a familiar rule-consequentialism: see R M Hare, *Moral Thinking: Its Levels, Method and Point* (Oxford: Oxford University Press, 1981).

[80] Compare Health and Safety at Work etc. Act 1974, ss. 2–3, on employers' duties to 'ensure, so far as is reasonably practicable', the health and safety of their employees and others.

such assurance in part by visibly following public safety-protecting rules, such as the speed limit.[81] Secondly, a driver who claims to know that he can safely ignore such rules claims a certain superiority over his fellows: *they* must obey these rules, because they cannot be trusted to decide for themselves, but *I* need not. What is wrong with such a claim is not that it is false (though it often will be), but that it is a denial of fellowship with my fellow citizens: a recognition of fellow citizenship (and of the dangers involved in allowing exemptions to the law's demands) should motivate me to accept such laws even if I believe (truly) that they are unnecessary in my case; at least so long as the demands the law makes on me are not that onerous, this is a modest burden that I ought to accept as an implication (and expression) of citizenship.

The arguments sketched here will not justify all the implicit endangerment offences that our laws currently contain—nor should they; but they can justify some such offences.[82]

Direct v Indirect Offences

Endangerment offences are *direct* if the relevant harm would ensue from the criminalized conduct without any intervening wrongful human action; they are *indirect* if the harm would ensue only given further, wrongful actions by the agent or by others. Thus dangerous driving standardly involves direct endangerment, as does causing a dangerous explosion.[83] Carrying firearms or offensive weapons in public, however, involves only indirect endangerment, since the relevant harms would normally ensue only if the firearms or weapons were then misused by the carrier or by others.[84] A complication arises when the intervening actions would be by children, or by people who are acting quite reasonably. If I supply a gun to a child,[85] or wave a gun at someone who does not know it is unloaded,[86] harm might

[81] Similar considerations also apply to the requirements that drivers be licensed, after passing a test, and that they carry at least third party insurance: these are ways of ensuring and assuring that drivers are minimally competent and that damage they cause will be paid for.

[82] But see D Husak, '*Malum Prohibitum* and Retributivism', in this volume, for a critique of this line of argument.

[83] See n. 61 above.

[84] Firearms Act 1968, s. 19; Prevention of Crime Act 1953, s. 1; Criminal Justice Act, s. 139 (these are also offences of implicit rather than explicit endangerment). Offences of possessing or supplying drugs are also offences of indirect implicit endangerment—and are controversial partly because of their uncertain relationship to criminally significant harm: see D Husak, *Drugs and Rights* (Cambridge: Cambridge University Press, 1992). Possession offences more generally provide good examples of the way in which the criminal law can be extended to capture kinds of conduct (or state) that are at worst indirectly dangerous: see M D Dubber, 'Policing Possession: The War on Crime and the End of Criminal Law' (2001) 91 *Journal of Criminal Law and Criminology* 829 and 'The Possession Paradigm: The Special Part and the Police Power Model of the Criminal Process', in this volume.

[85] Compare Firearms Act 1968, s. 24.

[86] See, e.g., *Thomas v Commonwealth* 567 SW 2d 299 (Kentucky 1978); *Commonwealth v Gouse* 429 A 2d 1129 (Pennsylvania 1981).

flow from what the child does with the gun, or from what the other person does to escape the perceived threat: but my conduct might still count as 'directly' dangerous, if we see the intervening agency as suitably 'innocent'. We should count endangerment as strictly 'indirect' only if the occurrence of the relevant harm would depend on a genuine, noninnocent, *novus actus interveniens*.[87]

Offences of direct endangerment are in principle unproblematic—or no more problematic than the doctrines of causation on which they depend. Offences of indirect endangerment are, however, more problematic, whether the occurrence of the harm would depend on the agent's own further actions, or on those of others.

What argues against criminalizing conduct that would become directly dangerous only in virtue of further actions by the agent herself is the general principle of respect for autonomy: the law should not prohibit intrinsically harmless conduct on the mere grounds that the agent might go on to create a risk of harm, since this fails to treat citizens as responsible agents who can be expected to recognise and respond to the good reasons that the law anyway offers for not going on to create such risk. This principle is qualified when the law criminalizes conduct that is preparatory to an intended attack,[88] but such a qualification is already controversial, as denying the agent a suitable '*locus poenitentiae*'.[89] If we also extend the law to cover cases in which what is in prospect is not an attack, but mere endangerment, we surely separate the law of endangerment too far from the wrongful harms that should be its primary focus.[90] The only other kind of case in which the principle might be qualified is that in which there is particular reason to think that the agent cannot be trusted to be responsive to reasons; an example might be the drunk-driving provision that criminalizes not just anyone who 'drives or attempts to drive', but anyone who 'is in charge of a motor vehicle' when over the limit.[91]

[87] On *novus actus interveniens*, see A P Simester and G R Sullivan, *Criminal Law: Theory and Doctrine* (2nd ed., Oxford: Hart Publishing, 2003), 91–103. See *Khaliq v H M Advocate* [1984] JC 171, *Ulhaq v H M Advocate* [1991] SLT 614. In both cases, the defendants were convicted of an offence of endangerment, for supplying materials that they knew would be used for glue sniffing. In *Khaliq*, the buyers were children, but the court did not rely on this, and in *Ulhaq* they were adults; the offence was thus treated as one of indirect endangerment.

[88] E.g. Criminal Law Act 1967, s. 4—doing 'any act with intent to impede [the] apprehension or prosecution of an offender'; Criminal Damage Act 1971, s. 3(a)—possession of something intending that it be used to damage another's property: J Horder, 'Crimes of Ulterior Intent', in Simester and Smith, n. 33 above, 153.

[89] See Duff, n. 2 above, at 35–7, 386–9.

[90] Bearing in mind that if the agent acts with the intention of going on to endanger others, his conduct is preparatory to an attack, not to mere endangerment: see at n. 26–31 above; and compare Explosive Substances Act 1883 s. 3(b), possessing or making explosives 'with intent by means thereof to endanger life'.

[91] Road Traffic Act 1988, s. 5(1)(b). It is worth nothing, however, that under s. 5(2) it is a defence for a person charged with this offence 'to prove that at the time he is alleged to have committed the offence the circumstances were such that there was no likelihood of his driving the vehicle' whilst he was over the limit.

Usually, of course, conduct that is indirectly dangerous in virtue of what the agent might do is also indirectly dangerous in virtue of what others might do. When the occurrence of a direct risk of harm would depend on the conduct of others, we must ask different questions about the extent of our responsibilities to assist in preventing crime: how far can a polity justifiably demand that its citizens constrain their own otherwise lawful conduct because of the risk that others might take advantage of it, or be encouraged or enabled by it, to commit crimes?[92] I do not have, and do not think we can aspire to, a general answer to this question: without the kind of detailed examination of different offences that we cannot embark on here, the most we can say is (vaguely) that we surely have some such responsibility, and that its precise scope will depend on weighing such factors as the onerousness of the restraint it involves, and the likelihood and seriousness of the offences that might then ensue.

My aim in this section has not been to answer the various questions, or to solve the various problems, that I have identified. My aim in the paper as a whole has rather been to clarify the character of endangerment as a distinctive kind of wrongdoing (distinct in particular from attacks), to show the different ways in which endangerment offences can be structured and defined, and to raise some of the questions that must be answered if we are to develop a just and acceptable criminal law of endangerment.

[92] See A von Hirsch, 'Extending the Harm Principle: "Remote" Harms and Fair Imputation', in Simester and Smith, n. 33 above, 259.

4

Malum Prohibitum *and Retributivism*

Douglas Husak*

1. Introduction

This volume is designed to help correct the indisputable fact that the special part of criminal law has received much less scholarly attention than its general counterpart. What is equally apparent, however, is that whatever emphasis the special part has attracted tends to focus on the same small handful of substantive offenses. Casebooks adopted in courses throughout the United States and the United Kingdom typically include chapters on homicide, theft, and (more recently) rape. Why are these few offenses so widely discussed while most others are ignored? The answer cannot be that these offenses consume the bulk of the workload of our systems of criminal justice. Other prohibitions—most notably, drug offenses—result in significantly greater numbers of arrests, prosecutions and convictions.[1] But even if the traditional focus were expanded to include drug proscriptions, I am confident that the kinds of offenses examined would still be what generally are called *core* crimes.[2]

Almost totally lacking is an examination of crimes outside the so-called core.[3] Which kinds of offenses are neglected? The answer is not altogether clear, since theorists differ about the conditions under which a crime should

* Professor of Philosophy, Rutgers University. I would like to thank the participants at the Special Part Conference at Louisiana State University Law School organized by Stuart Green and Antony Duff. These two organizers also provided me with thoughtful and detailed suggestions to improve my paper.

[1] Under current federal law, almost as many persons are punished for drug offenses as for all other crimes combined. See Bureau of Justice Statistics: *Sourcebook of Criminal Justice Statistics*, table 5.18 (2001).

[2] The idea that criminal law contains a core was introduced by George Fletcher, *Rethinking Criminal Law* (Boston: Little, Brown and Co, 1978). For further discussion, see Douglas Husak, 'Crimes Outside the Core' (2004) 39 *Tulsa Law Review* 101.

[3] According to William Stuntz, the criminal law has now become 'not one field but two. The first consists of a few core crimes . . . The second consists of everything else. Criminal law courses, criminal law literature, and popular conversation about crime focus heavily on the first. The second dominates criminal codes.' See William Stuntz, 'The Pathological Politics of Criminal Law' (2001) 100 *Michigan Law Review* 505, at 512.

be located within the core of the criminal law.[4] But each of the offenses scrutinized by theorists share at least three general features. First, they originated in the common law and thus have existed for a very long time in all jurisdictions. Secondly, they are codified in the enormously influential Model Penal Code. But mere longevity and codification do not explain why some offenses are emphasized while others are not. For present purposes, a third feature is especially significant. The crimes examined by theorists proscribe conduct that is morally wrongful prior to or independent of law. In other words, the particular offenses on which theorists focus are *mala in se*.

In this paper I will seek to rectify this imbalance by discussing *mala prohibita* offenses. I will not endeavor to describe and critique the various attempts commentators have made to draw the elusive distinction between these two kinds of crimes.[5] The problem of analyzing the concept of *malum prohibitum* is so formidable that it threatens to distract us from the topic I propose to address. I will construe an offense to be an instance of *malum prohibitum* when the conduct proscribed is not wrongful prior to or independent of the law that defined it as criminal. I hope that this rough characterization captures how most theorists understand the nature of *mala prohibita*.[6] Most importantly, this admittedly oversimplified description enables me to move directly to the substantive issue I will examine here.

An example of a *malum prohibitum* offense will prove helpful. In light of the notorious difficulty contrasting *malum in se* from *malum prohibitum*, no case can be expected to be wholly beyond controversy.[7] An illustration should satisfy two vague desiderata. First, it should not be patently silly or objectionable; it should not be a crime that almost no theorist would defend as a legitimate exercise of the criminal sanction.[8] In addition, it should not contain features that are unrepresentative of the category of *mala prohibita*

[4] For an example of a controversial position about what constitutes the core of the criminal law and the particular offenses that belong there, see George P Fletcher, 'Blackmail: The Paradigmatic Crime' (1993) 141 *University of Pennsylvania Law Review* 1617.

[5] I do not minimize this difficulty. After a lengthy investigation, however, I became convinced that a separate paper would be required to sort out the enormous confusions found in the literature.

[6] I am aware of several problems with this account, none of which (I believe and hope) raise grave difficulties for my project. One problem is that even *mala in se* offenses often appear to have a *malum prohibitum* component. The application of homicide offenses, for example, must specify when a victim is dead. The definition of death may be partly stipulative.

[7] Still, some candidates seem peculiar. Consider, for instance, Joshua Dressler's curious example of a *malum prohibitum* offense: selling adulterated foods. I trust that Dressler cannot believe that there is nothing wrongful about this conduct independent of and prior to law. Thus he must presuppose a different conception of *malum prohibitum*. See Joshua Dressler, *Understanding Criminal Law* (3rd ed., New York: Lexis Publishing, 2001), 145.

[8] For examples of silly laws and astute observations about why they proliferate, see Ronald L Gainer, 'Federal Criminal Code Reform: Past and Future' (1998) 2 *Buffalo Criminal Law Review* 45. His examples (at 66–7) include 'the transportation of alligator grass across a state line, using the slogan "Give a hoot, don't pollute" without authorization, pretending to be a 4-H Club member with intent to defraud, and including a member of the armed forces in a voter preference poll'.

offenses. An example that satisfies these desiderata—to which I will refer frequently—is the federal offense of money laundering. This statute imposes up to ten years' imprisonment on persons who knowingly engage in a monetary transaction (such as a bank deposit or withdrawal) of funds greater than $10,000 derived from specified unlawful activities.[9] This conduct seems likely to be *malum prohibitum*; although it is obviously wrongful to profit from conduct that is *malum in se*, it is hard to see why persons who deposit or withdraw these funds from banks commit a *second* wrong that is independent of or prior to law.[10] I see no reason why a defendant who deposits his ill-gotten gains in his account rather than concealing them under a mattress is culpable for greater wrongdoing and should be liable for an additional crime.[11] Unlike other possible examples of *mala prohibita* offenses that are rarely if ever enforced through criminal sanctions,[12] charges of money laundering are a staple of the ongoing war on drugs.[13]

Even those commentators obsessed with the general part of criminal law have a powerful incentive not to overlook such *mala prohibita* offenses. Whatever else the general part of criminal law may be, its content is derived largely by abstracting from offenses in the special part. Clearly, our views about the general part are shaped and influenced by the kinds of offense from which we generalize. Principles constructed from *mala in se* crimes are likely to be radically dissimilar from those derived from a broader sampling of offenses.[14] The existence of *mala prohibita* crimes has several

[9] 18 USCA § 1957 (West Supp. 2003).

[10] This example of *malum prohibitum* is best construed as an *ancillary* offense, designed to facilitate the prosecution and enforcement of a *malum in se*. These crimes are increasingly common. See Norman Abrams, 'The New Ancillary Offenses' (1989) 1 *Criminal Law Forum* 1.

[11] One commentator expresses his dissatisfaction with such offenses as follows: 'Sometimes the operating philosophy seems to be that, if government cannot prosecute what it wishes to penalize, it will penalize what it wishes to prosecute... Moving beyond penalization of collateral misconduct to the penalization of collateral, seemingly innocent conduct, that causes no real independent harm but that may be associated with either lawful or unlawful actions, raises jurisprudential questions that lawmakers have not frequently chosen to face.' See Gainer, above n. 8, at 63 n. 38.

[12] Federal prosecutors assure me that this statute is almost never construed as written, but is applied against those who act furtively or secretively. I have little doubt that exercises of prosecutorial discretion help to salvage many *mala prohibita* offenses. But I concur with those theorists who believe that prosecutorial discretion is a poor substitute for correctly formulating offenses in the first place. See Fletcher, above n. 2.

[13] Ironically, Stuart Green admits that the example he chooses to defend the justifiability of retributive punishment for *mala prohibita* offenders—the crime of tearing a tag off a mattress—has never actually been used to impose criminal sanctions. See Stuart Green, 'Why It's a Crime to Tear the Tag Off a Mattress: Overcriminalization and the Moral Content of Regulatory Offenses' (1997) 46 *Emory Law Journal* 1533, 1540–1, n. 7. I discuss Green's position at length below in § 3–4.

[14] For example, it seems unlikely that a theorist could have had *mala prohibita* offenses in mind when defining a crime as 'an act or omission and its accompanying state of mind which, if duly shown to have taken place, will incur a formal and solemn pronouncement of the moral condemnation of the community.' Henry Hart, 'The Aims of the Criminal Law' (1958) 23 *Law and Contemporary Problems* 401, 405.

implications for doctrines in the general part I cannot begin to explore here.[15] I will restrict my attention to a single problem that should disturb legal philosophers who adopt retributive theories of crime and punishment. I will question how we might justify the punishment of persons who commit *mala prohibita* offenses.

On the view I will presuppose, the normative problems associated with criminalization are intimately related to those surrounding punishment. I assume that conduct is defined as criminal when persons who engage in it become subject to state punishment, and the principle of legality ensures that no one becomes subject to state punishment unless he has engaged in conduct defined as criminal. Even if this biconditional relation between crime and punishment cannot be established as a conceptual truth, it surely is a close approximation I will not endeavor to defend here. If this presupposition is accepted, the notorious difficulty of justifying punishment is closely connected to the problem of defending a theory of criminalization. We cannot hope to justify punishment without attending to what individuals are punished *for*. Since persons who commit crimes become subject to punishment, and punishment must satisfy a stringent standard of justification, the state must be cautious before enacting a criminal offense. Unless the state would be justified in punishing persons who engage in a given type of conduct, that conduct should not have been criminalized in the first place. A defective theory of criminalization is likely to allow the state to proscribe conduct that will subject perpetrators to punishments that will prove difficult or impossible to justify.[16]

In the remainder of this Introduction, I make two (hopefully uncontroversial) observations about philosophical attempts to address these intimately related problems—to defend a theory of criminalization and to provide a justification of state punishment. First, the exponential growth in both the number of crimes enacted as well as the quanta of punishment inflicted makes solutions to these problems urgent. No one seems prepared to estimate the number of criminal offenses that exist in the United States today.[17] What is abundantly clear, however, is that the criminal law has

[15] Let me cite just one example. Any serious interpretation of the claim that persons are presumed to know the criminal law must wrestle with the issue of how defendants could reasonably be expected to be aware of the many *mala prohibita* offenses to which they are subject. See Douglas Husak and Andrew von Hirsch, 'Culpability and Mistake of Law', in Stephen Shute, John Gardner, and Jeremy Horder (eds), *Action and Value in Criminal Law* (Oxford: Clarendon Press, 1993), 157.

[16] Historically, some legal theorists have worried about imposing punishments on *mala prohibita* offenders, but the nature of their concerns tend to be unlike those expressed here. Francis Sayre, for example, complained that 'the vitality of the criminal law has been sapped' by punishments for *mala prohibita* offenses. See his 'Public Welfare Offenses' (1933) 33 *Columbia Law Review* 55, 80.

[17] For some astounding approximations, see John Coffee, 'Paradigms Lost: The Blurring of the Criminal and Civil Law Models—And What Can Be Done About It' (1992) 101 *Yale Law Journal* 1875.

grown far beyond its core, and now includes a plethora of proscriptions 'undreamed of by the drafters of the Model Penal Code'.[18] Until the middle of the nineteenth century, Anglo-American criminal law consisted almost entirely of *mala in se* crimes.[19] After all, there are only so many ways to behave wrongfully independent of and prior to law, and virtually all of these behaviors have been proscribed by the state for many years.[20] But there is no discernable limit to the number of *mala prohibita* offenses that might be enacted. Thus most of this phenomenal expansion in the criminal law is due to the proliferation of *mala prohibita* offenses.

Only a theory of criminalization can provide a principled basis to retard this expansion. Elsewhere, I have sketched the outlines of a theory of criminalization,[21] but I have not endeavored to apply it to *mala prohibita* offenses. My theory is motivated by what Andrew Ashworth aptly describes as criminal law *minimalism*.[22] Although it may be an unhelpful exaggeration to say that criminal sanctions should be employed only as a last resort,[23] I share the opinion of those many theorists who believe that punishment should be utilized only after a careful consideration of alternative means of social control.[24]

The growth in the size and scope of the criminal law has been accompanied by a massive increase in state punishment.[25] We live in the most punitive period in our history. Approximately two million people are

[18] See the discussion in Gerard E Lynch: 'Towards A Model Penal Code, Second (Federal?): The Challenge of the Special Part' (1998) 2 *Buffalo Criminal Law Review* 297, 299.

[19] Dressler, above n. 7, 144.

[20] Of course, it is easy to think of exceptions. According to one commentator, 'probably no area of criminal law has experienced more growth in recent years than intellectual property, at least in terms of legislative enactments'. Presumably, many of the new offenses to which the author refers are examples of *mala in se*. See Stuart Green, 'Plagiarism, Norms, and the Limits of Theft Law: Some Observations on the Use of Criminal Sanctions in Enforcing Intellectual Property Rights' (2002) 54 *Hastings Law Journal* 167, 235.

[21] See Douglas Husak, 'Limitations on Criminalization and the General Part of Criminal Law', in Stephen Shute and A P Simester (eds), *Criminal Law Theory: Doctrines of the General Part* (Oxford: Oxford University Press, 2002), 13; 'Guns and Drugs: Case Studies on the Principled Limits of the Criminal Sanction' (2004) 23 *Law and Philosophy* 437.

[22] Andrew Ashworth, *Principles of Criminal Law* (4th ed., Oxford: Clarendon Press, 2003), 32–7.

[23] See Douglas Husak, 'The Criminal Law as Last Resort' 24 *Oxford Journal of Legal Studies* 207 (2004).

[24] See Nils Jareborg, 'What Kind of Criminal Law Do We Want?' in Annika Snare (ed.), *Beware of Punishment* (Oslo: Scandinavian Research Council for Criminology, 1995), 17.

[25] The connection between the phenomenon of enacting too many criminal laws and that of inflicting too much punishment is not altogether obvious. Since most new statutes proscribe conduct that was already criminal under a preexisting law, the process by which greater numbers of prohibitions lead to greater amounts of punishments is complicated. As a result of overcriminalization, many defendants whose conduct intuitively amounts to a single crime actually commit several distinct offenses simultaneously. The availability of overlapping offenses leads to 'charge-stacking'. Since the risks of going to trial are greater when multiple offenses are charged, criminal defendants have enormous incentives to plead guilty as well as to agree to more severe punishments. See Stuntz, above n. 3.

confined in prisons and jails, a total that has nearly quadrupled since 1980. Since only about 8 million people are incarcerated throughout the world, one-quarter of these are jailed or imprisoned in the United States. Perhaps more worrisome is the fact that roughly 6.5 million Americans are presently under the supervision of the criminal justice system—which includes probation and parole. Prosecutorial restraint is the main reason these totals are not even higher.[26]

My second observation is that retributivism is the dominant school of punishment among contemporary legal philosophers. Admittedly, retributivism comes in many shapes and varieties, and some of its elements remain immensely controversial.[27] In any event, the problem on which I will focus is generated by very weak forms of retributivism to which the vast majority of philosophers subscribe.[28] Any defensible version of retributivism contends that punishment must be deserved, and desert is a backward-looking consideration with its base in something the agent has done. It is hard to see how punishment can be deserved unless what the agent has done—his desert base—is wrongful. Call this condition of justified punishment the *wrongfulness constraint*. The wrongfulness constraint is satisfied trivially when persons commit *mala in se* offenses like rape or murder. But the wrongfulness constraint becomes far more problematic when persons commit *mala prohibita* offenses. Retributivist theories of crime and punishment are at best embarrassed and at worst refuted by the existence of *mala prohibita* offenses.

Thus the task of reconciling *mala prohibita* offenses with retributive theories of criminalization and punishment is more pressing than ever. A comprehensive theory of criminalization must address the criteria by which to assess these offenses. Punishment will prove difficult or impossible to justify for those offenses that fail whatever criteria we ultimately defend.

2. Theoretical Neglect of the Problem

Since *mala prohibita* offenses are so numerous and weak forms of retributivism are so widely accepted, one would expect criminal theorists to have expended considerable ingenuity on the problem of justifying the punishments of persons who commit these crimes. In fact, however, relatively few such efforts have been undertaken. This oversight demands an explanation; I need to show that the difficulty on which I will focus is genuine. In this section, I will briefly examine six possible reasons why theorists may have neglected this issue.

[26] Anyone who peruses state or federal criminal codes would be astonished 'at their scope, by the sheer amount of conduct they render punishable'. Stuntz, *ibid.* 515.

[27] See John Cottingham, 'Varieties of Retributivism' (1979) 29 *Philosophical Quarterly* 238.

[28] See Larry Alexander, 'The Philosophy of Criminal Law', in Jules Coleman and Scott Shapiro (eds), *The Oxford Handbook of Jurisprudence and Philosophy of Law* (Oxford: Oxford University Press, 2002), 815.

Although none of these reasons is satisfactory, their failures are instructive, revealing much of interest about criminal theory generally.

I have already adverted to one explanation for this neglect. The very distinction between *malum in se* and *malum prohibitum* is hard to draw. As a consequence, many prominent theorists do not attempt to draw it at all.[29] No one needs to offer an account of a nonexistent contrast.[30] But we should not ignore a distinction because it is problematic and admits of innumerable borderline cases. As I have indicated, conduct may be described as *malum prohibitum* when it is not wrongful independent of or prior to law. Hopefully, few theorists would deny that some offenses conform to this description—such as my example of money laundering—while others do not.[31] *Some* such distinction *must* exist.

In addition, retributivists have been preoccupied with even more basic and fundamental questions. Although no one denies that a *malum in se* crime is wrongful, retributivists have struggled to explain exactly *how* and *why* the wrongfulness of such conduct makes persons deserving of state punishment.[32] Obviously, this task has proved daunting. If an account is difficult to defend even in cases of core criminality, it is not surprising that retributivists have barely begun to tackle the even more perilous job of extending their theory to crimes beyond the core.

Third, the difficulty of reconciling *mala prohibita* offenses with a retributivist theory of punishment is not a concern for those commentators who reject retributivism. Although I observed that the majority of legal philosophers subscribe to some version of retributivism,[33] the same cannot be said for theorists in related disciplines, most notably in criminology and

[29] In England, for example, Glanville Williams dismisses the distinction in a number of footnotes to his influential *Criminal Law: The General Part* (2nd ed., London: Stevens, 1961). A cursory discussion of *malum prohibitum* appears in the text of his subsequent *Textbook of Criminal Law* (2nd ed., London: Stevens, 1983). Here, Williams apparently equates (at 936) *mala prohibita* with 'quasi-criminal offences', 'public welfare offences', and 'regulatory offences', and subsequently laments: 'The difficulty with trying to establish a category of this kind is to say exactly what it means.' In the United States, the most influential book—George Fletcher's *Rethinking Criminal Law*—fails to include entries for *malum in se, malum prohibitum* (or even *regulatory offense*) in its index.

[30] Some commentators claim that 'the difficulty of classifying particular crimes as *mala in se* or *mala prohibita* suggests further that the classification should be abandoned'. See Wayne R LaFave, *Criminal Law* (3rd ed., St. Paul: West, 2000), 35–6.

[31] Stuart Green has suggested in correspondence that it may be misleading to categorize whole offenses as *malum prohibitum* or *malum in se*. Instead, it might be preferable to refer to given offenses as possessing *mala prohibita* elements to various degrees. See Green, above n. 13.

[32] According to one theorist, 'the central task [for retributivists] is to explain... this supposed justificatory relationship between past crime and present punishment'. R A Duff, 'Punishment, Communication, and Community', in Matt Matravers (ed.), *Punishment and Political Theory* (Oxford: Hart Publishing, 1999), 48. He continues (at 50): 'Antiretributivists make quite a meal [of] the general idea that crimes "deserve" punishment.'

[33] Of course, retributivism has had its detractors. See, for example, David Dolinko, 'Three Mistakes of Retributivism' (1991) 101 *Ethics* 537; and Russell L Christopher, 'Deterring Retributivism: The Injustice of "Just Punishment"' (2002) 96 *Northwestern University Law Review* 843.

criminal justice. Consequentialist theories, I am sure, encounter fewer problems justifying punishment for persons who commit *mala prohibita* crimes. Good results may follow from punishment regardless of whether conduct is *malum in se* or *malum prohibitum*, so consequentialists need not wrestle with the central problem I have posed. Indeed, nonretributivist accounts of crime and punishment might even reject the wrongfulness constraint itself. I would regard this rejection as a *reductio* of consequentialist theories, although I will not defend that position here.

Next, theorists may be reluctant to concede that *mala prohibita* offenses are 'true crimes' for which 'real punishments' are imposed.[34] Punishments need not be justified unless they are inflicted. This tactic is suggested by the Model Penal Code, which creates a category of 'violations' that are differentiated from crimes and are exempted from many of the doctrines in the general part.[35] I am skeptical of this approach generally, even though the contrast between punishments and other forms of unwanted deprivations is notoriously hard to draw.[36] Punishments require a justification even when they are not especially severe. Admittedly, real punishments involve both hard treatment and censure,[37] and the sanctions imposed for some *mala prohibita* offenses are not clearly designed to stigmatize. Still, these sanctions need to be justified, regardless of whether they are categorized as punishments.[38] In any event, this attempt to evade the fundamental issue is unsatisfactory when applied to all *mala prohibita* offenses. No one one can deny that a great many *mala prohibita* offenses *do* subject perpetrators to punishment by any reasonable definition. As I have indicated, persons convicted of money laundering may be imprisoned for as many as ten years.

Fifth, some philosophers have defended analyses of legal authority that might explain why disobedience to a *malum prohibitum* offense is wrongful. Joseph Raz has argued that law (under appropriate conditions) provides *pre-emptive* reasons for action.[39] According to his analysis, the many

[34] Some commentators state emphatically: 'An offense *malum prohibitum* is not a crime.' See Rollin M Perkins and Ronald N Boyce, *Criminal Law* (3rd ed., Mineola: Foundation Press, 1982), 886.

[35] American Law Institute, *Model Penal Code* § 1.04(5). Although the Code generally refrains from using the word 'punishment', violations are contrasted from crimes in that they do not subject offenders to terms of imprisonment. It is not hard to interpret the draftsmen as believing that violations, unlike crimes, do not give rise to punishments.

[36] The Supreme Court has struggled to differentiate punishments from deprivations imposed by the state that are non-punitive. One commentator describes the Court's effort as 'an incoherent muddle... so inconsistent that it borders on the unintelligible.' Wayne Logan, 'The Ex Post Facto Clause and the Jurisprudence of Punishment' (1998) 35 *American Criminal Law Review* 1261, 1268, 1280. Most recently, see *Smith v Doe*, 123 S.Ct. 1140 (2003) (deciding whether the Alaska version of 'Megan's Law', the Sex Offender Registration Act, is so punitive either in purpose or effect as to negate the State's intention to deem it as civil).

[37] See Andrew von Hirsch, *Censure and Sanctions* (Oxford: Clarendon Press, 1993).

[38] See Carol S Steiker: 'Foreword: The Limits of the Preventive State' (1998) 88 *Journal of Criminal Law & Criminology* 771.

[39] Joseph Raz, *The Authority of Law* (Oxford: Clarendon Press, 1979).

possible first-order reasons not to comply with a law, *malum prohibitum* or otherwise, are simply excluded from playing a role in practical reasoning. Raz's explication of legal authority has given rise to a massive literature, much of it critical, and I cannot begin to do justice to his theory here.[40] I simply assert without argument that no analysis of legal authority can hope to resolve the substantive question of whether retributive punishment is justifiably inflicted on persons who commit *mala prohibita* offenses.

Finally, theorists may be attracted by a deceptively straightforward solution to the problem of justifying punishment. It is tempting to suppose that the conduct prohibited by *mala prohibita* offenses is wrongful simply because it has been duly proscribed by the criminal law. According to the school of thought sometimes known as *legalistic retributivism,* persons are justifiably subjected to punishment whenever they have been given notice that their conduct falls under a criminal statute enacted by the state. This purported solution (if it does not evade the problem altogether) attempts to show that the wrongfulness constraint is satisfied *whenever* a criminal law has been enacted. The central problem I have posed is magically transformed into a matter of legality.

In the history of philosophical attempts to justify punishment, this solution is defended by J D Mabbott, whose views on the justification of penal sanctions are still included in textbooks that survey all of the possible varieties of retributivism.[41] According to Mabbott, criminals are justifiably punished simply because they have broken the law.[42] He explicitly indicates that the goodness or badness of either the government or the law is wholly irrelevant to whether punishment is just.[43] If Mabbott were correct, the problem of explaining how retributivists could justify punishments for *mala prohibita* offenses would be resolved easily. Unfortunately, the problem would be resolved *too* easily. Mabbott has elevated a necessary condition of justified punishment—that the defendant has violated a criminal law—into a sufficient condition. His theory breaches a second important constraint that an adequate theory of criminalization and punishment must satisfy. A viable theory of criminalization and punishment not only must specify the conditions under which the creation of a criminal law and the punishment of offenders would be justified, but also must describe the conditions under which they would *not* be justified. In other words, *some* offenses—including those that are *mala prohibita*—must be capable of being *un*justified.[44] I will call this second important constraint the *fallibility condition.*

[40] For an alternative analysis of authority that rejects the pre-emption model, see Scott J Shapiro: 'Authority', in Coleman and Shapiro, above n. 28, at 382.

[41] J D Mabbott: 'Punishment', in H B Acton (ed.), *The Philosophy of Punishment* (Macmillan: St. Martin's Press, 1969), 39.

[42] *Ibid.* 42.

[43] *Ibid.* 48.

[44] In a subsequent response to his critics, Mabbott allows that countervailing obligations might lead a judge *not* to impose a justified punishment. See J D Mabbott, 'Professor Flew on Punishment', in Acton, above n. 41, at 115, 124.

None of these six explanations is adequate to explain the neglect I will try to rectify. My fundamental objective is to try to understand how the enactment of *mala prohibita* offenses, and the punishments of persons who perpetrate them, are compatible with the wrongfulness constraint of even the weakest versions of retributivism. For the most part, my efforts will fail. I will survey the justificatory efforts of a number of prominent criminal theorists and conclude that they are largely unpersuasive. I am hesitant, however, to accept the full implications of my arguments. Rejecting masses of *mala prohibita* offenses is a radical step, even for a criminal law minimalist. Perhaps my reservations about many *mala prohibita* offenses will stimulate other commentators to undertake the formidable challenge of explaining how the state can be justified in punishing persons who commit them.

How *might* a given *malum prohibitum* offense satisfy the wrongfulness constraint and thus make perpetrators eligible for state punishment? No single answer to this question will suffice. The beginning of wisdom is to recognize the existence of several distinct *kinds* of *malum prohibitum* offense.[45] What makes different offenses members of a given kind?[46] If our objective is to reconcile *mala prohibita* offenses with the wrongfulness constraint of retributivism, the basis for assimilating different offenses into a single group should be relatively straightforward. Offenses should be sorted into a given kind because they are wrongful for the same reason. Once we have classified all of the possible reasons that an offense can be wrongful (without being an instance of *malum in se*), we will have produced an exhaustive inventory of the kinds of *malum prohibitum* offense that are needed for present purposes.[47] In the remaining sections I will describe two such categories—what I call hybrid offenses, and proscriptions arising from promises or a principle of fair play.[48] I attempt to decide whether and to what extent the wrongfulness constraint is satisfied when defendants commit offenses in each of these two categories.

3. Hybrid Offenses

In a recent article, Antony Duff has begun to address the problem I have raised. Although he does not pretend to offer a comprehensive account of how retributivists might justify the enactment of *mala prohibita* offenses or

[45] Admittedly, without a precise account of the distinction between *malum in se* and *malum prohibitum*, we may be unable to provide a complete description of the many ways that instances of the latter might be wrongful.

[46] Many distinct classificatory schemes might be provided. See, for example, the four categories developed in Eric Luna, 'Principled Enforcement of Penal Codes' (2000) 4 *Buffalo Criminal Law Review* 515, 528–33.

[47] Of course, a single *malum prohibitum* offense may be justified by distinct rationales, and thus be assigned to several different categories simultaneously.

[48] I do not claim that these categories exhaust the reasons a *malum prohibitum* offense might be wrongful.

the punishments of persons who commit them, he defends what he regards as a solution for one important kind of offense: a category of crimes he alleges to be 'neither purely *mala prohibita* nor purely *mala in se*'.[49] Instances of the kind of offense he has in mind 'involve a more or less artificial, stipulative determination of a genuine *malum in se*'.[50] Even though Duff himself does not give this category of proscriptions a name, I will call them *hybrid* offenses.

His examples of hybrid offenses—statutory rape and drunk driving—are illustrative.[51] Duff contends that the genuine *mala in se* behaviors that correspond to these hybrids are (roughly) 'having sexual intercourse with a young person who is not yet mature enough to be capable of making rational decisions about such matters', and 'driving when one's capacities are impaired by alcohol or drugs'. Instead of explicitly criminalizing *these* behaviors, however, the criminal law proscribes 'sexual intercourse with anyone under a specified age' or driving 'with more than a specified amount of alcohol in one's blood'.[52] These latter offenses are hybrids—neither purely *mala in se* nor purely *mala prohibitum*.[53] They are similar to but different from wholly *mala in se* or *mala prohibitum* offenses in the following respect. Persons *can* (and frequently *do*) commit these offenses without doing anything wrongful prior to or independent of law. This is not the case with pure *malum in se* offenses.[54] But some instances of these offenses *are* wrongful prior to or independent of law.[55] This is not the case with pure *mala prohibita* offenses.

No special difficulty justifying punishment arises when the conduct of a given defendant is both *malum in se* as well as *malum prohibitum*. That is, no difficulty arises when the sexual partner of a particular defendant is *both* below the age at which she is mature enough to consent *and* below the age

[49] R A Duff, 'Crime, Prohibition, and Punishment' 19 *Journal of Applied Philosophy* 97, 102 (2002).
[50] *Ibid.*

[51] These examples indicate that hybrid offenses represent a category of *malum prohibitum* distinct from crimes designed to solve coordination problems. For further discussion of the similarities and differences between these two classes of offense, see *infra* § 4.

[52] Duff, above n. 49, at 102.

[53] Notice that it may not be clear *what* particular *malum in se* is allegedly specified by a hybrid offense, or whether a genuine *malum in se* is specified at all. The first of the examples provided by Duff gives rise to this worry. Duff purports to 'leave aside the issue of whether [the act of having sexual intercourse with a young person who is not yet mature enough to be capable of making rational decisions about such matters] really is a *malum* that should concern the criminal law'. *Ibid.* 102.

[54] Unless, of course, persons who commit these offenses are *justified*. Justifications are extrinsic to offenses, but arise in circumstances in which the defendant's conduct is permissible despite satisfying each element of a criminal offense. Henceforth I ignore this complication, and assume that the criminal conduct in question is not justified.

[55] Or so I assume. Some theorists contend that crimes of risk imposition—such as drunk driving—are not wrongful in cases in which the risk does not materialize. For example, see Heidi Hurd, 'What in the World Is Wrong?' (1994) 5 *Journal of Contemporary Legal Issues* 157.

stipulated in the statute. The fundamental problem emerges, however, when the latter but not the former is true—when the conduct of the defendant is *malum prohibitum* without simultaneously being *malum in se*.[56] Some individuals, in other words, perpetrate a hybrid offense despite the fact that their conduct is not a *malum in se* of the appropriate kind. Because these offenses are hybrids, this outcome is all but inevitable. When the law proscribes sexual intercourse with anyone under a specified age, Duff admits 'we know that there are some individuals under that age who are fully capable of rational consent (more so than some above that age)'.[57] Moreover, when the law proscribes driving with a given blood alcohol content, 'we know that some people could still drive safely (more safely than many of those who are under the legal limit) when they are above the limit'.[58] In such circumstances—when a defendant commits a hybrid offense by engaging in conduct that is *malum prohibitum* even though it is not simultaneously *malum in se*—how can punishment be justified? More specifically, how can punishment be justified within a retributive theory that accepts the wrongfulness constraint?[59]

Duff's response invites us to consider why legislatures formulate these offenses as hybrids rather than as 'genuine *mala in se*'. He begins by listing many of the benefits of the foregoing 'artificial, stipulative determinations'. They facilitate convictions, curb discretion, and reduce abuse among law enforcement officials. But these advantages appear to be utilitarian; it is hard to see how they could satisfy a retributivist who (like Duff) contends that punishment must be grounded in the desert of the offender. The crucial issue, as he recognizes, involves 'considerations of principle. Our first question must be whether breaches of such regulations should *in principle* be made a criminal matter.'[60] Thus Duff advances what he calls 'a better reason [for criminalization]—that in these kinds of situations people should not try to decide for themselves whether what they would like to do is safe, since they cannot be trusted (and should not trust themselves) to do so'.[61] More specifically, 'a man excited at the prospect of sex with a young woman is ill

[56] In other words, hybrid offenses are *overinclusive*—perhaps necessarily so. For further thoughts on problems of overinclusion in the criminal arena, see Douglas Husak, 'Reasonable Risk Creation and Overinclusive Legislation' (1998) 1 *Buffalo Criminal Law Review* 599.

[57] Duff, above n. 49, at 102. [58] *Ibid.*

[59] I focus on the problem of overinclusion while ignoring the converse problem of *underinclusion*—that is, cases in which the defendant's conduct is *malum in se* even though it is not simultaneously *malum prohibitum*. In these cases, criminal liability is precluded by the principle of legality. Underinclusive statutes pose serious and unresolved difficulties for strong versions of retributivism that insist that each and every perpetrator of a moral wrong deserves to be punished. Michael Moore, for example, contends that 'legislators have reason to pass statutes prohibiting all actions that are morally wrong'. See Michael Moore, *Placing Blame* (Oxford: Clarendon Press, 1997), 72. It is unclear how Moore's retributivist objective can be achieved in a jurisdiction that accepts a principle of legality while allowing hybrid offenses to specify the content of a genuine *malum in se*.

[60] Duff, above n. 49, at 103 (emphasis in original). [61] *Ibid.*

placed to judge her maturity', and 'someone relaxing in a pub is ill placed to judge whether another drink might impair his capacity to drive safely'.[62]

How can these observations possibly help to justify punishment? Consider a person who has breached one of the hybrid laws Duff describes, even though his sexual partner is sufficiently mature to consent, or his driving is not seriously impaired. The difficulty is to show why such persons act wrongfully. Duff offers an original answer to this problem. He contends that punishment in such cases is justified because the defendant displays 'what we can call a kind of *civic arrogance*, which merits public censure and punishment'.[63] His position on this issue is worth quoting in full:

> Someone who insists that his sexual partner, although under the legal age of consent, is mature enough to decide about her own sex life, or that he can safely drive . . . after drinking an amount that puts him over the alcohol limit, might in fact be right. Indeed, he might *know* that his action is safe: his belief that it is safe might be true and well grounded. Nonetheless, if the assumption which underpins the law is correct, that these are contexts in which people cannot be trusted, and should not trust themselves, to make rational judgements, then this person arrogantly claims to be an exception to that rule. He claims that he can trust himself, and that we should therefore trust him, to make such judgements; he has no adequate basis for that claim. He might know that his conduct is safe—that it does not endanger the relevant interests: but he does not *know* that he knows this, and therefore cannot justifiably claim to be sure that he is not endangering any such interest. So even if his action does not in fact endanger any such interest, he takes an unjustified risk that it will do so; and he arrogantly claims the right to decide for himself on matters which he, like the rest of us, should not trust himself to decide. His claim is arrogant because it is unjustified—but also because it seeks to set him above his fellow citizens, in matters which affect their legally protected interests; and that is what merits the censure of the criminal law.[64]

Duff's argument contains several distinct threads. For simplicity, I will refer to it as the *civic arrogance* argument for punishing persons who commit hybrid offenses in circumstances in which their conduct is not *malum in se*.

The importance of Duff's civic arrogance argument in a comprehensive attempt to justify the enactment of *mala prohibita* offenses depends on how *many* crimes can plausibly be construed as hybrids—a matter of considerable dispute. It is hard to see how the crime of money laundering, for example, could be interpreted as specifying the content of a genuine *malum in se*. In any event, I will question whether the civic arrogance argument justifies punishment for those criminal offenses that unquestionably *are* hybrids. In the remainder of this section I will contend that Duff's civic arrogance argument probably succeeds in only a handful of cases—in only a small minority of the offenses to which it might be thought to apply.

First, Duff's position rests on an empirical claim for which no evidence is offered. Presumably, he regards this claim as uncontroversial, but I am

62 *Ibid.* 63 *Ibid.* 104 (emphasis in original). 64 *Ibid* (emphasis in original).

less certain. Doubts arise when we appreciate that the empirical claim in question is comparative. In other words, the real issue is whether the defendant is in a better position *than the legislature* to decide, for example, if a given amount of alcohol seriously impairs his ability to drive. A long tradition, dating at least to John Stuart Mill, holds that the individual himself, in his own circumstances, is in the better position to make these sorts of determinations.[65] Of course, Duff reminds us of the distortion in judgment produced by self-interest and wishful thinking. But we should not be persuaded to endorse the civic arrogance argument by comparing nonrational defendants with ideal legislatures.[66] A fair comparison must remain mindful of the factors that infect the quality of legislative determinations. Even the most casual experience with the political processes that have led states to lower the blood alcohol level required by the hybrid offense of drunk driving, for example, does not inspire confidence that legislatures have drawn the line in the right place for the right reasons.[67]

Moreover, both of the examples Duff selects involve what might be called *temptation* cases—situations in which a person's self-interest urges him to proceed while his judgement is clouded by lust, intoxication, or the like. In these kinds of situations, we all recognize the human tendency to err by permitting our own behavior. But temptation is not present in all cases in which the legislature provides content to a *malum in se* by enacting a hybrid offense. In fact, relatively few hybrid offenses seem designed to compensate for temptation. Federal law, for example, bars doctors from prescribing marijuana to their patients. Presumably, the relevant *malum in se* consists in prescribing substances that are ineffective as medicines and may even be harmful to those who ingest them. The law provides content to this *malum in se* by identifying the specific substances that meet this description. Regardless of whether the specification that precludes marijuana is correct or incorrect, there is no reason to believe that the judgements of doctors are distorted by temptation. In such a case, we need a better reason than Duff provides to conclude that defendants are less likely than legislatures to identify those instances of conduct that are *mala in se*. As a general matter, why should we believe that the legislature is better situated than the defendant to draw lines in the right place?

And where *is* the right place? This question goes right to the heart of my inquiry. No one could deny that *some* attempts to provide an 'artificial,

[65] Mill expresses these reservations in the context of rejecting paternalism. See John Stuart Mill, *On Liberty* (New York: E.P. Dutton/Everyman's Edition, 1951), 188.

[66] 'In law, the rules are designed by legislators or other authorities who are not any better at practical reasoning, by and large, than other individuals', Philip Soper, 'Legal Theory and the Claim of Authority' (1989) 18 *Philosophy & Public Affairs* 209, 226.

[67] See the discussion of the politics of drunk driving described in H Laurence Ross, *Confronting Drunk Driving* (New Haven: Yale University Press, 1992), 173–84.

stipulative determination of a genuine *malum in se*' are deficient.[68] Recall what I called the fallibility condition: an adequate theory of criminalization must identify when a given *malum prohibitum* offense would *not* be justified. The fallibility condition is no less important when the crime in question is a hybrid. Not just any amount of youth suffices to preclude maturity to give consent to sexual relations; not just any amount of intoxication suffices to seriously impair drivers.[69] The task of line-drawing is hardly arbitrary in the sense that any position is as good as any other; some specifications are obviously unacceptable.[70] Within obvious parameters, where should lines be drawn? Expressed concretely, the question is how the state should decide where to set the specific blood alcohol concentration of drunk driving, or the precise age at which adolescents cannot convey effective consent to sexual relations.[71] More abstractly, the question is how legislatures should decide to give content to the *malum in se* of a hybrid offense.

Duff responds with only the following hint. 'If the laws defining such offences are to be justified at all, it must be true that most of those who commit such offences will commit a *malum in se* of the appropriate kind.'[72] I construe Duff to mean that the *malum in se* should be specified so that the majority of those who commit the hybrid offense will also be guilty of a *malum in se*. In other words, more than half of those who commit the offense of statutory rape or drunk driving, for example, must be guilty of a *malum in se*. Let us call this proposal for specifying the content of a hybrid offense the *majoritarian condition*.

Recall that the point of raising my inquiry is to understand how persons who commit hybrid offenses act wrongfully and thus become eligible for retributive punishment when their behavior is not also *malum in se*. With this focus in mind, I strongly doubt that the majoritarian condition is adequate to justify impositions of the criminal sanction.[73] Should we really conclude that a given individual acts wrongfully when he commits a hybrid offense the content of which conforms to the majoritarian condition?

[68] The most obvious violations of the fallibility condition would occur when the conduct proscribed did not specify a genuine *malum in se*. If the state should not proscribe a given kind of conduct in the first place, we need not struggle to provide an artificial stipulative determination of that conduct.

[69] In many states, however, *any* amount of blood alcohol concentration is sufficient to allow adolescents (who are too young to drink alcohol legally) to be convicted of impaired driving. Presumably, these 'no tolerance' statutes fail (what I will later call) the majoritarian condition.

[70] Some commentators have suggested that conduct that is *malum prohibitum* can become *malum in se* 'depending on the degree of the violation'. See LaFave, above n. 30, at 34.

[71] I leave aside such difficult questions as whether the specification of the offense of drunk driving should consist in a blood alcohol concentration (BAC) at all. There is no obvious reason why the degree to which a driver's ability is impaired by intoxication should be defined by the amount of alcohol in his blood. See James B Jacobs, *Drunk Driving: An American Dilemma* (Chicago: University of Chicago Press, 1989), 61–2.

[72] Duff, above n. 49, at 102.

[73] Admittedly, Duff explicitly advances the majoritarian condition only as a *necessary* condition for deciding whether a hybrid offense is justified.

A person's act is not wrongful because it tokens a type that is wrongful when performed by the majority of agents. Only *personal* desert can render persons eligible for retributive punishment.[74] If the majoritarian condition were implemented, nearly half of all persons who were guilty of hybrid offenses would commit a *malum prohibitum* that would *not* also be a *malum in se*. This implication casts the net of punishment far too widely. No theorist who hopes to construct a minimalist theory of criminalization should welcome this result.

Moreover, the distribution of persons who commit hybrid offenses that conform to the majoritarian condition without simultaneously perpetrating a *malum in se* is not likely to be random. Some persons will have excellent reasons to believe that their behavior is not wrongful prior to or independent of law. In fact, some such persons will actually *know* that their conduct is not a genuine *malum in se*. Duff is aware that a given individual may know that his act-token is not a *malum in se* even though his act-type is wrongful more often than not. What is perhaps most intriguing about his argument from civic arrogance is his contention that the wrongfulness constraint of retributivism is satisfied even in such a case. Duff alleges that the agent acts wrongfully despite knowing that his conduct is not a *malum in se* because he does not *know* that he knows this.[75]

It is not entirely clear why many such agents could *not* know that they know their conduct is not a *malum in se*—analyzes of the state of knowing that one knows are highly controversial.[76] The more important question, however, is whether persons who fail to meet this lofty epistemological test act wrongfully and thus become eligible for retributive punishment. Why, in other words, should we conclude that an agent who *knows* his act is not wrongful prior to and independent of law nonetheless acts wrongfully simply because he does not know that he knows this?[77] As far as I can tell, the extraordinary epistemological standard Duff imposes is inapplicable anywhere else in the criminal law. In the well-known debate about whether a defendant can be justified in violating a law unless he knows he has a justification, for example,

[74] Many familiar doctrines in the criminal law are sensible only when desert is construed as personal. Each individual defendant, for example, may be convicted only when the quantum of evidence advanced in his case amounts to proof beyond a reasonable doubt. In light of the well-known objections to punishing the innocent, it is unclear why defendants should be liable for committing offenses that satisfy the majoritarian condition.

[75] Duff, above n. 49, at 104.

[76] On most *externalist* accounts of knowledge, persons may know without knowing that they know quite frequently. They may believe a true proposition *p*, have whatever justification for *p* is needed to elevate their justified true belief to knowledge, but not believe their justification to be adequate. In such a case, the agent would know without even believing that he knows; he certainly would not know that he knows.

[77] Duff alleges (above n. 49, at 104) that the claim of this defendant is 'unjustified'; indeed, his supposed lack of justification is crucial to why his claim is thought to be arrogant. But the defendant who knows his conduct is not *malum in se* must (on any standard account of knowledge) have a justification for his true belief; why doesn't whatever justifies him in believing that his conduct is not *malum in se* furnish the justification Duff alleges to be absent?

did anyone ever think that the defendant in question not only must know, but also must know that he knows he has a justification?

By hypothesis, Duff maintains that a defendant manifests *civic arrogance* when he commits a hybrid offense while knowing but not knowing that he knows his conduct is not a genuine *malum in se*. But three problems arise. First, where exactly is the arrogance? Duff alleges that our defendant claims an exception to a rule that others must follow, and seeks to set himself above his fellow citizens.[78] But no such privilege need be claimed. Presumably, our defendant would allow anyone who knows his conduct is not a *malum in se* to perpetrate the hybrid offense as well.[79] Secondly, why think that civic arrogance merits criminal punishment? Civic arrogance itself is not criminal, and no one, to my knowledge, has proposed to criminalize it. How can the supposed wrongfulness of civic arrogance substitute for the wrongfulness that is absent in these hybrid offenses? Finally, assuming that civic arrogance does merit some degree of punishment, how *much* punishment could it possibly merit? Since civic arrogance itself is not a crime, our defendant is punished *for* his hybrid offense, not for his civic arrogance. The punishments imposed for some such offenses—like that for statutory rape—can be incredibly severe. But civic arrogance, if it should be punished at all, does not seem especially serious. How can such severe punishments satisfy any reasonable test of proportionality?

I propose to illustrate this latter problem of proportionality by contrasting two statutory rapists, Jack and Jim. Jack has sex with a young woman he knows to be too immature to consent to sex. Jim has sex with a woman of the same age, but his partner is *not* too immature to consent. Moreover, Jim actually *knows* that his partner is sufficiently mature to consent. Jack commits a *malum in se*; Duff holds that Jim acts wrongfully as well, not because his conduct is a *malum in se*—indeed, it is not—but because he displays civic arrogance. As a result, both Jack and Jim are guilty of the very same hybrid offense, and (presumably) become eligible for comparable punishments.[80] This outcome seems manifestly unjust. Whatever quanta of punishment (if any) may be appropriate for displays of civic arrogance, they surely should be less severe than those deserved by statutory rapists who (like Jack) knowingly perpetrate a serious *malum in se*.

Finally, I fear that Duff's appeal to civic arrogance to attempt to justify retributive punishment may prove too much. It is hard to understand why a defendant who commits a hybrid offense that is specified in violation of the majoritarian condition displays any less civic arrogance than a defendant

[78] Duff, above n. 49, at 104 (emphasis in original).

[79] Duff is aware of this possibility. See *ibid.* at 108 n. 19.

[80] Of course, Duff could claim that Jim but not Jack qualifies for mitigation. Perhaps. But no one has ever explained why some circumstances that bear on culpability make defendants eligible for reduced punishments, while others preclude punishment altogether. Generally, see Douglas Husak, 'Partial Defenses' (1998) XI *Canadian Journal of Law & Jurisprudence* 167.

who commits a hybrid offense that conforms to this condition. If I am correct, Duff's only constraint on the justifiability of hybrid offenses cannot be reconciled with his general argument for punishing persons who commit these very crimes. In addition, although Duff mostly restricts his focus to hybrid offenses, one wonders why his civic arrogance argument lacks a wider, more general application to other categories of *malum prohibitum*. Why doesn't a defendant who knowingly engages in money laundering—not a hybrid offense—manifest civic arrogance as well? Duff's argument would be strengthened by providing examples of defendants who commit *mala prohibita* offenses *without* displaying civic arrogance. In other words, Duff must try to explain how his theory satisfies the fallibility condition. I do not insist that he could not possibly succeed. My own conclusion is more cautions and tentative. I invite theorists to show in greater detail how the punishment of persons who commit hybrid offenses is compatible with the wrongfulness constraint of retributivism.

4. Promises, Coordination Problems, and Fair Play

Stuart Green has made the most ambitious attempt to defend retributive punishment for pure *mala prohibita* offenses—those that cannot plausibly be construed as hybrids.[81] According to Green, the wrongfulness of breaking a promise or violating a duty of fair play 'frequently' explains why it is wrongful to commit a pure *malum prohibitum* offense.[82] Partly because of the well-known difficulties in distinguishing obligations that originate in promises from those that arise from fair play,[83] I will examine each of these arguments together in this section. For reasons that should become clear, I will also critically evaluate the claim that many *mala prohibita* offenses can be justified by the need to solve coordination problems. I will conclude that these strategies may succeed occasionally, but are unlikely to support retributive punishment for many *mala prohibita* offenders.

I begin with promises—the least controversial way to undertake a moral commitment the breach of which is *prima facie* wrongful. Green asks us to consider, for example, many of the criminal laws that govern an activity—like those pertaining to fishing, hunting or driving. He observes that individuals who apply for permits or licenses typically 'make an explicit promise to abide by certain applicable rules and regulations'.[84] He concludes that the wrongfulness of conduct that deviates from the terms or conditions of

[81] There is some difficulty in identifying this category of crime—a point to which I will return.

[82] Green, above n. 13, at 1586.

[83] For difficulties in categorizing John Locke's theory of political obligation, see A John Simmons, *Moral Principles and Political Obligations* (Princeton: Princeton University Press, 1979), 83–95.

[84] Green, above n. 13, at 1587.

these permits and licenses can often be derived from the immorality of breaking this earlier promise.

Green is careful to disassociate his position from that of theorists in the social contract tradition who aspire to defend a general obligation to obey the law. As global accounts of the wrongfulness of criminal behavior, social contract theories encounter many well-known difficulties to which Green's view may seem immune. In particular, he need not worry about how a binding promise might be inferred from nonverbal behavior, or could arise from what a rational person would do under ideal circumstances. The kinds of promise on which Green relies are *explicit,* not tacit or hypothetical. Nonetheless, I believe that some of the familiar objections to social contract theories also count against Green's more modest endeavor to explain why persons often are said to act wrongfully by committing *mala prohibita* offenses.

Admittedly, many persons *do* make explicit agreements in order to receive permission to engage in an activity. Notice, however, that individuals who fish or hunt *without* a permit or license, for example, have made no such promise. At best, Green's account pertains only to persons who breach the terms or conditions of the permits or licenses they have obtained. Thus it has no conceivable application to the most egregious violators—those who fish or drive without ever having bothered to apply for a license at all. Only those individuals who have taken the crucial step of receiving a permit could possibly be said to have promised to conform to its terms or conditions.[85]

Is Green's argument persuasive even for that class of persons who breach the terms or conditions of a permit they *have* obtained? Perhaps his strategy succeeds in a handful of cases. Still, consider the content of the promise that persons who receive a driver's license, for example, are likely to have made. Clearly, applicants do not explicitly agree to comply with each and every specific law that pertains to driving. They typically make a generic promise like 'the holder of this permit hereby agrees to conform to all of the current provisions in the Code of Motor Vehicles'. For several reasons, I am dubious that such generic promises can give rise to obligations. Consider, for example, a driver who fails to affix a validated inspection sticker he has obtained in the precise place on the windshield of his car. Can his generic promise to abide by the terms of his license possibly explain why his conduct is wrongful and renders him eligible for retributive punishment? Almost certainly, our driver would not be held to have breached a *contract* by neglecting to display his sticker. He may not even be aware of the particular regulation he has violated, and could not be said to have explicitly agreed to

[85] Although Green is aware of this problem—see *ibid.* 1590—he does not indicate how he purports to solve it. It is odd to think that persons act wrongfully only when they deviate from the terms of the licenses they have obtained, rather than when they engage in the same type of conduct but have not obtained a license at all. It is also peculiar to suppose that a *different* account of the wrongfulness of such conduct must be given in the two types of cases.

a condition of which he has no knowledge. This possibility is hardly remote. Almost no driver knows more than a tiny fraction of the literally thousands of rules to which he is subject. Ignorance of law may not excuse criminal liability generally, but it creates an insuperable obstacle to any attempt to explain why unlawful conduct is wrongful by appealing to an explicit agreement.

Perhaps more importantly, even those individuals who *are* aware of a specific term or condition would rarely be held to have breached a contract in the event of noncompliance. My skepticism draws from the philosophical foundations of contract law. The terms in a driving or fishing license might be described as 'boiler-plate', offered to applicants on a 'take-it-or-leave-it' basis. As with other contracts of adhesion, virtually all of the enforceable regulations governing fishing or driving are and ought to be a product of law, not of agreement.[86] The fact that these promises would not give rise to liability under contract law may not be *fatal* to Green's proposal. Surely, however, it is peculiar to hold that a promise that would not create an enforceable obligation in civil law would suffice to justify punishment in a criminal context. One would think that the standard of justification needed in the criminal arena would be at least as high, if not higher, than that in civil law.

Moreover, breaches of promise seldom are wrongs enforced through the criminal law. Green, of course, is aware of this fact, but contends that such statutes as the Mail Fraud Act and the Hobbs Act serve as models for punishing persons who default on their agreements.[87] But the fact that there is precedent for imposing criminal liability on those who break their promises does not establish that this approach should be adopted more broadly. Green does not recommend that *all* breaches of contract should be treated as criminal wrongs.[88] On what ground does he propose to be selective?

Finally, what I have called the fallibility condition represents another major hurdle in attempts to locate the wrongfulness of a *malum prohibitum* offense in a breach of promise. If a person behaves wrongfully in violating a term in a permit because he has defaulted on his agreement, how could *any* condition in a license *not* provide the basis for satisfying the wrongfulness constraint? How, in other words, does Green's analysis not prove too much? Green explicitly admits that the commission of some *mala prohibita* offenses might *not* be wrongful, but he does not explain why this concession does not undermine his entire account. His examples include 'nonsensical regulations prohibiting pineapple chunks from being colored green, honey from being added to peanut butter, and vitamins from being added to

[86] For the classic account, see Todd D Rakoff, 'Contracts of Adhesion: An Essay in Reconstruction' (1983) 96 *Harvard Law Review* 1174.

[87] Green, above n. 13, 1601.

[88] Green is certainly correct (*ibid* 1601) to note that 'the line between criminal law and civil law is not, and never has been, impermeable'. But this observation does not go very far to establish the general justifiability of retributive punishment for breaches of contract.

chocolate bars.'[89] It is easy to imagine, however, that a person might promise not to add color or honey in order to be allowed to sell pineapples or peanut butter.[90] As far as I can see, even these 'nonsensical regulations' are amenable to exactly the same analysis as Green provides for those laws to which he argues that persons have promised to conform. This conclusion leads me to suspect that the presence or absence of a promise may do less work in Green's theory than he is willing to admit.

I do not deny that promissory obligations might occasionally provide an adequate account of the wrongfulness of *mala prohibita* offenses. But I suspect that such an explanation will succeed infrequently; it cannot justify retributive punishment for the vast majority of *mala prohibita* offenders. It cannot explain the wrongfulness of violating the great bulk of traffic rules (that are not hybrids). Nor can it explain the wrongfulness of many other *mala prohibita,* such as my example of money laundering. Thus I turn to a related account—the principle of fair play that Green alleges to underlie the wrongfulness of several *mala prohibita* offenses.[91]

I begin indirectly, by examining the class of what might be called *coordination offenses*—criminal laws designed to solve coordination problems. Extravagant claims have been made about the jurisprudential importance of this category of crime. John Finnis, for example, has famously argued that the point or function of law is to coordinate activities for the common good, and that this objective provides a defense for a version of natural law theory as opposed to positivism.[92] Finnis' thesis, of course, is compatible with the belief that a great number of criminal laws do *not* serve this function. The immediate question is not whether entire *systems* of law should be construed as solutions to coordination problems, but to what extent this objective helps to show that significant numbers of *mala prohibita* offenses satisfy the wrongfulness constraint needed to justify retributive punishment.[93]

We cannot hope to resolve this matter unless we are clear about what a coordination problem *is*. According to Leslie Green's influential account, agents have a coordination problem 'where each must choose between exclusively alternative courses of action, the directly consequentialist returns

[89] *Ibid.* 1582, n. 157.

[90] I set aside such possible defenses as duress or unconscionability as irrelevant to my inquiry. Nothing need be unconscionable or coercive about a promise to abide by the 'nonsensical regulations' Green mentions.

[91] 'Even when there has been no promise to obey the law, a moral obligation might be derived from notions of fair play.' *Ibid.* 1589.

[92] John Finnis, *Natural Law and Natural Rights* (Oxford: Clarendon Press, 1980).

[93] Some theorists appear to have endorsed the claim that concerns us here. William S Boardman, for example, maintains that 'the law typically works by solving coordination problems'. See 'Coordination and the Moral Obligation to Obey the Law' (1987) 97 *Ethics* 546, 549. It is not exactly clear what degree of evidence would suffice to show that the function Boardman cites is *not* typical of law.

of which each depend on both his own choices and those of others'.[94] Green holds that a regularity *R* in the behavior of members of a population *P* in a recurring situation S represents a *solution* to a coordination problem if and only if, 'in (almost) any instance of *S*: (1) it is common knowledge in *P* that (2) (almost) everyone conforms to *R* because (2a) (almost everyone expects (almost) everyone else to conform to R; (2b) (almost) everyone prefers that any one conform to R on the condition that (almost) everyone conform to R; (2c) (almost) everyone prefers that everyone conform to some R rather than not conform to any R.'[95] The rule requiring motorists to drive on a given side of the road is everyone's favorite example of a coordination offense. When a solution to a coordination problem is proposed, each motorist increases his utility by driving on whatever side is required, and (almost) none could do better (and in fact would do worse) by driving on the other side.

This account enables us to appreciate that some but not all coordination offenses are hybrid offenses. The categories overlap substantially. Many traffic offenses, like those requiring drivers to stop at red lights at busy intersections, seem to be examples of both categories; they solve a coordination problem while providing content to the *malum in se* of reckless or dangerous driving. But many hybrids are not coordination offenses. No crime can qualify as an instance of a coordination offense in the absence of a preexisting coordination problem. A single solution—it may not matter which one—is preferable to the chaos that would ensue if no solution were found. The crimes of statutory rape and drunk driving do not solve preexisting coordination problems; there is (*inter alia*) no 'regularity R' to which persons conform because they expect that others will do likewise. In addition, some offenses—such as bans on price-fixing or insider trading—seem designed to *preclude* given solutions to coordination problems.[96] In any event, our central question is whether persons act wrongfully and become eligible for retributive punishment when they violate those laws that *do* solve coordination problems.

Leslie Green's account also helps to show why coordination offenses (as he construes them) do not provide a plausible model for understanding the alleged wrongfulness of many *mala prohibita* crimes. Although he raises a number of potential difficulties, I will mention only two that seem relevant for present purposes.[97] First and more importantly, conformity with a solution, although perhaps an issue of rationality, is not always an issue of

[94] Leslie Green, 'Law, Co-ordination, and the Common Good' (1983) 3 *Oxford Journal of Legal Studies* 299, 301.
[95] *Ibid.* 302.

[96] Leslie Green, *The Authority of the State* (Oxford: Clarendon Press, 1990), 117.

[97] Green points out that finding a particular solution may not be especially important; many coordination problems are unsolved, and persons do not seem especially worse-off as a result. Moreover, many coordination problems are solved without resort to law. Custom and informal arrangements frequently emerge to solve coordination problems—as in the case of a common language or calendar. These solutions emerged without unanimity or the existence of an authority empowered to establish them. 'Whether coordination problems call for legal solutions is thus a matter that is highly context-dependent; no general conclusions can be drawn.' Leslie Green, 'Positivism and Conventionalism' (1999) XII *Canadian Journal of Law & Jurisprudence* 35, 46.

morality. Persons do not act wrongfully (even if they act contrary to their self-interest) when they deviate from the solution to a coordination problem by, for example, speaking a different language, ignoring the conventional calendar, or resorting to barter rather than using the common currency. Even if the criminal law proscribed the failure to use the common currency, it is hard to see why those who committed this offense would act wrongfully. To be sure, persons act wrongfully when they drive on the wrong side of the street, but the immorality of this conduct can be fully explained by the fact that this offense is a hybrid that is not overinclusive. Why, then, is it wrongful to violate those coordination offenses that are pure cases of *malum prohibitum*? Noncompliance might be wrongful under *some* conditions—if, in Green's words, 'coordination is *preeminently* valuable, and if authority is the *only* feasible way of establishing a coordination convention, and if the authority of law is the *only* feasible sort.'[98] These stringent conditions will seldom be satisfied.

Second, coordination offenses seem unable to explain the importance of sanctions in motivating compliance. Threats of punishment typically function to dissuade individuals from pursuing their own interest by engaging in criminal activity. But this explanation does not apply to coordination offenses. No further need for coercion arises when a common solution to a coordination problem is beneficial to all.[99] If the obvious risks of deviating from the solution to a coordination problem (say, by driving through a red light) are insufficient to motivate compliance, it is unclear how threats of punishment will help to do so. This problem may not bother those retributivists who believe that consequences are wholly irrelevant to the justification of punishment, but any legal philosopher who finds room in his theory for deterrence will be puzzled by it.

Both these obstacles could be surmounted if pure *mala prohibita* offenses proscribed behavior (like prisoner's dilemmas) in which individuals were able to maximize their own utility by defecting while others cooperate. In these circumstances, sanctions could play their familiar role in helping to motivate compliance. Moreover, the wrongfulness of defection would be easier to explain. Persons who violate the law could be said to act unfairly by benefiting from the conformity of others; they would be *free riders*. The *principle of fair play* provides the most plausible account of the wrongfulness of such conduct. In its most general formulation, the principle of fair play states that 'those who benefit from the good-faith sacrifices of others, made in support of a mutually beneficial cooperative venture, have a moral obligation to do their parts as well (that is, to make reciprocal sacrifices) within the venture.'[100] The free-rider need not directly harm anyone or

[98] *Ibid.* 49 (emphasis in original).

[99] See David Lewis, *Convention* (Cambridge: Harvard University Press, 1969), 48.

[100] A John Simmons, *Justification & Legitimacy: Essays on Rights and Obligations* (Cambridge: Cambridge University Press, 2001), 29.

endanger the entire cooperative enterprise, but he acts wrongfully by abrogating to himself a privilege that cannot be extended to everyone who is similarly situated.

Philosophers disagree about the conditions under which the principle of fair play creates a moral reason in favor of given acts of reciprocity, but nearly all agree that the mere *receipt* of a benefit, although necessary, is not sufficient.[101] Whatever requirements are added to this condition—such as the reasonable opportunity to decline the benefit—almost certainly disqualify the principle as an adequate account of political obligation generally.[102] In all likelihood, these same requirements (whatever they may be) will also disqualify the principle from justifying many *mala prohibita* offenses. It may be true that *some* of the benefits conferred by *mala prohibita* offenses will satisfy whatever set of conditions is ultimately deemed sufficient. Still, such examples will almost certainly be unusual; many of the benefits conferred by *mala prohibita* offenses will *not* satisfy each of these necessary conditions. Admittedly, this conclusion cannot be supported without a more complete account of the principle of fair play than I will provide. Still, I suspect that the principle of fair play will succeed in explaining the wrongfulness of *mala prohibita* offenses in only a small handful of cases, leaving unresolved our central question of why persons deserve punishment in committing the vast majority of such crimes. Yet again, persons guilty of money laundering cannot be portrayed as free riders who benefit from the sacrifices of those who support a mutually beneficial cooperative venture. Presumably, those who violate this statute would be willing to allow similarly situated persons to deposit or withdraw their ill-gotten gains.

Stuart Green believes otherwise, and relies as much on the principle of fair play as on explicit promises in his efforts to account for the alleged wrongfulness of many *mala prohibita* offenses.[103] His own example is instructive, revealing what is defective about his analysis generally. He discusses taverns in a municipality that violate a local ordinance by selling alcohol on Sundays. According to Green, the owners who profit from these sales act wrongfully because they are *cheaters*.[104] 'Such establishments are profiting at the expense of, and obtaining an unfair advantage over, their law-abiding competitors.'[105] Clearly, Green is correct that these taverns 'increase their revenues in relation to their law-abiding rivals'.[106] But why do their profits not simply represent the fruits of capitalistic competition; what is the basis for describing the advantage gained by those establishments that sell alcohol on Sunday as an 'unfair' case of 'cheating'? Green

[101] But see Richard Arneson, 'The Principle of Fairness and Free-Rider Problems' (1982) 92 *Ethics* 624.
[102] See Simmons, above n. 100, at 31–6.
[103] Green, above n. 13, at 1589.
[104] More recently, see Stuart Green, 'Cheating' (2004) 23 *Law and Philosophy* 137.
[105] Green, above n. 13, at 1589.
[106] *Ibid.* 1590.

fails to defend the conclusion that these owners infringe an adequate formulation of the principle of fair play. These persons are not free-riders who exploit a system of mutual forbearance by abrogating to themselves a privilege they withhold from others who are similarly situated. Again, I assume they would allow (even though they would not prefer) all taverns to sell alcohol on Sundays. If we suppose that the law simply *defines* the parameters of fair competition, we could conclude that establishments that profit by breaching these conditions gain an advantage that is unfair. But where is the argument that these parameters are defined by law? As far as I can see, this *malum prohibitum* regulation has less to do with fair competition than with attempts to enforce religious morality.

Finally, recall Green's examples of nonsensical laws that are not wrongful to disobey. He writes: 'to the extent that such laws exist for no reason other than to give an unfair advantage to one or more market participants or to satisfy the whims of some regulator, it seems likely that there is no moral obligation to obey such laws.'[107] It is revealing that Green admits that some such regulations might be objectionable precisely *because* they are designed 'to give an unfair advantage to one or more market participants'. This concession indicates that Green could not believe that the terms of fair competition simply *are* those regulations the competitors are legally required to obey. Some such regulations, he admits, actually make the terms of competition *un*fair. Thus, there must be an antecedent standard of fairness and unfairness to which these regulations may or may not conform. If so, defendants need not breach these antecedent standards simply by committing a *malum prohibitum* offense. The case remains to be made that other examples of *mala prohibita* offenses implement a principle of fair play.

5. Conclusion

Too much conduct is criminalized and subjected to punishment. Can these punishments be justified? We cannot appreciate the full dimensions of this problem unless we expand our analysis of the special part of criminal law to include *mala prohibita* offenses. I have critically discussed the few attempts undertaken by legal philosophers to explain why the punishment of persons who commit these crimes might be compatible with the wrongfulness constraint of even the weakest forms of retributivism. I began by arguing that this problem is genuine, despite its neglect among all but a handful of criminal law theorists. My initial effort to solve the problem construed *mala prohibita* offenses as hybrids, designed to provide specific content to a vague *malum in se*. Next, I sought to ground the wrongfulness of pure *mala prohibita* offenses in promissory obligation or a principle of fair play. Each

[107] *Ibid.* 1582–3.

of these efforts might succeed in a small number of cases. If my criticisms are cogent, however, none of these attempts justify punishing those who commit the vast majority of *mala prohibita* offenses. They fail, for example, to provide a persuasive rationale for inflicting retributive punishment on persons convicted of money laundering. Does it follow that most of these crimes should be repealed as incompatible with our best theory of criminalization and punishment? Perhaps. I confess, however, that I am a bit reluctant to endorse this sweeping and radical conclusion, despite my sympathies for a minimalist theory of criminalization. I hope that the difficulties I have discussed will inspire commentators to rise to the challenge of explaining in greater detail how retributive punishment can be justified for those who commit *mala prohibita* offenses.

5

The Possession Paradigm: The Special Part and the Police Power Model of the Criminal Process

Markus Dirk Dubber*

1. Introduction

In *The Limits of the Criminal Sanction*, Herbert Packer distinguished between two models of the criminal process: the Due Process Model and the Crime Control Model.[1] In the Due Process Model, criminal defendants enjoy the familiar procedural protections, including a presumption of innocence. In the Crime Control Model, by contrast, the suppression of crime is given priority over a fastidious concern for defendants' rights. Effectiveness is key, rather than fairness.

In 1968, when Packer set up the contrast between these two models—ostensibly for analytic purposes—the Crime Control Model was seen as gaining ground on the Due Process Model. Packer's book reads like a last stand against a creeping erosion of the time-honored principles of the Due Process Model, which he apparently regarded as preceding the Crime Control Model, though he never set out a detailed historical sequence of principles gained and lost.

Within a few years of the publication of Packer's book, the Crime Control Model had come to dominate the American criminal process. More recently the Crime Control Model itself has given way to the Police Power Model, as the War on Crime of the past three decades has shifted the focus of the American criminal process from the control of interpersonal crime to the affirmation of state authority.[2]

* Thanks to Antony Duff, Stuart Green, Jeremy Horder, Kevin McMunigal, and Sophie Dubber for detailed comments and suggestions. Tony Dillof gets credit for renaming the 'Police Model' the 'Police Power Model' for purposes of this essay, to avoid confusion between the traditional broad notion of police as a power of government and the modern narrow notion of police as an institution of law enforcement.

[1] Herbert L Packer, *The Limits of the Criminal Sanction* (Stanford, CA: Stanford University Press, 1968).

[2] The role of the so-called victims' rights movement in this transformation is explored in detail in Markus D Dubber, *Victims in the War on Crime: The Use and Abuse of Victims'*

The Police Power Model derives its name from the power of government that is widely recognized as the foundation of criminal law, the police power.[3] In the United States, it is a commonplace that the states' authority to criminalize derives from their power to police.[4] The power to police is also generally acknowledged to be the most comprehensive, and least limitable, power of government.[5] It is 'the power to govern men and things':[6] its origins can be traced back to the householder's discretionary authority over his household resources, human and nonhuman, animate and inanimate alike.[7] The most influential definition of police, cited by American courts and commentators until well into the twentieth century, can be found in Blackstone:

> By the public police and oeconomy I mean the due regulation and domestic order of the kingdom: whereby the individuals of the state, like members of a well-governed family, are bound to conform their general behaviour to the rules of propriety, good neighbourhood, and good manners: and to be decent, industrious, and inoffensive in their respective stations.[8]

The Police Power Model of the criminal process is, like the Crime Control Model, concerned with eradicating crime, but it operates with a different concept of crime. The Crime Control Model still conceives of crime as the

Rights (New York: NYU Press, 2002). The Police Power Model can be seen as a radicalized descendant of the Crime Control Model, and contrasts with the Autonomy Model—which casts central features of the American criminal process as attempts to legitimate the practice of punishment by rendering it consistent with the idea of self-government—in much the same way that the Crime Control Model contrasted with the Due Process Model. While the Police Power Model captures the reality of the modern American criminal process, the Autonomy Model functions as a basis for normative critique. On the two models, see Markus Dubber, 'The New Police Science and the Police Power Model of the Criminal Process', in Markus Dubber and Mariana Valverde (eds), *The New Police Science: The Police Power in Domestic and International Law* (forthcoming 2006); Markus Dubber, 'The Criminal Trial and the Legitimation of Punishment', in R A Duff, et al. (eds), *The Trial on Trial* (Oxford: Hart Publishing, 2004).

[3] See generally Markus D Dubber, *The Police Power: Patriarchy and the Foundations of American Government* (New York: Columbia University Press, 2005). The power to police is not to be confused with the power of police. Modern police departments are but one institutional manifestation of police as a general mode of governance. See, e.g., Mark Neocleous, *The Fabrication of Social Order: A Critical Theory of Police Power* (Sterling, VA: Pluto Press, 2000); Mariana Valverde, 'Police Science British Style: Pub Licensing and Knowledges of Urban Disorder' (2003) 32 *Economy and Society* 234.

[4] The federal government enjoys an analogous de facto police power, despite the familiar fiction that the police power is the states' alone. See Ernst Freund, *The Police Power: Public Policy and Constitutional Rights* (Chicago: Callaghan & Co., 1904), 63.

[5] *Slaughter-House Cases*, 83 US 36, 49 (1873) (police power 'is, and must be from its very nature, incapable of any very exact definition or limitation'); 'Constitutional Law', *Am. Jur. 2d*, vol. 16A, § 317 ('the most essential, the most insistent, and always one of the least limitable of the powers of government').

[6] *License Cases*, 46 U.S. 504, 583 (1847).

[7] See generally Dubber, *The Police Power*, above n. 3.

[8] W Blackstone, *Commentaries on the Laws of England* (Oxford: Oxford University Press, 1769), vol. 4, 162; see *Commonwealth v Keller*, 35 D. & C.2d 615 (Pa. Ct. Com. Pleas 1964) (quoting Blackstone's definition in support of creating common law misdemeanor of 'indecent disposition of a dead body').

infliction of (criminal) harm by one individual upon another. The Police Power Model shifts the focus from protecting individual interests or rights to public interests. Chronically amorphous, public interests in turn require definition in the abstract and, at least as important, in each particular case. This task of definition, however, is performed by none other than the state. In the end, therefore, public interests are *what the state considers* public interests, and thus become functionally indistinguishable from the interests of the state itself. The criminal law process, then, is not concerned with the protection of individual rights, be they the offenders' or the victims', but with the protection of the authority of the state. The victim of criminal law is not the person, but the state.[9]

In short, the Police Power Model transforms criminal law from an institution for the regulation of interpersonal conflict to an administrative mechanism for the enforcement of state authority. Systematically, the Police Power Model prioritizes efficiency and is characterized by discretion and a general impatience for the principles of legality, including the principles of specificity, prospectivity, publicity, legislativity, and lenity, as well as the separation of powers, along with the 'common law' principles of procedural and substantive criminal law.

In procedural criminal law, the preferred disposition is the guilty plea. The preferred mode of trial is the plea bargain. The center of gravity lies at the front-end of the process; the prosecutor decides what to prosecute, what penalty to offer, and what concessions to demand. The defense attorney is a negotiator, rather than a trial attorney. In many cases, the best defense attorney is no defense attorney at all; the best advice a defense attorney can give her client is not to wait until he has spoken with an attorney, as the early bird gets the worm. The defendant who cooperates first is the defendant who stands to benefit the most, at the expense of other persons who may or may not be charged as co-defendants. The criminal process of the Police Power Model is *neo-inquisitorial* in that it consists of pleadings brought in secret before the prosecutor whose unreviewable decisions are then rubberstamped by a judge, who lends legal force to the executive judgment. Unlike the traditional inquisitorial model, the Police Power Model criminal process is not dominated by the judge, but by the prosecutor. The abandonment of the investigating judge has in fact had its desired effect; judges no longer assemble the evidence and then decide the case. Instead of judges, prosecutors now do the assembling and the deciding. The two functions thus are once again in the hand of one official; but the power of investigation and decision now lies not with the judiciary, but with the executive whose members have traditionally been—and so far remain—beyond external scrutiny.

In the general part of substantive criminal law, the Police Power Model has little use for the actus reus requirement, has few qualms about omission

[9] See generally Dubber, *Victims in the War on Crime*, above n. 2.

liability or vicarious liability; the mens rea requirement likewise does not stand in the way of strict liability, or presumptions of intent. Defenses, such as self-defense, necessity, infancy and insanity, viewed as dispensations of sovereign mercy rather than as rights or entitlements, are labeled affirmative, curtailed or eliminated.

In the special part of criminal law, the Police Power Model prefers broad offense definitions, narrow defense definitions (if it doesn't do away with a defense altogether), status offenses (over conduct offenses), conduct offenses (over result offenses), unlawfulness and lack-of-authorization offenses, inchoate offenses (over completed offenses), and endangerment offenses (over harm offenses). The scope of the special part is continuously expanded, not only for the sake of criminalization but also to provide prosecutors with ever greater discretion, to threaten, bring or dismiss charges in the plea process.

In this paper, I want to explore the role of the special part in the Police Power Model of the criminal process. To figure out how the special part in modern American criminal law works, I will focus on what I consider to be the paradigmatic offense of the Police Power Model: possession.[10]

In the following, I will focus on New York criminal law, with occasional references to the Model Penal Code to broaden the scope of the inquiry. (There will be similarities: the New York Penal Law was based on the Model Penal Code.) Studies in the special part of criminal law are peculiarly parochial. They require careful attention to statutory language and structure. Comparative analysis of the special part is more difficult than comparative analysis of the general part. Underlying traditional work on the big issues of the general part, responsibility, mens rea, justification, excuse, and so on, is the assumption that there is a common theoretical foundation that undergirds these doctrinal concepts.[11] No similar assumption of universality applies to the definition of murder, the distinction between larceny and fraud, or the list of controlled substances. There may be a general part of the special part, but it's not obvious what it would contain.[12] (After all, if an issue were truly of general application, presumably it would be in the general part.) One might investigate the various structural features of a special part, including the distinction between the general part and the special part, the grouping and ordering of offenses (and relatedly, the rights or interests to be protected by each offense and group of offenses),[13] the types of offense

[10] See Markus D Dubber, 'Policing Possession: The War on Crime and the End of Criminal Law' (2002) 91 *Journal Criminal Law & Criminology* 829.

[11] See W Naucke, 'Lücken im Allgemeinen Teil des Strafrechts', in R Lahti and K Nuotio (eds), *Strafrechtstheorie im Umbruch* (Helsinki: Finnish Lawyers' Pub. Co., 1992) 269, 277–8.

[12] On this question see Jeremy Horder, 'The Classification of Crimes and the Special Part of the Criminal Law', in this volume.

[13] See, e.g., Stuart P Green, 'Prototype Theory and the Classification of Offenses in a Revised Model Penal Code: A General Approach to the Special Part' (2000) 4 *Buffalo Criminal Law Review* 301.

elements, the specificity of offense definitions, and so on. One might even consider the scope of the special part, and ponder the question of what sort of conduct deserves to be criminalized or, for existing offenses, which legal interest or right (its *Rechtsgut*, as the Germans would say)[14] they are meant to protect.[15] Perhaps there is even room for the study of criminal codification, once considered a worthy science by Bentham and, with less fervor, many other Enlightenment criminal law scholars. A science of criminal codification might consider such questions as whether to codify, what to codify, where to codify, and how to codify.[16] The more emphasis is placed on the special part of criminal codes, however, the less room there would appear to be for comparative analysis involving legal systems that have not yet resolved the initial question of a science of codification, namely *whether* to codify. Perhaps, then, one effect of a move from the general part to the special part as an object of inquiry would be to align American criminal law more closely with continental systems, where criminal codes have long been the norm.

Much of this paper is an exercise in categorization. In order to develop a theory—or even a systematic account—of the special part, it would be helpful to put in a place a common vocabulary and to canvass the subject to identify topics for further investigation. Whether this taxonomical effort will serve any function other than itself remains to be seen. Perhaps there is little more to the study of the special part than jurisprudential botany. Partly this paper then represents an effort to see what a theory of the special part might contribute to the general project of a critical analysis of criminal law.[17]

2. A Taxonomy of Possession

Varieties of Possession

Possession offenses play a central role in the police action against crime (also known as the 'war on crime', though to call it a war risks importing basic notions of chivalrous conflict and mutual respect, codified in the 'rules of war', that are foreign to the essentially hierarchical nature of the Police

[14] See, e.g., C Roxin, *Strafrecht Allgemeiner Teil (Band I)* (3rd ed., Munich: C.H. Beck, 1997) § 2.

[15] See, e.g., Stuart P Green, *A Moral Theory of White Collar Crime* (Oxford: Oxford University Press, forthcoming 2006).

[16] See Markus D Dubber, 'Penal Panopticon: The Idea of a Modern Model Penal Code' (2000) 4 *Buffalo Criminal Law Review* 53.

[17] Note the limited ambitions of this essay. It contributes to the analysis of the criminal process in the hope that this analysis might lay the foundation for a normative critique of that process. It does not set out to provide this critique. For a critique of possession offenses in particular and of criminal law as police action in general, see Dubber, above n. 10; Dubber, *Victims in the War on Crime*, above note 2, pt. I; Dubber, above n. 3.

Power Model).[18] In New York criminal law, for instance, there are over 150 possession offenses, ranging from a violation (punishable by $100 fine) to an A-I felony (punishable by life imprisonment).[19] In 1998, over 100,000 possession arrests were made in New York and one in five prison or jail sentences were imposed for possession offenses.[20] Possession is not only an independent offense, it also triggers presumptions attaching to other offenses, including importation, manufacture, and distribution. (Various presumptions attach to possession itself, most important proximity to the item possessed.) Possession also enhances punishment for other offenses.

Possession is easy to detect and, once detected, easy to prove. Driven by enforcement concerns, possession is built for speed. The annals of American jurisprudence are filled with cases that began with an innocuous—or not so innocuous—traffic stop or pat down, and end up as a possession conviction. Possession is the ideal fall-back, or charge-down, option in today's criminal process. If nothing else sticks, possession will. A burglary suspect caught with the loot may escape a burglary conviction because of an inadmissible confession, but he will not be able to beat a conviction for possession of stolen property. And with suitable enhancements for being a 'scourge of the community', he will find himself in prison for life.[21]

Every prosecutor worth his salt will, without much difficulty, find a possession offense that fits the crime, and more important, the criminal. Here is a (woefully incomplete) list of items the possession of which is proscribed by criminal law:

- firearms and other weapons,[22] including toy guns,[23] air pistols and rifles,[24] tear gas,[25] and ammunition;[26]
- 'instruments of crime',[27] including body vests,[28] anti-security items,[29] and burglary tools;[30]
- stolen property;[31]
- drugs,[32] along with drug 'paraphernalia'[33] and drug precursors;[34]

[18] The distinction between a war on crime and a police action against crime, or rather against criminals, is further explored in Dubber and, 'The New Police Science', above n. 2. Of course, the war on crime has also been characterized by a depiction—and thereby exclusion—of offenders as enemies and the mobilization of bellicose sentiments against them For a brilliant early analysis of the criminal process as war, see G H Mead, 'The Psychology of Punitive Justice' (1918) 23 *American Journal of Sociology* 577.

[19] N.Y. Penal Law § 220.21 (criminal possession of a controlled substance in the first degree).

[20] State of New York, Division of Criminal Justice Services, Possession Related Offenses New York State (Feb. 4, 2000) (on file with author).

[21] *People v Young*, 94 NE2d 171 (N.Y. 1999).

[22] N.Y. Penal Law §§ 265.01–.05; Model Penal Code §§ 5.06 (Instruments of Crime; Weapons), 5.07 (offensive weapons) (1985).

[23] New York, N.Y. Admin. Code § 10-131(g). [24] *Id.* § 10-131(e).

[25] *Id.* § 10-131(h). [26] *Id.* § 10-131(i).

[27] Model Penal Code §§ 5.06 (Instruments of Crime; Weapons).

[28] N.Y. Penal Law §§ 270.20, 400.05. [29] *Id.* § 170.47. [30] *Id.* § 140.35.

[31] *Id.* §§ 165.40–.65; see also 625 Ill Comp. Stat. § 5/4-103(a)(1) (possession of stolen vehicle).

[32] N.Y. Penal Law arts 220, 221. [33] *Id.* § 220.50. [34] *Id.* § 220.60.

- graffiti instruments;[35]
- computer-related material;[36]
- counterfeit trademarks;[37]
- unauthorized recordings of a performance;[38]
- public benefit cards;[39]
- forged instruments,[40] as well as forgery devices [41]and credit card embossing machines;[42]
- slugs,[43] gambling devices,[44] and gambling records;[45]
- vehicle identification numbers [46]and vehicle titles without complete assignment;[47]
- usurious loan records;[48]
- prison contraband;[49]
- obscene material,[50] obscene sexual performances by a child,[51] and 'premises which [one] knows are being used for prostitution purposes';[52]
- eavesdropping devices;[53]
- fireworks;[54]
- 'noxious materials';[55]
- taximeter accelerating devices;[56]
- spearfishing equipment;[57] and
- undersized catfish (in Louisiana).[58]

Possession, then, functions like a modern sweep offense that sweeps far wider than the original sweep offense, vagrancy, as every day there are far more criminal possessors than there are vagrants and packs a far greater punch, with maximum penalties for possession alone extending to life imprisonment without the possibility of parole,[59] without mentioning the substantial possession enhancements for other crimes, as contrasted with the overnight jailings followed by a more or less formal order to 'get out of town' once common for those deemed vagrants.[60]

[35] N.Y. Penal Law § 145.65.
[36] *Id.* § 156.35 (possessing illegal copies of computer data or programs).
[37] *Id.* §§ 165.71–.73. [38] *Id.* §§ 275.15–.45. [39] *Id.* § 158.40.
[40] *Id.* §§ 170.20–.30. [41] *Id.* §§ 170.40–.50.
[42] *State v Saiez*, 489 So 2d 1125 (Fla. 1986). [43] N.Y. Penal Law §§ 170.55–.60.
[44] N.Y. Penal Law §§ 225.30–.35. [45] *Id.* §§ 225.00–.35, 415.00.
[46] *Id.* § 170.70. [47] 625 Ill Comp Stat § 5/4–104(a)(2) (1976). [48] *Id.* § 190.45
[49] *Id.* § 205.25.
[50] *Stanley v Georgia*, 394 U.S. 557 (1969); N.Y. Penal Law §§ 235.05–.07.
[51] N.Y. Penal Law § 263.11. [52] *Id.* § 230.40. [53] *Id.* § 250.10.
[54] *Id.* § 270.00. [55] *Id.* § 270.05. [56] *Id.* § 145.70.
[57] *Delmonico v State*, 155 So. 2d 368 (Fla. 1963).
[58] La. Rev. Stat. Ann. § 56:326(A)(7)(b) (*State v Wingate*, 668 So. 2d 1324 (La. Ct. App. 1996)). [59] See, e.g., *Harmelin v Michigan*, 501 U.S. 957 (1991).
[60] For a vivid description of this practice in late nineteenth-century America, see C G Tiedeman, *A Treatise on the Limitations of Police Power in the United States Considered From Both a Civil and Criminal Standpoint* (St. Louis: F.H. Thomas Law Book Co., 1886) § 49, at 124.

But how does possession perform this function? More specifically, how does possession fit into the special part of criminal law? Unlike vagrancy, possession does not stick out like a sore thumb. It does not wear its premodern origin on its sleeve, by breathlessly commingling acts with statuses in colorful centuries-old language:

> Rogues and vagabonds, or dissolute persons who go about begging, common gamblers, persons who use juggling or unlawful games or plays, common drunkards, common night walkers, thieves, pilferers or pickpockets, traders in stolen property, lewd, wanton and lascivious persons, keepers of gambling places, common railers and brawlers, persons wandering or strolling around from place to place without any lawful purpose or object, habitual loafers, disorderly persons, persons neglecting all lawful business and habitually spending their time by frequenting houses of ill fame, gaming houses, or places where alcoholic beverages are sold or served, persons able to work but habitually living upon the earnings of their wives or minor children shall be deemed vagrants . . .[61]

Possession offenses instead have all the trappings of a modern criminal offense. Rather than 'deeming' certain persons 'possessors', they set out the conditions under which a defendant is 'guilty' of 'possession'. They even come in different degrees. The New York Penal Law, for instance, a concededly degree-happy criminal code, recognizes no fewer than six degrees of 'criminal possession of a controlled substance', ranging from seventh degree possession (an A misdemeanor) to first degree possession (an A-I felony).[62] Possession offenses are integrated into articles and chapters dealing with a particular offense type. In the New York Penal Law, for instance, article 220 ('Controlled Substances Offenses') begins with a general definitional section, followed by seven sections on drug possession, six sections on drug distribution, one on possession, three on use, one on possession, and one on distribution.

And yet there is something odd about possession. A closer look reveals that possession does not fit comfortably within the taxonomy of the special part.

Conduct or Result Offense?

One common taxonomical device in the special part is the distinction between *conduct offenses* and *result offenses*. Possession, however, qualifies as neither a conduct nor a result offense. It is so heavy on attendant circumstances, and so light on result and conduct, that it instead might best be described as an *attendant circumstance offense*.

The Model Penal Code not only introduced the distinction between a general part and a special part to American criminal law, it also developed a quite sophisticated taxonomy of the special part. Having filtered general

[61] *Papachristou v. City of Jacksonville* 405 U.S. 156 at 156 n. 1 (1972).

[62] For whatever reason (perhaps a legislative oversight), there is no sixth degree criminal possession of a controlled substance.

principles (like actus reus, mens rea, and 'defenses') out of the special part, the drafters differentiated between three types of offense element, conduct, attendant circumstance, and result. They did not define these element types, but instead provided an illustration.

The 'circumstances' of the offense refer to the objective situation that the law requires to exist, in addition to the defendant's act or any results that the act may cause. The elements of 'nighttime' in burglary, 'property of another' in theft, 'female not his wife' in rape, and 'dwelling' in arson are illustrations. 'Conduct' refers to 'breaking and entering' in burglary, 'taking' in theft, 'sexual intercourse' in rape and 'burning' in arson. Results, of course, include 'death' in homicide.[63]

Possession offenses do not have a result element. Liability for possession does not require having caused harm or, in fact, any result whatever. Possession thus is a *resultless (or harmless) offense* (which is another way of saying it is not a result (or harm) offense).[64] To say that possession is a harmless offense is not necessarily to say that possession inflicts no harm in fact, but merely that possession is not defined so as to require the infliction of harm. Whether possession can be regarded as inflicting some harm in fact, if not in definition, depends on one's concept of harm. In the Police Power Model of the criminal process, criminal harm is not limited to harm inflicted on particular persons, or even groups of persons. The ultimate victim of crime is the state. In this conception, possession is neither harmless nor victimless, as every violation of a state norm offends the state by challenging its authority. A violation of a criminal statute, a statute backed up by the most severe type of state sanction, represents a particularly serious affront against the dignity of the state.

But even if we disregard the definition of harm (and victim) characteristic of the Police Power Model, the connection between possession and individual (or group) harm is worth exploring. For that connection, it turns out, is exceptionally loose. This is not to say that the looseness of the connection between possession and individual harm is unrelated to the shift in the definition of harm from individual to state harm. Instead, once the connection between criminal offenses and individual harm is rendered so remote as to render individual harm insignificant,[65] the Police Power Model is no longer merely *replacing* individual harm with state harm as the characteristic harm of criminal law. Harm, having been relegated to a background consideration rather than a prerequisite for liability, becomes a surplusage that could be defined in whatever way the state sees fit.

One way of thinking about the (individual) harmlessness of possession is in terms of the distinction between *endangerment offenses* and *harm*

[63] Commentaries § 5.01, at 301 n. 9 (emphasis added).

[64] As we'll see shortly, that's not to say that possession qualifies as a conduct offense.

[65] Cf. B E Harcourt, 'The Collapse of the Harm Principle' (1999) 90 *Journal of Criminal Law & Criminology* 109.

offenses.[66] Possession is not a harm offense in that it does not require—and in fact cannot require—the infliction of harm. Endangerment offenses can be divided into two kinds, *actual endangerment* and *abstract endangerment offenses.* Actual endangerment offenses require the creation of danger. The reckless endangerment statute in the New York Penal Law is an example; it criminalizes 'recklessly engag[ing] in conduct which creates a substantial risk of serious physical injury to another person'.[67] Reckless endangerment thus defined is a *specific actual endangerment offense*; it requires endangering a particular person (or arguably a specific group of persons).[68] By contrast, a *general actual endangerment offense* would require the creation of danger in general or to some undefined group ('community' or 'public').[69]

Unlike actual endangerment offenses, *abstract* endangerment offenses make no reference to danger. The prevention of danger instead is thought to account for the existence (if not the actual adoption) of the offense in the first place.[70] One reason why an offense might be classified as an abstract endangerment offense—even though it makes no mention of danger—is that the conduct in question is so inherently dangerous that a requirement and, more importantly, a showing of dangerousness in each individual case would be unnecessary.[71] Another reason might be that proving actual endangerment of a particular person (or group of persons) in a particular case might be difficult, if not impossible, or at least time-consuming, or that the conduct in question is *ordinarily* dangerous, even if it needn't be in each case. An experienced motorcycle rider who races down a deserted country road in the middle of nowhere may endanger no one (possibly excluding herself), but would be guilty of speeding nonetheless.

Now, possession clearly is not an actual endangerment offense. Whether it qualifies as an abstract endangerment offense would depend on the considerations motivating its adoption. There is some evidence that possession offenses are meant to prevent danger. Some American criminal

[66] Cf. Dubber, *Victims in the War on Crime*, above n. 2, at 21; Roxin, above n. 14, at § 2 VII.

[67] N.Y. Penal Law § 120.20 (reckless endangerment in the second degree).

[68] This distinction is familiar from the law of nuisance, which distinguishes between specific (private and civil) and general (public and criminal) nuisance. Cf. Dubber, above n. 3.

[69] The New York reckless endangerment statute can also be distinguished from the Model Penal Code reckless endangerment provision (upon which the New York statute, along with many others, is based). The Model Penal Code defines reckless endangerment as 'recklessly engag[ing] in conduct which places *or may place* another person in danger of death or serious bodily injury', § 211.2 (emphasis added). While the creation of danger thus is an element of the Model Penal Code version of reckless endangerment, the potential creation of danger suffices for criminal liability in the alternative. In this sense, the Model Penal Code provision can be viewed as a *potential actual endangerment offense*, which in turn may come in specific or general varieties, depending on the object of the danger created. (Thanks to Antony Duff for alerting me to this feature of the Model Penal Code reckless endangerment provision.)

[70] See, e.g., Roxin, above n. 14, at §§ 10–11.

[71] Abstract endangerment offenses thus resemble *potential* actual endangerment offenses in that they do not require proof of the endangerment of a particular persons or group of persons. Unlike potential actual endangerment offenses, however, they make no mention of danger in their definition.

codes include possession offenses among the *inchoate offenses* (as opposed to *completed*, or object, or substantive, offenses).[72] A common justification of inchoate (or preparatory or incomplete) offenses is that they prevent crime by identifying and incapacitating abnormally dangerous individuals. Strictly speaking, then, inchoate offenses target not dangerous acts, but dangerous actors. In fact, the modern trend in inchoate offense law has moved away from a focus on the act to a focus on the actor, as evidenced by the Model Penal Code's 'substantial step' test in attempt law which replaced the 'last proximate act' or 'dangerous proximity' tests, among others. The point of inchoate offenses then is no longer (only) to prevent a specific harm inflicted by a specific act, but more broadly to remove dangerous individuals from a position where they can pose a danger to others (outside prison walls).

Possession doesn't quite fit in among inchoate offenses, though in ways that are not necessarily inconsistent with its classification as an abstract endangerment offense. On its face, possession is not an inchoate offense, but a completed offense. It is not preparatory to any completed offense, as inchoate offenses are by definition (and often by name).[73] Possession is a self-standing offense, rather than being parasitic upon another, substantive, crime. Possession liability does not derive from another, object, offense codified in the special part. It is no accident that possession offenses can appear in the general part and the special part of the same criminal code.[74] In fact, perhaps possession can be viewed as an *abstract inchoate crime* because it does not include a reference to any crime yet to be committed, in analogy to abstract endangerment crimes that make no reference to a specific danger. At the same time, however, possession is a completed crime to which the traditional inchoate crimes can attach themselves (attempted possession, conspiracy to possess, etc.). Possession is thus both the most and the least inchoate of inchoate offenses.

That possession is farther removed from the infliction of harm or danger (or the commission of some other substantive crime) than ordinary inchoate offenses also becomes clear when we locate it within the spectrum of dangerousness in attempt law. As we noted above, attempt traditionally drew the line of criminal liability rather close to the completion of the offense. A preparation did not become an attempt, and thereby generate criminal liability, until the 'last proximate act' had been committed.[75] More recently that line has been pushed back considerably past the last

[72] See, e.g., Model Penal Code §§ 5.06 and 5.07.

[73] See, e.g., Texas Penal Code ch. 15 ('Preparatory Offenses').

[74] Compare Model Penal Code §§ 5.06 ('Possessing Instruments of Crime'), 5.07 (possessing offensive weapons) with Model Penal Code §§ 224.7 (possessing for use a false weight or measure), 230.3(6) (possessing with intent to sell abortifacents), 242.7 (inmate's possessing implements for escape), 251.4(2)(d) (possessing obscene material for purposes of sale).

[75] See, e.g., *People v Murray*, 14 Cal. 159 (1859) (attempt if conduct 'would end in the consummation of the particular offense, but for the intervention of circumstances independent of the will of the party').

proximate act to any behavior that amounts to a 'substantial step' toward completion of the crime.[76] This extension was consistent with an incapacitationist approach to attempt law which saw no reason not to intervene criminally when sufficient evidence of an actor's unusual dangerousness—in the form of a substantial step 'strongly corroborative of his criminal purpose'—was available. Possession law moves the *locus poenitentiae* yet farther away from the infliction of harm. For possession requires not even a substantial step for criminal liability. Possession is not preparation for another offense, nor an attempt to commit it. It is an offense in and of itself. The possession of some item already provides sufficient evidence of criminal dangerousness to warrant 'peno-correctional treatment'.

Note that possession offenses may appear in both the special and the general part. Inchoate offenses too straddle the line between the general part and the special part of modern American criminal codes, but they appear in either one or the other, rather than in both at the same time.[77] Traditionally, inchoate offenses like attempt and conspiracy were not offenses of general application. Only certain attempts were punishable. Conspiracy was an independent offense, rather than the inchoate version of some other offense. Much the same still holds in continental legal systems. While the German Penal Code, for instance, does define attempt in its general part, attempts to commit lesser offenses are punishable only if the offense defined in the special part says so.[78] Conspiracy is a substantive crime in the special part, not an inchoate version of all crimes.[79]

Perhaps, then, possession will go the way of attempt and be transformed into a general *proto-inchoate offense* that would attach to any crime defined in the special part. Rather than continuing the current practice of supplementing other offenses with possession provisions (forgery vs. possession of forgery devices), the state could simply include a general possession section in the criminal code's general part that criminalizes the possession of items for the purpose of using them to commit any crime. The Model Penal Code comes close:

Section 5.06. Possessing Instruments of Crime

(1) Criminal Instruments Generally. A person commits a misdemeanor if he possesses any instrument of crime with purpose to employ it criminally. 'Instrument of crime' means:
   (a) anything specially made or specially adapted for criminal use; or
   (b) anything commonly used for criminal purposes and possessed by the actor under circumstances which do not negative unlawful purpose.

[76] See Model Penal Code § 5.01(1)(c) and (2); see also *Commonwealth v Donton* 439 Pa. Super. 406 (1995) (exploring 'expansion of the crime of attempt' under Model Penal Code standard).

[77] Compare N.Y. Penal Law pt 3 tit G (anticipatory offenses) with Model Penal Code art 5 (inchoate crimes).

[78] StGB §§ 22 and 23.

[79] StGB § 129.

But possession offenses do more than function as proto-inchoate offenses. They operate not only prospectively, but retrospectively as well. Not only the possession of forgery devices is criminal, so is the possession of forged instruments. Possession provides evidence not only of future conduct, but also of past conduct. I may use the item in my possession in some harmful (or at least dangerous) way in the future, or I may have acquired the item in some harmful (or at least criminal) way in the past.

In fact, possession is not present conduct, but evidence of future or past conduct. Possession offenses lack not only a result element; they lack a conduct element as well. The absence of a conduct element, however, is more noteworthy than is the absence of a result element, for a *conductless offense* appears to fly in the face of the traditional act (or conduct) requirement in Anglo-American criminal law. That possession is not an act, but rather a status, or more precisely, a relationship between a person and an object, has been obvious enough for at least two centuries. Eighteenth-century English courts as a matter of course dismissed common law indictments for possession for that very reason.[80] It was only when cases began to be brought under the growing number of possession statutes that courts acquiesced, on the ground that the common law principle of actus reus didn't apply to statutory crimes.[81]Ever since then the conflict between possession and actus reus has been considered a question of statutory interpretation—or legislative prerogative. The currently favored solution is to simply declare possession an act, by (statutory) definition. The Model Penal Code, for instance, in a section entitled, among other things, 'Possession as an Act', announces that '[p]ossession is an act . . . if the possessor knowingly procured or received the thing possessed or was aware of his control thereof for a sufficient period to have been able to terminate his possession.'[82] The New York Penal Law likewise declares that possession 'means to have physical possession or otherwise to exercise dominion or control over tangible property', and counts as a voluntary act 'if the actor was aware of his physical possession or control . . . for a sufficient period to have been able to terminate it'.[83]

Possession, then, is not conduct, but evidence of future or past conduct. More precisely, possession is a sort of doctrinal shorthand for the acquisition of an object or the failure to distribute it. Insofar as—at least by definition—possession makes reference to conduct, without constituting conduct itself, one might describe it as a *constructive conduct offense*. Rather than criminalizing future or past conduct (use or distribution and acquisition), possession punishes present status as evidence of that future or past conduct.

[80] Cf. *Regina v Dugdale*, 1 El. & Bl. 435 at 439 (1853) (Coleridge, J).
[81] See, e.g., *Rex v Lennard*, 1 Leach 90 (1772) (applying 8 & 9 Will 3 c 26).
[82] § 2.01(4). [83] N.Y. Penal Law §§ 10.00, 15.00(2).

Note also that possession in fact combines within itself commission and omission liability. It is both a *(constructive) commission offense* and a *(constructive) omission offense*; in short it's a *commission-omission offense*. It is defined both in terms of the commission of acquisition and the omission of dispossession. Considered as an omission offense, possession straddles the familiar line between *indirect* and *direct* omission liability.[84] Direct omission offenses, like tax evasion, explicitly criminalize the failure to engage in particular conduct, like failing to pay taxes. The theory of indirect omission, by contrast, transforms any commission offense into an omission offense by reference to a duty to act set out elsewhere. So the failure to get medical attention that results in death is homicide if the victim is the perpetrator's child because parents owe their children a duty of care.[85] Possession appears as an *indirect* omission offense if one focuses on the definition of each possession offense, which makes no mention of the failure to distribute the item possessed. At the same time, it might appear to be a *direct* omission offense in that the general definition of possession makes explicit reference to the failure to distribute. If it is regarded as an indirect omission offense, it would have to rely on some duty (to dispossess), elsewhere defined, the violation of which could give rise to indirect omission liability. Terminating possession to avoid possession liability—by avoiding having one's relationship to an object be characterized as possession in the first place—turns out to be not as straightforward as it sounds. For the distribution of items the possession of which is criminalized tends to be criminal itself.[86]

Presumptions, Explicit and Implicit

So far we have focused on the retro- and prospective aspects of the *definition* of possession. But not only possession itself is both retro- and prospective; functionally speaking it also provides evidence of *other* conduct in the future and in the past. Once it has been established what possession is, the next question is what it means. Here the idea is that what we are punishing when we punish possession isn't 'really' possession itself but some objectionable future or past conduct, i.e. a particular form of distribution, use or acquisition. So possession really punishes importation (since all drugs originate abroad). Or possession really punishes distribution (since the

[84] On the distinction between direct and indirect omission offenses, see Markus D Dubber, *Criminal Law: Model Penal Code* (New York: Foundation Press, 2002), 35–7.

[85] See, e.g., *People v Steinberg*, 79 N.Y.2d 673 (1992) (finding common-law and statutory basis for parent's duty of care toward child).

[86] The most obvious example here is drug criminal law, which consists of prohibitions of distributing and possessing various 'controlled substances'. Occasionally a defendant may find himself charged with distributing (as a principal) and possessing (as an accomplice) the same drugs. See, e.g., *People v Manini*, 79 N.Y.2d 561 (1992) (throwing out the possession complicity charge on the ground that possession is 'necessarily incidental' to distribution).

possession of large amounts of drugs suggests that they are not kept for personal use). Or possession really punishes use (which—in the case of drugs, though not necessarily of guns—isn't criminal itself, but is nonetheless harmful in some sense).[87]

This evidentiary function of possession emerges most clearly in *compound possession offenses*. A compound offense is an offense that includes as one of its elements another offense, accompanied by some mental state (ordinarily, intent or purpose). Burglary (trespass with the intent to commit a felony) is a well-known example. Possession with intent to distribute is another. Possession with intent to distribute might be thought of as proto-inchoate distribution (proto-inchoate because it needn't rise to the level of an attempt). That's not to say, however, that *simple possession offenses* do not also serve this evidentiary function. In fact, possession of sufficiently large quantities of drugs is taken to be such convincing evidence of the intent to distribute that that intent is irrebuttably—and implicitly—presumed. Possession thus would give rise to a presumption of intent to distribute which, combined with possession, would provide sufficient evidence of future (or past) distribution. Simple possession of small, personal, quantities of drugs do not provide evidence of distribution, but instead bear the possibility of future *use*, which is said to have harmful primary and remote effects.[88]

In addition to these implicit presumptions at work in possession offenses, modern criminal law has surrounded possession offenses with a number of explicit presumptions. These too work backward and forward. A traditional example of a backward presumption is the presumption of larceny based on possession of stolen goods. Other retrospective presumptions include those of importation, manufacture, and transfer. Forward presumptions include a presumption of an intent to use.[89] (Contemporaneously, possession can also create a presumption of knowing possession).[90] And of course possession itself can be presumed, say, on the basis of proximity, (even if the proximity isn't itself criminalized).[91] In New York, as elsewhere, every occupant of

[87] As a matter of fact, one cannot use drugs without possessing them. As a matter of form, however, legislatures generally do not punish drug consumption, but drug possession. Possession is quite literally the core concept of drug criminal law. It lies at the hub of an implicit regulatory web that reaches not only consumption (or other use), but also acquisition (which, like use, is not separately criminalized) and distribution (which is).

[88] For a discussion of the remote harm caused—or threatened—by drug possession, see *Harmelin v Michigan*, 501 U.S. 957 (1991).

[89] See, e.g., N.Y. Penal Law §§ 158.00 (possession of five or more public benefit cards presumptive evidence of intent to use them for fraudulent purposes), 265.15(4) (unlawful use of explosive substance), 270.00(2)(c) (sale of fireworks), 270.05(3) (use of noxious material)); Model Penal Code § 5.06 ('purpose to employ [weapon] criminally').

[90] *Barnes v United States*, 412 US 837 (1973) (possession of stolen property as presumptive evidence of knowledge that property was stolen); N.Y. Penal Law §§ 165.55, 170.71, 225.35; see also *Id.* § 265.15(6) (defacement).

[91] See, e.g., Mass. Ann. Laws ch 94C, § 35 ('Unlawful presence at a place where heroin is kept or being in company of person in possession thereof').

a car, for instance, is presumed to knowingly possess any gun or controlled substance found in the car.[92]

So not only is possession a retro- and prospective presumption, it can be presumed itself, and then give rise to other retro- and prospective presumptions. Here possession offenses challenge the distinction between the law of evidence and substantive criminal law. Presumptions have long been disfavored under Packer's Due Process Model because they risk hollowing out statutory definitions without doing away with them altogether. So instead of removing a mens rea requirement from a possession statute—as occurs quite frequently—the state might establish a presumption of knowledge or instead of criminalizing proximity to 'contraband'—as also happens—it might establish a presumption of possession based on proximity.

Presumptions are driven by considerations of prosecutorial convenience. As a sweep offense in the Police Power Model of the criminal process, it is no surprise that the law of possession is filled with presumptions. Possession itself is, after all, shorthand for a whole host of other offenses (and some types of noncriminal conduct as well, like drug use).

Possession as Attendant Circumstance Offense

While possession offenses lack both a conduct and a result element, they do have at least one *attendant circumstance* element—the characteristics of the item possessed. In fact, many possession offenses consist almost entirely of a description of this attendant circumstance. Take, for instance, the definition of criminal possession of a controlled substance in the fourth degree, taken from the New York Penal Law:

Section 220.09. Criminal possession of a controlled substance in the fourth degree

A person is guilty of criminal possession of a controlled substance in the fourth degree when he knowingly and unlawfully possesses:

1. one or more preparations, compounds, mixtures or substances containing a narcotic drug and said preparations, compounds, mixtures or substances are of an aggregate weight of one-eighth ounce or more; or
2. one or more preparations, compounds, mixtures or substances containing methamphetamine, its salts, isomers or salts of isomers and said preparations, compounds, mixtures or substances are of an aggregate weight of one-half ounce or more; or
3. one or more preparations, compounds, mixtures or substances containing a narcotic preparation and said preparations, compounds, mixtures or substances are of an aggregate weight of two ounces or more; or
4. a stimulant and said stimulant weighs one gram or more; or

[92] N.Y. Penal Law § 220.25 ('The presence of a dangerous drug in an automobile . . . is presumptive evidence of knowing possession thereof by each and every person in the automobile at the time such drug was found').

5. lysergic acid diethylamide and said lysergic acid diethylamide weighs one milligram or more; or
6. a hallucinogen and said hallucinogen weighs twenty-five milligrams or more; or
7. a hallucinogenic substance and said hallucinogenic substance weighs one gram or more; or
8. a dangerous depressant and such dangerous depressant weighs ten ounces or more; or
9. a depressant and such depressant weighs two pounds or more; or
10. one or more preparations, compounds, mixtures or substances containing concentrated cannabis as defined in paragraph (a) of subdivision four of section thirty-three hundred two of the public health law and said preparations, compounds, mixtures or substances are of an aggregate weight of one ounce or more; or
11. phencyclidine and said phencyclidine weighs two hundred fifty milligrams or more; or
12. methadone and said methadone weighs three hundred sixty milligrams or more; or
13. phencyclidine and said phencyclidine weighs fifty milligrams or more with intent to sell it and has previously been convicted of an offense defined in this article or the attempt or conspiracy to commit any such offense; or
14. ketamine and said ketamine weighs four thousand milligrams or more.

Note that not even this detailed list of drug characteristics (quality and quantity) is exhaustive. The definitions of 'controlled substance'[93] and 'concentrated cannabis' appear not in the Penal Law, but in the Public Health Law. In this sense, drug possession offenses exemplify an increasingly common type of offense, the *multi-code offense*. Multi-code offenses are a form of *fragmented offense*, whose elements are dispersed among various provisions. In the traditional type of fragmented offense, one might find the definition of certain elements common to several offenses in a separate 'definitions' provision—*single-code fragmented offenses*.[94]

If we think of possession as an attendant circumstance (since it is not conduct, nor result) that describes a relationship between a person and a thing, assigning one the status of possessor and the other the status of possessed (or possession), then every possession offense provides a radical example of a single-code fragmented offense. For the very definition of possession appears not in offense definitions but in the general part of

[93] N.Y. Penal Law § 220.00(5) (citing N.Y. Public Health Law §§ 3302 and 3306).

[94] A modest example of this type of offense is the crime of larceny as defined in section 584 of the 1865 draft of the New York Penal Code: 'Larceny is the taking of personal property accomplished by fraud or stealth, or without color of right thereto, and with intent to deprive another thereof'. 'Personal property' then was defined in § 775 as including 'every description of money, goods, chattels, effects, evidences of rights in action, and all written instruments by which any pecuniary obligation, right or title to property, real or personal, is created, acknowledged, transferred, increased, defeated, discharged or diminished, and every right and interest therein.'

modern criminal codes.[95] Multi-code offenses blur the distinction between criminal and noncriminal law insofar as an essential part—and in the case of possession offenses, often *the* essential part—of an offense is defined in a noncriminal code. Consider, for instance, the element of unlawfulness that can be found in many possession statutes. This element—which can be viewed as an attendant circumstance attaching to the element of 'possession'—is defined not in the criminal code, but in some noncriminal code dealing with matters of 'public health': ' "Unlawfully" means in violation of article thirty-three of the public health law.'[96] In the Public Health Law, one finds a section 3304, which explains, somewhat unhelpfully, that '[i]t shall be unlawful for any person to . . . possess . . . a controlled substance except as expressly allowed by this article.' Possession of a controlled substance, in other words, is presumptively unlawful—and therefore, given the unlawful possession provisions in the New York Penal Law, also criminal—unless certain 'exemptions' apply. The Health Law thus does not set out the conditions for unlawfulness of possession of controlled substances, but the conditions for its lawfulness, provided the substance is in fact 'controlled'. We know already, however, that the Public Health Law, and not the Penal Law, determines which substances are controlled and which aren't.

The offense elements supplied by the Public Health thus consist of two lists, rather than definitions. The first list sets out the exemptions to the general presumption of unlawfulness of the possession (and therefore criminality); the second list sets out the conditions for 'controlledness' of the substance possessed. I will excerpt only the former as the latter consists of an even longer list of substances than that reproduced in section 220.09 above:

Section 3305. Exemptions.

1. The provisions of this article restricting the possession . . . of controlled substances . . . shall not apply:
   (a) to common carriers or to warehousemen, while engaged in lawfully transporting or storing such substances, or to any employee of the same acting within the scope of his employment; or
   (b) official duties requiring possession or control of controlled substances; or
   (c) to temporary incidental possession by employees or agents of persons lawfully entitled to possession, or by persons whose possession is for the purpose of aiding public officers in performing their official duties.
   (d) to a duly authorized agent of an incorporated society for the prevention of cruelty to animals . . . for the limited purpose of . . . possessing . . . , ketamine hydrochloride to anesthetize animals and/or sodium pentobarbital to euthanize animals . . . .

[95] Possession thus would count as a *multi-part single-code fragmented offense*. See N.Y. Penal Law §§ 10.00 (definition of possession), 15.00(2) (possession as voluntary act); Model Penal Code § 2.01(4) (possession as voluntary act).

[96] N.Y. Penal Law § 220.00.

3. The commissioner is hereby authorized and empowered to make any rules, regulations and determinations permitting the following categories of persons to obtain, dispense and administer controlled substances under such conditions and in such manner as he shall prescribe:
   (a) a person in the employ of the United States government or of any state, . . . possessing . . . controlled substances by reason of his official duties . . . .

Here, then, we have the state declaring a substance controlled. Having declared it controlled, it then proceeds to declare its possession unlawful. Only at this point do we leave the realm of public health law and enter criminal law; for having declared possession of the substance unlawful, the state then declares its unlawful possession criminal.

Note that the quoted excerpt from the Public Health Law illustrates another variety of fragmented offense, the *multi-branch offense*. The commissioner for public health, the head of an agency in the executive branch, is authorized in a code passed by the legislative branch to supply a crucial definitional element of the crime of drug possession (and other drug crimes), through 'rules, regulations and determinations permitting [certain] persons to obtain, dispense and administer controlled substances under such conditions and in such manner as he shall prescribe'.[97]

There are other types of multi-branch offenses of course. In the case of our drug possession example, the crime (of drug possession) still appears in the criminal code (though it is not exhaustively defined there). Yet more common are *noncriminal multi-branch offenses*, which appear in noncriminal codes. An example is the crime of 'wilful violation of health laws', defined in section 12-b of the New York Public Health Law:

1. A person who wilfully violates or refuses or omits to comply with any lawful order or regulation prescribed by any local board of health or local health officer, is guilty of a misdemeanor; . . .
2. A person who wilfully violates any provision of this chapter, or any regulation lawfully made or established by any public officer or board under authority of this chapter, the punishment for violating which is not otherwise prescribed by this chapter or any other law, is punishable by imprisonment not exceeding one year, or by a fine not exceeding two thousand dollars or by both.

In a well-known case, *People v Coe*,[98] a nurse at a senior citizens' home was convicted under this provision for frisking an elderly patient with a history of heart disease, who died shortly thereafter. Coe was held to have violated

[97] See N.Y. Comp. Codes R. & Regs. tit. 10, § 80.2 ('Exemptions'); see also *ibid.* §§ 80.3 ('Exceptions, reclassification and exemptions of scheduled controlled substances'), 80.125(b) ('Possession of a false or forged controlled substance prescription by any person other than a pharmacist in the pursuance of his profession shall be presumptive evidence of his intent to use the same for the purpose of illegally obtaining a controlled substance'.).

[98] 71 NY.2d 852 (1988).

section 2803-d(7) of the Public Health Law:

> [A]ny person who commits an act of physical abuse, neglect or mistreatment, or who fails to report such an act as provided in this section, shall be deemed to have violated this section and shall be liable for a penalty pursuant to section twelve of this chapter after an opportunity to be heard pursuant to this section.

'Physical abuse', in turn, was defined in a regulation as 'inappropriate physical contact with a patient or resident of a residential health care facility', where inappropriate physical contact includes, among other things, 'striking' and 'shoving'. In the same regulation, 'mistreatment' is defined as 'inappropriate use of physical . . . restraints on . . . a patient or resident of a residential health care facility.'[99]

The crime in *Coe*, then, was defined entirely outside the criminal code. What's more, while it appeared in a noncriminal code, several of its elements were defined not in a code, but in a set of executive regulations.[100] In fact, the crime, as defined in section 12-b, would apply directly to violations of executive regulations, without an intermediary statutory provision like section 2803-d(7). Section 12-b is an expansive version of a *blanket law*, a law that provides for criminal punishment but does not set out the elements of a criminal offense itself, and instead leaves the definition of the offense to other norms and—in the case of executive regulations and order—officials.[101] Executive officials, in fact, receive the backing of criminal sanctions not only for duly and centrally promulgated regulations, which are subject to procedural constraints of notice and comment and then published in a code of rules and regulations, but for any 'order . . . prescribed by any . . . local health officer'.

Like many blanket statutes, section 12-b includes two limitations, one on the scope of the offense and the other on its punishment. It authorizes a maximum penalty of one year imprisonment and a $2,000 fine. These punishments are by no means negligible, but they do not approach the punishment for a multi-code fragmented offense like drug possession, which can extend to life imprisonment (in New York) and to life imprisonment without the possibility of parole (in other jurisdictions).[102] Furthermore, the violation of a subsidiary norm referenced in the blanket law of section 12-b is criminal only if it is committed 'wilfully'. Wilfulness has been interpreted to require some degree of notice.[103] In *Coe*, for instance, the court held that in order to make out a wilful violation of section 12-b, the state had to

[99] 10 N.Y. Code Rules & Regulations § 81.1(a) and (b).

[100] *Coe* thus illustrates that multi-branch offenses are not limited to those that are defined in the criminal code and some executive regulations; their legislative component may be found in noncriminal codes as well.

[101] H-H Jescheck and T Weigend, *Lehrbuch des Strafrechts: Allgemeiner Teil* (5th ed., Berlin: Duncker & Humblot, 1996) 111 (Blankettstrafgesetz).

[102] See, e.g., *Harmelin v Michigan*, 501 U.S. 957 (1991).

[103] See also *Cheek v United States*, 498 U.S. 192 (1991) (criminal tax evasion).

establish that the defendant 'was aware that her conduct was illegal'. The court rejected a more onerous notice requirement, which would have limited wilful violations to cases where the defendant 'knew she was violating a specific statute or regulation'. In *Coe* the requisite awareness of illegality was present because the defendant had received a copy of the 'Patient's Bill of Rights' (itself codified in the Public Health Law) and attended lectures regarding its content. The Patient's Bill of Rights recognizes a patient's right to be free from having his privacy invaded, physically or mentally abused, and being forced to do anything against his will. This notice requirement may not be particularly toothful; still, other fragmented offenses, such as the multi-code drug possession offenses, have no notice requirement of any kind, however undemanding.

Multi-branch offenses thus blur the line between norms originating in the legislative and executive branch, just as multi-code offenses straddle the distinction between criminal and noncriminal law. In Anglo-American law, the distinction—and competition—between legislative and nonlegislative criminal norms of course played a central role for centuries. Traditionally, however, the nonlegislative origin of criminal norms was judicial, not executive. The arguments against judicial criminal lawmaking are familiar. Judicial crime definition is thought to violate the *principle of legality*, which encompasses the principles of *prospectivity, specificity*, and *publicity*. Executive crime definition faces similar, but not identical, problems.

Judicial criminal lawmaking is always retrospective, at least in the Anglo-American view of the judicial role, which is limited to deciding live cases or controversies. 'Advisory' judicial opinions do not raise prospectivity concerns. Executive criminal lawmaking needn't be retrospective, though it may be. The executive may decide to make its regulations prospective, but it is not required constitutionally to do so. It might be argued, in fact, that executive regulations are not criminal statutes and therefore are not subject to the principle of prospectivity in the first place. At any rate, executive regulations only become criminalized through the application of some blanket clause (like section 12-b of the New York Public Health Law). But the list of controlled substances, say, is not itself a criminal provision. It merely declares what substances are deemed 'controlled'. As long as the provision setting out criminal liability, then, is not applied retroactively, executive regulations promulgated under it, or criminalized by it, could be retroactive. Or should the prospectivity requirement attach only if the regulation is used as the basis for a criminal prosecution, but not if it is merely applied civilly? Whether the blanket law itself (or some other provision in a noncriminal code that provides for criminal penalties, such as imprisonment) would be considered criminal, and therefore subject to the principle of prospectivity, is another matter, of course. Here it may be relevant whether the blanket law—unlike section 12-b—appears in a criminal code.

In some ways, multi-branch offenses can *enhance* specificity. Executive regulations and orders, after all, can be seen as spelling out broad legislative commands that, without executive specification, would be hopelessly vague. An offense defined as 'unlawful possession of a controlled substance' would provide neither sufficient notice nor sufficient guidance to law enforcement, the traditional components of a 'void for vagueness' inquiry in American constitutional law. But to say that executive regulations may serve the ideal of specificity in fact is not to say that they are subject to a (constitutional) principle of specificity.[104] It may, for instance, be in the interest of the state to provide its executive with specific guidelines for enforcement for the sake of a more efficient operation of the state apparatus. The point of the specificity requirement, however, is not to make bureaucracies run more smoothly, but to provide notice to individuals about the criminality of their conduct and to prevent (or at least make more difficult) discriminatory or otherwise arbitrary, rather than incompetent, enforcement. The problematic presumption of notice that attaches to statutory texts is more fanciful when it is applied to executive regulations. Without a sophisticated dissemination and education campaign (as for instance a universal requirement of driving instruction by licensed instructors), not even the most detailed executive regulation buried in a code of rules and regulations can provide meaningful notice to anyone other than the sophisticated actor who operates in a specialized industry and has sufficient resources to devote to the monitoring of a fluid regulatory environment.

Whether executive regulations provide guidance to law enforcement officials if criminal statutes do not, is not quite clear. The problem here is not the lack of specificity of any particular regulation, but the mass of regulations as a whole. A blanket criminal law considerably, and with one stroke, expands the number of potential criminal violations. American criminal codes already feature a large, and growing, collection of criminal offenses; converting any and all executive orders or regulations promulgated by some member of the executive increases the discretion of executive officials not only in the creation of criminal norms, but also in their enforcement. Specificity only limits executive discretion if it is not achieved at the price of increasing the number of specific offenses. Today arbitrary enforcement is problematic not because of the arbitrary application of criminal norms, but because of the arbitrary *selection* of criminal norms among a virtually unlimited supply. In this way, the illusory specificity of executive regulations backed by criminal sanctions allows the state to make an end run around the concern with the uniformity—and therefore the legality—of executive participation in the criminal process that underlies the specificity requirement in the first place.

[104] Cf. *People v Lobianco*, 766 N.Y.S.2d 807 (N.Y. Crim. Ct. 2003) (rejecting vagueness challenge against offense of unlawful possession of a hypodermic instrument, N.Y. Penal Law § 220.45, where unlawfulness is defined in N.Y. Pub. Health Law).

Publicity traditionally has been considered an important component of the principle of legality, and a significant weakness of judicial criminal lawmaking. It is doubtful that the publication of executive rules and regulations in 'codes' of rules and regulations is superior to the publication of judicial decisions in court reporters. Then again, it is difficult to fault executive regulations for their lack of publicity if legislatively enacted criminal statutes have essentially been exempted from meaningful publicity inquiry themselves.[105]

There is another aspect of the legality principle that raises concerns about executive and judicial criminal lawmaking alike. The principle of *legislativity* insists that the criminal lawmaking power be limited to the legislature, on the basis of familiar concerns about democratic legitimacy (legislatures represent the constituents of the political community, they deliberate, they have staffs). One might suggest that executive criminal lawmaking is more consistent with the principle of legislativity than is judicial criminal lawmaking because the legislature explicitly delegated the task of criminal lawmaking to the executive when it declares, in a statute, that some administrative official is authorized to promulgate rules and regulations pursuant to some statute and that violations of these rules and regulations are deemed criminal (under certain circumstances). But does the fact of delegation resolve the theoretical (and constitutional) question of legitimacy? Presumably the problem of the illegitimacy of judicial criminal lawmaking could not be solved by the legislature passing a statute that authorized *judges* to create crimes. Perhaps the legislature might be allowed to instruct some agency charged with 'environmental protection' to set acceptable pollution levels, and then threatening exceeding these levels with punishment. But should it be permitted to simply declare any and all rules and regulations promulgated by that agency to constitute crimes?[106]

So much for the dispersed definition of attendant circumstances pertaining to the characteristics of the item possessed and of the possession itself. The attendant circumstances defining the *possessor* are perhaps more noteworthy still. Possession is, after all, a status offense. It requires not conduct, nor does it require a result. It instead defines the relationship of an individual with an object. That relationship is determined by the status of the possessor and of the possessed. Possession is an incapacitationist tool for the elimination of threats. The all-important status that lies at the heart of the crime of possession thus is dangerousness. Possession is criminalized if it poses a threat, and more precisely, under the Police Power Model of the criminal process, a threat to the authority of the state. Possessor and possessed are

[105] See, e.g., *United States v Casson*, 434 F.2d 415 (1970).

[106] A solid majority of the U.S. Supreme Court presumably would find no constitutional fault with this arrangement. See *Mistretta v United States*, 488 U.S. 361 (1989) (delegation of power to make punishment law to federal sentencing commission).

considered as a threat unit. The threat can either emanate from the possessor or from the possessed. Some objects are so dangerous that their *being possessed* is presumptively criminal. And some individuals are so dangerous that their *possessing* is presumptively criminal. The prime example of the possessed-driven possession offense is gun possession, which is criminal except for certain individuals deemed nondangerous to the state (through exemptions for state officials or licensing).[107] The prime example of the possessor-driven possession offense is universal possession prohibition in high-security prisons, where inmates are prohibited from possessing any object unless possession of that object has been permitted by the prison authorities.[108]

The presumption of dangerousness attaching to the possessor is either rebuttable or irrebuttable. In the case of gun possession, for instance, the presumption is irrebuttable if the possessor has the status of 'felon'[109] or 'alien'.[110] Other possessors can rebut the presumption of dangerousness in various ways. One common method of rebuttal is the license. If the state finds that the possessor is 'of good moral character', then it may, in its discretion, grant him the license to possess a weapon.[111] Receipt of the license is not a matter of right, but of grace.[112] Another common method of rebuttal, often neglected, is attaining the status of state official. The state has granted to certain of its officials, including police officers and soldiers, permission to possess guns. The licensee and the state official are those whose status translates into an 'exemption' from the general prohibition of gun ownership.[113] Much the same holds for drug possession offenses; there the status-based exemptions from the universal prohibition include state officials and licensed physicians.

The Possession Universe

Note, then, the complex structure of a possession offense. At first sight, possession offenses look straightforward enough: 'A person is guilty of criminal possession of a weapon in the fourth degree when ... [h]e possesses any firearm ...'[114] Possession of a particular object is criminalized without any reference to (offender) status (or conduct). The (very detailed) definition

[107] On licensing as a tool of modern governance, see Mariana Valverde, *Law's Dream of a Common Knowledge* (Princeton, N.J.: Princeton University Press, 2003), ch. 6.

[108] See Ted Conover, *Newjack: Guarding Sing Sing* (New York: Random House, 2000), 104–5 (prison contraband defined as 'any article that is not authorized by the Superintendent or [his] designee').

[109] See, e.g., N.Y. Penal Law § 265.01(4) (convicted of a felony or serious offense); cf. *United States v Leviner*, 31 F Supp 2d 23, 26–27 (D. Mass 1998) ('Felon in Possession of a Firearm is the prototypical status offense'.).

[110] *Id.* § 265.01(5).

[111] N.Y. Penal Law § 400.00(1)(a).

[112] *Shapiro v New York City Police Dep't* (License Division), 157 Misc. 2d 28 (N.Y. 1993).

[113] See N.Y. Penal Law § 265.20. This exemption attaches to persons, not acts. It therefore even applies to an off-duty police officer's possession of a deadly weapon with the intent to use it unlawfully against another. See *People v Desthers* 343 NYS.2d 887 (N.Y. Crim. Ct. 1973).

[114] N.Y. Penal Law § 265.01 (criminal possession of a weapon in the fourth degree).

of 'firearm', i.e. of the attendant circumstances that transform an object into 'contraband', appears elsewhere in the same article of the special part.[115]

The all-important definition of the relationship between the person and the object (i.e. the part of the statute that would ordinarily be occupied by its conduct element) can be found not in the special part, but in the general part of the criminal code. There possession is defined, as we've seen, in two places. Possession means either 'to have physical possession' or 'to exercise dominion or control over tangible property'.[116] Possession, in other words, is either *actual* or *constructive*. Elsewhere possession is said to qualify as a voluntary act—and therefore as subject to criminal punishment—if 'the actor was aware of his physical possession or control thereof for a sufficient period to have been able to terminate it'.[117] In the Model Penal Code, possession also includes, in the alternative, 'knowingly procur[ing] or receiv[ing] the thing possessed'.[118]

Having thus pieced together the scope of the universal prohibition on possession, the special part further complicates matters by setting out 'exemptions' to that prohibition. These exemptions must be carefully distinguished from ordinary 'defenses'. Not only do they not appear in the general part, but they are of a different quality altogether. Those who are exempt from criminal liability have no need to raise a defense. They are freed of even that prima facie criminal liability which ordinarily results from a match between one's conduct and all the elements of some criminal offense. They are free of criminal liability by definition, so to speak. Only after reviewing the status-based exemptions can we determine whether someone has in fact committed an offense.

Ordinarily at this stage, we would proceed to investigate the lawfulness of the facially criminal conduct (justifiability), followed by an inquiry into the responsibility of the person engaging in it (excusability). We would, in other words, proceed from our inquiry into the special part to one into the general principles of liability laid out in the general part. Possession offenses, however, resist this familiar mode of analysis. They are, in a sense, a *miniature code* unto themselves, with their very own, truncated, versions of the doctrines that we ordinarily associate with the general part.

The definition of possession creates a *sui generis* type of voluntary act that is both commission (acquisition) and omission (failure to dispossess) and, *in defining its actness*, makes references to requisite mental states, including knowledge and awareness.[119] Besides these miniature doctrines of actus reus and mens rea, the doctrine of possession features its own version of imputation, both as instrumentalization and as complicity. Constructive possession is established through control over a person or over an area. With

[115] N.Y. Penal Law § 265.00(3). [116] *Id.* 10.00(8). [117] *Id.* 15.00(2).

[118] § 2.01(4).

[119] This commingling of actus reus and mens rea can create difficulties of interpretation, particular in strict liability possession offenses. See *In re L*, 121 Misc. 2d 271 (N.Y. Fam. Ct. 1983).

constructive possession there is no need to invoke traditional doctrines such as involuntary act (where one person's conduct is so completely controlled by another as to render it involuntary) or duress (where one person's conduct is sufficiently caused by another as to render it excusable) or imputation by instrumentalization (the flip-side of duress) or imputation by complicity (where one person's conduct is sufficiently instigated or facilitated by another as to be imputed to the latter as his own).[120] It would be a mistake, however, to think of constructive possession as a form of vicarious or group liability in the traditional sense. While it radically simplifies traditional means of imputation, with their cumbersome actus reus and mens rea (purpose or at least knowledge) requirements, constructive possession turns on an altogether different type of imputation, from object to person, rather than from person to person. It is the connection with the object, and more precisely the match of the object's dangerousness with the dangerousness of the person, that ultimately gives rise to criminal liability. How could indirect possession liability rely on imputing conduct from one person to another, if possession is not conduct?

The miniature version of the doctrine of justification is the element of unlawfulness. Lawful possession is not prima facie possession that is justified on the basis of one or another of the familiar grounds of justification (self-defense, necessity, and so on). The doctrine of justification has been folded into the element of unlawfulness, which is defined by the state not in the general part, but in a definitional section setting out what substance is 'controlled' or which possessor is 'exempted' from criminal liability. For that reason, courts have hesitated to recognize general defenses to a charge of possession. Self-defense may be a defense to murder, but not to possessing the gun used in the homicide because 'a person either possesses a weapon lawfully or he does not'.[121] The justified self-defender thus may find herself acquitted of murder, but still convicted of gun possession, illustrating possession's function as a universal *fall-back* (or *Velcro*) *offense*, the offense that will stick if no other will.[122] Put another way, the defense of consent, properly reconceptualized as state-based, becomes the one and only 'justification' for a possession offense. If the state consents to a person's possession of an object the possession of which has been proscribed by the state, then no crime has been committed, as no offense has been taken.

[120] See, e.g., *People v Rivera*, 77 AD2d 538 (N.Y. App. Div. 1980) (defendant held to constructively possess a gun physically possessed by his brother because he had told him to get it).

[121] *People v Almodovar*, 62 N.Y. 2d 126 (1984); see also *People v Laramore*, 1 Misc. 3d 5, 764 N.Y.S.2d 299 (N.Y. App. Term 2003) ('We cannot conceive of a situation where an intent to use a kitchen knife unlawfully can ever be justified'.). Other—federal—courts have recognized, after much handwringing, a defense of justification to a gun possession charge 'in only extraordinary circumstances'. *United States v Deleveaux* 205 F.3d 1292 at 1297 (2000).

[122] See Dubber, *Victims in the War on Crime*, above n. 2, at 52, 77–8.

The law of possession thus is a closed universe that resists any attempt to connect questions of liability with a comprehensive account of criminal law, and thereby to subject it to critical analysis in light of the principles of the general part. Possession needs no general part; it comes with its very own *special general part*.

3. Conclusion

Possession, we have seen, defies traditional categories. Rather than struggle to shoehorn possession into the common law's familiar analytic framework of actus reus, mens rea, and the like, we might be better off thinking of possession as representing a new paradigm of offense within a new model of the criminal law process, the Police Power Model. Possession offenses appear both in the general part (as a variety of inchoate liability) and the special part (attached to particular offense categories), as a single broad offense (such as possession of criminal instruments) and as several specific offenses (such as possession of drugs, guns, stolen property, and so on). They collapse the distinctions between offense and defense (more specifically, between offense definition and justification) by including, within their definition, the concept of 'unlawfulness', 'illegality', or 'criminality', along with separate 'exemptions'. Possession offenses also do away with traditional notions of imputed (and 'group') liability, through the doctrine of constructive possession, which makes room for vicarious liability (through dominion over a person) and spatial liability (through dominion over an area). They are neither result nor conduct offenses and defy the traditional distinction between voluntariness and mens rea.

Possession offenses also straddle familiar distinctions among various aspects of the criminal process, definition, imposition, and infliction. Through the use of presumptions they incorporate procedural elements into substantive criminal law, thus breaking down the distinction between definition and imposition. Designed for ease of enforcement and imposition, possession offenses reflect an approach to criminal law that emphasizes crime control over just punishment, application over definition, results over rules, and ultimately the protection of state authority over the prevention and vindication of personal harm. In the possession paradigm, substantive criminal law (including its special part) is of instrumental significance as its traditional categories must give way to the exigencies of crime control.

Possession's failure to fit in might give rise to critique, at least insofar as the categories of the substantive criminal law can claim normative, and not merely taxonomical, significance. Given that the time-honored principles of Anglo-American criminal law, however, are founded more on tradition than on any coherent theory of legitimacy, mere noncompliance hardly means illegitimacy. The present analysis of possession offenses in the broader context of the Police Power Model of the criminal process is content to unearth new categories that may prove useful in assembling a more nuanced account of Anglo-American criminal law in general, and of its special part in particular.

6

The Distinctiveness of Domestic Abuse: A Freedom-Based Account

Victor Tadros*

Violence is the food and drink of criminal law. But as violence comes in different forms and degrees, there is a question about how the criminal law should differentiate between different forms of violence. Some theoretical debate has recently emerged which encourages us to think not only about degrees of violence but also about kinds of violence. Different forms of violence, it is argued, are morally distinct from each other. The criminal law, in constructing distinct offences of violence, ought to reflect those moral distinctions.[1] The way in which violence is perpetrated, the argument goes, is at least as central to distinguishing between offences as is degree. For example, if disfigurement is a kind of violence distinct from bruising, the criminal law ought to reflect that distinction. And that is at least as important as distinguishing between greater and lesser degrees of disfigurement or greater and lesser degrees of bruising, or perhaps even more so.

Domestic abuse is treated distinctively in the social and political realm as well as by the institutions of criminal justice. And yet domestic abuse has not featured very much in the literature on offences against the person by substantive criminal lawyers.[2] That is so even though the literature concerning domestic abuse in the fields of criminal justice and criminology is extensive. By far the most common way in which domestic abuse tends to appear in

* Many thanks to the participants in the workshop at the Louisiana State University and to the editors for helpful criticisms and suggestions that have resulted in substantial development of this chapter and, I hope, its improvement. Particular thanks go to Phil Bates, who was my commentator in Louisiana. Thanks also to Sharon Cowan and Niki Lacey for their insightful and knowledgeable comments on the piece close to completion, and to Elaine Reid and Jamie McLean for research assistance.

[1] See J Horder 'Rethinking Non-Fatal Offences Against the Person' (1994) 14 *Oxford Journal of Legal Studies* 335; J Gardner 'Rationality and the Rule of Law in Offences Against the Person' (1994) *Cambridge Law Journal* 502.

[2] An exception is N Lacey, C Wells and O Quick, *Rethinking Criminal Law: Texts and Materials* (3rd ed., London: Butterworths, 2003), 629–37.

discussions of substantive criminal law is in relation to victims of domestic abuse who kill their abuser, and the defences that might be available in such circumstances, cases that must be exceptional amongst those who are abused.

No doubt part of the reason for this lack of real interest in domestic abuse by substantive criminal lawyers is that there is no specific offence that distinguishes such behaviour in law. Domestic abuse tends to be prosecuted using other offences, including homicide offences, sexual or non-sexual offences against the person, or even breach of the peace. Undoubtedly these different offences mark out different kinds of domestic abuse. And yet domestic abuse has a character of its own, and is thought of as a social problem (or, by some, a non-problem) of a particular kind. Hence it is surprising that calls for a distinct offence of domestic abuse are infrequent.[3]

In this essay I hope to achieve two things. First, I hope to begin to ground discussion about whether domestic abuse ought to be recognized in the criminal law through the creation of a distinct offence. Does the argument concerning the moral distinctiveness of offences support the creation of a distinct offence to cover instances of domestic abuse? And if a distinct offence cannot be supported on those grounds, or those grounds alone, how are we to decide whether there should be a distinct offence concerned with domestic abuse? In order to address those questions I will develop some general thoughts about the project of distinguishing between offences.

In § 1, I will outline two features that mark out domestic abuse from other types of violent conduct. First, and obviously, domestic abuse occurs within the context of an intimate relationship. The second is that the abuse is systematic. In § 2, I will suggest that these two features of domestic abuse have the tendency to erode a distinctive kind of freedom that individuals ought to have. To show this I will use Philip Pettit's account of freedom as non-domination. Furthermore, I will argue that this erosion of the victim's freedom is particularly significant because it takes place through the violation of an expectation of trust. Section 3 will consider an objection to creating a distinct offence of domestic abuse based on the idea that distinct criminal offences ought to reflect distinctive wrongs. I will show that although there may be instances of domestic abuse which do not have the consequences outlined in § 2, that does not prevent those consequences from making the wrong of domestic abuse distinctive. Hence, domestic abuse may be considered distinctively wrong even though not all instances of domestic abuse will result in the negative consequences that make it distinctively wrong (this slightly opaque idea will be explained below). The conclusions will involve a discussion of the potential practical advantages and disadvantages of a distinct offence of domestic abuse. I will argue that a

[3] The idea of a distinct offence was mentioned, but rejected, in the UK Government's consultation paper *Safety and Justice: The Government's Proposals on Domestic Violence* (London: HMSO, 2003; Cm 5847). One example of a distinct offence being created is contained in the California Penal Code s. 13700.

distinct offence is unlikely to have very powerful consequences in altering patterns of behaviour. However, I will suggest that there are some reasons to be optimistic about the impact of creating such a distinct offence, at least to some degree, given the way in which criminal evidence works.

1. What is Significant About Domestic Abuse?

Domestic abuse is clearly demarcated from other instances of violence, both in popular perception and in institutional response, and this might be thought to contribute to an understanding of what is distinctive about it. Domestic abuse is considered a particular kind of social problem, which demands a particular kind of social response that is quite distinct from the response to violence in other contexts. Furthermore, institutional responses to domestic abuse are clearly different from institutional responses to other forms of violence. Cases of domestic abuse are probably less likely to result in arrest.[4] The victim is often less willing to see a prosecution go ahead,[5] or to testify if a prosecution does go ahead, than are victims of violence in non-domestic contexts. Domestic abuse may previously have been seen as 'less serious' than other instances of violence by the police and prosecuting services, although recent studies suggest that social and institutional evaluation of domestic abuse may well currently be in the process of change.[6] Some jurisdictions mandate,[7] or at least strongly recommend, arrest and/or prosecution in domestic abuse cases, which may explain some of the changes in trends in policing. This shows that institutions treat violence in the domestic context differently from violence in other contexts, although, of course, this may be in part an attempt to ensure that violence in the domestic context is taken 'as seriously' as violence in other contexts.

And yet, despite the fact that institutional responses to domestic abuse are clearly distinct from responses to other forms of violence, there is very

[4] For an overview of the literature in the USA, see R B Felson and J Ackerman, 'Arrest for Domestic and other Assaults' (2001) 39 *Criminology* 655.

[5] According to the Crown Prosecution Service guidelines, developed in 2001, prosecutions will go ahead against the victim's wishes, especially in serious cases of domestic violence. In her 1998 study Carolyn Hoyle showed the significance of a lack of victim participation in prosecution decisions: see C Hoyle, *Negotiating Domestic Violence: Police, Criminal Justice, and Victims* (Oxford: Oxford University Press, 1998). However, lack of victim participation ought not to make the evidentiary burden insurmountable in all cases: see L Ellison, 'Prosecuting Domestic Violence without Victim Participation' (2002) 65 *Modern Law Review* 834.

[6] Felson and Ackerman's study (n. 4 above) suggest that the reason for the apparent leniency is not tolerance for domestic abuse, but rather lack of cooperation on the part of victims. See also L Feder, 'Police Handling of Domestic and Nondomestic Assault Calls: Is There a Case for Discrimination' (1998) *Crime and Delinquency* 335.

[7] For example, the Utah Code Ann. Section 77-36-2.2(2)(a) provides that 'in addition to the arrest powers described in Section 77-7-2, when a peace officer responds to a domestic violence call and has probable cause to believe that an act of domestic violence has been committed, the peace officer shall arrest without a warrant or issue a citation to any person that he has probable cause to believe has committed an act of domestic violence'.

little legal recognition of any distinction between domestic abuse and non-domestic violence, at least as far as offence categories are concerned. The offences prosecuted in cases of domestic abuse are, as we have seen, identical to those prosecuted in violence outside the domestic context.

The fact that the institutions of criminal justice have been seen as relatively ineffective in controlling domestic abuse can contribute to the case for a distinct offence, as we shall see. To pre-empt a fuller argument, it may be that the historic failure properly to respond to domestic abuse should motivate the legislature to consider creating an offence simply for the reason that it would encourage better practice in policing and prosecution. However, that case will be strengthened if there is something distinctively wrongful or harmful about domestic abuse. For this reason, criminological studies into domestic abuse ought to be supplemented by normative analysis. Empirical research alone cannot tell us what constitutes the particular wrong of domestic abuse, if anything. That is a moral question rather than a purely empirical question, albeit (as we shall see) one whose answer may build upon empirical observation.

Obviously the principal way in which domestic abuse is to be distinguished from other forms of violence has to do with the social context in which violence occurs. The term 'domestic' may suggest that the primary distinguishing mark of domestic abuse is its location: it occurs in the family home. However, that is not the best way to understand how domestic abuse is distinctive. Domestic abuse is clearly not marked out by the occurrence of violence in the home: violence in the course of a domestic burglary is not domestic abuse, and violence that takes place between husband and wife in public may still contribute to a pattern of domestic abuse. Domestic abuse takes place in the context of a relationship between the abuser and the abused, and a particularly intimate relationship at that. That is its distinctive feature. To regulate domestic abuse is to regulate relationships, not locations.[8]

This also suggests that, as far as domestic abuse goes, there is no important distinction to be made between the public and the private sphere. That distinction may be important when it comes to regulating freedom of expression, for example, but it is not relevant to distinguishing between different forms of non-consensual violence. To that extent, this essay builds upon the insights of feminist scholars who have mounted a critique of the traditional liberal distinction between public and private.[9] Domestic abuse

[8] The word 'domestic' in the phrase has also been criticized for making the violence seem 'cosy'. See Lacey, Wells and Quick, n. 2 above, 630.

[9] See, for example, S M Okin, 'Gender, the Public, and the Private', in D Held (ed.) *Political Theory Today* (Oxford: Polity Press, 1991); N Lacey, 'Theory into Practice? Pornography and the Public/Private Dichotomy', in her *Unspeakable Subjects: Feminist Essays in Legal Theory* (Oxford: Hart Publishing, 1998). In the context of domestic abuse, see T A Açikalin, 'Debunking the Dichotomy of Nonintervention: The Role of the State in Regulating Domestic Violence' (2000) 74 *Tulane Law Review* 1045.

is not particularly a private matter, both in the sense that it ought to be the subject of political concern,[10] and in the sense that it may occur in public. It is only private in the sense that the relationship may be said to be particularly private. For this reason, the word 'domestic' in the phrase 'domestic abuse' is perhaps unfortunate. There is nothing particularly *domestic* about domestic abuse. Despite this weakness, I will continue to use the term 'domestic abuse' due to its familiarity.

Domestic abuse, then, is characterized by the fact that violence occurs within the context of a relationship. One difficulty in determining the boundaries of the idea has to do with demarcating which relationships count for the purpose of domestic abuse and which do not. There may be violence between spouses or between parents and children, between non-married partners, between siblings,[11] or between those in more distant familial relationships. But violence may also take place in the context of other ongoing relationships, such as between work colleagues or between friends. Whilst the latter instances of violence may share some of the characteristics of domestic abuse, they do not fall within the popular idea of domestic abuse. Whilst the term 'domestic' is misleading, it does indicate something else that is generally regarded as significant in understanding domestic abuse: the abuse occurs within the context of the family, or related relationships. As suggested above, if cases of violence at work, bullying at school or violence between friends turn out to constitute the same kind of wrong as domestic abuse, there is no particular wrong of domestic abuse. Domestic abuse would merely be an instance of a broader wrong, the domestic context making a difference that is not sufficiently significant to be marked out by the distinction between offences. I will have more to say about that question later.

However, whilst the relationship between the accused and the victim is one central distinguishing feature of domestic abuse, there are other features of such abuse that mark it out socially. Perhaps the most important of these is that violence in the domestic context is generally seen as being much more likely to be repetitive and systematic than violence in the non-domestic context;[12] indeed, that is considered a reason why the institutional and other social responses to domestic violence ought to be distinct from responses to other forms of violence.[13]

[10] On the changing social and political climate which made domestic abuse part of public concern, see N Lacey, 'Unspeakable Subjects, Impossible Rights: Sexuality, Integrity and Criminal Law' in *Unspeakable Subjects*, n. 9 above.

[11] Whether this case falls within the popular paradigm of domestic abuse is controversial, but we shall see some reasons why it should so fall below.

[12] The criminal law does not often criminalize systematic behaviour, but see the Protection from Harassment Act 1997 for an example.

[13] See, for example, J Stubbs, 'Domestic Violence and Women's Safety: Feminist Challenges to Restorative Justice', in H Strang and J Braithwaite (eds), *Restorative Justice and Family Violence* (Cambridge: Cambridge University Press, 2002).

The repetitive nature of the abuse is also part of the paradigm of domestic abuse. There is no doubt that a single instance of violence within the context of a relationship may be very serious. However, at least part of the reason for this is that a particular instance of violence is often predictive of further instances of violence in the context of a relationship. An instance of violence may be seen as indicative of further underlying features of the relationship, particularly of male dominance. A recent Home Office study reports that the average number of incidents of assault perpetrated on a victim of domestic violence is around five per year.[14] A single assault within the context of a relationship is probably not sufficiently distinct from single assaults in other contexts to justify criminalization as a distinct offence. Furthermore, there are good reasons, grounded in the presumption of innocence, for the criminal justice system not to label the perpetrator as a systematic abuser on the basis that one incidence of violence in the domestic context is an indication of a pattern of abuse. The victim of a single instance of violence in a domestic context ought, of course, to have recourse to the law. But the proper offence to charge, in such a case, is assault.

There are two central features of domestic abuse, then. The first is that the abuse occurs within the context of an intimate relationship. The second is that the abuse is systematic. These features of domestic abuse help to explain problems that criminal justice agencies have encountered when dealing with domestic abuse, as well as revealing some of the reasons why their responses have tended to be inadequate.

First, the unwillingness of the police to intervene in intimate relationships is commonly cited to explain the failure of the criminal justice system properly to regulate domestic abuse. This may be at least in part a rational response by criminal justice agencies. If the relationship between the accused and the victim is ongoing, it will often be difficult to secure a conviction. Convictions in such cases normally depend on the victim providing evidence against the accused, which they may be reluctant to do. This may be because of the victim's fear of the accused, or because the victim actively wants the prosecution not to go ahead. Of course, the police may play a role short of securing convictions which helps to control domestic abuse.

However, as a consequence of these inadequacies of the criminal justice system, responses to domestic violence sometimes focus on negotiation within the domestic context in an attempt to prevent re-offending without having to resort to the processes and agencies of criminal justice at all. Some scholars are critical of this approach, however, claiming that restoration

[14] C Mirrlees-Black, *Domestic Violence: Findings from a New British Crime Survey Self-Completion Questionnaire* (London: HMSO, 1999). See also E Stark, 'From Battered Woman Syndrome to Coercive Control' (1995) 58 *Albany Law Review* 1973. It is sometimes claimed that domestic abuse is cyclical (see L Walker *The Battered Woman* (New York: Harper & Row, 1979)), although that is not characteristic of all domestic abuse situations: see Royal College of Psychiatrists, *Domestic Violence* (Council Report CR102, 2002).

within the private sphere fails properly to recognize both the nature of domestic abuse, and the social context which helps to foster and support it.[15]

But it may also be the case that domestic abuse fails to attract an appropriate response from the police for reasons that are more difficult to sympathise with. It may still be that domestic abuse is thought of as 'less serious' than other instances of violence. There may be an extent to which the police see regulating intimate relationships as beyond their central role; a lack of training might leave police officers with little confidence in their ability to respond adequately or effectively to violence in intimate relationships.[16]

Secondly, the systematic nature of domestic abuse is often seen as particularly problematic in terms of prosecution and conviction. It has generally been regarded as a difficulty in prosecution that the courts are unable to 'see' the systematic nature of abuse for the reason that any instance of violence is often prosecuted either in isolation, or as one of a short series of instances. This may lead to lenient sentences where the particular instance of violence that results in prosecution and conviction is not very severe in isolation, but appears much more severe in context. It is often difficult to prove beyond reasonable doubt that any particular injury suffered by the victim was an instance of domestic abuse, particularly where the victim is unwilling to testify or does not provide very effective evidence. It is therefore likely to prove difficult to convict the accused of the full range of abusive conduct even where that conduct constitutes a series of criminal offences. And even where a conviction is achieved, it becomes difficult to impose the kind of sentence that would effectively protect the victim from further abuse.

Once again, there may well still be practices of prosecutors and of courts which are more difficult to sympathize with. As with the police, there may still be a tendency to treat domestic abuse as less serious for the purposes of prosecutorial decision-making and sentencing than assault on strangers. And in some cases it may be that prosecutors and sentencers are motivated to save relationships that are not worth saving either by deciding not to prosecute or by imposing light sentences. This has sometimes led to legislation which mandates prosecution, even against the wishes of the victim,[17] and severe sentences in domestic abuse cases.

2. Freedom and Domestic Abuse

There are two distinctive elements of domestic abuse, then. First, domestic abuse occurs in the context of an intimate relationship. Secondly, domestic abuse is systematic. In this section I will suggest that the combination of

[15] See, for example, D Coker, 'Transformative Justice: Anti-Subordination Processes in Cases of Domestic Violence', in Strang and Braithwaite, n. 13 above.

[16] For a balanced view, see Hoyle, n. 5 above, 98–9.

[17] For discussion, see D Coker, 'Crime Control and Feminist Law Reform in Domestic Violence Law: A Critical Review' (2001) 4 *Buffalo Criminal Law Review* 800.

these two features of domestic abuse makes it distinctively wrong. I will argue that a particular kind of freedom is often undermined by domestic abuse, and that this effect of domestic abuse is a significant reason to create a distinct offence for dealing with domestic abuse. It should be noted that, at this stage, this constitutes only an indication of an approach that may be taken, an approach that rests on generalizations from empirical research that may turn out to be wrong.

As noted above, domestic abuse tends to be characterized by the fact that it is systematic, and this perception of domestic abuse is supported by empirical data. High levels of repeat violence are reported, and are often coupled with violent threats and other forms of psychological abuse. Domestic abuse, then, is properly characterized not merely as an incident of violence in the context of an intimate relationship, but rather as a course of conduct perpetrated in the context of an intimate relationship. This feature of domestic abuse is key to understanding the values that it attacks.

To see how this is so, I will use a conception of freedom that has been developed by Philip Pettit. Pettit argues that, in order to determine how free someone is, the significant question concerns not the range of options that that person has, but rather the extent to which, and the way in which, that person's range of options tracks their interests. Options, Pettit notes, can be restricted either arbitrarily or non-arbitrarily. Restriction of an option is non-arbitrary, in Pettit's view, when that restriction is 'forced to track the interests and ideas of the person suffering the interference'.[18] What freedom requires is protection against arbitrary control over options, rather than against non-arbitrary control over options.

The first thing that is worth noting about this conception of freedom is that it is only indirectly concerned with options. The important question is not what options a person in fact has, but rather the conditions under which others can *control* his options. In line with the republican tradition in which Pettit places himself, this conception of freedom is most appropriate to show why slavery undermines freedom. As Pettit argues, the slave may in fact have a broad range of options, but another, the master, is in the position arbitrarily to control that range of options: to diminish or increase them as he sees fit. That the slave is not regarded as free cannot be a result of the lack of options that he has: he may have a benevolent master who in fact grants him a broad range of options. Even under such conditions, however, the slave is not free: his options are under the control of another. Freedom, Pettit concludes, is to be in a condition of non-domination rather than non-interference.

There are two ways in which Pettit's analysis of freedom is misleading. First, the idea that restrictions on options ought to reflect the 'interests and

[18] P Pettit, *Republicanism: A Theory of Freedom and Government* (Oxford: Oxford University Press, 1998), 55.

ideas' of the agent is vague and problematic. Surely the value of a person having an option is dependent not simply upon his interests and ideas, but on his *legitimate* interests and ideas.[19] This criticism is restricted to the context of political theory and I will not develop it here. Secondly, and more importantly for our purposes, Pettit sees his conception of freedom as supplanting rather than supplementing the traditional liberal view of freedom as non-interference. However, we ought to distinguish between the question of how free someone is and the question of whether a particular restriction on freedom has a negative impact upon them. Restrictions on options are surely restrictions on freedom, although some restrictions on our options might not have disvalue, and may even have value.

It is sometimes argued that having an option to *v* can never be bad, as one can always not *v*.[20] But that is not true.[21] Having an option may have disvalue without the exercise of that option.[22] Being a slave may be bad, but being a slave owner is bad as well. In being a slave owner, one has a degree and kind of control over another that one ought not to have or want to have. Having that kind of control defines one's relationship to others in a way that has active disvalue. In becoming a slave owner, my freedom increases, but that increase in freedom is of disvalue to me. As that increase in my range of options does not track my interests, Pettit does not see it as an increase in freedom at all. That is surely wrong. My freedom has expanded, albeit not in a way that is valuable to me.

Now, my claim in this section is that very many warranted and properly constructed criminal offences are concerned with protecting freedom against the reduction of options. However, what distinguishes domestic abuse is that it may well be concerned with freedom of the kind characterized by Pettit as non-domination. Domestic abuse can result in the victim not only having a limited range of options, but also having her options subject to the unwarranted and arbitrary control of another person, or having her ability to recognize her range of options, assess them and choose between them diminished arbitrarily by that other person. The victim of domestic abuse, on this account, is a person whose options, and whose capacity in relation to her options, are controlled by another: the other has the kind of power over her options that he ought not to have, and deprives the victim of the kind of perceptual and evaluative control over her options that is required for true freedom.

One example of this is the typical phenomenon in cases of domestic abuse that the perpetrator responds with extreme jealousy to his partner meeting

[19] Pettit's view is usefully scrutinized and fleshed out in H Richardson, *Democratic Autonomy: Public Reasoning about the Ends of Policy* (Oxford: Oxford University Press, 2002), ch. 3.

[20] See J Rawls, *A Theory of Justice* (Cambridge Mass.: Harvard University Press, 1972), 143.

[21] For an expanded account of the potential disvalue of an increase of freedom, see V Tadros, *Criminal Responsibility* (Oxford: Oxford University Press, 2005), ch. 7.

[22] Grounds for this position other than the one that I use here are developed by Gerald Dworkin, *The Theory and Practice of Autonomy* (Cambridge: Cambridge University Press, 1988), ch. 5.

other people.[23] In such cases, the wrong that is done is not just that the partner's liberty to meet certain people is limited, but also that she does not know who it is that she is entitled to meet and who she is not entitled to meet. The fact that the perpetrator responds in an irrational fashion to her social life is not only restrictive of the options that she has for social interaction; after all, there may be those who live in isolated areas who suffer equally on that score. It also restricts the extent to which her social life is within her control, or is sensitive to her character and choices. This has an impact not only on the relationships that she is not permitted to pursue, but also on those that she is permitted to pursue.

Furthermore, this impact is strengthened by the fact that victims of domestic abuse tend to overestimate the degree of power and control that perpetrators have over their lives; to see the perpetrator as omnipotent. It is common for victims of domestic abuse to fail to recognize that there are options available to them to move on from the abusive relationship.[24] Undoubtedly, this perception is sometimes accurate,[25] but there is also a reported tendency for victims to underestimate the liberty that they have. From this we can see that the wrong that is done through domestic abuse is not just that the defendant denies the victim options, but also that he denies her the freedom to recognize and exploit the options that she has.[26]

Finally, victims of domestic abuse tend to blame themselves for instances of violence by the perpetrator, and such a tendency is likely to discourage such victims from seeking professional help.[27] Clearly, such a tendency does not involve a diminution in the victim's liberty, as traditionally understood. However, the fact that such an evaluation is clearly, and tragically, absurd is also evidence of a diminution of freedom in the distinct sense that I am using here. Perhaps such self-blame is the result of the misperception that the relationship with her abuser is within her control, or of a desperation that it will be so; that she has, or will have, dominion over what happens to her; that she is, or will be, in a relationship of mutual respect and trust. But the absurdity of self-blame in such circumstances indicates the extent to which this is not so. It also indicates that the victim's capacity for evaluation tends to be undermined by domestic abuse; but such a capacity is central to a fully autonomous life.[28]

The reliability of the socio-psychological literature on domestic abuse is clearly central to the plausibility of this claim. The psychological literature provides at least significant evidence that victims of domestic abuse perceive

[23] See R E Dobash, R P Dobash, K Cavanagh and R Lewis, *Research Evaluation of Programmes for Violent Men* (Edinburgh: Scottish Office Central Research Unit, 1996).

[24] See C Hoyle and A Sanders, 'Police Response to Domestic Violence: From Victim Choice to Victim Empowerment?' (2000) 40 *British Journal of Criminology* 14.

[25] *Ibid.*

[26] See Royal College of Psychiatrists, *Domestic Violence*, n. 14 above.

[27] See Mirlees Black, n. 14 above 40–1; Hoyle and Sanders, n. 24 above.

[28] On the relationship between the capacity for evaluation, autonomy and responsibility, see Tadros, n. 21 above, ch. 2.

that their options are dominated by their abusive partners, such that they experience the perpetrator as having control over their options.[29] Sometimes, it is suggested, this appears to create the impression in the mind of the victim that what appeared to be an option is in fact not an option. If this is to be believed, the ability of the victim to assess and choose has been undermined by the perpetrator. Once again, it is not, or not only, the existence of choice that is reduced by the perpetrator of domestic abuse, but rather it is the psychological state required to make choices that is diminished. Paradoxically, then, the victim of domestic abuse appears to blame herself for the abuse at the same time as overestimating the power that her abuser has over her.

But, as suggested earlier, this is still insufficient to mark out domestic abuse as morally distinctive. For it may be that such psychological effects are caused in other social contexts. There are other sources of autonomy and integrity that are threatened in a comparable way by wrongdoing. For example, many people may develop autonomy and integrity at work. Such development may be threatened by bullying in the workplace. Many people may regard a peaceful home environment as important in a similar way. But that may be undermined by abusive and noisy neighbours. This may suggest that there ought to be a more general offence which includes such long term abuse within it.

Does this press us to criminalize the creation of the kinds of experience that victims of abuse suffer, rather than tying the offence particularly to the context of 'domestic' relationships? There is a further reason why this should not be done. It may be that abuse outside the context of an intimate relationship can result in the same diminution of autonomy that is characteristic of victims of domestic abuse. But the context of a relationship is particular in another way: long term relationships, be they with sexual partners, or between parents and children, are often at least hoped to be the site of intimacy and trust, features which are central to the development of autonomy and personal integrity, but which are also valuable in themselves.

That is not to say that autonomy and personal integrity cannot develop outside those relationships, or that other forms of relationship are not equally important and legitimate in the lives of some people. But the trust and intimacy of long term relationships is central to the development of autonomy and integrity in many lives. In recognizing the significance of such relationships, the state does not foreclose other possibilities. It merely reflects the current source of much that is of value in our society.

[29] This idea is not intended to reflect the specific claim made by Lenore Walker in *The Battered Woman* (New York: Harper Row, 1979) and *The Battered Women Syndrome* (New York: Springer, 1984) that such women suffer from 'learned helplessness'. Walker's claims are contested: see R Schopp, B J Sturgis and M Sullivan, '*Battered Woman Syndrome, Expert Testimony, and the Distinction between Justification and Excuse*' (1994) *University of Illinois Law Review* 45; D L Faigman and A J Wright, 'The Battered Woman Syndrome in the Age of Science' (1997) 39 *Arizona Law Review* 67.

Intimacy is valuable in itself. It is central to the depth of one's relationships. Intimacy requires trust. The expectation of trust in intimate relationships is obviously dashed through abuse. And there is also good reason to suppose that this tends to corrode the self-esteem that is required for autonomy and integrity in one's life in a particularly powerful way.

Hence, although there is certainly some merit to the idea that there are different ways in which autonomy and integrity are undermined by systematic abuse beyond the context of intimate relationships, there is also good reason to suppose that domestic abuse is distinctive both in its nature and its consequences. Not only does the freedom of the victim tend to be eroded in a distinctive way, but this is done through the demolition of trust, which is a central value of intimate relationships.

The fact that intimate relationships are often central to an individual's perception both of their autonomous identity and of their value, and that perception of autonomous identity and value is often undermined by domestic abuse, provides at least some good reason to mark out domestic abuse as worth recognition as a particular kind of offence. That such a diminution of freedom, in Pettit's sense, through destruction of a relationship that is intended to be built on trust, is common in cases of domestic abuse constitutes good reason to distinguish domestic abuse from other kinds of assault.[30]

Now, the argument developed so far might give rise to a concern that has become familiar in discussions about the use of psychological evidence of the effects of domestic abuse in the context of criminal defences. There has been scepticism in that context about whether there is such a thing as battered woman syndrome, and the implications of such a syndrome if indeed it is properly identified. None of the argument so far is intended to support diagnosis of such a syndrome.

It may be that such terminology wrongly pathologizes victims of domestic abuse, and through that stigmatizes them.[31] However, there is some reason to be cautious about such claims. The fact that those suffering from domestic abuse show a tendency to misperception and mis-evaluation of their circumstances ought not necessarily to be regarded as stigmatic, particularly given the explanation for that tendency. The fact that such

[30] For an argument that criminal offences ought implicitly to reflect the diminution of what is valuable in human life in the context of the offence of rape, see Lacey 'Unspeakable Subjects, Impossible Rights', n. 10 above. See also my related analysis in 'No Consent: A Historical Critique of the *Actus Reus* of Rape' (1999) 3 *Edinburgh Law Review* 317. Of course, that is not to say that the criminal law should become involved *whenever* there is a diminution of such intimacy. We will see below why the value of intimacy can help to ground the wrong of domestic abuse in spite of this.

[31] The claim is very common, so common as to have become almost casual: see, for example, A M Coughlin, 'Excusing Women' (1994) 82 *California Law Review* 1; J Dressler, 'Battered Women Who Kill Their Sleeping Tormenters', in S Shute and A P Simester (eds), *Criminal Law Theory: Doctrines of the General Part* (Oxford: Oxford University Press, 2002).

misperception and mis-evaluation are common ought to suggest that they are also ordinary human responses to systematic violence in the domestic context. Recognizing a syndrome, however, does not necessarily suggest otherwise.[32] Furthermore, scepticism about the use of such medical terms might itself flow in part from a worrying tendency to regard having a syndrome, and any lack of capacity that may result from such a syndrome, as stigmatic in and of itself.[33]

That said, there are undoubtedly some flaws in the original methodology and the conceptual framework that Lenore Walker used when developing the concept of battered woman syndrome, which have been exposed in the literature.[34] Such criticisms require at least a substantial revision of the way in which battered woman syndrome is to be understood, or possibly the abandonment of that concept. Many of those criticisms, however, are levelled specifically at the use of the concept of battered woman syndrome as evidence to support defences for battered women who kill their abusive partners, which is not my interest here. That battered women often fail effectively to evaluate the options that are available to them, overestimate the power that their partner has over them and blame themselves for the violence that they suffer have not been shown to be false and are well supported by social and psychological studies. Whether these phenomena are sufficient to ground a syndrome is another question which is beyond the scope of this chapter.

3. The Principles of Definition

So far I have suggested two features of domestic abuse that make it distinctive: the context of an intimate relationship and its systematicity. And I have argued that the socio-psychological effects of domestic abuse tend to diminish the freedom of the victim in a distinctive way. In this section I will consider an objection to creating a distinct offence of domestic abuse on these grounds. There are instances of domestic abuse which indeed have these consequences, it will be admitted. But there may also be instances of domestic abuse that do not. When identifying criminal wrongs, however, we ought to be searching for what is *intrinsically* wrong about a certain form of conduct. A mere *tendency* to have a particular negative effect is insufficient to mark out a distinct wrong that is worthy of recognition by the creation of a new criminal offence. Against this I will argue that an element may be definitional of a particular kind of wrong without being present in all instances of that wrong. That there are cases of domestic abuse that do not

[32] For a similar point, see J Horder 'Killing the Passive Abuser: A Theoretical Defence' in Shute and Simester, n. 31 above.

[33] See Tadros, n. 21 above, ch. 5 for a more extended discussion on the relationship between lack of capacity and stigma.

[34] See n. 29 above.

undermine freedom and integrity in the way I have suggested does not entail that the erosion of freedom and integrity is not central to identifying the definitional features of the wrong.

Domestic abuse normally involves some kind of extant criminal offence being committed. Given that, why create a new criminal offence? One common reason that is given for distinguishing between offences has to do with fair labelling. When the accused is convicted of a criminal offence, he is not only labelled as a criminal in general, he is labelled in relation to a particular offence. It is therefore important that his conduct is identified in the appropriate way, and properly defining criminal offences is the most obvious way to do this.

One way in which we might begin to think about the principles that govern the definition and classification of criminal offences has to do with the distinction between different kinds of wrong. Two wrongs may differ from each other either in degree or in kind. Stealing £100 differs only in degree from stealing £10. But stealing £100 is a different kind of wrong from punching someone in the face. The special part of the criminal law, it might be argued, ought to track the differences that there are between kinds of wrong. The principle of fair labelling, it might be claimed, requires that offence definitions communicate about kinds of wrong rather than mere degree. On this account, to justify the creation of a distinct offence of domestic abuse, it must be shown that domestic abuse is different in kind from other criminal wrongs rather than just different in degree.

It should be noted that I do not think that it is inappropriate for the criminal law to distinguish offences simply on the basis of degree as well as of kind. As Andrew Ashworth puts it, the principle of fair labelling requires 'that offences are subdivided and labelled so as to represent fairly the nature *and magnitude* of the law-breaking'.[35] It might be fair to represent differences in the magnitude of criminal offending even where there is no difference in the nature of that offending. Hence, there might be good reason to have an offence of petty theft to distinguish it from grand theft simply on the basis of the value of what is stolen. So even if domestic abuse is merely assault multiplied, that would not rule out the creation of a distinct offence on the grounds of fair labelling. Nevertheless, if domestic abuse is wrongful in a distinctive way, that would at least fortify the case for a distinct criminal offence.

How are we to identify kinds of criminal offending? I have already identified two features that mark out domestic abuse from other kinds of wrongful conduct: that it takes place as part of an intimate relationship, and that it is systematic. But merely to identify such features is not yet to establish a difference in kind. We might distinguish assaults of blue-eyed

[35] A J Ashworth, *Principles of Criminal Law* (4th ed., Oxford: Oxford University Press, 2003), 89–90 (emphasis added).

people from assaults on others. But there is no difference in the kind of wrong perpetrated as between assaults on those with blue eyes and assaults on others. Wrongs must be distinguished on the basis of characteristics that are significant.

The relevant kind of significance here is *moral* significance. It may be that there are distinctions between instances of wrongdoing that are considered significant socially, but that are not morally significant. It may also be that there is a failure socially to recognize moral differences. Against this, it might be argued that liberal democracies ought to reflect in their policies the view and values of the citizenry. But liberal democracies must also protect minorities and those without a strong public voice. The fact that states have a responsibility to protect the vulnerable and minorities may constitute a reason to criminalize wrongful conduct directed against those groups, particularly in circumstances where the nature of the wrong is not recognized, even by victims themselves.[36]

Domestic abuse has always been understood to be distinct from other kinds of violence, but for the wrong reasons. It has been treated as less serious, or even as justified or excused violence. Perhaps it will be argued that the proper response to this fact is to encourage the criminal justice system to treat domestic abusers in the same way as other violent offenders are treated, which would militate against a distinct offence. In response, when assessing the moral significance of a feature of criminal offending, we ought to be careful not to ignore historical and social factors. At least in this context, Nicola Lacey is right that theoretical scholarship in criminal law ought properly to be connected to scholarship in criminal justice and social history.[37] The very fact that domestic abuse has been treated as less serious than other forms of assault might help to justify the creation of a distinct offence. There are at least three further reasons why this might be so.

First, the creation of a distinct offence might be a way to encourage similar treatment of domestic abusers and other perpetrators of violence. The creation of a new offence, with the appropriate publicity and prosecuting and sentencing guidelines, might encourage officers in the criminal justice system who think and act as though domestic abuse is 'less serious' to reassess their views, or at least to change their behaviour.

Secondly, the creation of such an offence will send out a message to perpetrators and victims of domestic abuse that such criminal offending is to be taken seriously, and is the proper subject of public condemnation. There

[36] Hence it is misleading for Ashworth to claim that distinctions between criminal offences must reflect kinds and degrees of wrongdoing that are 'widely felt': *Principles of Criminal Law*, n. 35 above, 89.

[37] See N Lacey, 'In Search of the Responsible Subject: History, Philosophy and the Social Sciences in Criminal Law Theory' (2001) 64 *Modern Law Review* 350. I have offered some reasons to qualify this suggestion in the context of theoretical writing about the general part in 'The System of the Criminal Law' (2002) 22 *Legal Studies* 448.

may be a tendency amongst abusers and victims to see domestic abuse as outside the realm of the criminal justice system altogether,[38] and the creation of a distinct offence may help to change those beliefs.

Thirdly, the creation of a new offence might be a way for the state to recognize past failures of the criminal justice system to regulate domestic abuse in a proper way. The creation of a new offence, with the appropriate sentencing guidelines and publicity, would be a way to express the fact that the state no longer tolerates domestic abuse, whereas doing nothing might indicate to some that the state accepts the *status quo*. Of course, the creation of a distinct offence is not the only way in which this could be achieved. Sentencing guidelines for existing offences perpetrated in the domestic context, and legislation concerning arrest and prosecution might be other ways to achieve the same thing.

Thus even if there is no significant difference, in the nature of the wrong committed, between domestic abuse and various other kinds of criminal violence, a distinct offence might be created simply to mark the fact that domestic abuse has not been properly policed by the criminal justice system in the past. Socio-historical research into domestic abuse is relevant, then, in supporting the case for a distinct offence. That research has shown both just how common domestic abuse is, and the inadequacy of the response to such abuse by the criminal justice system. Those facts are relevant in defending the case for a distinct offence.

These arguments for a distinct offence, however, are only intended to supplement the main claim that I am defending in this paper: that domestic abuse is wrongful in a sufficiently distinctive way to merit criminalization. So far I have developed that argument using some empirical claims about the socio-psychological effects that domestic abuse tends to have, and I have suggested that these effects diminish the freedom of the victim in a particular respect. The point is not only that the options that the victim has are reduced, but also that her control over those options, and her ability to appreciate and evaluate them, is reduced. Furthermore, I have argued that this diminution is especially significant when it occurs in the context of an intimate relationship. Now I will consider a complex objection to creating a distinct offence of domestic abuse on these grounds. The objection concerns both the use of such socio-psychological research, and an argument concerning the intrinsic nature of wrongs.

It is sometimes claimed that the experience of those suffering wrongs can tell us relatively little about the nature of wrongs. For example, in the context of the law of rape, John Gardner and Stephen Shute rightly point out that the mere fact that a particular event is experienced as a violation does not entail that it is a violation. And rape is a particular kind of wrong

[38] See particularly Black, n. 27 above, ch. 7. Her research finds that only 17% of victims of domestic assault considered that a crime had been perpetrated against them.

because the victim *is* violated rather than because she *experiences* that violation as a violation. After all, it may be that some actions are seen as a violation which are not in fact violations, and that other violations go unnoticed. That a violation has occurred is quite distinct from the experience of that violation. This is shown most clearly from the fact that a person can be raped without knowing that they have been, for example whilst unconscious through drugging.[39]

This might lead one to the suggestion that in order to investigate whether there should be a distinctive offence of domestic abuse we ought to ignore the effect of domestic abuse on victims. This might be thought to be a consequence of the fact that victims may systematically over- or under-react to domestic abuse. A consequence is that the nature and significance of the wrong, if any, cannot be understood *simply* by investigating the effects of domestic abuse.

Nevertheless, we should not be too quick to dismiss the value of empirical research into the experience of victims of domestic abuse. We should distinguish the victims' evaluations of their circumstances from the general psychological effects of those circumstances on the victims. To generalize from the argument by Gardner and Shute, the fact that victims evaluate a particular form of conduct as a distinct and significant wrong obviously cannot lead us directly to recognize it as such. Victims do not have special authority to evaluate wrongs. They may be systematically misled, as Western society was once systematically misled to thinking that interracial marriage was wrong.

However, that a particular response is common amongst victims of a certain kind of behaviour might at least to put us on notice that a certain kind of wrong has been perpetrated, even if that response is not sufficient to demonstrate the distinctiveness or significance of that wrong. In this context, the fact that it is not uncommon for victims of domestic violence to experience a diminished sense of freedom, not only through the practical consequences of that violence, but also through psychological erosion, ought to lead us to consider whether the wrong of domestic violence constitutes a special kind of attack on the freedom of the victim, as I have been arguing here that it does.

But this might give rise to a further objection. It might be argued that although domestic abuse *tends* to have certain psychological consequences, it will not necessarily have those consequences. If we only identify the consequences that conduct tends to have, we do not identify any intrinsic feature of that conduct that could help to identify it as a distinctive wrong.

Once again, compare Gardner and Shute on rape. The particular wrong of rape is identified, Gardner and Shute claim, if one can perceive such

[39] J Gardner and S Shute, 'The Wrongness of Rape' in J Horder (ed.), *Oxford Essays in Jurisprudence* (4th series, Oxford: Oxford University Press, 2000).

wrongful conduct in the absence of any of the harmful consequences of that conduct. Hence, they argue that the 'pure' case of rape is the case of rape which is 'entirely stripped of distracting epiphenomena' such as the victim's psychological response.[40] That would be the case if the rape went entirely unnoticed by the victim, if she was unconscious during the episode and never found out. Harms such as the psychological trauma of victims can only be judged as rational or understandable if they are understood as responses to the pure wrong of rape. 'If nothing was wrong with being raped apart from the fact that one reacted badly afterwards, then one had no reason to react badly afterwards,'[41] they argue.

Similarly, we might seek to identify what is wrong with domestic abuse in the absence of the psychological trauma that is suffered by victims. Perhaps it will be claimed that the 'pure' case of domestic abuse is the case in which the victim is not traumatized by the abuse, where she does not suffer the kind of psychological reaction that is common in cases of abuse. But I think that would be a mistake. The fact that there may be cases of this sort ought not to incline us to think that psychological trauma is not central to what is wrong with domestic abuse. That there are instances of domestic abuse without psychological trauma does not make psychological trauma merely epiphenomenal to the wrong of domestic abuse, just as the fact that there are trunkless elephants does not make trunks merely epiphenomenally related to elephants in the way that dirt is a mere epiphenomenon of elephants.

This idea is reflected in the nature of concepts in general. A family of particular instances may properly fall under one conceptual umbrella where there are overlaps between each instance under that umbrella, but no single feature that is present in all instances that is sufficiently distinctive to define the ambit of the concept. In the context of distinguishing criminal offences, the same argument holds water. It is not necessarily an objection to the creation of a distinct criminal offence that there is no set of necessary and sufficient conditions that define the wrong that the offence is intended to track. A criminal offence might quite properly reflect overlapping values, or vices, whereby two instances of behaviour that fall within that offence do not share all of the salient and distinctive elements that make any particular token of the offence wrongful.[42] For example, it is not necessarily problematic to include both intentional but provoked killings and reckless killings within the category of manslaughter, even if these killings are wrong in quite different ways. That the killing was intentional (although provoked) is constitutive of the wrongfulness of the defendant's conduct where the defendant utilizes the defence of provocation, even if an intention to kill

[40] 'The Wrongness of Rape', 197. [41] *Ibid.*

[42] See particularly Stephen Mulhall's interpretation of Wittgenstein in *Inheritance and Originality: Wittgenstein, Heidegger, Kierkegaard* (Oxford: Oxford University Press, 2001), 84–7. In the context of the criminal law the same point is made in A L Bogg and J Stanton-Ife, 'Protecting the vulnerable: legality, harm and theft' (2003) 23 *Legal Studies* 402.

is not a necessary condition for properly convicting any defendant of manslaughter.

Or it might be that there is a paradigm of an offence, where conduct which is sufficiently close to the paradigm is also worthy of conviction of that offence, even if a significant element of the paradigm case is missing in cases beyond the paradigm. So it might be that the paradigm of assault involves physical harm, even if psychological harm, or the threat of physical harm, is sufficient in some cases where physical harm is not present. Once again, in the paradigm case physical harm is constitutive of the wrongfulness of the defendant's conduct even if it is not a necessary condition of properly convicting any defendant of assault. That is not to say, of course, that Gardner and Shute are mistaken in their analysis of rape in particular, although I suspect that the infliction of psychological trauma is best thought paradigmatic of the wrong of rape. What is clear is that the idea of pure cases ought not to be considered a method by which the nature of criminal wrongs can be investigated in general.

Finally, it might be objected that if the wrong that is being perpetrated by domestic abuse is the diminution of freedom in the distinctive way that I have suggested, that ought also to be a condition of being convicted of any new offence. The prosecution, it might be argued ought to have to show not only that there was an intimate relationship between the defendant and the victim, and that there was systematic abuse within that relationship, but also that the victim's freedom was undermined in the way that I have suggested.

I think that this ought not to be required of the prosecution. First, it is worth noting that many other criminal offences have a loose association with the harm which they are ultimately intended to prevent. For example, s. 19 of the Firearms Act 1968 makes it a criminal offence to carry a firearm together with ammunition in a public place without lawful authority or reasonable excuse. Now obviously the central reason why that offence was created is the potential use of the firearm rather than mere possession. That firearms kill and maim is used to justify the possession offence, but mere possession itself does not kill and maim. But that is no objection to the definition of the offence. That possession offences do not always lead to the harm that they are intended to control does not mean that possession ought not to be criminalized at all.[43] A very strict reading of the harm principle might lead some to the conclusion that such offences are contrary to principle. I have some doubts about whether the harm principle is a proper principle of criminal law at all. But even if it is, it does not seem difficult to provide an argument that possession offences such as this help to prevent harm: consider even the psychological harm that would be done

[43] See D Husak, 'The Nature and Justifiability of Nonconsummate Offenses' (1995) 37 *Arizona Law Review* 151.

were everyone to know that possession of firearms and ammunition in public places was permitted.[44]

Or consider s. 28 of the Offences Against the Person Act 1861, which makes it an offence unlawfully and maliciously, by explosive substance, to burn, maim, disfigure, disable, or do grievous bodily harm to any person. Let us consider disfigurement alone for a moment. There is good reason to think that it is wrong in a particular way to disfigure another. But disfigurement is significantly wrong because of the particular value that people generally attach to their physical appearance. Now, if there are cases of disfigurement which cause no distress, say because the victim likes the look of his scars, surely that is not a reason to acquit the assailant of the offence created by s. 28.

Similarly in this case, the fact that there are instances of domestic abuse that do not lead to the diminution of freedom in the way that I have suggested does not entitle the perpetrators of such abuse to an acquittal. The diminution of freedom is central to the wrong, and yet the natural tendency of such conduct to lead to that diminution is sufficient to justify conviction. The defendant has perpetrated conduct which often leads to such a diminution of freedom. Indeed, such an effect is arguably paradigmatic of domestic abuse. That such a diminution does not in fact come about cannot save him from being liable for the same offence as those whose conduct in fact has the relevant harmful consequence.[45]

4. Conclusions

The response of the criminal justice system to domestic abuse has long been considered problematic, and for good reason. Domestic abuse initiatives, such as training programmes for police officers, show that progress can be made in this area. Creating a nominate offence of domestic abuse can only make a small contribution to improving the situation further. Ensuring that the substantive criminal law expresses an appropriate categorization of offences is important, and other decisions, such as policing decisions, prosecution decisions and sentencing decisions, reflect offence categorization at least to some degree. But changes in the way in which offences are categorized, even quite radical changes, may well not have much of an impact

[44] That is not to say that possession offences have not been extended far too widely: for discussion, see M D Dubber, 'The Possession Paradigm: The Special Part and the Police Power Model of the Criminal Process', in this volume. Furthermore, consideration has to be given to the presumption of innocence, a principle which is at least sometimes violated by some possession offences. See V Tadros and S Tierney, 'The Presumption of Innocence and the Human Rights Act' (2004) 67 *Modern Law Review* 402.

[45] None of this should be taken to mean that I am in favour of a strict version of the correspondence principle. The consequences of one's actions are often relevant in attributing criminal responsibility. See Tadros, n. 21 above, ch. 3 for an argument why this is so.

on policing, prosecution rates, conviction rates or sentencing in the context of domestic abuse.[46]

However, even if the impact of a new offence in improving the lives of victims of domestic abuse would be modest, that is not to say that a new offence should not be created. There are what we might call 'symbolic' as well as practical reasons for creating a new offence. By creating such an offence, at least if it is done in the appropriate way, the state acknowledges the seriousness of domestic abuse, and its history of failure in dealing with such abuse.

Nevertheless, we can speculate about one or two ways in which the creation of a new offence might have a practical as well as a symbolic impact. First, nothing that I have been advocating here ought to be thought of as necessarily ruling out other approaches, within or without the criminal justice process. Clearly, if other methods of tackling the problem of domestic abuse are effective in reducing the frequency with which the conduct is perpetrated, there is good reason to use those methods. Other methods might include using existing offences, or using institutions outside the criminal justice process altogether. Obviously, any new offence ought to be a supplement to existing offences rather than a replacement. And the existence of a new offence should not be thought to preclude prosecution using existing offences.[47] A distinct domestic abuse offence is another string to the bow of the criminal justice system, and can supplement social responses to domestic abuse beyond that system.

That being said, as has been implied, there are some reasons to use the criminal justice process that go beyond its effectiveness in tackling rates of offending in the most direct way. The criminal justice process has unique power to mark a public recognition of the wrongful nature of a particular kind of conduct, and to stigmatize those who perpetrate that conduct. Taking domestic abuse outside the criminal justice system is likely to create or reinforce the perception that domestic abuse is less 'serious' than other kinds of assaults, when what has been argued here is that domestic abuse is often very serious, and serious in a way that distinguishes it from other kinds of assault.

It is against this background that I would like to consider one important evidential issue that might lead us to conclude that a specific offence could have some, albeit probably relatively slight, impact on conviction rates. Superficially, there seems a straightforward reason not to pin too much hope on an offence that is concerned with a course of conduct. The argument is as

[46] See, for example, the sober analysis of radical reform of the law of sexual offences in J Temkin, *Rape and the Legal Process* (2nd ed., Oxford: Oxford University Press, 2002): 'radical reformers did not sufficiently reckon with the attitudes and practices of those who administer the law, from police officers to jurors' (at 186).

[47] This deals with the problems mentioned by the UK government in *Safety and Justice* n. 3 above.

follows. Achieving a conviction for any single assault in domestic abuse cases is often difficult enough. This is particularly so given the reluctance of some victims of domestic abuse to testify.[48] Proving a course of conduct is likely to be all the more difficult. Hence, the argument goes, a new offence is very unlikely to prove useful to prosecutors.

Against this, I would argue that there will be cases in which it is *easier* to prove a course of conduct by the defendant against the victim than it is to prove a single incident. Consider a victim who, seven times in the last year, has been admitted to hospital with bruising. Each time, when asked how the bruising came about, she reports that the injury was accidental. There is evidence from the neighbours that sometimes there are aggressive fights, but no further evidence of violence. The victim refuses to testify. Now, for any one of the seven incidents it might be impossible to prove beyond reasonable doubt that the bruising was caused by an assault on the victim by her partner. In each case taken individually it might be plausible that the bruising was caused by an accident, as the victim reported it. However, despite this, there might be proof beyond reasonable doubt that more than one incident was caused by an assault on the victim by her partner. Where there are seven instances of bruising, there may be no reasonable possibility that six of them were the result of an accident, even if there is a reasonable doubt about the cause of any one of the seven.

Now in order to convict the accused for assault, it would normally have to be proved that one particular incident was an assault. At least in Scots law,[49] there is a requirement for a conviction for any offence that the date, time and circumstances of the offence must be specified in the indictment. Whilst there is some flexibility as to how this is done, there is no authority for a conviction where the prosecution has not made out, beyond a reasonable doubt, that the circumstances of the offence, as specified in the indictment, occurred. But to prove that a defendant has engaged in a course of conduct of domestic abuse against the victim, it might not be necessary to prove beyond reasonable doubt which incidents were assaults, rather than accidents. Even where the victim refuses to testify, then, there may be sufficient evidence in such cases to convict the accused of an offence of domestic abuse, characterized by a course of conduct, when there is insufficient evidence to convict him of any single assault.

Of course, the evidential problem would be lessened still further, in such a case, if a conviction of assault was possible without proving which event

[48] Mandating prosecution against the wishes of the victim may have some impact on recidivism. See Coker, n. 17 above. Some argue that mandating prosecution in such circumstances is problematic: the victim becomes a victim not only of her partner, but also of the state, the argument goes. However, if freedom is diminished by domestic abuse in the way that I have suggested, merely fulfilling the wishes of the victim is likely to be too crude a way of respecting the victim's autonomy.

[49] For discussion, see A V Sheehan and D J Dickson, *Criminal Procedure* (2nd ed., London: LexisNexis, 2003), 122–3.

constituted the assault. But there may be difficulties in jumping over the evidential hurdles presented in such a case in this way. If there is insufficient evidence to prove beyond reasonable doubt that any particular incident was an assault, it would be a breach of the presumption of innocence to warrant the conviction of the defendant for an assault.[50] But that argument cannot apply to the case of domestic abuse. There, the nature of the offence has to do with engaging in a course of abuse against the victim, and, on the facts suggested above, there is proof beyond reasonable doubt that the defendant was engaged in such a course of conduct against the victim.[51]

In summary, we should not think that the only good reason for creating a new criminal offences is to identify a particular, distinctive kind of wrong. There is a broader range of concerns that ought to guide the way in which criminal offences are identified and divided up. First, the social context of a particular kind of conduct cannot be ignored. The fact that a certain kind of conduct has not been properly recognized, or that it is not properly recognized today, can constitute a reason for creating a new criminal offence. States have a duty to protect the vulnerable, the less vocal, and minorities, particularly those who have suffered historically. A lack of public recognition of the wrong perpetrated, or of the consequences of that wrong, can, therefore, be as much a reason to criminalize as public recognition.

Furthermore, that a particular kind of conduct generally has a certain kind of consequence may be enough reason to criminalize that kind of conduct distinctively, even if that kind of conduct does not always have those consequences. This is true of domestic abuse. It may be that not all victims of domestic abuse experience a reduction in freedom in the way that I have suggested, but that it is a reasonably frequent consequence of domestic abuse may be sufficient to mark out domestic abuse as sufficiently distinct to warrant criminalization independently of other kinds of assault. And those reasons stand even if such an experience of a loss of freedom may come about in other ways.

If this is a good reason to mark out domestic abuse as sufficiently distinctive to warrant an independent offence, thought needs to be given to the practical implications of the creation of a new offence. I have suggested that we ought not to be overly optimistic about the impact that the creation of a new offence might have on offending rates. However, I have suggested that there is at least some reason to think that a new offence might help to overcome some of the evidential hurdles that are faced by those prosecuting domestic abuse. The problem of domestic abuse no doubt ought to be tackled by a broad ranging set of reforms in the criminal justice system as

[50] For a thorough analysis of evidential problems and solutions where a single assault is prosecuted, see Ellison, n. 5 above.

[51] For an account of the relationship between the nature of a criminal offence and the presumption of innocence, see Tadros and Tierney, n. 44 above.

a whole, and beyond the criminal justice system. Some of those reforms are under way and, at least to a degree, have promoted more effective and adequate responses to domestic abuse. I hope that I have done enough to establish that there is some good reason to think that the creation of a new offence might have at least some part to play in such a programme of reform.

7

What's Wrong With Bribery

Stuart P Green*

In 1998, attorney John V Wachtel, of Wichita, Kansas, had a provocative idea. He was representing the appeal of a defendant named Sonya Singleton, who had been convicted of money laundering and conspiracy to distribute cocaine.[1] At trial, the government's case had rested largely on the strength of testimony offered by Singleton's alleged co-conspirator, Napoleon Douglas, who, under a standard plea agreement, had agreed to testify in return for the government's promise of leniency. Watchtel's idea was as follows: By offering Douglas 'something of value' in return for his testimony, the government had violated the gratuities provision of 18 U.S.C. § 201, the federal bribery statute[2]; and for this reason, he argued, Douglas's testimony should have been suppressed. Surprisingly, a three-judge panel of the U.S. Tenth Circuit Court of Appeals agreed with his argument and reversed Singleton's conviction. 'If justice is perverted when a criminal defendant seeks to buy testimony from a witness', Judge Paul J Kelly, Jr. wrote for the panel, 'it is no less perverted when the government does so'.[3]

Almost overnight, the decision caused a storm of controversy. Prosecutors, for their part, warned that categorically excluding testimony obtained in exchange for promises of leniency would undermine the system of plea bargaining in use throughout the United States. Defense attorneys, on the other hand, took pleasure in noting that they had always known that there was something fishy about testimony obtained under such circumstances. The case also generated a flood of scholarly commentary, most of it focused

* I am grateful to Vera Bergelson, Hugo Bedau, Antony Duff, John Kleinig, and the participants at the LSU Special Part conference for their comments on an earlier draft.

[1] *U.S. v Singleton*, 144 F.3d 1343 (10th Cir. 1998), *rev'd by* 165 F.3d 1297 (10th Cir. 1999) (*en banc*), *cert. denied*, 527 U.S. 1024 (1999). The story of Wachtel's representation of Singleton is told in Mark Hansen, 'Shot Down in Mid-Theory' 85 *ABA Journal* 46 (May 1999).

[2] Section 201 contains two distinct, but closely related, offenses. The first offense, bribery, makes it a crime to 'corruptly' give or receive 'anything of value' in return for influence of an official act. The second offense, giving or receiving gratuities, makes it a crime to give or receive anything of value 'for or because of' an official act. For purposes of the discussion here, I will focus on the question whether the government in *Singleton* committed bribery. If it can be shown that it did, then *a fortiori* it would also have committed gratuities.

[3] *Singleton*, 144 F.3d at 1346.

on the issue of prosecutorial ethics.[4] As a practical matter, however, the controversy did not last long. Six months after the panel issued its decision, the Tenth Circuit, sitting *en banc*, reversed, reinstating Singleton's conviction and holding that Section 201 did not apply to prosecutors in such circumstances.[5] All of the other circuits that have considered the issue have more or less agreed, and, for the moment at least, the issue seems settled.[6] Despite its lapse in topicality, however, the *Singleton* case continues to pose important questions about the deeper nature of bribery. In this chapter, I want to use the facts of *Singleton* as a reference point for my broader analysis of bribery—what its limits are, and why it's morally wrong.

In §§ 1–2, bribery is conceived as an agreement in which a briber promises to give a bribee something of value in return for the bribee's promise to act in furtherance of some interest of the briber's. The focus here is on questions such as who can be a bribee, who can be a briber, what the bribee must give, and what she must receive in return. Sections 3–6 then seek to get at the underlying moral content of bribery, by distinguishing between taking a bribe and offering a bribe. The former act, I suggest, involves a breach of loyalty owed by the bribee arising out of her office, position, or involvement in some practice, while the latter involves inducing another to breach such a duty. Throughout my analysis, I return to the facts of *Singleton* as posing a particularly problematic case for the theory of bribery, inasmuch as the putative bribee, by agreeing to offer true testimony as a fact witness in a criminal trial, does what is, in effect, the 'right thing'.

1. Bribers and Bribees

Before we can consider why bribery is wrong, we need to have a preliminary idea of what bribery is. But there is an inevitable potential for circularity here: ultimately, a determination of its precise contours will turn on an understanding of why bribery is wrong.

One problem is that there are hundreds of bribery and corruption provisions in force throughout the United States,[7] the United Kingdom,[8] and in

[4] See, e.g., David A Sklansky, 'Starr, *Singleton*, and the Prosecutor's Role' (1999) 26 *Fordham Urban Law Journal* 509; Michael S Ross, 'Thinking Outside the Box: How the Enforcement of Ethical Rules Can Minimize the Dangers of Prosecutorial Leniency and Immunity Deals' (2002) 23 *Cardozo Law Review* 875; George C Harris, 'Testimony for Sale: The Law and Ethics of Snitches and Experts' (2000) 28 *Pepperdine Law Review* 1.

[5] 165 F.3d 1297 (10th Cir. 1999). The court's reasoning is described below, text accompanying n. 20.

[6] E.g. *U.S. v Jenkins* 178 F.3d 1287 (4th Cir. 1999); *U.S. v Pullins* 238 F.3d 425 (6th Cir. 2000); *U.S. v Murphy*, 193 F.3d 1 (1st Cir. 1999); *U.S. v Hunte*, 193 F.3d 173, 174 (3rd Cir. 1999).

[7] For a helpful overview of the American law of bribery, see Sarah N Welling, et al., *Federal Criminal Law and Related Actions: Crimes, Forfeiture, the False Claims Act and RICO* (St. Paul, Minn: West Group, 1998), vol. 1, ch. 7.

[8] In England and Wales, the leading bribery statutes are the Public Bodies Corrupt Practices Act 1889 and the Prevention of Corruption Acts 1906 and 1916. There are also a number of

virtually every other legal system around the world[9]—and there is a good deal of variation among them. Although I will be giving special consideration to several of the most interesting and problematic aspects of the leading American bribery statute, 18 U.S.C. § 201,[10] my overarching interest here will be in articulating a deeper, more universal conception of bribery, one which is correlated only imperfectly with the concept of bribery that can be found in any specific statute.

As a framework for analysis, then, I propose the following working definition of bribery: *X* (a bribee) is bribed by *Y* (a briber) if and only if: (1) *X* accepts, or agrees to accept, something of value from *Y*; (2) in exchange for *X*'s acting, or agreeing to act, in furtherance of some interest of *Y*'s; (3) by violating some duty of loyalty owed by *X* arising out of *X*'s office, position, or involvement in some practice.[11] This section focuses on the questions of who can be a bribee and a briber. The next section focuses on bribery as an agreement.

Like offenses such as conspiracy and dueling, a completed act of bribery requires the voluntary concerted criminal participation of two parties. In order for there to be a bribe, there must be both a briber and a bribee (or at least an intended briber and bribee).

Who Can Be a Bribee?

For most of the history of bribery, the only kind of person who could be a bribee was a public official.[12] And, indeed, the only kind of public official that could be bribed for much of that history has been a judge—a fact that is illustrated by references to bribery in both the Hebrew Bible[13] and early

special offenses covering matters such as bribery in elections. The English law of corruption is described in David Lanham, 'Bribery and Corruption', in Peter Smith (ed.), *Criminal Law: Essays in Honor of J C Smith* (London: Butterworths, 1987), 92; Peter Alldridge, 'Reforming the Criminal Law of Corruption' (2000) 11 *Criminal Law Forum* 287; G R Sullivan, 'Reformulating the Corruption Laws: The Law Commission Proposals' (1997) *Criminal Law Review* 730. In Scotland, bribery is both a common law and statutory offense, the former apparently being limited to the bribery of judicial officials. Gerald H Gordon, *The Criminal Law of Scotland* (3rd ed., Michael Christie; Edinburgh: W. Green, 2001), vol. 2, 692–3.

[9] See Hearings Before the Committee on Banking, Housing and Urban Affairs, U.S. Senate, 94th Congress, Second Session, April 5, 1976 (research by the Securities and Exchange Commission failed to identify a single country in which it was not a crime to pay a government official money to induce him to enter into a contract with a private firm).

[10] See above n. 2.

[11] My formulation of this definition and the analysis that follows were influenced by a reading of the following: Kendall D'Andrade, 'Bribery' (1985) 4 *Journal of Business Ethics* 239; Thomas L Carson, 'Bribery, Extortion, and "The Foreign Corrupt Practices Act"' (1985) 14 *Philosophy & Public Affairs* 66; John R Danley, 'Toward a Theory of Bribery' (Spring 1983) *Business & Professional Ethics* 19; Michael Philips, 'Bribery' (1984) 94 *Ethics* 621; Michael S Pritchard, 'Bribery: The Concept' (1998) 4 *Science & Engineering Ethics* 281.

[12] See generally John T Noonan, Jr., *Bribes* (Berkeley: University of California Press, 1984).

[13] See, e.g., *Exodus* 23:9 ('Do not take bribes, for bribes blind the clear-sighted and upset the pleas of those who are in the right'); *Deuteronomy* 16:19 (similar). It is worth noting that, under the original Israeli law of bribery, bribe-taking by judges was considered a more serious offense than bribe-taking by other kinds of government officials. Cf. Penal Law Revision (Bribery and Rewards) Law, 1950 § 1(a) with § 2.

English common law.[14] Over time, however, the universe of people considered capable of being bribees has grown considerably, in two ways: First, the class of people who are considered 'public officials' has grown. For example, under Section 201(a), the term 'public official' is now broadly defined to include members of Congress, virtually all officers and employees of all three branches of government, jurors, and persons who act 'for or on behalf of' the federal government, such as private employees who receive federally administered funds.[15] Second, despite the non-applicability of Section 201 itself to private party bribees, the law is increasingly moving in the direction of criminalizing commercial bribery. For example, other provisions of federal law now make it a crime for investment advisers, contestants in broadcast quiz shows, bank employees, sellers of alcoholic beverages, labor union officials, railroad employees, and radio disc jockeys to receive bribes of various sorts.[16] There are also numerous other provisions, in the United States and elsewhere, that make it a crime to bribe employees of private firms.[17] In short, although, historically, bribery could be committed only by public officials, and many leading statutes continue to be restricted in this way, cases in which payments are received by department store buyers, contest judges, athletes, and other private sector actors are now, arguably, as central to the concept of bribery as those involving more traditional bribees such as judges and legislators.

So should witnesses qualify as potential bribees? Under Section 201(b)(4), bribery is explicitly defined to include cases in which a person corruptly receives something of value 'in return for being influenced in testimony

[14] See, e.g., Henry de Bracton, *On the Laws and Customs of England* (trans. Samuel E Thorne; Cambridge: Harvard U. Press, 1968), vol. 2, 302–03 (citing biblical sources).

[15] 18 U.S.C. § 201(a); *Dixson v U.S.*, 465 U.S. 482 (1984) (applying statute to employee of private nonprofit corporation that administered subgrant from municipality's federal block grant). One of the most notable aspects of Section 201(b) is that it prohibits bribery of officials who work for the federal government, but not those who work for state and local governments. When the federal government wants to prosecute state and local government officials for bribery and other forms of corruption, it frequently charges them, under the Hobbs Act, 18 U.S.C. § 1951, with the offense of extortion 'under color of official right'. It can also use 18 U.S.C. § 666, which prohibits bribery of state and local officials of entities that receive at least $10,000 in federal funds. See also *Krichman v U.S.*, 256 U.S. 363, 366–68 (1921) (concluding that earlier federal bribery statute did not reach federal employees such as 'window cleaners, scrubwomen, elevator boys, doorkeepers, pages . . . or baggage porters'). Although the Court has not had occasion to revisit the question, the prevailing view in the lower courts is that the current bribery statute is not limited in the same way as the earlier statute, and that every federal employee should be regarded as a 'public official' for purposes of Section 201. Welling, et al., above n. 7, vol. 1, at 201 and n. 3.

[16] E.g. 18 U.S.C. § 215 (bribery of bank employees); 27 U.S.C. § 205(c) (bribery in alcoholic beverage industry); 29 U.S.C. § 186 (bribery of labor representatives); 49 U.S.C. § 11907 (bribery of railroad employees). Commercial bribery can also serve as a predicate offense under the mail fraud, wire fraud, RICO, and Travel Act statutes.

[17] See *Perrin v U.S.*, 444 U.S. 37, 44 notes 9 and 10 (1979) (listing statutes); Gunter Heine, et al. (eds), *Private Commercial Bribery: A Comparison of National and Supranational Legal* Structures (Freiburg: International Chamber of Commerce, 2003) (study of laws in thirteen OECD countries).

under oath or affirmation as a witness'. Clearly, then, the statute would apply to a witness who agreed to give perjured testimony in return for payment. But would it apply to a witness who agreed to give truthful testimony? Such a witness might have an argument that, rather than receiving something of value in return for being influenced in his role *as a witness*, he was actually receiving something of value in return for his being influenced to *become* a witness. As such, there was (as we shall see below) no positional duty for him to violate. His act would thus be analogous to a private person's accepting payment in return for deciding not to run for some political office[18]—an act that would not on its face appear to constitute receiving a bribe.

Who Can be a Briber?

Having considered who can be a bribee, we can now look at who (or what) can be a briber. Section 201 says simply that bribery is committed by 'whoever' gives or receives something of value in return for influence over an official act. The term 'whoever', in turn, is defined (along with 'persons') in Title 1, Section 1 of the U.S. Code, the 'Dictionary Act', to include 'corporations, companies, associations, firms, partnerships, societies, and joint stock companies, as well as individuals'.

Given the breadth of this definition and the all-encompassing manner in which the term 'whoever' has been interpreted in other federal criminal statutes,[19] it is hard to see how any person or legal entity could be held incapable of being a briber. Nevertheless, this is exactly what the Tenth Circuit *en banc* opinion held in *Singleton*. Indeed, the court was so anxious to avoid the conclusion that a promise of leniency in return for testimony might constitute a crime that it gave a wholly implausible answer to the 'who can be a briber' question (or, more precisely, the 'who can be a gratuity-giver' question).

The court's argument, as best it can be summarized, was as follows: The prosecutor in federal criminal cases works not on behalf of herself, but rather on behalf of the U.S. Government. The Government cannot prosecute 'itself'. Therefore, a federal prosecutor, acting in her capacity as a representative of the 'sovereign', cannot be prosecuted for a crime that is committed in the course of her regular duties. And, because a prosecutor who promises leniency in return for true (as opposed to false) testimony is functioning within 'the limits of his or her office', she cannot be prosecuted under Section 201.[20]

[18] See generally Daniel H Lowenstein, 'Political Bribery and the Intermediate Theory of Politics' (1985) 32 *UCLA Law Review* 784, 791–5.

[19] Cf. Stuart P Green, 'The Criminal Prosecution of Local Governments' (1994) 72 *North Carolina Law Review* 1197, 1215–17 (concerning application of federal environmental crime statutes to municipalities).

[20] *Singleton*, 165 F.3d at 1302 and n. 2.

This argument reflects at least four major flaws. First, it is simply wrong that a government-initiated prosecution against a federal prosecutor acting in her official capacity would constitute a prosecution by the government of 'itself';[21] the government and its representatives are, and always have been, viewed as distinct. Secondly, it obviously begs the question to say that a prosecutor who offers leniency in return for testimony is functioning within the limits of her office; whether a prosecutor who offers such a deal is acting illegally is precisely the issue the court was called upon to answer. Thirdly, the court offers no explanation for why a government prosecutor is incapable of bribing a witness to tell the truth, but fully capable of bribing a witness to lie. Fourthly, the decision fails entirely to address the deeper question of whether and how such conduct can be distinguished from conduct that should properly be regarded as bribery. This is a question that will be addressed below.

2. Bribery as an Agreement

In this section we consider two related issues: (1) how bribes differ from gifts, tips, and campaign contributions; and (2) what it means for the briber to give the bribee 'something of value' in return for the bribee's acting on the briber's behalf.

Bribes vs. Gifts, Tips, and Campaign Contributions

The supposed difficulty of distinguishing bribes from gifts, tips, rewards, and campaign contributions has frequently been noted.[22] Although it may well be difficult to make the distinction in practice, in theory it is clear: Bribes involve an agreement to exchange something of value in return for influence, while gifts, tips, and campaign contributions involve no such agreement.[23]

A bribe involves a bilateral agreement between two parties in which something of value is given or promised *in exchange for* the bribee's acting on the briber's behalf. There can be no completed bribe without a meeting of minds. Thus, as in the case of conspiracy,[24] if the briber or bribee is intoxicated or is mistaken, or is an undercover agent feigning agreement (as

[21] I have previously dealt with the supposed problem of self-prosecution in Green, above n. 19, at 1209–10.

[22] See, e.g., Noonan, above n. 12, at 687–90; James Lindgren, 'The Theory, History, and Practice of the Bribery-Extortion Distinction' (1993) 141 *University of Pennsylvania Law Review* 1695, at 1707.

[23] A similar distinction is made in Susan Rose-Ackerman, *Corruption and Government: Causes, Consequences, and Reform* (Cambridge: Cambridge University Press, 1999), 93; and Philips, above n. 11, at 632.

[24] At common law, the traditional rule was that there was no conspiracy unless the plurality requirement was satisfied—i.e. unless at least two persons possessed the requisite intent to conspire. See *Morrison v California*, 291 U.S. 82, 92 (1934) (Cardozo, J.).

in the notorious Abscam case),[25] the bribe would be incomplete. Therefore, assuming for purposes of discussion that *Singleton* is right, and that government attorneys acting within the scope of their office are incapable of committing bribery, it would seem to follow that, if a witness who accepts consideration from such a person in return for testifying is a bribee at all, he is party to an *incomplete* bribe (though it should be noted that, for all practical purposes, Section 201 makes no real distinction between 'choate' and 'inchoate' bribes).

In contrast to bribes, gifts, tips, rewards, and donations are unilateral; they are given without any agreement to reciprocate. This is not to deny, of course, that gifts are often given either in return for some service that has already been rendered (as in the case of tips or rewards), or in expectation of receiving something in return (as in the 'exchange' of family gifts at holiday time). We have all encountered circumstances in which such ambiguity is manifest.[26] Nevertheless, there is, at least as a conceptual matter, a significant difference between 'exchanging' goods or services through an agreement and doing so gratuitously. Similarly, there is a significant conceptual difference between completed bribes and gifts.

What the Briber Gives: 'Something of Value'

Bribery statutes typically say that a bribee must accept, or agree to accept, 'something of value' in return for some service rendered to the briber. Although the idea of bribery typically conjures up images of fat envelopes stuffed with hundred dollar bills, the thing of value given by the briber to the bribee need not, of course, be money. Bribes have been premised on a wide range of things of value, such as offers of future employment, unsecured short-term (and subsequently repaid) loans, restaurant meals and tickets for athletic events, ostensibly valuable (but actually worthless) stock certificates, and even sexual favors.[27] Indeed, in the Talmudic tradition, bribes could be effected even by means of 'pleasant words' of flattery.[28]

On the other hand, as I have discussed elsewhere in the context of theft law, the term 'thing of value' cannot always be taken literally.[29] We need to

[25] Described in Stuart P Green, 'Federal Bribery Statute', in Brian K. Landsberg, *Encyclopedia of Major Acts of Congress* (New York: Macmillan, 2003).

[26] See, e.g., *The Simpsons: Lisa's Substitute* (Fox television broadcast, April 25, 1991) (Homer is bemused to learn that while local art museum does not charge 'admission' per se, patrons are expected to give a 'donation' upon entering).

[27] See, respectively, *Biaggi*, 909 F.2d 662, 684–5 (2d Cir. 1990); *U.S. v Gorman*, 807 F.2d 1299, 1304–5 (6th Cir. 1986); *U.S. v Sun Diamond Growers* 526 U.S. 398, 401–2 (1999); *U.S. v Williams*, 705 F.2d 603 (2d Cir. 1983), 623; *Scott v State*, 141 N.E. 19, 23 (Ohio 1923).

[28] See Babylonian Talmud, Ketubbot 15b; Meir Tamari, Al Chet: *Sins in the Marketplace* (Northvale, NJ: Aronson, 1996), 137.

[29] See Stuart P Green, 'Plagiarism, Norms, and the Limits of Theft Law: Some Observations on the Use of Criminal Sanctions in Protecting Intellectual Property Rights' (2002) 54 *Hastings Law Journal* 167, at 211–21.

think about the term in relation to the underlying purposes and policy concerns of the relevant statute. In the case of bribery, we would need to inquire into the extent to which an expansive interpretation of 'things of value' might create a chilling effect in the context of, for example, dealings between department store buyers and suppliers, political fundraising activities, and the social lives of government officials.

An interesting context in which the 'thing of value' question arises is provided, yet again, by a case in which a prosecutor made a deal with a witness to give something in return for testimony. In *United States v Medina*, the defendant, charged with drug trafficking, sought to exclude testimony given by a cooperating government witness who had, in exchange for his agreement to testify on behalf of the government, received not only a promise of leniency but also cash payments of over $105,000.[30] In ruling on the motion, the court seemed reluctant to follow the approach used by the Tenth Circuit in *Singleton*, and refused to hold that prosecutors acting within the scope of their duties could never violate Section 201. Instead, the *Medina* court distinguished between prosecutorial promises of leniency and payments of cash, arguing that while there was a long 'tradition' of giving witnesses the former, the ethical issues raised by the latter were 'troubling'.[31] In essence, the court said, while cash is a 'thing of value' for purposes of the bribery statute, prosecutorial leniency is not.

What the Bribee Gives Back: Influence

Section 201(b)(2) requires that the bribee agree to accept something of value 'in return for... being influenced in the performance of any official act'. As we shall see below, it is this 'being influenced' requirement on which the moral wrongfulness of bribery largely depends, and in which the moral ambiguity inherent in some cases of bribery chiefly resides.

For the moment, we can simply observe that the federal courts have interpreted the 'being influenced' requirement quite broadly, upholding convictions despite the fact that the act had already been contemplated before the bribe was solicited.[32] The courts have also read broadly the requirement that the bribe relate to acts that are 'official', rejecting, for example, the claim by a defendant congressman that such acts must occur exclusively within the legislative process itself.[33]

[30] 41 F. Supp. 2d 38 (D. Mass. 1999).

[31] Nevertheless, the court ultimately denied the motion on the grounds that the witness was being paid not for his testimony as a witness but rather for his help as an informant. 41 F. Supp. 2d at 48–53. *See also U.S. v Murphy*, 193 F.3d 1, 9 (1st Cir. 1999) (recognizing distinction between offering witnesses leniency and 'just pay[ing] witnesses money for their testimony'); *U.S. v Condon*, 170 F.3d 687, 689 (7th Cir. 1999), *cert. denied*, 526 U.S. 1126; *U.S. v Hunte*, 193 F.3d 173, 176 note 4 (3d Cir. 1999).

[32] *U.S. v Quinn*, 359 F.3d 666, 675 (4th Cir. 2004).

[33] *U.S. v Biaggi* 853 F.2d 89, 97–9 (2d Cir. 1988), *cert. denied*, 489 U.S. 1052 (1989).

In this context, it is worth asking whether a witness who receives consideration in return for agreeing to testify truthfully as a fact witness in a criminal trial would satisfy the 'being influenced' requirement of the statute. Such a witness would presumably want to argue that she was not being influenced in her act, since she would have given the same true testimony regardless of whether she received consideration for doing so. Moreover, it could be argued that the service the witness was providing was not giving *true* testimony per se but, rather, waiving her right not to testify in the first place. In any event, to really understand what it is the bribee must give back to the briber, we need to look more deeply at why bribery is a morally wrongful act.

3. The Moral Content of Bribery

As I have described elsewhere, the moral content of any given criminal offense can be divided into three basic kinds of (often overlapping) elements. *Culpability* reflects the mental element with which an offense is committed, such as intent, knowledge, or belief. *Harmfulness* reflects the degree to which a criminal act causes, or risks causing, harm to others or self. And *moral wrongfulness* reflects the way in which the criminal act involves a violation of a specific moral norm or set of norms, such as deception, cheating, coercion, exploitation, stealing, promise-breaking, disobeying, or disloyalty. I will here follow this basic tri-partite division.[34]

Culpability

Under Section 201, a thing of value must be given or received 'corruptly' in order for such act to constitute bribery. Indeed, the requirement of 'corruptness' is often said to be the principal factor that distinguishes bribery from the lesser offense of giving or receiving gratuities.[35] In reality, corruptness is as much a form of moral wrongfulness as it is of culpability. But because the courts tend to regard it as a form of mens rea, and it appears in the leading statute as such, I will treat it as a form of culpability here. The question is, what exactly does 'corrupt' mean in the context of bribery?

Under American law, the term 'corruptly' has been interpreted to mean that the defendant desires that, in exchange for something of value, the public official will perform some act.[36] Thus, the briber must presumably intend that the bribee be influenced, while the bribee must intend that she herself be influenced.

[34] For a discussion of its rationale, see Stuart P Green, 'Why It's a Crime to Tear the Tag Off a Mattress: Overcriminalization and the Moral Content of Regulatory Offenses' (1997) 46 *Emory Law Journal* 1533, at 1547–52.

[35] See, e.g., *U.S. v Muldoon*, 931 F.2d 282, 287 (4th Cir. 1991).

[36] Welling et al., above n. 7, at § 7.4, at 210–11.

An interesting question arises in cases in which the bribee takes money from a briber with no intention of allowing herself to be influenced. For example, in the Abscam case, the defendant, Congressman Michael Myers, argued that although he had been captured on videotape ostensibly agreeing to introduce a private immigration bill in return for a payment of fifty thousand dollars, in fact he had merely been 'playacting', and had never actually intended to follow through on his promise.[37] In rejecting what it characterized as a 'bizarre defense', the court said simply that it understood the agreeing to 'be influenced' language of the statute to refer not to the bribe taker's 'true intent', but rather to 'the intention he conveys to the briber in exchange for the bribe'.[38]

The court's reasoning in *Myers* is surely wrong. One who accepts money ostensibly in return for performing an official act he has no intention of performing has no more accepted a bribe than one who accepts money ostensibly in return for committing a killing he has no intention of carrying out has conspired to commit murder. An official who takes money in exchange for a service he does not intend to carry out has presumably committed not bribery, but fraud. On the other hand, an official who accepts money to perform an official act that she does intend to perform, but is unable to do so, either because she lacks authority, or because the act has already been performed, could properly be held to have accepted a bribe.[39]

Harmfulness

Much of the literature on bribery and other forms of corruption focuses on the numerous ways in such acts are believed to be harmful to society.[40] Bribery 'corrupts' political and commercial life by inviting inappropriate grounds for decision-making.[41] It creates political instability, distorts markets, undermines legitimacy, retards development, wastes resources, undercuts confidence in decision-making institutions, and leads to injustice, unfairness, and inefficiency. In the Talmudic view, even a wise person who accepts a gift but otherwise intends to maintain objectivity in the case before him will find that his judgement is distorted.[42]

The precise nature of the harm that a given act of bribery causes will vary depending on the nature of the official act that is compromised, whether by judge, legislator, administrator, juror, witness, executive, or other official. Consider, for example, the difference in harm between cases in which, in

[37] *U.S. v Myers*, 692 F.2d 823 (2d Cir. 1982), *cert. denied*, 461 U.S. 961 (1983). A similar case, from South Africa, is *S. v Van Der Westhuizen* [1974] (4) SA 61. *See also R v Dillon* [1982] VR 434.

[38] 692 F.2d at 841–2 and n. 19.

[39] See, e.g., *U.S. v Carson*, 464 F.2d 424, 433 (2d Cir 1972) (bribe taker had no authority to take the requested action), *cert. denied*, 409 U.S. 949 (1972); *U.S. v Heffler* 402 F.2d 924 (3d Cir. 1968) (similar), *cert. denied*, 394 U.S. 946 (1969).

[40] See, e.g., Rose-Ackerman, above n. 23; and sources cited below n. 69.

[41] See Noonan, above n. 12, at 3.

[42] See sources cited n. 28 above.

return for payment: (1) a military officer agrees to share secrets that could result in loss of life, and (2) a waiter agrees to give a patron a better table in his restaurant (if in fact the latter case involves a bribe at all).[43]

Of course, none of this is to say that every act of bribery will necessarily lead to any actual bad decisions. As we shall see below, a legislator or judge can be bribed into making the same correct decision she would have made absent the bribe. All that is required is that the decision-making process itself be corrupted by the payment of the bribe.

Moral Wrongfulness

So far, we have been talking about 'bribes' as if they were single, unidirectional transactions. In fact, however, bribes involve two distinct parts: a bribe must be given (or at least offered) by a briber; and it must be received (or at least solicited) by a bribee. Although the modern American statutory approach is to impose the same penalty for bribe-taking and bribe-giving, there is some evidence that the general public regards bribe-taking as the more serious offense,[44] and it is in fact treated as such in some foreign statutes.[45] In terms of understanding why bribery is morally wrongful, the distinction is crucial. In the analysis that follows, I focus first on the moral wrongfulness of *receiving* a bribe, and then on the moral wrongfulness of *giving* a bribe.

4. Loyalty and Disloyalty

In this section and the next, I consider the idea that the bribee, by taking something of value in return for doing an act on the briber's behalf, *violates a duty of loyalty arising out of the bribee's office, position, or involvement in some practice*. It is important to recognize, however, that the moral wrongfulness entailed by receiving a bribe, though consisting in large part of disloyalty, is not limited to disloyalty, and should also be understood to include elements of deception, cheating, stealing (in the sense that the bribee sells something he has no right to sell),[46] and the wrongful commodification

[43] See discussion in text preceding n. 69.

[44] In a recent study, respondents were asked which they regarded as more serious: a public official accepting a bribe, or a private citizen giving a bribe to a public official. Seventy-four percent said they regarded the former as more serious; 12 percent said the latter was more serious; 14 percent said they were equal in seriousness. Training and Research Institute, National White Collar Crime Center, *The National Public Survey on White Collar Crime* (2000), available at <http://www.nw3c.org/research_topics.html>. Of course, it should be pointed out that such data could also be consistent with the view that what respondents thought was more serious was corrupt action by officials (whether offering or taking bribes) as opposed to corrupt action by private individuals.

[45] E.g. Israel Penal Law Revision (Bribery and Rewards) Law, 1950 § 3 (person giving bribe is liable for only half the penalty applicable to person accepting bribe).

[46] Cf. *A-G for Hong Kong v Reid* [1994] 1 AC 324 (because proceeds of bribe given to agent of principal are property of principal, failure to turn over such proceeds constitutes theft).

of government—concepts that I have discussed elsewhere in other contexts and will not repeat here.[47]

The Duty of Loyalty

Before we can consider what it means to *violate* a duty of loyalty, we first need to consider what it means to *have* a duty of loyalty. To be loyal involves being true or faithful to someone or something—having a 'persevering commitment to some associational object', as John Kleinig has put it.[48] But what kind of object? Some commentators, such as Marcia Baron and John Ladd, have argued that loyalty must be interpersonal—that is, that one can be loyal only to an individual, or group, or institution.[49] Under this view, loyalty is founded on a specific kind of relationship or tie defined by membership in a group and differentiation within that group.[50] It is typically defined by social roles, rather than any particular characteristics of individuals: Thus, I am loyal to *my* family, *my* friends, and *my* colleagues because of their relationship to me, rather than because of any particular qualities they might possess.

Other commentators, including, most prominently, Josiah Royce, have suggested that the proper objects of loyalty are ideals, causes, and practices, rather than individual people or institutions. Thus, for Royce, loyalty consists in the 'devotion of a patriot to his country', 'the devotion of a martyr to his religion', and 'the devotion of a ship's captain to the requirements of his office'.[51]

The best view, it seems to me, is that one can be loyal to both people *and* causes or ideals (or, to put it homophonically, to both princip*als* and princip*les*).[52] Loyalty creates in one a prima facie obligation to act *in the best interests* of a particular person or cause, even when doing so would be against one's own self-interest. It helps define many of our most important human relationships, and indeed our very identities as persons. To be loyal is to be guided by such concerns for the relevant others in our dealings with family, friends, colleagues, communities, and nations, and in the pursuit of

[47] Stuart P Green, 'Broadening the Scope of Criminal Law Scholarship' (Summer/Fall 2001) 21 *Criminal Justice Ethics* 55 (criticizing Peter Alldridge's argument that bribery should be conceptualized as wrongful commodification of government); Stuart P Green, 'Lying, Misleading, and Falsely Denying: How Moral Concepts Inform the Law of Perjury, Fraud, and False Statements' (2001) 53 *Hastings Law Journal* 157; Stuart P Green, 'Cheating' (2004) 23 *Law and Philosophy* 137.

[48] This phrase appears in an in-progress draft of a book of Kleinig's entitled *Loyalty and Loyalties*, of which I am grateful to have had the opportunity to read a chapter.

[49] Marcia Baron, *The Moral Status of Loyalty* (Dubuque, IA: Kendall/Hunt, 1984), at 5; John Ladd, 'Loyalty', in Paul Edwards (ed.), *Encyclopedia of Philosophy* (London: Routledge, 1967), vol. 5, 97.

[50] Ladd, *ibid.* at 97.

[51] Josiah Royce, *The Philosophy of Loyalty* (New York: Hafner Publishing Co., 1908), 17.

[52] Whether one can also properly be said to be loyal to a product or brand, and whether dogs and other animals can truly be said to be loyal, are questions which, for present purposes, need not be answered. *See generally* Kleinig, above n. 48.

our most important projects. As Andrew Oldenquist has suggested, 'it is likely that loyalties ground more of the principled, self-sacrificing, and other kinds of nonselfish behavior in which people engage than do [other kinds of] moral principles and ideals'.[53] Take away loyalty and our lives would be empty indeed.

In some cases, we choose our own loyalties. When I decide to marry a particular person, work for a particular employer, or join a particular club, I knowingly and voluntarily assume the moral obligations that go with such relationships. In other cases, loyalties arise involuntarily: We are all born into a web of familial, social, national, ethnic, cultural, religious, ideological, and political relationships. As adults, we may be theoretically free to reject those ties and choose others in their place, but such early bonds are usually strong ones.

Loyalty and Moral Conflict

Sometimes, a person ostensibly subject to a duty of loyalty is forced to choose between acting in a way that is consistent with such duty and complying with some competing moral obligation. In sorting out such conflicts, it will be helpful, first, to distinguish between what we can refer to as (1) loyalty in the factual (or descriptive or empirical) sense, and (2) loyalty in the normative (or moral) sense.[54] Loyalty in the factual sense consists in a certain mental attitude that *X* has towards the object of his loyalty: it requires that *X* view himself as obligated to act, and in fact be inclined to act, in the best interests of his principal; and that he be willing to persevere in such an attachment despite the difficulties that might be involved. Loyalty in this sense does not require that the object of one's loyalty be a good person or right cause.

By contrast, to think of loyalty in the normative or moral sense is to think of loyalty as a virtue; it requires not only that *X* work in the best interests of his principal, but also that such principal in fact be a good person or right cause, or at least not a thoroughly bad person or wrong cause. Thus, whereas one could be loyal in the empirical sense to a Hitler or to the ideology of Nazism, one could not be loyal to such objects in the normative sense.[55] In such cases, we say that one's loyalties are misplaced.

Loyalties, in either form, are not absolute. Loyalty is only one of a series of competing factors, a prima facie consideration, which people take into account in making moral decisions.[56] Sometimes our loyalty to one person

[53] See Andrew Oldenquist, 'Loyalties' (1982) 79 *Journal of Philosophy* 173.

[54] Cf. Peter Westen, *The Logic of Consent* (Aldershot: Ashgate Publishing, 2004) 4–7 (distinguishing between 'factual' and 'legal' senses of 'consent'); Robert Nozick, 'Coercion', in *Socratic Puzzles* (Cambridge, Mass: Harvard University Press, 1997) (distinguishing between coercion in the 'empirical' sense and coercion in the 'moral' sense').

[55] Cf. Robert E Ewin, 'Loyalty and Virtues' (1992) 42 *Philosophical Quarterly* 403.

[56] Cf. Marcia W Baron, 'Loyalty', in Lawrence C Becker and Charlotte B Becker (eds), *Encyclopedia of Ethics* (2nd ed., New York: Routledge, 1992), vol. 2, 751, 752.

or cause conflicts with our loyalty to another person or cause.[57] The obligations of loyalty can also come into conflict with other kinds of moral obligations. For example, if one were questioned by the police about what one knew of criminal wrongdoing by one's spouse or child, the demands of loyalty might well require that one violate one's competing moral (and legal) obligation to tell the truth.[58]

Inasmuch as it is potentially at odds with liberalism, loyalty can seem a disfavored or outmoded virtue. Liberalism in its various forms assumes that all people should be regarded as equal, that they should be treated with like concern and respect, and that moral judgments should be impartial. The ethic of loyalty, by contrast, involves a preference for people in my family or my group over those who are outside it.[59] In some cases, the conflict between the two approaches can be acute. Adherence to the ethic of loyalty has the potential to negate our critical edge, cause complacency, lead us to accept what our political leaders do unquestioningly, and to be intolerant of those who are not part of our group. In its most perverse forms, loyalty can lead to bigotry and xenophobia.

Indeed, there are cases in which individuals are encouraged, or even required, to place adherence to some supposedly higher principle (one might even say 'loyalty' to some higher principle) over loyalty to a friend or employer. For example, rules against nepotism require hiring decisions to be made on the basis of what is in the best interest of an institution, rather than according to personal loyalties.[60] Similarly, the Code of Ethics for federal government employees states that such employees should 'expose corruption wherever uncovered', 'pay loyalty to the highest moral principles', and 'put country above loyalty to persons, party, or Government department'.[61] And the *qui tam* provisions of the U.S. Federal Civil False Claims Act create significant financial incentives that encourage 'whistle-blowing' employees to betray the interests of their employees, when such betrayal would serve the larger interests of the public.[62]

[57] Compare Forster's famous remark that, 'If I had to choose between betraying my country and betraying my friend, I hope I should have the guts to betray my country'. E M Forster, 'What I Believe', in *Two Cheers for Democracy* (Harmondsworth: Penguin, 1965), 75 at 76.

[58] On the ethics of 'snitching', see Stuart P Green, 'Uncovering the Cover-Up Crimes' (2005) 42 *American Criminal Law Review* 9, at 32–3.

[59] This point is emphasized in George P Fletcher, *Loyalty: An Essay on the Morality of Relationships* (New York: Oxford University Press, 1993), 11–16. For commentary, see 'Symposium: Loyalty' 12 *Criminal Justice Ethics* 34–70 (Winter/Spring 1993).

[60] See, e.g., 5 U.S.C. § 3110(b) (barring officials from appointing relatives to positions in agencies over which the public official exercises jurisdiction or control).

[61] Code of Ethics for Government Service, passed by the U.S. House of Representatives in the 85th Congress, 1958, quoted in Sissela Bok, *Secrets: On the Ethics of Concealment and Revelation* (New York: Oxford University Press, 1984), at 211–12.

[62] False Claims Act, 31 U.S.C. § 3730; *see also* Public Interest Disclosure Act 1998 (UK) (protecting employees from retaliation for whistle blowing).

Disloyalty

Disloyalty consists of more than merely the absence of loyalty. Just as promise-breaking requires that *X* be bound by a promise, disloyalty presupposes that *X* be bound by some duty of loyalty. George Fletcher has described loyalty as a rejection of alternatives that undermine the principal bond: 'A loyal lover is someone who will not be seduced by another. A loyal citizen is someone who will not go over to the enemy in a time of conflict. A loyal political adherent will not 'sell out' to the opposition.'[63] Disloyalty, then, can be defined as the pursuit of alternatives that undermine the principal bond.

Disloyalty comes in various gradations. Imagine that third parties are speaking negatively about someone to whom one has an obligation of loyalty. Failing to say anything in the face of such criticism may be seen as disloyal. Adding one's own negative comments seems even more so. And if others are working actively to harm the object of one's loyalty, then it may be disloyal to fail to work against their doing so, and even more disloyal to assist them. In its most virulent form, disloyalty becomes betrayal.

The extent to which one can be said to be disloyal turns on context-specific determinations. Some conservatives seem to think that it is disloyal to criticize one's government, its leaders, or its policies, especially in times of war. In contrast, liberals believe that one can be highly critical of one's country without being disloyal. Indeed, the liberal view is that true loyalty *obligates* one to criticize one's country when it is in the wrong.

Context may also determine the difference between disloyalty and a mere shift in loyalties. For example, while *X* is working for company *C*, it would presumably be disloyal for him to work simultaneously for its chief rival, *R*. On the other hand, once *X* leaves his job at *C* and goes to work for *R*, he is free (and, indeed, morally and legally required) to shift his loyalties to *R* (even though he continues to be ethically and legally constrained from divulging trade secrets learned while working for *C*). What is less clear, however, is whether and when it would be disloyal for *X* to leave *C* and go to work for *R* in the first place.

Disloyalty vs. Promise-Breaking and Breach of Fiduciary Duty

In what respects is the concept of disloyalty I have described distinguishable from other forms of moral wrongfulness, such as promise-breaking and breach of fiduciary duty? Disloyalty is both broader and narrower than promise-breaking. If I enter into a contract in which I promise to sell my butterfly collection to a stranger over eBay, and then renege on that promise, I have not been disloyal. Loyalty involves a complex web of obligations and duties arising out of certain kinds of identifiable social relations: friend-to-friend, sibling-to-sibling, employee-to-employer, and so forth.

[63] Fletcher, above n. 59, at 8.

Such relations are not easily reducible to an identifiable promise or set of promises. Moreover, although one who is disloyal will often have made a promise to be loyal, this is not always the case. For example, people are generally thought to have a duty of loyalty to their families even though they will not normally have made any specific promise as such.

The concept of disloyalty is also both broader and narrower than that of breach of fiduciary duty. Unlike loyalty, which is primarily a concept of morality, fiduciary duty is primarily a concept of law; it refers to a set of obligations that the law imposes on parties who stand in a position of trust in relation to other parties, such as agents to principals, lawyers to clients, and doctors to patients. There are obviously cases in which one can have a duty of loyalty without a corresponding duty to a fiduciary. For example, while I certainly have a duty of loyalty to friends and relatives outside my immediate family, I generally owe them no legally enforceable fiduciary duty.

The harder question is whether fiduciary duties are always reducible to duties of loyalty. There is a great deal of debate in the literature about exactly what lies at the core of fiduciary duty. Courts and scholars have variously described fiduciary duty as (1) involving a 'duty of care', (2) fundamentally contractual in nature, and (3) nothing more than a collection of specific, narrower duties, such as avoidance of conflicts, and the obligation to treat beneficiaries of the same class equally and beneficiaries of different classes fairly.[64] There is also an interesting strand of thought that does in fact view loyalty as the foundation of fiduciary duty.[65] While it is beyond the scope of this study to resolve this issue in the law of agency, for the moment it is enough simply to raise the possibility of a connection between a loyalty-based theory of fiduciary duty and a (dis)loyalty-based theory of bribery.[66]

5. Disloyalty and Bribery

In this section, I want to show how the concept of disloyalty just sketched might inform our understanding of the offense of receiving a bribe.

Receiving a Bribe as a Form of Disloyalty

In thinking about receiving or soliciting a bribe as a form of disloyalty, let us begin with what is presumably a paradigm case: *L* is a legislator who has

[64] For a sampling of the vast literature on fiduciary relationships, see Robert Flannigan, 'The Fiduciary Obligation' (1989) 9 *Oxford Journal of Legal Studies* 285; Tamar Frankel, 'Fiduciary Law' (1983) 71 *California Law Review* 795; Deborah A DeMott, 'Beyond Metaphor: An Analysis of Fiduciary Obligation' (1988) *Duke Law Journal* 879.

[65] Gordon Smith, 'The Critical Resource Theory of Fiduciary Duty' (2002) 55 *Vanderbilt Law Review* 1399, at 1406–11.

[66] The connection between fiduciary duty theory and the law of corruption is made explicit in Kathleen Clark, 'Do We Have Enough Ethics in Government Yet?: An Answer from Fiduciary Theory' (1996) *University of Illinois Law Review* 57.

been elected or appointed to represent a particular constituency. *L* is offered a substantial sum of money by *X* in return for *L*'s agreeing to vote for some piece of legislation that *X* favors, but which is directly contrary to the interests of *L*'s constituents. *L* accepts the payment and votes in favor of *X*'s favored legislation. In this case, we can clearly see that *L* has been disloyal to his constituents and to the ideals of his job. Loyal public officials are expected to resist the temptations that may come their way. They are expected to work in the best interests of their constituents or institutions, rather than in the interests of third parties who tempt them. Loyalty faces its most important test when temptation is strongest. To accept a bribe is to give in to such temptation, and therefore be disloyal.

Now let us change the facts a bit and see how far the idea of disloyalty will take us. Suppose that *J* is a judge presiding over a case involving *X* and *Y*, and that *J* accepts money from *X* in return for deciding the case in *X*'s favor, rather than on the merits (which would have favored *Y*). Clearly, *J* has violated her duty to decide cases impartially. She has *misused* her office. But has she been disloyal, and, if so, to whom or to what? The first thing to note is that, although *J* surely wrongs or harms *Y* by denying him the decision he deserves, *J* has not been disloyal to *Y*, since *J* never had a duty of loyalty to *Y* to begin with. Instead, we should say that *J* has been disloyal to her judicial office, to the ideal of impartial justice, or to the public. But in order to accept this characterization of the case, we need to believe that one can be loyal not just to other people but also to principles or ideals—an issue that has generated some controversy, as we saw above.

Next, let us imagine that *B* is a boxer who accepts a payment to throw a fight to his opponent. Unlike *L* and *J*, *B* holds no official office. But, as Michael Philips has put it in analyzing such a case, what *B* is 'paid to do is act in a manner dictated by some person or organization rather than to act according to the understandings constitutive of' his practice.[67] In this sense, we can say that *B* has been disloyal to the practice of boxing or to the ideals of athletic competition. But once again, this move is available only if we believe that it makes sense to talk about loyalty to ideals or principles, and not just to persons or groups of persons.

Distinguishing Between Breaches of Loyalty and Other Kinds of Breach

The kind of wrongfulness associated with accepting a bribe needs to be distinguished from two other kinds of moral wrongfulness with which it might be confused. First, it is not disloyal to accept payment to violate a 'non-positional' moral duty. That is, the act that is committed must involve a breach of duty arising out of some office or position or involvement in

[67] Philips, above n. 11, at 623.

some practice. Thus, it is not bribery for a hired killer to accept payment in return for violating her duty not to kill, since the duty not to kill does not arise out of a position or practice.[68]

Secondly, not even every breach of positional duty involves disloyalty. Judges, legislators, and other office-holders clearly breach positional duties when they abandon impartiality or make decisions on the basis of frivolous or selfish reasons. Witnesses also breach a positional duty when they lie on the witness stand. All of these acts are wrongful in their own way, but none of them involves disloyalty per se. Disloyalty requires that the agent charged with being loyal 'go over' to the other side: that is, act in a way that is intended to further the interests of someone or something other than the party or cause to which he is charged with being loyal. Where the official or witness is merely being lazy or malicious, and no third party is involved, there is no disloyalty.

Disloyalty Defined in Reference to Scope of Positional Duty

In determining whether someone has committed bribery, it is necessary to determine whether he has in fact violated a positional or practice-related duty. For example, if *W*, a waiter in a restaurant, accepts money from *C*, a customer, in return for giving *C* a better table than he otherwise would have received, we cannot know whether *W* has accepted a bribe unless we know exactly what *W*'s position entails, including whether he is under any duty to assign tables 'impartially'. It may be that *W*'s duty is merely to provide adequate service to some designated group of customers. On the other hand, if *W* accepted money from *C* in return for ignoring all of the other customers and attending exclusively to *C*, then it seems that *W* would have breached a positional duty.

Focusing on the scope of the alleged bribee's positional duty is also helpful in understanding what appears at first glance to be a kind of cultural variation in attitudes towards bribery. It is often assumed that bribery is less tolerated in modern Western democracies than, say, in Russia or certain countries in the Third World.[69] And, indeed, one of the goals of legislation such as the U.S. Foreign Corrupt Practice Act and the OECD Anti-Bribery Convention is to encourage the proliferation of anti-bribery norms that will apply universally.

So, are people in such societies really more inclined to commit bribery, or more tolerant of the act, than people in the West? At the risk of armchair

[68] This point is also made by Philips, above n. 11, at 622.

[69] E.g. Gunnar Myrdal, 'Corruption as a Hindrance to Modernization in South Asia' in Arnold J. Heidenheimer, et al. (eds), *Political Corruption: A Handbook* 405 (New Brunswick, NJ: Transaction Pub. 1989); John Girling, *Corruption, Capitalism and Democracy* (London: Routledge, 1997); Richard T De George, *Competing With Integrity in International Business* (Oxford: Oxford University Press, 1993); Sabrina Tavernise, 'A Russian Tilts at Graft' *N.Y. Times*, Feb. 10, 2003, at A3 (in Russia, business owners pay public officials an estimated $33 billion in bribes yearly).

anthropologizing, let me suggest that the cultural differences here may have less to do with the degree to which bribery and disloyalty are tolerated than with the different ways in which positional duties are defined in various systems.[70] For example, if a customs agent at the border crossing between (let us say) Nigeria and Cameroon is more likely than her counterpart at LAX to 'look the other way' in return for a cash payment, it may be simply because the two agents have different understandings of the duties their respective positions entail, rather than because they have different views about the wrongfulness of bribery (or disloyalty) itself.

Accepting a Bribe to Do the 'Right Thing'

In this section, I want to consider several additional cases that may at first seem problematic for my (dis)loyalty-based theory of bribery. First, imagine that *L*, a legislator, accepts a payment to do precisely what is in the best interests of her constituents and, in fact, in the best interests of the polity as a whole. Secondly, imagine that *G*, a prison guard at Auschwitz, accepts payment in return for agreeing to allow a prisoner to escape. Thirdly, consider the *Singleton* scenario itself, in which the witness Douglas was given something of value in return for a promise to offer (true) testimony in a criminal trial. In all three cases, it might be argued, the bribee has taken money to do 'the right thing'. Which, if any, of these cases can properly be said to involve taking a bribe?

In the first case, does it make sense to say that *L*, who was doing what was in fact in the interests of his constituents, was disloyal? In arguing that bribery involves a form of disloyalty, I have adopted a view that is similar to that adopted by the English Law Commission's 1997 *Consultation Paper on Corruption*.[71] According to that paper, the paradigm of bribery involves three parties: *A*, the briber; *B*, the recipient of the bribe ('the bribee'); and *C*, *B*'s principal. The purpose of *A*'s bribing *B* is to cause *B* to act in *A*'s interest, which in turn is likely to involve *B*'s acting against the interests of *C*, to whom *B*, as *C*'s agent, owes a duty of loyalty.

Curiously, however, the *Consultation Paper*'s characterization of the 'essential character of corruption' was rejected by its successor, the Commission's 1998 *Report on Corruption*.[72] According to the latter, 'an agent can act corruptly by doing something which is not, and which the agent knows is not, contrary to the principal's interest'. One example is where the agent 'demand[s] a bribe for doing what the agent's duty to the principal already requires the agent to do'. Another is when 'of a range of choices open to the agent, two or more appear equally advantageous to the

[70] A similar argument is offered in Danley, above n. 11, at 22.

[71] Law Commission, *Consultation Paper No. 145: Legislating the Criminal Code: Corruption* (1997), at paras. 1.12–1.15.

[72] Law Commission, *Report No. 248, Legislating the Criminal Code: Corruption* (1998), at paras. 5.4–5.10.

principal, and the agent is bribed to choose one of these acceptable options rather than another'. Indeed, the *Report* views these hypotheticals as so problematic that it 'conclud[es] that a definition [of corruption] couched in terms of breach of duty, or even in terms of the principal's best interest as the agent perceives them, would be too narrow'.[73]

In my view, the *Report* is wrong to suggest that these hypotheticals undermine a loyalty-based theory of bribery. The *Report*'s understanding of what loyalty entails is overly narrow. In cases such as those hypothesized, the wrongfulness of *L*'s conduct comes not from the actual decision that *L* makes, but rather from the fact that *L* makes her decision based on the wrong sorts of reasons.[74] The duty of loyalty that *L* owes to her principal is not to make one particular decision or another, but to make decisions *because* they are in her principals' interest. If *L* accepts money from a briber to do an act that is in the briber's interest, but which also happens, fortuitously,[75] to be in the interest of her principal, it is hard to see how we can say that she has been true to her principal.[76] Accordingly, I would conclude that *L* would be liable for bribery under a loyalty-based theory, notwithstanding the fact that she voted 'correctly'.

In the second case, *G*, the prison guard, accepts money to allow a prisoner to escape from Auschwitz. Can we say that *G* has been disloyal and that he has therefore taken a bribe? Recall the two senses in which 'loyalty' and 'disloyalty' are used: to the extent that *G* has taken money to work against the interests of the Nazis, he is being disloyal in the descriptive or empirical sense of the term, but not in its moral or normative sense, since one cannot be loyal in the moral sense to a thoroughly evil principal. Thus, in determining whether *G* has taken a bribe, we need to know which kind of disloyalty bribery entails—descriptive or normative. I suggest that the offense of bribery should be understood as entailing disloyalty in the normative sense, since it would be a perverse use of the criminal sanction to prosecute someone for betraying a

[73] Law Commission, *Report No. 248, Legislating the Criminal Code: Corruption* (1998), at 54.

[74] Cf. R A Duff, 'The Limits of Virtue Jurisprudence' (2003) 34 *Metaphilosophy* 214 ('A judge's duty is to decide the cases that come before her through a process that accords with the requirements of justice.... [A] judge who decides in favour of the party who is legally entitled to win only because she was bribed to do so has failed to observe a basic requirement of natural justice, that she attend only to legally relevant considerations in making her decision' at 219).

[75] I say fortuitously, although one could imagine a legislator or judge who would accept a bribe only in circumstances in which he was able to vote the 'correct' way.

[76] Maimonides, the great twelfth century Talmudic commentator, makes a similar point: bribery involves an intention to pervert justice, and such intention exists even when the judge is bribed to acquit the innocent or convict the guilty. Maimonides, *Mishnah Torah*, Sanhedrin 23:1 (described in Menachem Elon, 4 *Jewish Law: History, Sources, Principles* 1640 (trans. Bernard Auerbach and Melvin J. Sykes; Philadelphia: Jewish Publication Society, 1994), 1641). Thus, it is not surprising that modern Israeli bribery law makes explicit 'that the crime of bribery takes place not only when the purpose of the bribe is to induce an unlawful act or to pervert justice, but also when the object is to obtain performance of a lawful act which it is the duty of the recipient to perform in any case.' Israeli Penal Law, Art. 5, § 293(7).

loyalty that was so misplaced from the start. To be sure, *G*, by doing the right thing for the wrong reasons—that is, allowing the prisoner to escape because he was paid to do so, rather than out of any genuine moral commitment—acts in a manner that is formally similar to the way in which *L* acted in the previous hypothetical. But if I am right that bribery requires disloyalty in the moral sense, then we should say that *G* has not accepted a bribe.

Finally, let us consider the case in which a witness such as Douglas agrees to offer (truthful) testimony in return for a promise of leniency. Like *L* (the legislator who accepted money from a third party to do an act which, fortuitously, was in the best interest of his constituents), Douglas seems to have done the right act for the wrong reason. Witnesses are supposed to offer true testimony in order to aid the truth-finding function of the trial, not because they are paid to do so.[77] But to recognize this, is different from saying that Douglas has been disloyal. The problem is that, unlike *L*, who violated a well-defined duty to act in the interest of his constituents, a witness's duties are much less clear. Douglas, a private citizen with knowledge of a crime, agrees to waive his right to silence and testify in return for something of value. At a stretch, we could perhaps say that Douglas has somehow been disloyal to himself. But if this really is disloyalty, it is of the most elusive kind,[78] and not the sort of disloyalty that is, or should be, the concern of bribery law.

Coerced and Coercive Acceptance of Bribes

There are two final situations I want to consider in which the moral status of receiving a bribe may deviate from the norm. The first occurs when the putative bribee is also the victim of the briber's coercion. The second occurs when the bribee herself uses coercion against the briber. (Cases in which the putative *briber* is the victim or user of coercion are considered below.)

Consider the case of retiring Congressman Nick Smith, whose son, Brad, was running to take his father's seat. In the midst of an intense lobbying effort by the Bush administration to pass its Medicare bill, Nick was allegedly told that certain 'business interests' would give Brad $100,000 in return for his father's vote.[79] When Nick declined, he was allegedly told that fellow Republican House members would make sure that Brad would never win his race for Congress.[80] Thus, in addition to being *offered* something attractive if he cooperated, Nick was also *threatened* with something unattractive if he did

[77] Of course, as the existence of expert witnesses suggests, one can presumably testify both for money and in order to promote truth-finding.

[78] Cf. my brief discussion of the extent to which moral duties to self are comparable to moral duties to others, in 'Cheating', above n. 47, at 154 and n. 31.

[79] Sheryl Gay Stolberg, 'Inquiry Set on Bribery Claim in Medicare Vote' *N.Y. Times*, March 18, 2004; Timothy Noah, 'Nick Smith Recants: Did the Pressure Get to Him?', *Slate*, Dec. 5, 2003, http://www.slate.msn.com/id/2092054/.

[80] Robert Novak, 'GOP Pulled No Punches in Struggle for Medicare Bill', *Chicago Sun-Times*, Nov. 27, 2003.

not. Had he accepted the alleged bribe, would the fact that he was pressured into taking it give him a defense? The case is a complex one. Recall that the real test of loyalty is temptation. Had Nick given in to temptation and agreed to vote against the best interests of his constituents under such circumstances, he would surely have been disloyal to those constituents. On the other hand, it seems that Nick's loyalty to his constituents was in competition with the loyalty he presumably owed to his son. Moreover, had the threat been more dire—say, if his colleagues had threatened to kill Brad unless Nick voted their way—then we might well conclude that such coercion should relieve him of whatever competing moral or legal duties he might have.

Now let us turn the tables and imagine a case in which a police officer, *P*, offers, in return for a payment, to forgo arresting *D* for a crime that *D* has committed.[81] (Another way to put it is that *P threatens* to arrest *D* for a crime that *D* has committed unless *D* pays *P*.) Here, *P*, the would-be bribee, is using coercion to obtain a bribe. As such, *P* has simultaneously committed bribery and some additional offense, such as extortion, criminal coercion, or blackmail.[82]

6. What's Wrong with Offering or Giving a Bribe?

So far, we have been focusing on the moral wrongfulness of *accepting* a bribe. At this point, we need to change gears and inquire into the moral wrongfulness of *offering* a bribe, which under modern law merits an equivalent punishment. Because the briber typically breaches no duty of loyalty,[83] our analysis of moral wrongfulness will have to follow a different course. The question I want to ask is: what exactly is wrong with offering or giving a bribe? In this section, my focus is on the idea that offering a bribe involves inducing another to do a wrongful act.[84]

Inducing Another to Be Disloyal

Most of the theoretical literature on the wrongfulness of inducing another to do wrong focuses on the wrongfulness of doing so by means of coercion or exploitation. But while there certainly are bribes that involve coercion and

[81] The hypothetical is James Lindgren's, above n. 22.

[82] On the non-mutual exclusiveness of bribery and extortion, see Lindgren, above n. 22. On the differences between extortion, blackmail, and criminal coercion, see Stuart P Green, 'Theft by Coercion: Extortion, Blackmail, and Hard Bargaining' (forthcoming, 2005) 44 *Washburn Law Journal*.

[83] I say 'typically' because there could be cases in which a briber's offer of a bribe violates a duty of loyalty to the *briber's* principal—for example, if the briber were subject to ethical guidelines that forbade the offering of bribes.

[84] For other possible theories of why accepting or giving a bribe is morally wrong, see text accompanying nn. 46–7 above.

exploitation, neither device is necessary. Thus, for the moment I want to ask two less frequently asked questions. First, why is it wrong to induce another to do wrong, or attempt to induce another to do wrong, even when one does so without engaging in coercion or exploitation? Secondly, is there something in particular wrong about inducing another to do wrong by offering such person something of value in return?

As a start, it seems obvious that the wrongfulness of inducing another to do wrong is in some way derivative of the wrongfulness of the act being induced. Thus, it is clearly worse to induce *X* to commit murder than to induce her to park in a no-parking zone. On the other hand, we should not assume that inducing another to do a wrongful act and doing the act are necessarily morally equivalent. As bad as it is to induce another to kill, it is likely that we would reserve our most serious condemnation for the actual killer, since it was she who made the ultimate decision to pull the trigger.[85] In comparing the wrongfulness of inducing a wrongful act and doing the act, we will certainly want to assess the circumstances of the relationship between inducer and doer, particularly the balance of power between the parties, and the extent to which one party can be viewed as the moving force behind the wrongdoing. (In the case of bribery itself, such nuances are captured in part by the particular choice of words we make in describing a bribe as having been 'solicited' 'taken', 'sought', 'demanded', 'accepted', or 'received'.)

The criminal law must often confront questions about how to treat parties who influence, solicit, provoke, incite, advise, counsel, command, encourage, procure, instigate, or persuade others to commit a crime.[86] It is not possible here to sort out all of the complex differences among solicitation, attempt, conspiracy, and accomplice liability, except to say that inducers are sometimes treated as seriously as those they induce to engage in wrongdoing, and sometimes not.[87]

In the case of bribery, assessment of the briber's wrongfulness is, in theory at least, fairly straightforward. If *X* offers *Y* money in the belief that doing so will induce *Y* to breach a duty of loyalty, then *X* has done a morally wrongful act. But if *X* does not believe that his offering *Y* money will induce *Y* to breach a duty of loyalty, then it would seem to follow that *X* has not done a wrongful act. Of course, in practice, determining whether *X* has such an intention in a case in which, for example, he has made a large contribution to the re-election campaign of a judge before whom he often appears, is likely to be difficult.[88]

[85] Presumably, this intuition is reflected in laws that prohibit the application of the death penalty to non-trigger persons. See generally *Tison v Arizona*, 481 U.S. 137 (1987).

[86] This list of terms is derived from Sanford H Kadish, 'Complicity, Cause and Blame: A Study in the Interpretation of Doctrine' (1985) 73 *California Law Review* 323, 343.

[87] See generally Herbert Wechsler, et al., 'The Treatment of Inchoate Crimes in the Model Penal Code of the American Law Institute: Attempt, Solicitation, and Conspiracy', 61 *Columbia Law Review* 571 (1961).

[88] See generally Daniel H Lowenstein, 'When is a Campaign Contribution a Bribe?' in William C Heffernan and John Kleinig (eds), *Private and Public Corruption* (Lanham,

Thus, returning to an earlier hypothetical in which the duties of a customs official in Cameroon were assumed to be different from the duties of her counterpart in Los Angeles, I would argue that a Western business person who gives a 'grease payment' to a Cameroonian customs officer in such circumstances has not induced a breach of loyalty, and therefore should not be viewed as having committed bribery either.

Coerced and Coercive Giving of Bribes

In the discussion of why it is wrong to accept a bribe, I considered one case in which a putative bribee was coerced and another case in which a bribee did the coercing. Now, in the interest of completeness, I want to consider those circumstances in which being coerced and coercing are relevant to the moral status of the *briber*.

First, let us return to the case in which a police officer, *P*, offers not to arrest (or threatens to arrest) *D* for a crime that *D* has committed if (or unless) *D* pays *P* some amount of money. In the event that *D* agrees to pay *P* the money demanded, it would appear that *D* has satisfied the formal requirements of being a briber. But, from a moral perspective, it may seem harsh to hold *D* to account, given that he has been the victim of coercion.

Secondly, there are also cases in which bribers themselves use coercion. In the Nick Smith case described above, it is arguable that his fellow congressmen committed not only the morally wrongful act of inducing him to breach his duty of loyalty to his constituents, but also the morally wrongful act of using coercion to get him to do so. Once again, in such cases there should be no theoretical bar to charging the briber with both bribery and extortion.[89]

7. Conclusion

In the foregoing discussion, I have sought to describe some of the moral complexity that surrounds our conception of bribery. One of the keys to understanding, I have argued, is to recognize the distinction between

MD: Rowman & Littlefield, 2004), 127. For a discussion of a recent case that presents this ambiguity in dramatic fashion, see Andrew Longstreth, 'Mississippi Maelstrom' *American Lawyer*, August 2004, 76 (concerning controversial bribery prosecution of Paul Minor, a prominent Mississippi lawyer who gave campaign contributions to local judges). See also *U.S. v Brewster*, 506 F.2d 61 (D.C. Cir. 1974) (discussing application of bribery statute in context of putative campaign contributions); *U.S. v Biaggi*, 909 F.2d 662, 695 (2d Cir. 1990), *cert. denied*, 499 U.S. 904 (1991) (distinguishing between campaign contributions and illegal transactions by considering evidentiary factors such as 'whether the contribution was reported, whether it was unusually large compared to the contributor's normal donations, whether the official threatened adverse action if the contribution was not made, and how directly the official or those soliciting for him linked the contribution to specific official action').

[89] The extortion aspects of the Nick Smith case are dealt with in my article, 'Theft by Coercion', above n. 82.

bribe-taking (which involves a breach of loyalty) and bribe-giving (which involves inducing another to breach such a duty). Such distinctions, I believe, are of more than merely academic interest. As the analysis of the *Singleton* case illustrates, there are very real issues of doctrine that turn on fairly fine features of moral analysis, such as whether a witness should be viewed as having taken a bribe if he accepts something of value in return for doing what is arguably 'the right thing'. As I hope to have shown, only if we are clear about exactly why it's wrong to commit bribery can we be clear about exactly where the outer limits of the offense should lie.

8

On the Nature and Rationale of Property Offences

A P Simester and G R Sullivan*

There are a number of offences that we think of as being concerned primarily with the protection of proprietary interests. To be sure, many of the wrongs and setbacks that can accompany the invasion and loss of proprietary interests may also occur in circumstances not involving property. Harry may say, 'It's not that I mind Jane seeing Dennis, it's the fact that she does not tell me that hurts.' A similar damage to the security and depth of their personal relationship may occur when Diane truthfully reports: 'I would have given Bob far more than that had he asked; I can afford it and wanted to help. But he just took the money without telling me and that I cannot accept.' In these cases, the loss of trust, respect, and psychological security may follow similar emotional pathways and, for Harry and Diane, the salient outcome may be the same: Harry no longer trusts Jane and Diane no longer trusts Bob. Diane may feel no economic privation; in substance, her economic condition may be wholly unaffected by Bob's conduct. But theft by Bob it was and it was only the deprivation of Diane's property that made it so.

To the extent that proprietary interests are their *marque*, it is tempting to think that property offences are less serious than are crimes regulating injury to a person's body. This may often, in practice, be the case, but it is not obvious they are systemically of a different order of seriousness. If a person were forced to choose between suffering a minor assault and losing his house, for instance, it is plausible that he would prefer the former. At least from a liberal perspective, and in common with any criminal offence, the protection of property rights must be justified ultimately in terms of the interests of persons. Suppose a company collapses following some massive corporate accounting fraud. The most important concern in such cases is not the fraud *per se* but its widespread and real implications for the lives of human beings: employees who lose their jobs, shareholders, pension fund

* We are grateful to Robert Cryer, Jeremy Horder, and Paul Roberts, and to the editors and participants at the Louisiana conference for their many valuable comments.

holders, and the like. Whether or not the crime involves property, the same questions must always be asked about its legitimacy: how is enactment of this crime justified by reference to the interests of persons, either as individuals or as members of the community?[1] What rationale underpins the claim to state intervention on behalf of V and/or V's community, to the detriment of D?

Moreover, the answers to those questions must satisfy the demands of the Harm Principle. In a liberal society, it is important that the state respect its citizens by fostering their opportunities to pursue goals and values which they have adopted for themselves. But criminal law constrains the choices available to us. It is an intrusive and expensive method of regulating the behaviour of a society's citizens. Each new crime is inevitably framed in general terms, thereby inhibiting a wide variety of possible acts by individuals and restricting their opportunities to shape their own conduct, both short and long term. In so doing, it limits the range of prospects for autonomous and free choice, and has the potential to inhibit successful engagement with a person's own, constitutive goals, regardless of whether those goals are themselves valuable.

Of course, this is only a *prima facie* reason against coercing someone to behave as the state would like. Battery, for example, is rightly prohibited, because there are reasons not to hurt others that defeat any autonomy-based reasons for permitting such activity. Yet this illustrates the very point of the Harm Principle: state coercion can be justified, but only when it is to prevent harm to other persons. The existence and enforcement of a crime harms D and others like D, both *ex ante* by restricting D's freedom of action and *ex post* by penalising D when she transgresses. According to the Harm Principle, state intervention of this nature can be justified only by showing that acts of this type lead, directly or indirectly, to harm to other persons. As such, the principle mediates conflicting individual interests within a society. I should be left free to act, at least until my acts collide with yours. And even when such a collision occurs, regulation may not be a matter for the criminal law—it may suffice for the protection of those interests to rest with civil remedies.

Any defence of property crimes, therefore, requires us to identify some harm that is addressed by each crime, and to show that the harm is sufficiently important to outweigh countervailing considerations, including considerations of individual liberty, which militate against state intervention. Moreover, while it is, on this view, no part of the state's role to enforce morality *per se*, the account must also show how it is that the victim of the crime has been wronged.[2] The Harm Principle provides for protection

[1] Where one's interests, we take it, comprise the things that make one's life go well. See J Feinberg, *Harm to Others* (New York: Oxford University Press, 1984) 34; A P Simester and A von Hirsch, 'Rethinking the Offense Principle' (2002) 8 *Legal Theory* 269, 280–1.

[2] Cf. J Raz, 'Autonomy, Toleration, and the Harm Principle' in R Gavison (ed.), *Issues in Contemporary Legal Philosophy* (Oxford: Oxford University Press, 1987), 313, 328.

against only those losses and setbacks that D was not entitled to inflict on V. Suppose that D steals an old shirt from V. The shirt is worthless and of no use to V; in fact, V normally throws out his old clothing and has forgotten about the existence of the shirt.[3] Its misappropriation affects him not at all. Further, D is destitute and in great need of clothing. Yet V is wronged by D; and V wrongs no-one if, later, he discovers the loss and selfishly recovers his garment from D. V's act of reclamation falls outside the scope of the Harm Principle because, although D's welfare is damaged when he is deprived of the shirt, he has lost nothing to which he had a right.

1. Protecting the Regime of Property

In our view, it does not suffice to point to the violation of the property right *per se* as the wrongful harm that warrants state intervention. That would lead to a circularity about the application of the Harm Principle to violations of such rights because, in most modern societies, property rights are not pre-legal. This is not to deny that the legal structure of property rights may, analytically and historically, be a development of pre-legal norms and rights: conduct aimed at achieving dominion over resources and territory may exist before (or outside) any legal recognition of proprietary interests. Rather, our claim is that the recognition and delineation of proprietary interests is itself a matter of legal rules, and moreover of rules that have varied considerably across different periods of social and common-law development. As a formal category, property is quintessentially legal. I don't need the law to know that this arm is mine; but I do need the law to know that this is my table, or that this house is yours. Indeed, in the case of non-corporeal assets such as patents and shares, the very identification of such things as susceptible of ownership is dependent on law. Within the terms of the Harm Principle, interference with another's property rights constitutes a *prima facie* harm. But it constitutes a harm the existence of which depends on a determination by the state—and, without more, its legitimate protection by the criminal law would be weakened by circularity. To invoke the Harm Principle successfully, we must demonstrate that the protection of property by the criminal law rests on values other than protecting property rights for their own sake.

It might be thought that this is mistaken: that it is one question whether the state justifiably creates and maintains an institution of property, where

[3] Related examples are discussed by J Gardner and S C Shute, 'The Wrongness of Rape' in J Horder (ed.), *Oxford Essays in Jurisprudence* (4th series, Oxford: Oxford University Press, 2000), 193, 201 and A P Simester and A von Hirsch, n. 1 above, at 282. A practical illustration is the Scottish case of *Dewar v H.M. Advocate* 1945 SLT 114 (HJC), drawn to our attention by Victor Tadros. D, the manager of a crematorium, was convicted of theft for removing (and putting to 'various lucrative uses') the lids from coffins immediately before they, and their contents, were consigned to the furnace.

the answer to that question need not rely on the Harm Principle; and that it is a second, distinct, question whether that institution of property should be protected, in part, by the coercive power of the criminal law. For most liberals, the Harm Principle is obviously crucial to that second question. Yet some might doubt whether there is vicious circularity in appealing to a harm whose existence is determined, not by the criminal law (clearly *that* would be circular), but by the state's pre-criminal institutions.[4]

Yet the circularity remains, and it is revealing to see why. Even on a two-tier analysis, the *state's* claim to deploy criminal law remains self-justifying, so long as the occurrence of the harm depends on law. Separating the institution of a property regime from its enforcement cannot evade that difficulty. However, it does suggest a way forward. The circularity can be dissolved once it is seen that, notwithstanding Feinberg's formulation, the Harm Principle constrains other forms of state intervention besides penal legislation. Mill's parameter for state action, that 'the only purpose for which power can be rightfully exercised over any member of a civilized community, against his will, is to prevent harm to others',[5] applies also to the coercive sanctions of the civil law.[6] Hence the state ought not to give effect to a regime of property at all, even through the civil law, unless to do so is consonant with the Harm Principle.

The move away from circularity is therefore made by establishing that, in the circumstances of the particular jurisdiction under discussion, the law of property facilitates the creation of forms of welfare and human flourishing that would become unattainable should that institution be lost. Where this is so, the Harm Principle is brought into play by the property regime itself. The regime itself serves our well-being; it provides a reliable means by which we can pursue a good life, through the voluntary acquisition, use, and exchange of resources. Having such a system may promote our well-being even if the particular form of the regime is imperfect, provided the community as a whole benefits by having a predictable, reliable, set of rules with which to organise their lives.[7] Assuming minimum standards of just distribution of property, the proprietary regime is a public good.

Absent state intervention, however, the regime would be ineffective, and its ineffectiveness would result in lost opportunities for personal and social advancement through reliable coordinated economic activity, and for other forms of welfare and personal realisation that only the peaceful ownership and possession of property can deliver. Preventing that community-wide harm justifies state intervention to enforce the institution of property. Thus

[4] Thanks to Antony Duff for pressing us to address this objection in greater detail.

[5] J S Mill, *On Liberty* (1859), ch. 1.

[6] See, e.g., the discussion by Stephen A Smith, 'Towards a Theory of Contract' in Horder, n. 3 above, 107.

[7] See, e.g., Jules Coleman, *Risks and Wrongs* (Cambridge: Cambridge University Press, 1993), 350–4.

misappropriating V's old clothes harms not only the interest, if any, that V has in the clothes; it also undermines the regime by which V's property right in the clothes is recognised. It does so even if the survival and functioning of that regime is ultimately, on this occasion, unaffected by D's wrong. The undermining is both immediate—through D's denying, or at least failing to recognise and respect, the demands of that regime—and indirect: absent some reason for treating D's case as special (e.g. in circumstances of necessity or emergency) the widespread replication of such conduct by others would tend to damage the operation of the regime itself.

By prohibiting crimes such as theft, the criminal law both protects individuals from any particular loss they may suffer, and safeguards the regime of property law more generally. Those who steal attack the practices of creating and exchanging property rights. In doing so, they set back the dependability of proprietary entitlements; which, in turn, restricts the ability of property owners to plan their own lives, relying both on the property rights they have already and on the expectation of being able to improve their lives by formulating proprietary transactions in the future. Protecting against these outcomes is an appropriate use of the criminal law. Even though the civil law provides a regime for the enforcement and defence of property rights, those rights receive extra protection and security from the criminal law. No doubt V can sue D in the civil courts for the unlawful taking of, say, his car. Sometimes, however, leaving V to his own devices in terms of self-help and civil redress would inadequately protect his property and, by extrapolation, the system of property rights as a whole.[8] This is partly a pragmatic point: mobilising public resources to protect private property augments deterrence and means that V can report his loss to the police who, at least in theory, will assume the task of seeking out D and the stolen property while V gets on with his own affairs. But it is also symbolic: the proprietary regime is reinforced by public denunciation of proprietary usurpations.

As we intimated earlier, our argument accepts that violation of a property right may harm the victim directly. However, the harm is parasitic. It provides a justification for intervention only once it is accepted that the institution of property should be defended by the state. Once the case for a *regime* of property rights is accepted, further more specific harms may be crystallised by the rights themselves. Those more specific harms do not justify state intervention unless and until the regime by which they are created is itself justified. They cannot stand by themselves. Suppose, for example, that D rejects her society's convention that persons may be owned and sets out to usurp V's ownership of some slaves by helping them to escape. Although, within the terms of that civil legal system, V's interests are set back, any version of the Harm Principle rooted in liberal, inclusive values cannot justify the proscription of D's conduct.

[8] Cf. *Dewar*, discussed above, n. 3.

On the other hand, once the case is made for establishing (and then reinforcing) a system of proprietary rights, the more specific harms crystallise and can be relied on to justify particular offences. If D steals V's car, he wrongs V because the car is V's—only in virtue of this legal fact does V have a right that D not take the car without V's consent. Yet once that right is acknowledged, and the state has regime-based reasons for enforcing rights of that sort, V in particular can then claim to be harmed by D's theft. The existence of this harm creates a further reason for coercive state intervention. V has lost a valuable resource, diminishing the means and opportunities with which he may enjoy a good life. As such, V's proprietary rights need not be ends in themselves, they function not only to mark out what conduct by D counts as a wrong but also to allocate the instrumentally valuable resources that conduce (at least in standard cases) toward V's well-being.

In what follows, we take preliminary steps on two projects. In § 2, we discuss the nature and rationale of what might be regarded as the paradigm proprietary offence, theft. In light of our arguments concerning the importance of property regimes, we will consider the legitimate boundaries of theft and its subordination to the civil law of property. The remainder of the paper then builds on the discussion of theft, by investigating what work there is to do for other property offences. In § 3, we consider criminal damage and the grounds for distinguishing other property offences from theft before closing, in § 4, with a brief survey of the justification, within the constraints of the Harm Principle, for enacting other familiar property offences.

2. THEFT

Theft is one of the few 'pure' property offences, in that the wrong of theft is intimately bound up with the harm. It is the very misappropriation of property, without claim of right to it (or any other justification or excuse), that constitutes the gist of the offence. Of course, the statute books know many other offences that protect proprietary interests, and which are defined in terms of specific ways of acquiring or causing loss of property. One commits an offence, for example, if one dishonestly obtains property by deception.[9] Robbery is perpetrated if force or the threat of force is used to take property from another.[10] An offence of burglary occurs if a building is entered with intent to steal.[11] D is guilty of blackmail if he makes a demand for money backed by threats.[12] Although these offences are very much part

[9] See, e.g., Theft Act 1968 (UK), s. 15; Crimes Act 1961 (NZ), s. 246. Except where otherwise indicated, references to the Crimes Act 1961 (NZ) are to the Act prior to overhaul of the part containing the property offences in 2003.

[10] See, e.g., Theft Act 1968 (UK), s. 8; Crimes Act 1961 (NZ), s. 234.

[11] See, e.g., Theft Act 1968 (UK), s. 9; Crimes Act 1961 (NZ), s. 241.

[12] See, e.g., Theft Act 1968 (UK), s. 21; Crimes Act 1961 (NZ), ss. 238–9.

of the law's protection of proprietary interests, none of these offences is a 'pure' property offence in the manner of theft. The nature of wrongdoing implicit in these offences is exemplified by rather than limited to the gain or loss of property. D1 can deceive V either into giving her money or into a ceremony of marriage. D2 can threaten force in order to either take V's money or make V have sex with him. D3 can trespass in V's house with intent either to steal her record collection or to inflict bodily injury on her. D4 can threaten to expose V's criminal past either to gain money from him or to induce him to fire D4's rival for an upcoming post.[13] Unlike the taking of property in theft, these wrongs, and these offences, are not bound up purely with the violation of proprietary rights. It is with the intrinsically proprietary offence of theft that we begin.

The Gist of Theft

The essence of theft is to misappropriate, with intent to deprive,[14] property to which one is not legally entitled, and to do so without justification or excuse. As such, theft is concerned directly and primarily with protecting the legal structure of proprietary entitlements. Imagine V, a misanthropic billionaire who has inherited and not created any of his wealth. He has withdrawn all his money from his investments, trusts, and bank accounts and stacked the cash away in cardboard boxes that litter the floors of his grim mansion. He is determined that no-one shall have any use or pleasure from his wealth and has resolved that when his time is nigh, he will immolate himself and his cash.[15] D is V's selfless home-carer. Although paid a pittance by V, out of the goodness of her heart she ministers to V's needs beyond any call of duty. From time to time, she takes cash from one or other of the boxes, never for herself, but to ease the path of friends and acquaintances who are in dire economic straits. There is no profligacy in this: she takes enough, just enough, to stave off the worst consequences of the privations that afflict the people she helps. D is a thief; a thief despite the fact that V knows nothing of D's takings and is unharmed psychologically by what D has done, and despite the fact that, for him, the financial loss is *de minimis* in every conceivable sense. She has misappropriated V's property, usurped his property rights without his consent; no more is required. This conclusion follows, as we shall argue, even where D acts with a degree of selflessness and concern that

[13] Prior to 2003, this alternative would have fallen outside the terms of ss. 238–9 of the Crimes Act 1961 (NZ); but it now lies within the scope of s. 237.

[14] In most jurisdictions, with intent to deprive *permanently*. Contrast, in Scotland, *Strathern v Seaforth* 1926 JC 100. The exclusion from theft of dishonest borrowing is partly, we take it, designed to prevent liability for *de minimis* interferences with property. For discussion, see A P Simester and G R Sullivan, *Criminal Law: Theory and Doctrine* (2nd ed., Oxford: Hart Publishing, 2003), § 13.7(i)(a).

[15] We disregard any complications that may arise from offences of destroying currency.

would be vindicated as ethically correct under many versions of communitarian morality.

The example illustrates that the immediate victim of a theft may be harmed in a wholly conventional sense, without suffering any substantive disvalue or setback of human interests. Across a range of different cultures and circumstances, outcomes such as death, injury, physical and emotional pain, extreme discomfort, paralysing fear, bereavement, etc., are unequivocal—and pre-legal—harms. Although it does not follow that the infliction of such harms is always wrong, or that their categoric prohibition is justified, it may readily be agreed without reference to the law that a person who is badly physically or emotionally hurt is, while that condition endures, worse off than when her usual circumstances obtain. By contrast, and while D's conviction for theft may be justified in terms of protecting the proprietary regime itself, V is a victim only formally.

Violations of the ownership, control, or possession of property need not always set back the interests of an agent whose rights have been contravened.[16] Of course, sometimes a loss of property may have devastating consequences for the nature and quality of an agent's life. Yet the accretion of property may have no beneficent effect on the quality of life or moral standing of an agent. Take the misanthropic billionaire: no doubt from Aristotelian and communitarian perspectives his life and moral standing would improve immeasurably if, after some ghostly visitation, he were to give away the bulk of his fortune in well-judged and effective acts of philanthropy. Moreover, it may be argued from these moral perspectives that, absent any re-enactment of *The Christmas Carol*, D, his housekeeper, *should* have taken even more of V's money and redistributed it to the needy. It seems an inversion of sound moral judgment to castigate her as a thief. If she is to be criticised at all, it might be for her failure to take more of his money before he, his mansion, and the money went up in smoke.

Immorality, Redistribution, and Dishonesty

How might one bring a claim that the housekeeper has not acted wrongly within the ambit of a denial that she has committed the wrong of theft? Characteristically, conviction for theft requires proof that, in appropriating

[16] Provided 'interests' is given meaning beyond a circular definition that refers to the loss of property rights *per se*: above, n. 1. Contrast Feinberg's discussion of bare trespass in *Harm to Others* (n. 1 above) 107, criticised in Simester and von Hirsch, n. 1 above, at 284. Even so, it may be that such wrongs *standardly* cause harm. Given that criminal prohibitions are unavoidably rough-grained, it may be necessary to frame prohibitions in terms of benchmark cases. (Similarly, prohibitions of dangerous activities, such as speeding, tend to be framed on the basis of typical risks, it being uneconomic to enforce laws that accommodate the contextual detail of every transgression.) As such, if theft normally harms its immediate victims, and provided the property regime is defensible generally, we have reason within the terms of the Harm Principle to enact a general prohibition.

V's property with intent to deprive V of that property, D acts *dishonestly*.[17] *Prima facie*, it is this mens rea requirement that introduces the element of moral obloquy into theft, making the wrong of theft something more than a mere usurpation of V's property rights. Remedying mere usurpations, it might be thought, is the task of the civil law. Criminal law, by contrast, requires something more: a moral wrong, sufficient to mark out that usurpation as deserving condemnation and punishment.

Curiously, however, 'dishonesty' is an amorphous concept that lacks clear delineation. The English statute, for example, offers only a partial definition of *non*-dishonesty: a finding of dishonesty cannot be made if D takes property in the belief that it is lost property and the owner cannot reasonably be found; or that he has the right in law to take and keep the property; or that the owner would consent to his taking the property.[18] It will be noted that none of these negations of a finding of dishonesty involves any challenge to the justice or conscionability of any particular ownership of property or, in general terms, to the overarching societal distribution of property rights. All these negations fit snugly with the legal proprietary framework: the property was lost, or thought by D to be his own, or taken with V's assumed consent.

But these provisions determine only some cases where findings of dishonesty cannot be made. In other situations, the issue whether D was dishonest is left at large. To the extent that it admits of further definition at all, the general test for dishonesty is said to go beyond a mere examination whether D believes his conduct is *legally* innocent or justified. In England, the fact finder should ask whether what was done was dishonest according to 'the ordinary standards of reasonable and honest people'; and if so, whether D realised that what he was doing was, by those standards, dishonest.[19] It will readily be understood that this test could be applied to exonerate the housekeeper, D.[20]

Yet, assuming that V is a competent adult, the finding that his property may be taken by others acting without his consent and without a claim of (legal) right, in anything other than tightly defined emergency situations, amounts to a rejection on broad moral grounds of the incorrigibility of V's rights to his property.[21] D's claim is subversive of the proprietary regime,

[17] At least historically: see, e.g., Theft Act 1968 (UK), s. 1; Crimes Act 1961 (NZ), s. 220 ('fraudulently'). But contrast Model Penal Code, § 223.2; Crimes Act 1961 (NZ), s. 217 (as amended).

[18] Theft Act 1968, s. 2(1).

[19] *Ghosh* [1982] QB 1053, 1064.

[20] Similarly, in New Zealand prior to 2003 it sufficed to exculpate the defendant that she genuinely believed she was justified in departing from her legal obligations, such that the jury might conclude that her legally wrong conduct was never the less honest: *Firth* [1998] 1 NZLR 513, 519 (CA); *Williams* [1985] 1 NZLR 294, 308 (CA); *Coombridge* [1976] 2 NZLR 381, 387 (CA). This possibility has now been excluded by a statutory definition of dishonesty: see s. 217 (as amended) of the Crimes Act 1961 (NZ).

[21] This is, in effect, the view taken by the New Zealand legislature (*ibid.*), which now defines the theftuous requirements that D act 'dishonestly and without claim of right' as acting, respectively, without belief that consent has been given and without belief that the act is legally permitted.

the regime it is a function of the law of theft to uphold; it is, in effect, a claim to be a legitimate agent of distributive justice. The sheer cogency of her claim (and a myriad of similar claims) that the persons she helped required and deserved help demonstrates why such a plea cannot be allowed. It is of interest that the test of dishonesty in English law, while giving rise to musings about a 'Robin Hood' defence, has been circumspectly applied. In practice, it is available only when D takes V's property while still acknowledging V's ownership. So, a strapped-for-cash employee may be able to contest her dishonesty if she takes an unauthorised advance payment of wages, acknowledging her taking by an accurate I.O.U. and believing that she will be able to make repayment. While leaving cases of that kind to the jury has been criticised for undue laxity,[22] at least outright claims to V's property on the grounds of moral entitlement are avoided.

The criminal law, as currently conceived, cannot readily accommodate claims of moral entitlement or disentitlement to property.[23] It takes as a datum those property rights recognised and enforceable at civil law. Acknowledging claims to have acted honestly, even in cases as extreme as the billionaire and the housekeeper, imports a moral element into the security of property ownership. It is exceedingly difficult to place limits on this morally driven incursion into property rights. This is not to say that the recognition of property rights is normatively insensitive: but issues of distributive justice are questions affecting the design of a property law system and the recognition of rights within that system, not questions to be revisited at the point of protection and enforcement of that system. They are matters for property law, tax law, and the like; not for the criminal law. Within the framework of theft, harm (both to V and to the proprietary regime) is constituted by the unauthorised appropriation of V's property; it becomes a wrong simply in virtue of being deliberate and with intent to deprive. The wrong is, thus, derived from the harm—it is because the property is V's that D wrongs V when she interferes with it. With the exception of defences arising out of, for example, emergency and mistake, the criminal law must accept the distribution of property recognised and enforceable at civil law and protect that property through its blaming and coercive mechanisms.

This can show the criminal law in its most unattractive light. The saying, 'possession is nine-tenths of the law' is, suitably adapted for this context, an understatement. Some extreme forms of libertarianism will defend all measure of material inequality to the hilt. By contrast, one need not hold with Proudhon that all property is theft to be discomfited by the posture of Anglo-American criminal law as the unyielding custodian of the proprietary rights of unequal, divided societies. Admittedly, one may point to the

[22] E Griew, 'Dishonesty: The Objections to *Feely* and *Ghosh*' [1985] Crim LR 341.

[23] An egregious exception is *Police v Minhinnick* [1978] NZLJ 199; discussed in A P Simester and W J Brookbanks, *Principles of Criminal Law* (2nd ed., London: Sweet & Maxwell, 2002), § 19.4.2(1).

destabilising, even tumultuous, effect on civic order that any 'help yourself' message may bring if issued by an authoritative court, however guarded and circumspect the terms of the message might be: changes in the distribution and ownership of property should be determined by the political and legislative process and not by the courts. But if the existing, asymmetrical, distribution of material goods in a society is unjust, the criminal law can only compound that injustice. In all important respects, the law of theft is the protector of the status quo. That status quo is, in large part, defined by the civil law.

Theft and the Boundaries of Property Law

We have suggested that, in terms of the recognition and protection of property, the criminal law is dependent upon and posterior to the civil law. In so far as the actus reus of theft is defined in terms of 'property',[24] the range of economic interests buttressed by the criminal law will expand or contract according to developments in the civil law. For example, the taking of a bribe might formerly have led only to liability for offences of corruption. But receiving a bribe may now also be theft, following a common law decision that the proceeds of a bribe given to the agent of a principal are the property of the principal:[25] hence the retention of the property by the agent against his principal falls within the compass of theft.

The civil law of property is constantly evolving, leading inevitably to speculation whether particular forms of economic value constitute forms of *property*. Against that backdrop, it may on occasion be appropriate for the criminal law to resolve by stipulation whether, for the purposes of the law of theft, certain interests are to be regarded as proprietary in nature, especially where the question is contested at civil law.[26] Such 'deeming' provisions are useful for the avoidance of doubt that may arise at the margins of property law. In the absence of stipulative provision, moreover, it is appropriate for criminal courts to resolve any doubts about the coverage of the civil law in favour of the accused. For instance, it may be that there are property rights in certain kinds of confidential information. None the less, a criminal court can legitimately decline to rule about so contested a civil law matter and assume a state of the civil law favouring acquittal; as when it is assumed that for a student illegitimately to borrow a confidential examination paper, and return it after photocopying the contents, does not comprise the theft of any property.[27]

[24] See, e.g., Theft Act 1968 (UK), s. 4(1) ('money and all other property, real or personal, including things in action and other intangible property'); Crimes Act 1961 (NZ), s. 217 (everything 'which is the property of any person').

[25] *A-G for Hong Kong v Reid* [1994] 1 AC 324; see Simester and Sullivan, n. 14 above, § 13.5(1)(b).

[26] See, e.g., Theft Act 1968 (UK), s. 5(2)–(4); Crimes Act 1961 (NZ), ss. 218–19.

[27] *Oxford v Moss* (1978) 68 Cr. App. Rep. 183.

These interstitial clarifications do not alter the essential dependence and subjugation of the law of theft to the civil law of property. If, as we have argued, the harm of theft is the misappropriation of a person's property and the wrong of theft is to take property without claim of right to it and intending to keep or dispose of it, the subservience of the criminal law to the civil law comports with this state of affairs.

It is logically possible, however, for the criminal law to be more profoundly at odds with the civil law in respect of the protection it may extend to certain sorts of proprietary *interests*. For instance, a legislator might appease certain pressure groups by, say, legislating that the taking of a person's money earned by way of gambling, prostitution, or the performance of abortion, is not to be regarded as theft; so that the criminal law has different standards from the civil law and will not protect property rights obtained in certain ways. Yet while it may be possible logically to provide that certain property rights can only be enforced by way of self-help and civil redress, and that other public resources will not be mobilised in their defence, the overarching policy of the law as a whole would be undermined by this move. In a state where the law of theft had been amended in that way, D could enter the house of V, a prostitute, in order to take her money without perpetrating the crime of burglary: if he believed her money to be the proceeds of prostitution he would not intend to steal and would commit only a tort of trespass. V, presumably, could use reasonable force to protect her property, but could not call upon the police to help her prevent the commission of a crime if D intended to take the proceeds of prostitution and nothing else. While such a state of affairs is legally possible, there are cogent reasons for thinking it undesirable. The underlying rationale for protecting property rights via the criminal law applies to these cases too: arguments about the recognition of property rights belong in the civil law, and their resolution there should be authoritative.

An even more subversive possibility is the obverse scenario, contemplated recently in the English case of *Hinks*,[28] where the House of Lords was prepared to put the criminal law directly at odds with the civil law concerning the rules of ownership. D was convicted of stealing cheques and money from V. It was accepted that the property passed from V to D by way of gifts valid at civil law; so that, in civil law, D owned the money she stole. How, then, had she stolen it? Because, apparently, within the domain of criminal law, title to the money remained with V at the point of the theft. One may concede that, in the circumstances, it was dishonest of D to solicit and accept the gifts. (V was said to be a gullible man of somewhat limited intelligence.) Yet even if we acknowledge D's dishonesty, how, at one and the same time, could title to the money be vested in D under civil law yet remain with V for the purposes of the criminal law? One might defend this

[28] [2001] 2 AC 241.

possibility by arguing that the policies and protected interests of the civil and criminal laws can diverge: the civil law may be concerned primarily with certainty and the security of transactions, whereas the criminal law may be more concerned with the protection of the vulnerable and the punishment of dishonesty. Hence, in the civil law, property could be vested in D while still belonging to V, for the purposes of the criminal law, in order to convict D of theft. *Hinks*, in effect, invents a new category of property that can be owned solely by one person at civil law and owned simultaneously by another person at criminal law. The criminal law property right will trump the civil law right, at least in criminal proceedings held to determine whether D stole from V when acquiring a valid title to the property.

The disruptive potential of this possibility may be illustrated by an example discussed in *Hinks* itself. Suppose D sells his roadside petrol station to V, without disclosing that planning permission has been granted for the building of a bypass road—which, when built, will divert most of the traffic. The contract would be valid under English law; there was no special relationship between the parties, no duress or undue influence, no misrepresentation. Yet a majority of the House of Lords was prepared to accept that, if dishonest, D could have stolen the consideration he receives.

The argument has so far been made that it is in the nature and rationale of the law of theft to protect the proprietary status quo, a status quo consisting of the proprietary rights recognised by civil law. *Hinks* turns this on its head, placing the criminal law in opposition to the civil law where acquisitions of property through indefeasible civil law transactions contravene community standards of honesty. While the academic response to *Hinks* has been predominantly hostile,[29] the decision has its defenders.[30] In the eyes of its supporters, its major merit is the very lack of subjugation of the criminal law to the civil law that has been argued for here. The decision has been perceived as a wedge whereby communitarian and public values of the criminal law (as assumed) can militate against the private and commercial concerns of the civil law. Which, of course, they can, in specific targeted contexts such as consumer protection legislation. But not by the law of theft. If the behaviour in *Hinks* was wrong, it was a wrong of exploitation. It was not the wrong of stealing.

For those who criticise the decision, one ground of complaint is the deployment of the concept of dishonesty to segregate non-criminal from criminal transactions. And it is, we think, undesirable for rule of law reasons that this amorphous and vague concept should bear very significant weight.

[29] See, e.g., the notes by J C Smith at [2001] *Crim LR* 162; A T H Smith, 'Theft Or Sharp Practice: Who Cares Now?' (2001) 60 *Cambridge LJ* 21; J Beatson and A P Simester, 'Stealing one's own Property' (1999) 115 *LQR* 372.

[30] S C Shute, 'Appropriation and the Law of Theft' [2002] *Crim LR* 445; A Bogg and J Stanton-Ife, 'Protecting the Vulnerable: Legality, Harm and Theft' (2003) 23 *Legal Studies* 402. See also S Gardner, 'Property and Theft' [1998] *Crim LR* 35.

Yet the deeper concern about this possibility is the threat it poses to the coherence of the scheme of property protection provided by the legal system as a whole. A manageable law of theft can, in substance, concern itself only with corrective justice. That is to say, it must respond to situations where D has misappropriated V's property lacking any belief in a claim of right or any other justification or excuse. It cannot, reverting to the housekeeper and the misanthropic billionaire, deflect allegations of theft by hearing arguments that those for whom D acted were more deserving of the property than V; it cannot, in other words, listen to arguments based on distributive justice, particularly in cases of self-help.

The ramifications of the approach in *Hinks* lead one rapidly into destabilising questions of distributive justice. Consider, in our earlier example of the sale of the petrol station, the position of T who is aware of all the circumstances of the sale. He knows D will use the proceeds to purchase T's yacht. By accepting this money, does T commit the crime of handling stolen goods? If the answer is affirmative, this effectively lays down rules of just distribution rather than correcting any wrong done to V. We assume here that V cannot recover the money at civil law from D or from anyone who accepts the money with notice: if the transaction between D and V is valid at civil law that assumption should follow. Yet were we to hold that a civil law transaction involving theft by one of the parties is thereby vitiated, we would indeed be in a vicious circle. We would then be committed to holding that the dishonest acquisition of any property is theft because there is no entitlement to such property at civil law. The cart would be driving the horse.

Theft, Fraud, and Property

Historically, theft—larceny—required a physical interference with tangible goods.[31] The paradigm case of larceny exhibited 'manifest thievery', an overt unauthorised taking of another's property.[32] Larcenous incidents had implications for safety and security; they were unsettling interruptions to the normal flow of events. By contrast, fraudulent conduct was something that required investigation to reveal its true nature.

In modern societies, however, a myriad of valuable assets take incorporeal form, and theft now includes the appropriation of intangible property. Consequently, there may be nothing 'manifest' about many acts of theft. Suppose that a bank official knowingly transfers funds electronically from a customer's account to an account in another bank opened by a company in which he has a financial interest. His conduct may be indistinguishable externally from the conduct of normal business; yet it may be

[31] Cf. Larceny Act 1916 (UK), s. 1(1) ('takes and carries away').
[32] George Fletcher, *Rethinking Criminal Law* (Boston: Little, Brown, 1978), 33–5.

described either as a theftuous taking or as a fraudulent abstraction with no significant loss of nuance. In modern economies, theft is an important offence to be used in combating commercial fraud.

This raises the question: is it intrinsic to theft that it requires an appropriation of *property*? The line between intangible assets constituting property and other, non-proprietary, forms of economic value can be very hard to draw.[33] Furthermore, when drawing that line, the question of the appropriate parameters of theft is rarely at issue. Typically, the matter is determined by civil law considerations such as the intention of the parties, commercial expectations, priorities in liquidation, taxation implications, and like. That classification decision may have no bearing on D's culpability, or on the measure of harm done to V. Suppose, for example, that D manages a series of investment schemes from which, over a number of years, he abstracts millions of pounds for his own use. D is charged with the theft of this money.[34] Proof of this charge would require that investors retain an equitable proprietary interest in the money that they place in these funds. If, instead of proprietary rights, they merely have a contractual right to payment of dividends and lump sums when departing from the scheme, theft cannot be shown because D will not have appropriated property belonging to another.[35] Depending on fine points of the deed of investment, D might leave court a free man despite massive depredations of the funds and the ruin of many of his clients. Either way, moreover, the gist of his wrongdoing remains the same: dishonest abstraction of funds to the detriment of his investors.

Should, then, theft embrace the appropriation of all forms of intangible economic value and not just property—should a general fraud offence be spliced into the crime of theft? The boundary between proprietary and non-proprietary intangibles is frequently tentative and mutable, and may not track any principled divide between those appropriations that should be made criminal and those best left (if at all) to civil law redress. A conceptually coherent and morally defensible version of theft could admit non-proprietary abstractions within its ambit.

None the less, there are pragmatic reasons for confining theft to property. There may be considerable dispute whether certain forms of intangible economic value should be protected by the criminal law or, if so, protected by an offence more specific and fine-grained than theft. For example, a case can be made that existing copyright and patent regimes inadequately control the misuse of valuable information (such as confidential client lists). Yet misconduct such as exploiting confidential information can raise complex

[33] G R Sullivan 'The Particularity of Serious Fraud', in P B H Birks (ed.), *Pressing Problems in the Law* (Oxford: Oxford University Press, 1995), 99, 103–4.

[34] *Barlow Clowes (No. 2)* [1994] 2 All ER 316 (HL).

[35] Neither need he have committed any other offence; investors need not have been induced to invest by any deception, and there need be no collusion with others to support a charge of conspiracy to defraud; false accounting charges and other financial regulatory offences are often hindered, as they were in this case, by the offshore location of the funds.

issues of fair competition, access to markets, free movement of employees, and freedom of speech. To the extent that such questions are significantly more complex in the realm of non-proprietary economic value, they may be better mediated by more fine-grained and specific legislation, and not simply overpainted by the broad brush of theft.

A move of this sort would reflect the fact that, even in commercial transactions, the classification of criminal wrongs will not always track the definitions of 'property' that serve the aims of the civil law. Many wrongs that arise in property-related contexts, such as exploitation or unfair competition, are not themselves proprietary wrongs and should not be categorised as such. Insider trading, for example, is not theft. It is not really a property offence at all. Rather, it is a covert transactional wrong of exploiting market conditions through unequal access to information. D does not violate V's property rights in the shares. He buys them. But he cheated.

3. How Many Property Offences other than Theft do we Need?

One might question whether, if sufficiently widely defined, 'theft' is the only form of property offence required by legal systems in the Anglo-American tradition. To be sure, the protection of property would be incomplete without supporting inchoate and substantive-inchoate offences. Offences of conspiracy and attempt are supplemented by the offence of going equipped for stealing, for example. Additionally, we require offences proscribing conduct ancillary to theftuous activity, such as false accounting and suppression of documents. Necessary too is an offence of handling stolen goods, to discourage commerce in stolen goods. There are also offences that deal with non-proprietary forms of value. Yet, in terms of core property offences, one might think that a sufficiently widely drawn offence of theft, with its supporting offences, is arguably all that the law needs to cover wrongful violations of property rights.

Is that enough? It seems to us that there are ways of interfering with property which manifest wrongs distinct from the wrong of theft. Further, some varieties of proprietary wrongdoing lead to particular harms that differ from theft generally. As such, these wrongs should be reflected in the calendar of offences; particularly where they merit, on a systematic basis, more (or less) severe punishment than theft.

A Second Core Offence: Criminal Damage

One of the most important instances is criminal damage. Like theft, criminal damage may be regarded as a 'pure' property offence, in that it is intrinsically bound up with the violation of property rights. The intentional or reckless damaging of another's property suffices to establish the wrong. Moreover, like theft, criminal damage may be perpetrated whether or not there is any setback to the interests and well-being of the immediate victim. Assume, for instance, that the mansion of our misanthropic billionaire is situated on an enormous estate. V has instructed his housekeeper to keep to the paths. None the less, she regularly walks across a patch of grass to take a substantial shortcut to her work. Consequently, the grass on the route that she takes becomes flattened and bruised. V does not know this as he never ventures out; indeed, because he receives no visitors only D is aware of the despoliation. There is no impact on the economic value of the mansion and grounds. Yet D has committed the offence of criminal damage,[36] a result that can be defended, *mutatis mutandis*, on the same grounds that defend her conviction of theft when she takes V's money.

Even though theft and criminal damage are not coextensive (as our example in fact illustrates), their rationales are similar: like theft, criminal damage typically involves both a direct violation of V's proprietary rights and an indirect undermining of the proprietary regime. Why not, then, proscribe them with just a single, unified, crime? To deprive the owner of a chattel by destroying it can be the actus reus of a theft;[37] why not broaden this result to cover damage as well, by enacting (say) a generic offence of criminal interference with property?

One reason is that the manner of deprivation is characteristically different. While criminal damage *can* be committed in the pure form conjectured above, many typical instances of criminal damage involve forms of vandalism employing percussive force, fire, or explosions, conduct that may well cause alarm and concern even to bystanders lacking any proprietary interest in the property being damaged. To that extent, the offence becomes part of the family of offences concerned with restraining violence and disorder—concerns generally outside the ambit of theft, save for lootings in circumstances of civil tumult. And, to the extent that it is associated with these different forms of wrongful conduct, criminal damage is a less pure form of property offence than theft. Vandalism frequently has an expressive dimension, communicating a contempt for society, and for the victim, which goes beyond a mere trespass upon property rights; that further wrong is, in turn, more clearly captured by classifying offenders with a label distinct from theft.

Not all types of vandalism share this feature—think, for instance, of defacing a book. Yet it may well be a sufficiently familiar concomitant to give criminal damage a moral resonance going beyond its association with proprietary wrongs. This is, of course, a contingent matter. But all cases of vandalism share a second, more general, intrinsic feature: criminal damage

[36] *Gayford v Chouler* [1898] 1 QB 316 (DC).

[37] *Cabbage* (1815) Russ & Ry 292, 168 ER 809; Crimes Act 1961 (NZ), s. 219(1)(b) (as amended).

is concerned with the item of property *per se*, and not just with another's rights over that item. When D steals V's book, she does not attack the item itself but, rather, pre-empts V's rights to use and exchange the book. The book itself remains usable and exchangeable; indeed, it is simply the subject of an involuntary exchange. By contrast, when E destroys V's book he attacks the use- and exchange-value of the item in anyone's hands and not merely V's. Its value is lost *tout court*, not just to V; society's store of wealth is diminished. In this respect, the harm of criminal damage differs from that of theft.

Given the overlap, there will be borderline cases; especially where the focus of D's concern is 'purely' to destroy V's property and D's conduct has no public manifestation beyond that which affects the interests of the victim. In such cases, there may be shared territory with the law of theft and unclearness about which charge is the more appropriate. Imagine that, in the course of a furious row with V, D throws V's book into the household fire. This case seems straightforwardly one of criminal damage: D's conduct may violate V's ownership and use of the book yet his conduct lacks the connotation of underhandedness and acquisitiveness normally associated with theft. But suppose instead that, in the course of this row, D takes V's diamond brooch from her jewellery box and throws it into the river beneath the apartment? We may assume that the brooch is irrecoverably lost to V—yet, somewhere in the murky depths, it rests in pristine condition. What charge to bring? A charge of theft is somewhat artificial, for the reasons applicable to the book example. But as the brooch is neither damaged nor destroyed, a charge of criminal damage seems unfounded. If one considers (and we do) that such conduct should fall within the criminal law, it must be theft. The example illustrates the difficulty of framing laws to meet marginal cases, especially where offences and their rationales overlap. By placing the brooch irrevocably out of reach, D's action seems to be a special case of criminal damage, falling more within the rationale of that crime than of theft. But it shares with theft the wrong of deprivation and, it being often undesirable to manipulate offence definitions for the sake of peripheral cases, is appropriately treated as such.

Distinguishing Proprietary Criminal Wrongs

We have seen that theft is a paradigmatic offence, in that the proprietary harm is connected directly to D's wrong. The same is true, *mutatis mutandis*, of criminal damage; but we can identify differences, including a further expressive wrong, in typical ways in which the harm is inflicted. Other property offences may also affect V's resources; but they involve either a different wrong, a different harm, or both. It is for this reason that they are rightly separate offences. Obtaining by deception may, for example, lead to much the same immediate harm as does theft—a straightforward diminution of V's resources—but the wrong is different. Moreover, it does not undermine the proprietary *regime* in the same way as does theft. On the other hand, burglary (as we shall see) involves a different harm. In looking to explain and justify the existence of each of these offences, it is necessary to identify what harm, and what wrong, is addressed by each crime. Structurally, in turn, each can only be defended as a distinct form of criminality if it captures a distinctive harm or wrong. Moreover, distinctions between different harms and wrongs will only acquire salience for a criminal justice system if to override the distinctions will send misleading or incomplete communication, either (*ex ante*) as guidance to potential offenders or (*ex post*) from the fact of conviction, and/or will suppress considerations that should inform the kind and range of sentence.

English criminal lawyers will recognise this claim, about the importance of drawing distinctions, as an extension of the principles of fair warning and fair labelling.[38] *Ex ante*, citizens need to know where they stand. They need advance warning concerning their actions; in particular, about whether what they are going to do is a crime and, if so, what sort of crime it is. *Ex post*, offenders ought to be labelled with an adequate degree of precision, in order that the criminal record identifies the gist of D's criminal wrongdoing. Both principles require that each offence is labelled and defined in such a way that it conveys to citizens an accurate moral picture of the prohibited conduct, one that is neither misleading nor unduly vague or over-generalised. Offences should, so far as is practical, reflect meaningful distinctions in the public mind between different types of culpable wrongdoing. This requires that they are drawn up in such a way that they capture, and differentiate, significant differences in the harmfulness, wrongfulness, and/or culpability of various types of action.

By way of illustration, the differences between murder, maiming, and criminal damage are significant because the harms (and indeed the wrongs) at stake are quite different. Their differences are clearly sufficient to warrant enacting separate offences, since the meaning and moral significance of each action is clearly distinguished in the public mind. Attempted murder, too, is rightly distinguished from murder on the grounds of harm. Likewise, although the harms of theft and of criminal damage are similar, the manners in which they are inflicted involve two different forms of wrongdoing; forms that, as we have argued, are sufficiently distinct in the public mind to warrant independent recognition by the criminal law. Occasionally, too, there may be a case for distinguishing between two harmful activities on the grounds of culpability. An assault being negligent with regard to any consequential risks to life would typically lack the same culpability as an assault being reckless about those same risks—and, if ever worthy of being criminalised as form of a homicide (which we doubt), ought surely

[38] See, e.g., Simester and Sullivan, n. 14 above, §§ 2.3–2.4, and references there cited.

to be a separate offence and not lumped in with murder or reckless manslaughter.

Not every difference is worthy of capture. Even though many U.S. states follow the common law in drawing a rudimentary distinction between petty and grand larceny, nobody would suggest that there should be a much more refined series of theft offences, graded in minute detail (say, theft of less than £50 value; theft of less than £100 value; theft of less than £200 value; and so on). Excessively specific offences risk clogging the trial process with unmeritorious technical argument, and obfuscating the moral clarity of the law's communications. At least in the context of non-specialist activities such as property offences, people (both *ex ante* and *ex post*) need to know the law's requirements *in gist* and not precisely. As such, meaning is better conveyed through publicly-shared moral distinctions that are broadly rather than narrowly significant, provided those broader distinctions communicate an adequately nuanced statement of the prohibited wrongdoing.

The degree of specificity that the law should adopt when distinguishing various harms and wrongs is, therefore, a trade-off. The fragmentation of the particular must be balanced against the vagueness of the general. Moreover, while that balance is contextual, in that it is affected by the range of differentiation that informs the public imagination concerning each family of offences, that context can itself be affected by law. Whereas, some decades ago in England, driving after drinking was treated as minor matter (if a wrong at all), it is now widely perceived as very wrong indeed. The moral salience of the label has been informed and shaped by criminal prohibitions.

Identifying Non-Proprietary Rationales

People are, we think, right to treat drunk-driving more seriously than once they did. But sometimes public understandings can be misled by the law. Sometimes, on closer investigation, it turns out that an offence historically associated with the protection of property is in fact—like insider trading—not really a property offence at all; or at least should not be. One example of this is blackmail, which under English law is a (substantive-inchoate) property offence, in that the gain to D or the loss to V that D seeks, when he makes an unwarranted demand on V fortified by menaces, must be a gain of money or property.[39] But a closer examination of the harm and wrong of blackmail shows that this scope is unconnected to its rationale.

In our view, the restriction to money or property is, normatively speaking, arbitrary. The wrong of blackmail has no connection to the sorts of wrongs addressed by an offence such as theft. Consider a case where D and V are employed by the same company. D threatens to expose V's criminal past to the company's management unless V makes regular payments to him from

[39] Theft Act 1968 (UK), s. 21.

her salary. This might be described as the dishonest appropriation of property belonging to another and, therefore, under that description, a case of theft. But to describe the conduct in those terms is to miss the mark. From the perspective of the victim, this is something very different from finding a purse missing from her desk, however much money in the purse. The pressures inducing a surrender to these threats may well be, according to the circumstances, enormous, and succumbing may well entail a form of life that comes close to servitude. It is D's preparedness to put his victim through that experience—to subjugate V to his will—which is the essence of his wrongdoing. Blackmail, therefore, is in truth a serious offence against the person even where the threat is one of exposure rather than violence. The wrong of blackmail is committed by making the (conditional) threat, *whether or not* any property ultimately is transferred. Moreover, the same wrong is perpetrated even if the condition has nothing to do with payment; if, say, D threatens exposure unless V fires a colleague or herself resigns. It is this wrong, together with the need to protect citizens from unjustified coercion by others, which brings blackmail within the scope of the Harm Principle independent of any proprietary character that, at least under English law,[40] it may happen to possess. Perhaps the English limitation is designed to narrow the practical scope of the offence: but the *concept* of blackmail is free of property.

4. Other Property Offences

Limitations of space permit only a sample discussion of other property offences besides theft. In what follows, we offer some indicative remarks concerning their distinctive natures and rationales.

Deception

Is there need for an offence separate from theft of obtaining property by deception? Many jurisdictions maintain a clear distinction between the two offences.[41] Apart from the obvious distinction that the offence requires that one make a false representation, and that one do so with mens rea, a deception offence may be committed even though property is obtained with the consent of the owner, whereas the paradigm wrong of theft involves an adverse interference with the owner's property, a usurpation in violation of V's rights. This distinction has been undermined in English law,[42] such that virtually all cases of obtaining property by deception are now also cases of theft. Is, then, the better approach to follow the Model Penal Code and

[40] Contrast the Crimes Act 1961 (NZ), s. 237 (as amended).
[41] See, e.g., Theft Act 1968 (UK), ss. 1 and 15; Crimes Act 1961 (NZ), ss. 220 and 246.
[42] *Gomez* [1993] AC 442; *Hinks* [2001] 2 AC 241.

collapse obtainings of property by deception into the offence of theft, and thereby to abolish any separate deception offence related to the obtaining of property?[43]

We think not. First, however, it must be conceded that in certain circumstances acts of obtaining property by deception and simple acts of theft may be, in substance, much the same. Suppose that D1, an employee of a bank, sets up an automated payments system which skims off very small amounts from a great number of accounts, to be paid into accounts in which he has an interest. D2, on the other hand, is an employee of a company that purchases various forms of services; he arranges for companies in which he has an interest to invoice the employer for services never to be performed. If charges of theft were brought in response in each of these cases, nothing of substance would be lost even though the latter circumstances could also sustain a charge of obtaining property by deception. In substance, each case involves abstractions of money from an employer, wrongdoing adequately reflected in charges of theft.

Be that as it may, in other cases deception is at the heart of the wrongdoing and something would be lost if a charge of theft rather than deception were brought. Suppose, for instance, that V will happily provide funds for D to buy books for his studies but not to bet on dogs and horses. It may be that V is very well off and is in no sense perturbed by the loss of her money. What does make her angry is that she realises she has been lied to when she discovers the betting slips in D's pockets. On occasions like this, only a deception offence will capture the gravamen of the wrong: here, obtaining property by deception is a property offence, in that property must have been obtained by D, but it is the *means* by which he obtained the money that constitutes the wrong, and not the obtaining *per se*.[44]

Indeed, the *obtaining* need not be wrong at all. Just as the element of deception is lacking in theft, the element of misappropriation is, conversely, lacking in deception. The thief bypasses ordinary mechanisms for allocating and transferring property. The deceiver exploits them. By his deception, he induces V to initiate a transfer and wrongs her in doing so. The transfer, however, is V's choice. Moreover, she is ordinarily free to refrain, thereby protecting herself from the predations of V. Unlike theft, obtaining by deception does not drive a coach and horses through the regime of property law. Yet even if it does not undermine the ownership, use, and enjoyment of one's possessions, obtaining by deception characteristically affects the confidence one may have in property *exchanges*. One who has sold goods in

[43] Model Penal Code, § 223.

[44] See S C Shute and J Horder, 'Thieving and Deceiving—What is the Difference?' (1993) 56 *MLR* 548; C M V Clarkson, 'Theft and Fair Labelling' (1993) 56 *MLR* 554; L Koffman, 'The Nature of Appropriation' [1982] *Crim LR* 331; L Leigh, 'Some Remarks on Appropriation' (1985) 48 *MLR* 167; S Gardner, 'Is Theft a Rip-Off?' (1990) 10 *OJLS* 441; A Halpin, 'The Appropriate Appropriation' [1991] *Crim LR* 426. Contrast P R Glazebrook, 'Thief or Swindler: Who Cares?' [1991] *CLJ* 389.

return for a bad cheque may well hesitate to make such a transaction again. To the extent that it undermines the trust we can have in transactions, the wrong of obtaining by deception not merely harms V directly but harms the community more generally.

Handling (or Receiving) Stolen Goods

Typically, conduct that amounts to handling will also be misappropriation of the stolen goods by the handler. Accordingly, handlers also commit theft against the persons from whom the goods were originally stolen. None the less, the maximum penalty is frequently greater for the former than for the latter.[45] This difference is defensible only if it can be maintained that handling stolen goods is distinct from and, systemically, a more serious crime than theft.

In our view, handling *is* distinct from theft, even if all cases of handling are also cases of theft. Very common forms of handling will be sales at a discount of stolen goods to friends and acquaintances of the thief. By buying goods that he knows T has no right to sell, D will be committing theft against the rightful owner. Yet there is something technical about this conclusion. D's subsequent purchase of V's goods does not, in any substantive moral sense, compound or duplicate the original theft from V. At the time of D's purchase it is most unlikely that V will see her goods again. In many instances, D will know that if he does not buy, the person standing alongside him will do so instead. The essence of the wrong of handling seems to lie in the purchase of the goods themselves; in the idea that stolen goods are a form of contraband, like drugs or counterfeit currency, which law-abiding persons should not, knowingly, acquire.

Given that this wrong is distinctive, is it systemically worse than theft, justifying the higher penalty? Although moral judgements are not a matter of counting heads, one may be confident that, from a normally distributed sample of citizens, there will be significantly more persons prepared to buy stolen goods than initially to steal those same goods.[46] To a degree this can be explained by perceptions of risk about arrest and punishment. But there is also a familiar 'distancing' phenomenon, a greater ease of conscience in benefiting from a wrong perpetrated by someone else compared with directly committing the wrong. Many persons may decline a career in, say, the arms industry, despite possessing relevant skills and aptitudes. They might happily, however, benefit from a large bequest in the will of a successful but now deceased arms-dealing relative (or, indeed, work for a university receiving such bequests).

[45] Contrast Theft Act 1968 (UK), ss. 1 (theft—seven years' imprisonment), 22 (handling—fourteen years), with Crimes Act 1961 (NZ), ss. 220 and 258 (both seven years).

[46] Cf. *Sainthouse* [1980] Crim LR 506, where a lay (i.e. non-professional) receiver was prepared to plead guilty to handling but not to theft.

Perhaps the greater seriousness is instrumental—in virtue of the scale of the harm to which handling conduces. There is a symbiotic relationship between theft and handling: 'there would not be so many thieves if there were no receivers.'[47] No doubt, if there were no handlers, there would still be thieves. But if society were to eliminate handling, the incidence of theft surely would drop dramatically. One reason why the crime of handling deserves independent criminalisation is because of the important role that 'fences'—and indeed end-purchasers—of stolen goods play in the business of theft. In modern society, the explosion of property offences is largely a matter of economics: in the market for stolen goods, supply is responsive to demand. Dealers in stolen goods are the brokers who make that market: handling is the channel through which commercial forces drive theft.[48] Moreover, those who deal in stolen goods also provide the means by which merchandise can be 'laundered', so that the tangible evidence of theft effectively disappears.[49] Mass-produced items, once sold on, cannot normally be traced. By providing an outlet for the efficient disposal of such items, handlers reduce the risk that theft will be detected. Thus one, largely unrecognised, role that professional fences perform is the obstruction of justice.

Does it follow that there should be a heavier maximum penalty for handling? Under English law, the maximum penalty of 14 years is double the maximum for theft. Where a particular handler of stolen goods is a large scale organiser of theftuous activity by others, there may be strong instrumental reasons to punish the handler more severely than members of his team of thieves. There may even be intrinsic reasons, in that his culpability for the harm that these thefts inflict may be greater than anyone else's. He alone may be complicit in the totality of the theftuous conduct.

Heavier penalties may be apt to such cases. More typically, however, the handler acquires goods from the thief (or dealer) for her own consumption. In such cases there might be deterrence-based reasons for punishing purchasers of stolen goods more severely than the initial takers; but if this consideration were to underpin systematically heavier penalties for all forms of handling, we would be in the realm of instrumental penalties unmediated by individual culpability. Indeed, the culpability of a handler may be lesser than the initial thief's. Suppose H buys a DVD player from T in the knowledge that the player was stolen by T from V. H buys opportunistically; the player was not stolen to order. He is aware that the player will never find its way back to V and that there are other persons who will readily buy the item though aware of its provenance. What, precisely, does H do wrong?

[47] *Battams* (1979) 1 Cr. App. R(S) 15, 16; though see C B Klockars, *The Professional Fence* (London: Tavistock, 1974), 165–6.

[48] Cf. Klockars, *ibid.*; G R Blakey and M Goldsmith, 'Criminal Redistribution of Stolen Property: The Need for Reform' (1976) 74 *Mich LR* 1512.

[49] D Chappell and M Walsh, 'Receiving Stolen Property: The Need for a Systematic Inquiry into the Fencing Process' (1974) 11 *Criminology* 484, 494.

Arguably, H shares in the initial wrong done to V by T, in that he is prepared to benefit from T's theft. (Indeed, handling was originally criminalised as a form of accessoryship to theft).[50] However, he did not encourage or assist in the theft and his conduct, without more, does not amount under modern principles to being an accessory after the fact. Is it wrong *per se*, over and above the wrong of the original theft, to buy something known to be stolen? An affirmative answer may be given if we are confident, as we surely can be, that without willing end-purchasers of stolen goods there would be less theft.[51] To that extent handlers, even of the petty nature of H, are members of the class of persons whose activities undermine the security of ownership and possession, something that is wrong in itself apart from any further instrumental considerations. Yet there are no reasons of principle to punish H more severely than T.

Burglary

A typical burglary occurs when D breaks into V's premises in order to commit a further crime, such as theft. Of course, breaking into V's building is a significant physical step by which D commits herself to carrying out the theft, and it might warrant criminalisation as an attempt to commit a crime (say, theft) that itself standardly involves harm. Indeed, entry as a trespasser is not, by itself, an offence. It is D's intent to commit (or commission of) the ulterior crime that radically changes the nature of her legal wrong. Given this, it might be thought odd to enact a crime of burglary when D could, on the same facts, be convicted of an attempt to commit the ulterior crime directly. Paul Robinson asks:[52]

> One may wonder, then, why burglary is retained as an offense in modern codes. Conviction for criminal intrusion and for attempt to commit the intended offense would seem adequately and properly to punish the conduct constituting burglary.

It is certainly true that the gist of burglary is not trespass. However, neither is it the ulterior crime at which D aims (or ultimately commits). Burglary is not merely an aggravated form of theft etc. It is a wrong in its own right. The trespassory entry by D not only exposes V to risk of the further crime; it also, in so doing, violates V's private life.

The strongest case of this—often subject to distinctive labelling or sentencing provisions—is where the premises are a dwelling-house.[53] Interaction with and exposure to other members of society is integral to public life;

[50] 3 & 4 W. & M. c. 13 (1692).

[51] A similar argument is often made concerning end-purchasers of child pornography: although they themselves do not wrong the child victims, they create incentives for those wrongs to be perpetrated by others.

[52] P H Robinson, *Criminal Law* (New York: Aspen, 1997), 778.

[53] Theft Act 1968 (UK), s. 9(3)(a); Sentencing Act 2002 (NZ), s. 9(1)(b). This was originally the only variety of burglary known to the common law. See 3 Coke Inst. 63.

conversely, our sense of identity and well-being as individuals depends upon our being able to reserve private space, from which other persons can be excluded. It is through controlling our private environment that we are able to have 'breathing space' from interactions with other people. Burglary compromises that space. It is hardly surprising that house burglary, in particular, causes victims great distress even if they were absent at the material time. The victim of such a burglary cannot be sure of the peaceable and secure enjoyment even of her own home. For most people, when the integrity of their private space cannot be taken for granted, one of the foundations of their well-being is destroyed.

An analogous if less powerful claim can be made for burglary of other buildings. One of the main functions of structures such as warehouses, offices, and the like is to help safeguard people and property by establishing a physical separation from the public environment. Within that secured space, people can relax at least some of the precautions they may take when in public, by putting down their handbags, remaining late to work, and the like. Conversely, if that space is not perceived to be fully secure, such practices become disrupted. Even in these non-domestic contexts, the existence and control of a realm of quasi-private space affects the manner in which we live.[54]

The existence of secured private space also influences how we organise our property. Just as at home, goods in warehouses and offices can be arrayed or stocked without securing each individually. Thus a related harm of burglary is that it gives D unparalleled access to take (or damage) a whole range of V's goods, whether domestic or commercial, in a way that, say, pickpocketing does not.[55] Here too, the case of a domestic burglary is an aggravated one: the goods to which D has access tend to include our highly personal things (underclothes, private letters, and the like) as well as things with high sentimental value—something that reinforces the sense of 'violation' experienced by burglary victims.

The arguments outlined here are supplemented by consequentialist considerations. Entry into a building is a significant physical step by which D commits herself to carrying out the ulterior crime. In effect, it ups the stakes, making it more likely that the ulterior offence will be committed. Moreover, because the activity occurs inside a building, it increases the probability that incidental violence will ensue should D be chanced upon by someone else.[56]

For all these reasons, burglary deserves its status independently as a serious crime. Notice, though, that the normative core of burglary we have identified is concerned with the protection of real property rather than with

[54] The argument here suggests a proposition we embrace: that a space open to the public, such as a shop floor during trading hours, should not be susceptible of burglary (e.g. by a shoplifter who enters the shop with intent to steal). See n. 59 below.

[55] We are grateful to Jeremy Horder for help with this point.

[56] Cf. Note, 'A Rationale of the Law of Burglary' (1951) 51 *Col LR* 1009, 1026.

the particular offence that is intended or committed therein. For this reason, it seems to us anomalous that in English law the crime is confined to only a few specified ulterior crimes.[57] The rationale of burglary extends to penalising persons who make trespassory entries into a building and intend or commit *any* serious (say, indictable) crime.[58] The gravamen of the offence is both to be a trespasser *and* to intend or commit an indictable offence in the place wherein one has trespassed.[59] In its aggravated domestic version, burglary is most truly a property offence in that such conduct radically undermines the enjoyment of a vital proprietary interest. In other contexts, burglary becomes more obviously associated with proscribing conduct likely to result in the commission of a serious offence; yet there too it undermines the use and purposes of the premises themselves.

Robbery

Simply put, robbery—where force is used or threatened in order to steal—is a species of theft that is aggravated by assault. Thus it is to some extent unusual, in that it combines a property offence with an offence of violence against the person, with penalties more severe than the punishments for those individual offences. Partly, this is because the introduction of force makes theft more likely to succeed and, conversely, the object of theft makes the assault more highly motivated, arguably exposing the victim to a greater risk of injury.[60] More importantly, however, the use of force to complete a theft changes the moral character of D's action, such that it is legitimate to criminalise D's wrong specifically by the 'combined' offence of robbery. What is significant about robbery is not merely that D usurps V's property rights, but how she does so. The victim of a theft suffers a loss of property: in robbery, V *experiences* the deprivation. The psychological harm V suffers in so doing may go far beyond any immediate injury and loss. Conversely, the use of force differs from an ordinary assault in that, whereas many assaults are perpetrated for their own sake—perhaps a violent upshot of interactions in which the victim may even have participated—the robber purposively targets or victimises V for the sake of an ulterior goal. V is not addressed as a human being; rather, his interest in personal integrity is subordinated for the sake of material gain. By her actions, D communicates to V that, in her eyes, V matters not as a person but only as a source of wealth. Moreover, their interaction is, for V, involuntary. The best that V can do is minimise the risk of its recurrence. Indeed, even the *prospect* of a mugging undermines our

[57] Theft Act 1968 (UK), s. 9(1)–(2).

[58] As in New Zealand: Crimes Act 1961, s. 231 (as amended).

[59] These are separate elements: *contra* English law (*Smith and Jones* [1976] 3 All ER 54), the status of trespasser should not be accorded merely on the basis of intending to commit a crime on the premises concerned. See the criticism by Glanville Williams, *Textbook of Criminal Law* (2nd ed., London: Stevens, 1983), 847 ff.

[60] Note, 'A Rationale of the Law of Aggravated Theft' (1954) 54 *Col LR* 84, 102.

willingness to move freely through public spaces, such as parks, especially by night. Our expectations of personal and property security are preconditions of a stable, meaningful life, for both individuals and society. Robbery undermines *both* of these expectations. Thus it is misleading to suggest that robbery is a species of aggravated theft, or even a form of aggravated assault.[61] Robbery is a distinct wrong. The difference is not one of degree.

[61] Or to suggest with Robinson that, like burglary (above, n. 52, at 780), 'the situations to which the offense of robbery apply might as easily and logically be punished by conviction for both assault and theft'.

9

Is Strict Liability Rape Defensible?

Kyron Huigens

1. Introduction

The conventional account of strict criminal liability makes little sense.[1] Strict liability offenses are said to be those that do not require proof of criminal intent or negligence. Strict liability offenses are also said to be unjust because they authorize punishment for crime without proof of culpability, blameworthiness, or (in the term preferred here) criminal fault. But if the second claim is meant to follow from the first, as it usually is, then the conventional analysis of strict liability is a spectacular non-sequitur. The familiar list of fault elements—general and specific intents, purpose, knowledge, recklessness, negligence—does not exhaust the category of criminal fault. Positive law fault elements bear a complex relationship to the concept and norm of criminal fault—much more complex than is reflected in the conventional analysis of strict liability. The use of intentional states of mind to denote fault has less to do with the conceptual or normative features of fault than it does with rule of law values. Objective or (in the term preferred here) non-intentional fault extends beyond negligence; in fact, it is

[1] The 'conventional account of strict liability', as I use that term here, reflects a simplistic but widespread idea. As Justice Robert Jackson articulated it: 'The contention that an injury can amount to a crime only when inflicted by intention is not a provincial or transient notion. It is as universal and persistent in mature systems of law as belief in freedom of the human will and a consequent ability and duty of the normal individual to choose between good and evil': *Morisette v United States*, 342 U.S. 246 (1952). There is much buried complexity in both the formal part of the conventional account of strict liability (regarding the absence of an intentional state of mind from the offense definition) and in the substantive part (regarding strict liability's objectionable nature). This paper will not do either part justice. For thorough explanations of the formal and substantive dimensions of strict liability, see Kenneth W Simons, 'When Is Strict Criminal Liability Just?' (1997) *Journal of Criminal Law & Criminology* 1075; Stuart P Green, 'Six Senses of Strict Liability: A Plea for Formalism', in A P Simester (ed.), *Appraising Strict Liability* (Oxford: Oxford University Press, 2005). This paper merely advances, in Simons's terms, 'a substantive approach [that accepts] strict liability, if the criminal offense expresses substantive fault despite the formal absence of a culpability term' (Simons, above, at 1188). The argument here could also be described without reference to strict liability at all as a defense of an extreme form of non-intentional fault (or 'objective culpability' to use a common but ambiguous term).

pervasive in the criminal law. Moral fault is not irrelevant to legal fault, and judgements of legal fault conform to judgements of moral fault at significant points. Any analysis of strict liability that does not take these features of the criminal law into account is bound to be inadequate.

In this paper, I will make three points that do take these features into account. First, strict liability rape is criminal liability imposed on the basis of non-intentional fault. The common description of strict criminal liability as the imposition of punishment without any proof of criminal fault fails to describe any legal punishment at all. Secondly, the non-intentional fault criterion in the definition of rape often consists, not of some familiar non-intentional fault criterion such as negligence or malice, but instead of the set, or some sub-set, of the offense's material elements. In other words, either alone or in some combination, rape elements such as minority, non-consent, threat, force, or victim incapacity are themselves fault criteria, of the non-intentional kind. Third, the use of non-intentional fault criteria consisting of the set or a sub-set of the material elements of the offense of rape is morally defensible at least in cases of reasonable mistake about non-consent.[2] Whether it is morally defensible in cases of sexual conduct with a minor, or in cases in which the victim is mentally or physically incapacitated, are separate questions that might be subjected to the analysis that I describe below, but that will not be examined here.

2. Theoretical Premises

The arguments of this paper draw on a highly articulated conception of criminal fault that is a feature of a comprehensive *aretaic*, or virtue ethics, theory of punishment. Despite its density, complexity, and relative novelty, I will not defend this theoretical account of criminal fault here. I will only sketch it, so that we can move on to the analysis of fault in rape. Interested, outraged, or puzzled readers may wish to pursue the footnote references.

Criminal fault is an inference, drawn in the course of the adjudication of wrongdoing, to the effect that the practical reasoning of the defendant is deficient. This assessment of the quality of the defendant's practical reasoning is not limited to the defendant's reasoning in connection with the

[2] For example, in *Comm. v Lopez*, 745 N.E. 2d 961 (Mass. 2001) the Supreme Court of Massachusetts upheld a conviction for rape following a trial in which the defendant's reasonable mistake instruction was refused, saying: 'Historically, the relevant inquiry has been limited to consent in fact, and no mens rea or knowledge as to the lack of consent has ever been required.' The court added: 'Any perception (reasonable, honest, or otherwise) of the defendant as to the victim's consent is consequently not relevant to a rape prosecution.' This is commonly described as 'strict liability' rape in the literature, using what I have called here the 'conventional account' of strict liability. Robin Charlow, for example, cites *Lopez* (among other cases) in support of her claim that 'in a number of states, courts seem to treat the nonconsent element as one of strict liability, requiring no mens rea for conviction': Robin Charlow, 'Bad Acts In Search Of A Mens Rea: Anatomy Of A Rape' (2002) 71 *Fordham Law Review* 263, 280–1.

offense—even if 'in connection with' is given a very broad construction. It extends, in addition, to an assessment of the defendant's set of standing motivations, or ends—to their acquisition, development, maintenance, and ultimate issuance in the alleged offense. From an opposite perspective, criminal fault is an aspect of criminal wrongdoing. That is, the manner, circumstances, and specifics of the individual instance of wrongdoing alleged against the defendant are the subject matter of the adjudicative assessment of the quality of his practical reasoning that I have just described.[3] This conception of fault is an aretaic conception of fault in part because it supposes that one's ends are the subject of rational deliberation, and that one can, therefore, be held responsible for the state of one's ends. The imposition of responsibility for the state of one's ends is part of a system of just punishment in part because the proper disposition of individual actors' ends is one of the objectives of punishment.[4]

Three important points follow from this aretaic conception of criminal fault. First, criminal fault is not identical with any intentional state of mind. Rather, intentions are indicators of criminal fault that we incorporate into the positive law definitions of criminal offenses for rule-of-law reasons that are exogenous to fault (though not to just punishment). The jury can be directed by positive law to draw the inference of fault pursuant to (variously) rules, standards, or an unspecified permission to do so. This legal rule, standard, or permission might turn on (variously) the intentional or desiderative states of the defendant; the manner, circumstances, or specifics of his actions; or the consequences of his actions. At one extreme, the jury can be left to draw the inference of fault from all of the evidence, without any guidance whatsoever from positive law. This permissive option might violate the rule of law, but the other options in various combinations form a spectrum stretching back to an opposite pole represented by (say) a set of rules strictly requiring proof of an intentional state of mind with regard to each material element of the offense. The choice of the appropriate point on this spectrum in the definition of each element of a criminal offense—the choice of the relative legality[5] of each fault inquiry—is determined with an eye to a value in the criminal law that is in tension with the value of legality. This competing value is fine-grainedness, defined as a low level of under- and over-inclusiveness in our rules of criminal liability, relative to a background justification of moral desert; or defined, alternatively, as a high degree of congruence between our legal judgments of desert and our moral judgements of desert. If legality is the rule of law as a law of rules, then the

[3] Kyron Huigens, 'The Dead End of Deterrence, and Beyond' (2000) 41 *William & Mary Law Review* 943, 1022–34.

[4] Kyron Huigens, 'Virtue and Inculpation' (1995) 108 *Harvard Law Review* 1423, 1456–67.

[5] Not in the sense of its legal validity, but in the sense of its conforming more or less to rule of law requirements. In other words, I use the word 'legality' as it is used in the term 'the principles of legality'.

pursuit of fine-grainedness requires a relaxation of legality. The pursuit of legality, on the other hand, entails a loss in fine-grainedness and at least the risk of a loss in the credibility and prestige of the criminal justice system.

Secondly, there is a distinction to be made between the proof and finding of positive fault elements, on one hand, and interstitial fault determinations on the other. Rules about intentional states of mind do not exhaust the concept and norm of legal fault, but the addition of non-intentional fault elements does not do so either. Fault is not confined in its operations and effects to ex ante, positive criteria. To say, as I did at the outset, that legal fault is an inference drawn in adjudication, is to acknowledge the limits of ex ante definition. Because fine-grainedness is an important value in criminal law and because moral judgements about deserved punishment are context-sensitive value judgements, the particulars of each case must be taken fully into account before any final determination on legal fault is made. This requires the introduction of evidence, which means that fault is to a great extent an ex post facto determination. One familiar example of this process is the jury's determining the specific content of the reasonable person standard preliminarily to applying it to the defendant's conduct, in a case turning on negligence. But the ex post facto operations of legal fault go well beyond determinations of negligence. There is necessarily a limit to the amount of guidance that can be provided to the jury ex ante by positive fault elements, whether in rule or standard form, and adjudication necessarily involves determinations of interstitial fault—judgements about legal fault that are made ex post, in the interstices of positive law. For example, both a contract killer and a loving husband who asphyxiates his terminally ill and gravely suffering wife act with an intent to kill and premeditation. But we assess their legal fault quite differently, and we do this in the interstices between those positive law fault elements. While judgements about interstitial fault have their greatest scope and effect in sentencing, they also play a large role in decisions to prosecute and they make even conviction more or less likely at the margins.

These first two points have implications for the relationship between legal fault and moral fault, and they should be briefly spelled out here. Interstitial legal fault and moral fault are quite alike, differing mostly in context. Interstitial legal fault is like moral fault in its informality and might be identical with moral fault in its subject matter and normative content from case to case; but it is inferred by legal actors for legal purposes within a legal institutional framework. Because the value of fine-grainedness pertains to the level of congruence between our respective judgments of legal and moral fault, this similarity between interstitial legal fault and moral fault has an important effect: our drawing the boundary between positive fault and interstitial fault in the choice and drafting of fault criteria sets the balance between the competing values of legality and fine-grainedness in the offenses that feature those fault criteria. For example, a fault criterion such as negligence—a non-intentional standard—will make an offense in which it is used fine-grained: negligence captures most of our moral judgements of fault in positive law and leaves few of our moral judgements about fault in the interstices of the law. In contrast, a fault criterion such as premeditation—a rule about intentions—will make an offense in which it is used coarse-grained: premeditation captures relatively few of our moral judgements in positive law, and leaves many of our moral judgements in the interstices of the law to operate as interstitial judgements of legal fault.

The third and final point of this Part is that fault is to be distinguished from fair candidacy for punishment, also known (in the United States) as non-excuse or (in Britain) as the conditions of responsibility. If an insane person purposely causes the death of someone whom he knows to be a human being—say he believes himself to be John Wilkes Booth, the victim to be Abraham Lincoln, and the murder of Lincoln to be a requirement of history—then (assuming a standard definition of murder) he has acted with criminal fault. But he is not a fair candidate for punishment, because he lacks the grasp of reality and the freedom from internal duress that we require as a condition of criminal responsibility. In the language of the Model Penal Code, he does not have a defense of diminished capacity, but he does have an insanity excuse.[6] Criminal fault concerns the quality of the defendant's practical reasoning. Fair candidacy, in contrast, has to do with the defendant's capacity for practical reasoning. Criminal fault is indifferent to moral luck—one is held responsible for the state of one's ends and practical reasoning on the ground, in part, that deliberation on ends is a feature of an ordinary moral life. Fair candidacy for punishment, in contrast, is sensitive to moral luck; to the fact that not all moral lives are ordinary, and that deliberation on ends is sometimes difficult and sometimes simply impossible. Criminal fault is framed in positive law along a spectrum defined by competing values of legality and fine-grainedness. Fair candidacy, in contrast, is framed in positive law along a different spectrum: we accommodate moral luck in the criminal law only within limits imposed by the essential functions of law—public safety, social coordination, economic efficiency, and so on. A determination of fault is an endogenous (to wrongdoing), adjudicative complement to the legislative definition of an offense—and is therefore a highly context- and fact-specific, ex post facto, normative determination by the jury. In contrast, decisions about fair candidacy are exogenous (to wrongdoing) side-constraints on punishment. They are set by the legislature and implemented in adjudication by means of the application of a rule to adjudicated facts about the defendant's capacities.

[6] Compare, for example, § 2.04 of the Model Penal Code with § 4.01. Note that the terminology of diminished capacity and diminished responsibility is substantially different in the United States as compared to Britain. The text takes the American view that the defense of diminished capacity consists of a mental disease or defect's negating a positive fault element.

3. Non-Intentional Fault and Strict Liability in Rape

The essential starting point in the analysis of fault in rape is the case of *DPP v Morgan*.[7] Morgan, an NCO in the British Air Force, invited a group of junior airmen to have sex with his wife. He told them to ignore any objections from her, because his wife enjoyed rape fantasies and wanted to have sex with a number of men at one time. Mrs. Morgan did object when the airmen raped her, and the airmen duly ignored her. On trial for rape, they requested an instruction to the effect that their good faith belief in Mrs. Morgan's consent was a ground for acquittal. If the offense of rape requires an intentional state of mind regarding non-consent, then their genuine good faith belief in her consent precluded their having any such state of mind. If it never occurred to them that Mrs. Morgan was non-consenting, then the rape could not have been an intended or an intentional act—done with purpose, knowledge, or even advertent recklessness—with regard to her non-consent.[8] The trial court refused to give this instruction, the *Morgan* defendants were convicted, and the Law Lords affirmed the conviction. But the House of Lords affirmed the conviction only under a harmless error rule. The trial court did err in refusing to give the instruction, the Lords said, because rape requires an awareness of at least the risk of non-consent. In American terms, the *Morgan* defendants were entitled to their instruction because the law requires at least recklessness regarding non-consent to sexual intercourse, in accordance with the principle of Model Penal Code § 2.02(3).

Had the *Morgan* defendants received the instruction to which they were entitled, their acquittal still would have required very credible testimony on their part, an extremely persuasive argument from defense counsel, and the willingness of the jury to adhere strictly to its instructions. Most commentators read the harmless error portion of the opinion to say that such a perfect storm of exemplary trial practice would never occur, and that the convictions should be affirmed because no jury would ever acquit these defendants. But even if this is a correct description of the Law Lords' reasoning, it remains the case that the reasoning is wrong. To analyze harmless error by predicting an outcome invades the province of the jury. A proper harmless error analysis is far more deferential to the jury and far more likely to result in a reversal. Furthermore, not only do juries often follow their instructions conscientiously to outcomes that their members, as citizens, don't personally endorse; appellate courts are bound to assume that juries do this. And finally, it is not at all impossible to imagine the *Morgan*

[7] *DPP v Morgan* [1976] AC 182.

[8] The terms 'intended' and 'intentional', are explained in R A Duff, *Intention, Agency and Criminal Liability* (Oxford: Basil Blackwell, 1990), 76–87.

defendants' testimony in a plausible light. Suppose that, to a man, they took the stand and showed themselves to be callous, immature, self-absorbed, and stupid—as the facts indeed suggest they were—so that their claim to have had a good faith belief in consent was credible. On these quite plausible assumptions, the *Morgan* defendants not only should have received their instruction, they should have been acquitted.

Clearly, something has gone wrong here.[9] It goes beyond the relatively common, perhaps unavoidable situation of a court's being driven to adopt implausible reasoning to avoid an unpalatable outcome. The Law Lords in *Morgan* were driven to adopt patently erroneous reasoning in order to escape an apparently insoluble dilemma. They were simultaneously committed to the principle of intentional states fault and to the notion that such morally bad men should not escape criminal liability. They could have jettisoned the latter of these commitments—as Glanville Williams would have had them do—on the ground that the legal treatment of the case should be kept distinct from the moral treatment of the case. Or the Law Lords could have remanded the case in the hope and trust that the jury would convict the *Morgan* defendants. While many would have condemned this outcome, were it acknowledged, as a nullifying conviction for crime on moral grounds, others would defend it as a traditional and proper jury function: the quiet, invisible resolution of just such conflicts between law and morality.

The dilemma should be solved by grabbing the other horn and rejecting the intentional states conception of criminal fault. Think, first, of what the intentional states approach to fault says about the *Morgan* defendants. If they had intercourse with Mrs. Morgan out of callousness, immaturity, self-absorption, and stupidity, then the law grants them an acquittal because they were callous, immature, self-absorbed, and stupid. Mistake doctrine grants an acquittal, not because of the erroneous belief as such, but because of the reasons behind the erroneous belief. If I take another person's umbrella from the restaurant's vestibule because it looks exactly like mine, then I am not guilty of theft, because I am not at fault. I am not at fault because the reasons behind my mistake—good reasons that do not even suggest the deficient practical reasoning that otherwise might justify punishing me—not only explain my acquittal on a charge of theft, but also justify my acquittal. The problem in *Morgan* was that the reasons behind the defendants' genuine good faith belief in consent were not good reasons. Their belief in consent, that belief's negation of recklessness regarding non-consent, and the defendants' logical claim on acquittal were all the direct products of their callousness, immaturity, self-absorption, and stupidity. To apply standard mistake doctrine to their case is to suggest

[9] One indication of this is the fact that *Morgan* is no longer good law. Current law requires proof that the defendant 'does not reasonably believe' that the victim consents to sex, so that an unreasonable mistake such as that claimed by the *Morgan* defendants would support a conviction, not an acquittal: see Sexual Offences Act 2003, s. 1.

that these reasons behind their mistake justify an acquittal—which is, of course, absurd.

If, as is often assumed, people have no rational control over their own characters, then one might argue that an acquittal is appropriate. After all, the argument would go, it was not their fault that they were callous, immature, self-absorbed, and stupid. But to reason this way about *Morgan* would be to replace an analysis of fault with an analysis of fair candidacy, and with an utterly implausible analysis of fair candidacy at that. When we set side constraints on punishment on fair candidacy grounds—in recognizing a defense of insanity or duress, for example—we never draw the balance between acknowledging moral luck and serving the basic functions of law so much in favor of the former value. As an analysis of fault, however, to point to callousness, immaturity, self-absorption, and stupidity as reasons not to find fault in someone's actions is, to say the least, implausible.

Following *Morgan*, British courts developed several strategies for dealing with the dilemma that the *Morgan* court dodged by means of its harmless error holding. Principally, they recognized a second interpretation of 'reckless' as it was used in the definition of rape. As the Law Commission summarized these holdings in a report on sex offenses:

> On the question of recklessness, case law is that, in rape and other sex offences, the defendant is reckless if he does not have a belief that the other person is consenting, in circumstances in which he either knows there is a risk she does not consent or his attitude is one of indifference whether she consents or not. Thus it covers the situation where he knows that there is a risk that she does not consent and carries on regardless. It also appears to apply where the defendant has not specifically considered whether she consents, could not care less whether or not she is consenting, but presses on regardless. To put it another way, if a jury is sure that the defendant was indifferent to the wishes and feelings of the victim, aptly described as 'couldn't care less', then, in law, he is 'reckless' for the purpose of sex offences.[10]

The 'knows there is a risk' version of recklessness is fundamentally different from the other, 'attitude of indifference' version of recklessness. The former definition is consistent with the *Morgan* defendants' being entitled to an acquittal. The latter definition is not so consistent. It could have been said of each of the *Morgan* defendants that 'his attitude is one of indifference whether she consents or not'. The difference between these two definitions of 'reckless' is that the former describes recklessness as an intentional state of mind, whereas the latter describes recklessness as inadvertence with an attitude.

Significantly, this solution to the *Morgan* dilemma cannot be reduced to negligence. The 'attitude of indifference' of this putative recklessness standard might be accompanied by unreasonableness, and it might lead to

[10] The Law Commission, *Consent in Sex Offences: A Report to the Home Office Sex Offences Review* (http://www.lawcom.gov.uk/files/consent.pdf), para. 7.8 (emphases and footnotes omitted).

inadvertence. But if an attitude of indifference is singled out and equated with advertent recklessness, then it hardly seems that the defendant's fault lies in either his unreasonableness or his inadvertence, both of which are characteristics of negligence, not recklessness. On the contrary, the phrase 'could not care less' seems to condemn an attitude of indifference as such, and the association with advertent recklessness pegs this kind of fault at a step above mere negligence. The point is to highlight the defendant's callousness instead of his cluelessness. When we allow the jury to convict on this basis, we have premised fault on an attitude instead of either an intentional state of mind or negligence. There is nothing wrong with this. An attitude of indifference is not an unfamiliar criterion of criminal fault. The Model Penal Code provides that a homicide committed recklessly under circumstances manifesting an 'extreme indifference to the value of human life' constitutes murder instead of manslaughter.[11] Like the Law Commission Report, the Code describes indifference differently from unreasonable inadvertence, and treats indifference as evidence of a greater fault than negligence. The Code associates extreme indifference with recklessness, and uses indifference, in combination with recklessness, to indicate fault for one of the most serious offenses. 'Indifference' is a perfectly defensible addition to the doctrinal palette of fault criteria.

The question is whether it makes sense to call a rape committed out of an attitude of indifference a case of strict liability. It certainly meets the conventional definition of strict liability, in that it is a case of criminal liability secured without the proof of an intentional state of mind or negligence. But this is hardly satisfactory. We have just seen several good reasons to take an attitude of indifference as indicative of criminal fault. There is no reason we should not associate an attitude of indifference toward non-consent with recklessness, if it seems that such an attitude is as blameworthy as the conscious disregard of a risk of non-consent. Both intentional states and negligence are criteria of fault, not constitutive of fault, and there is no reason that an attitude cannot serve as a fault criterion just as well as an intentional state of mind or an inquiry into reasonableness. But if we do associate an attitude of indifference with recklessness, then there is no reason to think of a rape so committed as a case of strict liability. In light of this conclusion, a slight shift away from the conventional definition of strict liability may be in order. If we define strict liability as criminal liability obtained without proof of legal fault, and if an attitude of indifference is a kind of criminal fault, then a rape committed with an attitude of indifference would not be a case of strict liability.

However, there is a further difficulty lurking here. This modified definition of strict criminal liability—liability obtained without proof of legal fault—produces an empty set. Criminal fault is an aspect of wrongdoing,

[11] Model Penal Code, § 210.2(1)(b).

consisting of those features of the wrongdoing that are taken to be indicative of the quality of the defendant's practical reasoning. Because both legal wrongdoing and the deficiency of the offender's practical reasoning as an aspect of that wrongdoing are part of the justification of punishment—not of the practice of punishment, but of punishment in individual cases[12]—proof of criminal fault is always and necessarily required in the legal adjudication of a criminal offense. Some aspect of the offense is used as a fault criterion in every case of legal punishment—whether as a positive fault criterion or an interstitial fault consideration. Therefore, any case of criminal liability—the authorization of legal punishment because of a violation of a legal prohibition—necessarily entails legal fault.

What, then, is strict liability if it is neither criminal liability obtained without proof of a state of mind or negligence, nor criminal liability obtained without proof of legal fault? The way out of this difficulty is to describe those cases that we think of as strict liability cases in terms of non-intentional fault. An offense definition might prescribe proof of fault by reference to an intentional state of mind or negligence, or it might prescribe proof of fault by reference to an attitude such as indifference, or it might prescribe proof of fault by reference to only the offense's material elements. A 'strict liability' offense is one that falls in this last category. In other words, in a case of strict liability it is by reference to the offense's material elements alone that both the deficiency *vel non* and the relative deficiency of the defendant's practical reasoning is assessed in the adjudication of, and in the decision to punish because of, an instance of that offense.

This kind of fault can offend against the rule of law. In a prosecution for an offense with no express fault elements, the adjudication of fault might consist of nothing but the adjudication of interstitial fault. That is, the material elements of the offense might be few, and not particularly to the point on the question of the quality of the defendant's practical reasoning, so that it is in the interstices of the offense's elements, and only there, that the jury could and would find fault. This presents a danger that the defendant's apparent moral fault will overwhelm the legal fault inquiry. Or, to put the point another way, the moral assessment of the defendant's act threatens to bleed through the boundary between moral norms and legal norms entirely, and to determine the disposition of the legal case against him. From this perspective, the fundamental objection to strict liability offenses is that fine-grainedness threatens to overwhelm legality, to a morally unacceptable degree.

The notorious case of *Prince* exhibits this pattern:[13] the defendant's reasonable mistake about the age of a girl whom he removed from the

[12] This is a basic difference between consequentialist and virtue ethics theories of punishment. I describe the difference with reference to H L A Hart's consequentialist theory in Huigens, 'Dead End of Deterrence', above n. 3, at 978–80, 1028–31.

[13] *R v Prince* (1875) 13 Cox C.C. 138.

custody of her father could not serve as a defense, because unreasonableness was not an element of the offense of which he was accused. However, the Crown, the jury, and the Law Lords were all able and quite willing to rest legal liability on Prince's moral fault in his conduct with the girl, as that fault appeared from the evidence. Prince was not convicted without any proof of legal fault. As we have seen, this is impossible: because legal fault is merely an aspect of legal wrongdoing, a jury infers that the defendant's practical reasoning is deficient in any case of criminal liability. The problem in *Prince* was instead insufficiently formal proof of fault. The finding of legal fault occurred in the interstices of the offense definition, in such a way that the jury was never required to distinguish moral fault from legal fault. This left Prince with no formal avenue to argue that he was not legally at fault, regardless of his apparent moral fault. It is important to note that, under this analysis, Prince's legitimate objection to his conviction for a strict liability offense was an objection about the rule of law, instead of an objection about punishment in the absence of proof of fault as such.

It might seem to follow from this analysis of strict liability in terms of non-intentional fault that strict criminal liability is always unjust, in that it always involves a violation of the principle of legality. But the material elements of strict liability offenses are not always poorly suited to performing the functions of fault. A strict liability offense might consist, instead, of a coherent, systematic set of non-intentional fault elements that are implicitly dedicated to the task of fairly adjudicating the quality of the defendant's practical reasoning in the context of his alleged commission of an offense. Even without making reference to customary fault elements (such as intentional states or negligence) or relatively novel fault elements (such as indifference) some set of the offense's material elements might organize an inquiry into fault that is sufficiently formal to constitute a legal inquiry into fault. Depending on how an offense statute is written, its material elements alone might enable a person in much the same situation as Prince nevertheless to cabin the arguments of the prosecution and the discretion of the jury with sufficient formality to avoid a simple equation of moral and legal fault.

4. Rape, Reasonable Mistake, and Defensible Strict Liability

Suppose that a convicted serial rapist escapes from prison. His escape and his record are widely publicized, along with warnings that he is armed and dangerous. One night while the escaped rapist is still at large, Dirk and Violet meet in a dim and smoky bar, and flirt with one another. Eventually, they leave the bar together. Then, under the glare of a streetlight, Violet realizes that Dirk matches the description of the escaped rapist. Seized with terror, she accedes to his every suggestion and request, culminating in sexual intercourse with him. During the entire ordeal, Violet maintains an appearance of calm and complaisance, and even pretends to enjoy sex with Dirk—but only because she fears for her life. She never freely consents to sex, but is instead coerced into sex by the threat of serious bodily injury or death. Needless to say, Dirk turns out not to be the escaped rapist, and indeed is unaware that an escaped rapist is at large. Furthermore, Violet's feigned consent is so utterly plausible that it never occurs to Dirk that she has not actually consented to sex or that she fears for her safety.

Dirk has a genuine, good faith belief in consent of the kind that the *Morgan* defendants claimed, even though he is clearly mistaken about Violet's consent. Because there was no force and no resistance, his claim of a good faith belief in consent is more plausible than theirs was. Dirk can argue persuasively that he did not rape Violet because he was not advertently reckless regarding her non-consent. It never occurred to him that there was even a risk she might not consent. If the jury were to be instructed that Dirk was 'reckless' if he had an 'attitude of indifference' or 'couldn't have cared less' about the woman's consent, Dirk still would have a strong argument for acquittal. He was not indifferent to her consent. Instead, he tried to get it in the usual ways that one tries to get consent to sex in clubs and bars. And Dirk inferred that he had consent, based on the social signals that he sent Violet and that he seemed to receive from her in return. The *Morgan* defendants, in contrast, received no such signals and had no reason to think that they had, apart from the implausible tale told by the victim's husband. Finally, Dirk was not negligent. He continued to flirt with Violet and to otherwise take the trouble to seduce her after she left the bar. We can infer from this that Dirk recognized a risk of confusion about non-consent, and addressed it with conversation and social signaling. By the same token, if Dirk made a mistake about non-consent, he has a good argument that the mistake was reasonable. Not only did the victim not resist, she did not refuse; and not only did she not refuse, her conduct seemed to Dirk to welcome his attentions. Sex with a partner who is a relative stranger is a common enough occurrence, and usually does not involve rape.

The present question is whether a rape definition that does not explicitly provide Dirk an opportunity to argue either his lack of intent or his reasonable mistake can meet the requirements of legality. Before addressing the legality question, however, I want to describe how such a strict liability definition of rape might serve the countervailing value of fine-grainedness—defining a 'strict liability' offense, again, as one that turns on a non-intentional fault criterion consisting of the material elements of the offense, or some sub-set of them. By examining the value of fine-grainedness first, we will get a sense of the interstitial fault criteria that might threaten to overwhelm the legal fault criteria; and of the moral fault that might bleed through and threaten to determine the question of legal fault.

We can assume that, because Dirk's mistake is reasonable, he would be acquitted of rape on a negligence standard. But it is not perfectly clear that this is the correct result—in the sense that it might not be the result that will track the moral assessment of the case sufficiently well to preserve the public credibility of the criminal justice system. Even if Dirk is reasonable, his insensitivity to the victim's non-consent might be considered a sufficient failing to constitute criminal fault and to support his punishment for rape. (As I will explain below, this insensitivity is distinct from negligence.) Sexual intercourse is the most intimate transaction between human beings, and only an extraordinary and troubling insensitivity could cause a man not to detect a woman's actual non-consent to sex. It might seem that criminal punishment is a heavy price to pay for insensitivity, but this may or may not be so, depending on what it is that the defendant is insensitive to. Fault is but an aspect of wrongdoing. The insensitivity involved in forgetting a wedding anniversary does not call for legal punishment. The insensitivity involved in having sex with an actually unwilling partner might well call for legal punishment.

Dirk lacks something that Aristotle called *aisthesis* and that David Wiggins translates as 'situational appreciation'.[14] A virtuous or law abiding person will see the circumstances that are the relevant starting points to normative deliberations; and he or she will also competently perceive when required to do so by moral or legal norms—as one might do when acting under a practical norm such as 'Take the bread out when it is brown enough'.[15] Conversely, one whose practical reasoning is deficient in *aisthesis* or situational appreciation might be neither virtuous nor law abiding. If this failure of situational appreciation occurs as part of some criminal conduct, then the actor will be criminally at fault.[16]

In Dirk's situation, a failure of *aisthesis*, of situational appreciation, is an adequate indication of fault—of disordered ends, and of the chronic failures of practical reasoning that are required to achieve and maintain that disorder. The insensitivity of a man who cannot detect the difference between feigned and genuine consent to sexual intercourse reflects a deficiency in practical reasoning that raises a legitimate public concern about the fitness of the individual to participate in society on a free and equal basis. The most likely explanations for Dirk's insensitivity reflect poorly on his character. If Dirk could not detect even a brief flicker of fear at the moment Violet thought she recognized him as a rapist, then it seems that he pays little

[14] David Wiggins, 'Deliberation and Practical Reason' in Amelie Rorty (ed.), *Essays on Aristotle's Ethics* (Berkeley: University of California Press, 1981), 232–3.

[15] T H Irwin, 'Ethics As An Inexact Science: Aristotle's Ambitions For Moral Theory', in B Hooker and M Little (eds), *Moral Particularism* (Oxford: Clarendon Press, 2000), 127–9.

[16] Just as the criminal law does not require virtue, but only law-abidingness, so not only vice, but also *akrasia*—a chronic failure to do the right thing even when one knows the right thing to do—can constitute fault. Kyron Huigens, 'On Aristotelian Criminal Law: A Reply to Duff' (2004) 18 *Notre Dame Journal of Law, Ethics & Public Policy* 465, 492–3.

attention to the interior lives of others. If, in spite of his not being indifferent to Violet's consent, Dirk was unable to sense her true wishes at any point during the extended period of time in which he flirted, engaged in foreplay, and had intercourse with her, then the likely explanation is that he is not good at ascertaining others' true wishes. If Dirk failed to spot Violet's non-consent in spite of her being as completely exposed to him as one's partner is during sex, then it seems fair to conclude that Dirk was too self-absorbed really to perceive Violet as human being instead of as a sexual device. If during foreplay and intercourse Dirk was so completely caught up in his own sexual response that he was oblivious of his partner in producing that response, he simply seems immature.[17] Dirk's insensitivity to Violet's actual non-consent calls into question the ways in which he values things and has arranged his standing motivations or ends. Regardless of the state of his intentions toward her non-consent on the occasion of his conduct, and also regardless of his reasonableness or unreasonableness regarding her non-consent on that occasion, Dirk's practical reasoning was deficient in a deeper, more persistent way that can constitute criminal fault, and that can support criminal liability—provided, as always, that this fault is determined in a way that meets the requirements of legality.

It is tempting to collapse the fault of insensitivity into the fault of negligence by saying that Dirk's insensitivity to the woman's condition constitutes his negligence toward her non-consent. But this is not quite right. Dirk was not, strictly speaking, unreasonable. Dirk is a sympathetic figure in this hypothetical in part because it appears that, had Dirk perceived his situation fully and accurately, then his deliberations, conclusions, and resulting actions would have stayed within morally and socially acceptable limits. Had he known that Violet thought he was the escaped rapist—perhaps had he even known there was an escaped rapist—Dirk would not have had sex with Violet. Dirk's failure was specifically and exclusively a failure of perception. Negligence is, in contrast, a failure to meet a standard of conduct—a failure to which misperception might contribute, but which is more centrally a failure to reason or to reason correctly in the face of *accurate* perception. Notice, on this point, that an actor is both more negligent and more clearly negligent as he is shown to have had more and more knowledge of his actual situation, while he persists in producing prohibited results or engaging in prohibited conduct. Negligence involves inadvertence, but insensitivity is only one potential cause of inadvertence. Furthermore, negligence by definition entails inadvertence regarding consequences and conduct, but only sometimes involves inadvertence toward the situation that presents the starting points of normative deliberations. Unreasonableness

[17] Incidentally, though it might read too much into the hypothetical to say so, if there was no point during sexual intercourse at which Violet could have realized that Dirk was too considerate and giving as a lover to be a rapist, then one almost has to conclude that Dirk was callous and obtuse in just the ways I have described.

and insensitivity are distinct failings—as is an attitude of indifference, as is an intention toward a prohibited act or result—and they indicate fault in different ways. The analysis of non-intentional fault will be better served if we distinguish insensitivity from unreasonableness, instead of conflating them under the heading of 'negligence'. Our palette of fault criteria is too limited as it is, and we would be unwise to use negligence as a catch-all category for many different kinds of non-intentional fault. Furthermore, it will be more difficult accurately to assess the adequacy of any fault criterion as a matter of legality if we lack a precise and accurate understanding of the criterion that is supposed to pick fault out.

With this understanding of the fault that might be found in Dirk's case, the question now is whether a set of offense elements that does not reference intentions, indifference, negligence, or any other explicit fault criterion can possibly perform the functions of fault and also meet our rule of law requirements. The danger to Dirk in this situation is that he will be convicted under a strict liability definition of rape, and to show that this will not necessarily follow is the best way to show that a strict liability rape definition does not offend against legality. Generally, however, the rule of law does not require offense definitions to tend toward producing either conviction or acquittal. The rule of law danger that concerns us, the danger specific to the definition of criminal offenses, is the danger that the moral assessment of the case will bleed though to the legal assessment of the case in a way that deprives the defendant of an effective legal defense to the criminal charge. Many criminal law scholars have thought that the most effective way to forestall this danger is to confine the jury's discretion to a descriptive finding of a state of affairs, specifically an intentional state of mind regarding the more prominent features of the prohibited conduct or result. *Morgan* demonstrates that this requirement is too rigid in rape cases (though perhaps not for other offenses), and that it concedes too little to the countervailing value of fine-grainedness. A negligence requirement concedes more to fine-grainedness, but perhaps not enough, for the reasons I have given above. Any alternative approach to the adjudication of fault in rape, however, must still meet the requirements of legality. The goal is balance. The question in the definition of rape is whether there is some set of material elements that can adequately, as a matter of legality, provide for the adjudication of fault in rape, without reference to either intentional states of mind or negligence.

To begin with, it is helpful to examine the nature of Violet's non-consent. Her non-consent is not due to literal involuntariness. Unlike the unconscious rape victim, she retained her capacity for choice throughout. She always had the option of refusing sex, and retained the capacity to refuse sex, even though the alternative (as she thought) was to be assaulted or killed. Her case is one, instead, of hard choice involuntariness. She is in the position of the bank employee with a gun being held to his head. He has the choice to refuse to open the vault and to have his head blown off instead. We describe his opening the vault as 'involuntary' because this is not much of a choice. So it is with Violet. Furthermore, Violet's refusal to have sex probably would have required (under the assumptions she was making at the time) physical resistance. It is possible the rapist would kill her instantly upon her saying 'No', but given that he is a crazed rapist and not a crazed murderer, we can assume that he would try to get what he really wants, sex, before killing his victim—and if the sex comes with a violent struggle, perhaps so much the better for him. Both of these considerations tell us that Violet's non-consent is inextricably bound up with another common element of rape: the use or threatened use of force.

It is hardly surprising, from this point of view, to discover that non-consent and force are often similarly bound up in the definition of rape. And yet the inclusion of force in the definition of rape sometimes has been thought to be problematic. Indeed, cases such as Violet's are thought to be paradigmatic of the problem. The inclusion of force as a necessary part of the proof means that rape cannot be proved in a case in which the defendant found it unnecessary to use force on the victim, even though she did not truly consent to sex with him. This describes a troubling number of cases in which we would otherwise say that rape has occurred. It may frequently be the case that the defendant has a well-established reputation for violence and is significantly larger in size than the victim is, and knowing that resistance to the defendant's demands would be futile, the victim gratifies him for only that reason. To add 'a threat of force' to the offense definition does not entirely solve the problem. Suppose the defendant has power, prestige, and authority to wield over the victim, and he successfully uses it to extort sex. Or, suppose the defendant has damaging information against the defendant and uses it to blackmail her, for sex. In order to treat these cases as the rapes they seem to be, at least one state has eliminated both force and threat of force as an element of rape by holding that proof of those elements of rape requires no more than proof of intercourse itself.[18]

Most states, however, have retained a force element, and it is worth our while to consider why they have done so. Surely the elimination of force or threat from the offense definition would expedite conviction in cases such as those I have just described. However, if the elements of force and non-consent can be woven together in the definition of rape in a way that brings out their complementarity instead of their conflict, then the offense definition will be more responsive to the particulars of individual cases and more likely to produce an acquittal or conviction that matches the informal, moral assessment of the case. In other words, it will serve fine-grainedness. More important, for present purposes, a rape definition that weaves together force and non-consent in the right way will facilitate the fair

[18] State ex rel. M. T. S., 609 A. 2d 1266 (N.J. 1995).

adjudication of the offense, because it will expand and complicate the prosecution's proof. It will offer the defendant not only additional opportunities to argue a failure of proof, but more generally an adequate formal mechanism to contest legal fault. In other words, the right combination of non-consent and force in the offense definition could serve the value of legality. Even without making reference to customary fault elements (such as intentional states or negligence) or relatively novel fault elements (such as indifference) the material elements of the offense could organize an inquiry into non-intentional fault that cabins the arguments of the prosecution and the discretion of the jury with sufficient formality to avoid a simple equation of moral and legal fault.

California's rape statute offers an example. In California, consent is defined as 'positive cooperation in act or attitude pursuant to an exercise of free will. The person must act freely and voluntarily...'[19] The extent to which this definition of consent is dependent on the notion of force becomes clear when one reads the related provisions that give meaning to the terms 'free will' and 'freely and voluntarily' in this context. Sexual intercourse is rape in California if, inter alia, 'it is accomplished against a person's will by means of force, violence, duress, menace, or fear of immediate and unlawful bodily injury on the person of another'.[20] Duress, in turn, is defined as:

> ...a direct or implied threat of force, violence, danger, or retribution sufficient to coerce a reasonable person of ordinary susceptibilities to perform an act which otherwise would not have been performed, or acquiesce in an act to which one otherwise would not have submitted. The total circumstances, including the age of the victim, and his or her relationship to the defendant, are factors to consider in appraising the existence of duress.[21]

An alternative definition of rape further provides that sexual intercourse is rape:

> Where the act is accomplished against the victim's will by threatening to retaliate in the future against the victim or any other person, and there is a reasonable possibility that the perpetrator will execute the threat. As used in this paragraph, 'threatening to retaliate' means a threat to kidnap or falsely imprison, or to inflict extreme pain, serious bodily injury, or death.[22]

Under these definitions, Violet's case, like the other cases involving non-consent but no force, can unquestionably be prosecuted and punished as rape. Because it draws on a multiplicity of force concepts—especially the assessment of 'retribution' in light of 'the total circumstances'—and then weaves non-consent and force together, the California statute overcomes the problem of the force element's simply undercutting the non-consent element and the vindication of sexual autonomy that proof of non-consent is meant

[19] California Penal Code § 261.6.
[20] California Penal Code § 261(a)(2).
[21] California Penal Code § 261(b).
[22] California Penal Code § 261(a)(6).

to provide. This complex weave of force and non-consent concepts ensures a fine-grained fault inquiry—one that tends to produce legal assessments that square with our moral assessments of the cases. More to the present point, however, the complex weave of force and non-consent structures the fault inquiry in such a way as to serve the countervailing value of legality as well.

In Violet's case, the prosecution might allege that rape was accomplished against her will by means of duress, menace, or fear in that the threat of force or violence from the escaped rapist (as she thought) coerced her to perform an act which otherwise would not have been performed. Alternatively, the prosecution might allege that rape was accomplished against her will by means of a threat to retaliate against her; specifically a threat to inflict extreme pain, serious bodily injury, or death. The most obvious line of defense for Dirk is that he had no intentional state of mind—no purpose, knowledge, intent to, intent that, or advertent recklessness—toward Violet's acting against her will; toward a threat, violence, or danger; toward threatened retaliation; and so on. If the statute were to be interpreted as not requiring the prosecution to prove any such intentional state of mind, but only to prove negligence, Dirk would still be in good shape. The fact that Dirk was unaware that there was a rapist on the loose would permit him to argue his innocence under a negligence standard.

The question we need to answer is whether Dirk can defend himself adequately without recourse to either of those arguments. He can. Sexual intercourse 'accomplished against a person's will ... by means of duress' etc., does not describe an act of Dirk. Likewise, in the alternative version, sexual intercourse 'accomplished against a victim's will ... by threatening' does not describe an act of Dirk. Dirk engaged in sexual intercourse and Violet engaged in sexual intercourse against her will, but it misdescribes Dirk's actions to say he *accomplished* sex against Violet's will. Violet acted against her will as a result of duress, fear, threat, and so on, but it misdescribes Dirk's action to say that he engaged in sex *by means of* any such thing. In short, it is not accurate to say that Violet *was* coerced—as opposed to her *feeling* coerced—if we cannot also say that Dirk did coerce her.

Now, it is true that the easiest way to convey that the acts described in the offense definition are misdescriptions of Dirk's act is to say that Dirk had no intention such that 'accomplished' and 'by means of' are accurate descriptions of his act.[23] This is why, in defining the act of rape, to require proof of such intentions might be our first choice. It will be most clear that the victim was coerced when we also can say that the defendant had an intention to coerce. Under a definition of rape that references an intention, Dirk would have a clear and powerful argument that the prosecution cannot prove its case. However, the question here is the general definition of rape, and in another case that we would assess morally as rape, a definition that requires

[23] Intentions are best thought of as part of act descriptions. Duff, above n. 8, at 129–35.

proof of such intentions will create a troubling and apparently intolerable gap between the legal assessment of rape and the moral assessment of rape. In other words, because of the prospect of a case such as *Morgan*, we will give up something on the side of legality in order to gain something on the side of fine-grainedness in our definition of rape.

The requirement that the prosecution prove negligence regarding the elements of rape might provide a better balance between legality and fine-grainedness, as *Morgan* certainly suggests. We have excluded negligence as a possible fault criterion for purposes of our analysis, but we should take a moment to examine how it provides this balance. A negligence requirement forces the prosecution to match its proof to a description of Dirk's act that does not refer to intentions, but that refers instead to a very wide range of factual, evaluative, and normative features of his act. The prosecution must show that Dirk failed to meet a standard of due care when he engaged in sex with Violet, based on the state of his knowledge at the time. The proof of this broader description of the act of rape serves fine-grainedness, but it also serves legality. It gives the defendant ample opportunity to deny that his act meets the description of the prohibited act. He can argue that his knowledge—including his not being aware even that an escaped rapist was at large—would not have led anyone to recognize a risk that Violet's consent might not be genuine. From this, he can argue against the inference that he ought not to have engaged in sex with Violet because of such a risk. The threat or duress that Violet experienced is undeniable, but it is insufficient to make Dirk's act of sexual intercourse rape under a negligence standard regarding non-consent.

Now the critical point: even without the kind of act description featured in a negligence requirement, the definition of rape in the California statute still gives the defendant opportunities to deny that his act matches the law's description of the prohibited act. The threat or duress that Violet experienced will be undeniable, but the prosecution will find it necessary as a practical matter to portray Dirk's act in such a way as to comprehend both this threat or duress as a feature of wrongdoing and also some aspect of that threat or duress that can be attributed to him. Otherwise, the prosecution runs the risk of acquittal—perhaps a nullifying acquittal, but one no less to be avoided for that. More significantly, the danger of a nullifying acquittal indicates that the value of fine-grainedness and the necessity of balancing legality with fine-grainedness constrain the prosecutor as well as the legislature. The prosecution cannot prosecute a case based on a hyper-technical, legalistic interpretation of the offense definition without undercutting the credibility of the criminal justice system—a danger brought home in the threat of a nullifying acquittal.

Barring argument based on intentions or negligence, the most plausible way for the prosecution to frame the act description of the offense in a way that will match the description of Dirk's act is the argument I described above, which links the threat or duress experienced by Violet to Dirk's act of sexual intercourse by means of an appeal to his apparent insensitivity. In other words, the prosecution will attempt to expand the statute's act description so that it comprehends not only the intercourse, non-consent, and force, duress, or threat, but also insensitivity. This appeal to interstitial fault will make the legal offense of rape almost perfectly congruent with a moral offense of rape so that fine-grainedness is served. However, the interstitial fault of insensitivity to non-consent in rape is highly dependent upon and effectively defined by the material elements of the offense. Dirk still has formal, legal means to argue that he was not insensitive in a way that matches even this fine-grained offense definition. He was insensitive to Violet's non-consent, perhaps, but the statute defines non-consensual sex only in terms of the victim's will being overborne by threat, duress, retribution, and so on. If Dirk is to be found guilty of rape under this offense definition, the prosecution will have to show that he was insensitive, not to non-consent, but instead to Violet's feigned or putative consent as it is specifically born of threat, duress, or retribution. Put another way, non-consent simpliciter is not an element of the proof of rape because it does not appear as such in the offense definition. Only non-consent resulting from particular causes appears in the offense definition, and the act description of the offense therefore refers only to those particular kinds of non-consent. Dirk can argue that he was not insensitive to that kind of non-consent, even if he may have been insensitive to non-consent more generally.

So long as Dirk has a formal opportunity to defend the legal case against him with the arguments in the preceding paragraph, the legal offense of rape does not completely collapse the legal assessment of Dirk's act as rape into the moral assessment of Dirk's act as rape, so as to deprive him of adequate formal avenues of defense in the criminal case. He has an opportunity to defend because of the way in which the definition of rape weaves non-consent and duress, retribution, and threat together into a complex act description that arguably does not match Dirk's act very well. (Note that the qualifiers in that sentence do not undermine the contention that legality is satisfied because Dirk has some formal opportunity to defend under the offense definition.) The arguments that Dirk must make against this criminal charge of rape will be substantively the same arguments that he will make against a moral charge of rape arising from the same incident. But so long as the legal definition of rape permits him a formal opportunity to make those arguments in the criminal case, the legal offense has not completely collapsed into the informal moral offense.

To see this more clearly, imagine Dirk's trial. Assuming, plausibly, that Dirk has no criminal record, he will be able to take the witness stand and describe his actions from his own point of view. A sharp prosecutor will object on relevance grounds to any express statement such as 'I honestly believed she consented', or 'I was careful to make sure that she consented'.

But a good defense attorney would still have ample opportunity to portray Dirk as anything but the callous, uncaring person the prosecution has portrayed in its case. Furthermore, a good defense attorney would be alert to evidence and argument from the prosecution that suggests that Dirk was anything more than callous and uncaring. If the offense definition does not premise rape on intentions or negligence, then evidence suggesting intentions or negligence is irrelevant, and argument addressing intentions or negligence is improper—no matter which side of the case it comes from. If the case is well tried from both sides in these respects, then the only reason to think that Dirk has committed rape will be that he was insensitive to Violet's fear and fear-inspired consent. That we do not know whether this argument would succeed or could be defeated on these facts tells us nothing more than the limits of hypothetical cases.

This trial scenario demonstrates that even a strict liability definition of rape—defined as rape premised on a non-intentional fault criterion consisting of (some of) the material elements of an offense—can structure the proof of rape so as to serve the value of legality. But an important corollary of my analysis lurks in this scenario, and it should be spelled out because it provides a doctrinal reason to adopt the analysis—and thereby provides another reason to think that strict liability offenses need not offend against legality. Because strict liability on the conventional understanding is seen as relief from the requirement to prove fault, instead of as a different kind of fault criterion, it seems that the prosecutor need not prove intentional fault or negligence, but that she may do so if she wishes. It is not at all clear, on the conventional understanding of strict liability, that she should be barred from suggesting that the defendant acted intentionally, with indifference, or with negligence. My analysis of strict liability makes it clear that any suggestion of intentional fault, indifference, or negligence from the prosecution should be barred from evidence, and why this is so. Strict liability is not the absence of criminal fault, and a strict liability offense does not simply relieve the prosecution of the necessity of proving criminal fault. Strict liability offenses turn on a different kind of criminal fault—different from intentions, indifference, and negligence. The prosecution is required to prove the fault prescribed by the offense, and it cannot be permitted do so by proving a different kind of fault. If the prosecution's proof of fault suggests intentions, indifference, or negligence, then it should be objected to and excluded as irrelevant and prejudicial.[24] If this is done—as it is in the trial of Dirk's case that I imagined above—then the proof of fault in rape will be structured in such a way as to serve the value of legality well.

Even accepting that legality is served by this strict liability definition of rape, it does not follow that strict liability rape ought to be adopted. That

[24] In other words non-intentional fault criteria—and especially those that consist of a set or sub-set of offense elements—do not 'nest' as intentional states are said to do in, for example, Model Penal Code § 2.02(5).

question, as I have suggested, turns on whether the values of legality and fine-grainedness are brought into a morally acceptable balance in the offense definition. One could well argue that the definition of rape that I have described above concedes too much to fine-grainedness. The moral case for treating Dirk's actions as rape that I have outlined is, perhaps, one that few would endorse even as a moral assessment. If so, then to accommodate it in the legal definition of rape might seem to be unnecessary or morally wrong. Negligence might serve us better. However, the substantive disposition of that moral controversy is beyond the scope of the present paper. It suffices for present purposes to conclude that a sound argument can be made for strict liability rape, properly understood.

5. Conclusion

Is strict liability rape defensible? Yes, at least one particular kind of strict liability rape is quite defensible, even if we might conclude, ultimately, that we do not wish to adopt it. The same might be said of strict liability rape premised on minority; or on the mental or physical incapacitation of the victim; or even on a different set or subset of rape's material elements. Each of these rape definitions has to be assessed separately for the moral adequacy of its balance between legality and fine-grainedness. For now, however, we know that the answer to such an inquiry is not necessarily 'no'.

10

Merger and Felony Murder

Claire Finkelstein*

1. Introduction

Felony murder has been controversial among American commentators for years.[1] They see American criminal law as uncivilized, relative to other English-speaking nations, and urge the United States to follow the example of Great Britain, which abolished felony murder by legislation,[2] and Canada, which found it unconstitutional.[3] The central objection American criminal law scholars level at the doctrine is that it is a form of strict liability, and they see strict liability for serious crimes as morally unacceptable.[4] What makes matters worse, from their point of view, is that no one has a clear view of the purpose of the felony murder doctrine.[5] This makes it difficult to resolve borderline cases, as there are no underlying principles to guide their determination. The result is that the felony murder rule ends up being intolerably ad hoc.

Nevertheless, there seems little chance the felony murder rule will be abolished in the United States any time soon. It is a much favored tool of American prosecutors, and is available in the vast majority of American jurisdictions.[6] Despite their grave misgivings about the doctrine, then, it might behoove criminal law scholars to consider ways of improving the rule and its application, rather than treating current practice as an all-or-nothing

* The author wishes to thank Antony Duff, Kim Ferzan, Stuart Green, and Leo Katz for comments on various drafts of the present work.

[1] See J C Jeffries and P B Stephan, 'Defenses, Presumptions, and Burden of Proof in the Criminal Law' (1979) 88 *Yale Law Journal* 1325, 1387 (noting 'at least fifty years of sustained academic and judicial hostility' to felony murder). George Fletcher, *Rethinking Criminal Law* (Boston: Little, Brown, 1978), § 4.4; James J Hippard, Sr., 'The Unconstitutionality of Criminal Liability without Fault: An Argument for a Constitutional Doctrine of *Mens Rea*' (1973) 10 *Houston Law Review* 1039, 1045.

[2] Homicide Act 1957.

[3] *Regina v Martineau* (1990) 58 C.C.C. (3d) 353 (Alta. C.A.).

[4] Nelson E Roth and Scott E Sundby, 'The Felony Murder Rule: A Doctrine at Constitutional Crossroads' (1985) 70 *Cornell Law Review* 446, 448.

[5] For a thorough account of the historical origins of the American felony murder, see Guyora Binder, 'The Origins of American Felony Murder Rules' (2004) 57 *Stanford Law Review* 59.

[6] See Kevin Cole, 'Killing During Crime: Toward a Discriminating Theory of Strict Liability' (1990) 28 *American Criminal Law Review* 73, 74, 77.

proposition. What follows is a suggestion toward such incremental improvement.

It is the contention of this chapter that the greatest source of inconsistency in the application of the felony murder rule lies in the tests used to identify which felonies can serve as predicate felonies. There are two requirements that are commonly imposed in American jurisdictions. The first is that the felony must be 'inherently dangerous', a requirement that has mostly been articulated in jurisdictions where the basis for the felony murder rule is common law, rather than statutory. In these jurisdictions, a felony like fraud or theft will not support a charge of felony murder, even if it gives rise to death, because, considered in the abstract, fraud is not a dangerous act.[7] In states where the felony murder rule is statutory, the same principle has been adhered to in the legislatively specified list of acceptable predicate felonies, which is restricted to acts that would count as inherently dangerous in their common law cousins.

The second is the requirement that the predicate felony not merge with the homicide. The doctrine of merger restricts acceptable predicate felonies by treating certain felonies as inseparable from the homicides to which they give rise. The paradigm case is the killing that takes place in the course of an assault. The doctrine of merger says that the assault 'merges' with the homicide, with the result that prosecutors cannot avoid proving the *mens rea* for murder by tying the murder charge to the assault charge. Armed robbery, by contrast, will usually support a charge of felony murder, since the predicate felony is sufficiently distinct from the homicide.

My focus in what follows will be on the merger doctrine. It is here that the felony murder rule encounters its greatest source of confusion, with results that sometimes border on incoherence. In particular, the rule often has the effect of making it easier for prosecutors to prosecute defendants who have committed less severe crimes, as compared with those who have committed more serious ones. The person who assaults his victim with a deadly weapon can only be convicted if prosecutors can prove he *intended* to kill or had one of the other acceptable mental states for murder, such as knowledge or reckless indifference. The person who burgles a home in order to steal the television set, and accidentally kills the homeowner who happens upon him in fright, by contrast, can be convicted of murder on the basis of the burglary and the death of the victim alone. Worse, the parent who intentionally beats his child, causing the child's death, cannot be convicted of murder unless prosecutors can show that he intended to kill or at least knew he

[7] *People v Phillips*, 414 P. 2d 353 (1966). A minority of jurisdictions, however, apply a more liberal version of the 'inherently dangerous' test. Such jurisdictions require that the felony be dangerous 'in the particular' rather than in the abstract. For example, in *State v Goodseal*, 553 P. 2d 279 (Kan. 1977), the court said that one should consider 'both the nature of the offense in the abstract and the circumstances of its commission in determining whether a particular felony was inherently dangerous to human life'.

probably would. But the parent who is guilty of neglecting his child by failing to feed her, thus causing death, can often be convicted of murder without the prosecutor's having to prove the *mens rea* for murder. The result is that defendants will be acquitted of murder in a number of more serious cases, where they would often have been convicted had they committed a less serious crime that could serve as the predicate felony for a felony murder prosecution.

Not only do such results seem ad hoc, but it is hard even to imagine what a rationale for a doctrine with such wildly inconsistent outcomes could look like. Felony murder cannot be charged unless the predicate felony is sufficiently *serious*, under the inherently dangerous rule. But if the predicate felony is in the class of assault-like offenses, the merger doctrine will make felony murder unavailable again. The felony murder rule thus appears to make prosecution in the absence of *mens rea* possible in a middle tier of cases. What could the rationale for such a rule be? If the rationale were that such cases are *particularly* serious and so call for putting a thumb on the prosecution's side of the scale, it would not make sense to exempt crimes like assault from the list of predicate felonies. If, on the other hand, one were to argue that strict liability for murder should be acceptable in such cases because murders in this category are *less* serious, imposing the inherently dangerous rule would make little sense. In many jurisdictions, moreover, it is not the case that felony murder is punishable less severely than intentional murder. Thus distinguishing such cases at the level of *mens rea* is a curious thing to do.

Over the years, courts in various jurisdictions have proposed a number of quite different tests for solving the merger problem. There seems to be general agreement that assault and assault-type felonies should merge with the homicide, while felonies like armed robbery should not. But there are a host of grey area cases, such as burglary, felony child abuse, kidnapping, poisoning, and arson, where results are highly variable, both across jurisdictions and within a single jurisdiction. There are also a number of related doctrines, such as misdemeanor-manslaughter, where courts have been uncertain whether merger should apply. Adding to the overall inconsistency is the fact that some jurisdictions have eliminated the merger doctrine all together.

In what follows, I shall argue that courts fail to perceive the only possible rationale for the merger rule that makes any sense of the doctrine. In particular, they often take a functionalist view of merger—relating it to the general deterrence aims of the criminal law. I shall argue, by contrast, that the reason for having a merger doctrine is not functional but structural: if we are to have a form of liability in which we punish a person for killing in the process of committing a felony, the defendant must have done two things—performed a separate felony and killed. Once we understand what is required in philosophical terms for this to be the case, the doctrine will no longer seem so mysterious and the range of its application will be substantially clearer. The approach to merger I shall develop will not eliminate all the objections to the felony murder rule. In particular, it will do nothing to cure the basic objection of those who think it immoral to punish for serious offenses in the absence of *mens rea*, and it fails to address sources of inconsistency other than merger. But if I am correct that the merger doctrine currently provides the greatest source of inconsistency in the application of the felony murder rule, straightening out mergers should improve felony murder substantially. Moreover, once we understand the underlying logic of the merger doctrine, we will see that the problem of merger bears important affinities to other criminal law problems, such as double jeopardy, common law merger, and the voluntary act requirement. The merger doctrine itself will thus appear to descend from a set of more general principles relating to divisions among criminal acts.

2. Prevailing Approaches to Merger

The doctrine of merger is often traced to the California case of *People v Ireland*.[8] In that case, the defendant drew a gun and shot his wife, killing her. The jury was instructed that it could find the defendant guilty of second degree felony murder if it determined that the homicide occurred during the commission of an assault with a deadly weapon. The California Supreme Court struck down the conviction, on the ground that this approach allowed for a kind of 'bootstrapping': it allowed prosecutors to convert what would ordinarily be a straightforward murder case, involving only one crime, into a felony murder case, by separating off an assault and treating the killing as the result of the assault. Instead, the court maintained that 'a second degree felony murder instruction may not properly be given when it is based upon a felony which is an integral part of the homicide and which the evidence produced by the prosecution show to be an offense included in fact within the offense charged'.[9]

Ireland was quickly extended to more far-reaching situations. In *People v Wilson*,[10] the defendant broke into his estranged wife's apartment with a shotgun, where he fatally shot a man he encountered in the living room. He then proceeded to the bathroom where he killed his wife. His conviction for felony murder for both killings was reversed under *Ireland*. The argument was that the predicate felony of burglary was established solely in virtue of the fact that the defendant entered the apartment with intent to commit an assault with a deadly weapon, a felony that would normally merge with the homicide. The court held that this use of the felony murder rule involved the same kind of bootstrapping condemned in *Ireland*,

[8] 70 Cal. 2d 522 (1969). [9] *Id.* at 539. [10] 1 Cal. 3d 431 (1969).

and that the deterrent purpose of the felony murder rule is only relevant in application to a felony that is independent of the homicide. And in *People v Sears*,[11] the defendant broke into a dwelling for the purpose of killing his estranged wife, and ended up accidentally killing her daughter when the latter intervened. The lower court thought the burglary with intent to assault the wife could serve as the predicate felony for killing the daughter. The California Supreme Court, however, thought it anomalous 'to place the person who intends to attack one person and in the course of the assault kills another inadvertently or in the heat of battle in a worse position than the person who from the outset intended to attack both persons and killed one or both'.[12] Accordingly, the court once again applied the merger doctrine, rendering prosecution for felony murder unavailable.

The *Sears* court was of course correct that the results of applying the merger doctrine in that case would have been anomalous. Why should a person who kills accidentally find himself in a worse position than one who kills intentionally? Yet the anomalousness of the doctrine is not avoided by taking the *Sears* approach to burglary. For it will still be possible to construct side-by-side cases whose differential treatment seems ad hoc in this same way. Consider, for example, the varying approach to felony child abuse. The best known case in this area is *People v Smith*,[13] in which a child of two underwent severe beatings and other physical abuses from which she died later that day. The California Supreme Court applied the *Ireland* rule, saying that merger should apply where the purpose of the child abuse is the 'very assault that resulted in death'.[14] Furthermore, following a post-*Ireland* case involving armed robbery,[15] the court said that the defendant must have had an 'independent felonious purpose' in committing the predicate felony. The court pointed out that to refuse merger would allow the prosecution to bootstrap this case into murder 'merely because the victim was a child rather than an adult'. The court distinguished, however, cases of passive child abuse like *People v Shockley*, where the child's death followed from malnutrition and dehydration. Here the court found that the felony was 'independent' and 'not related to the assault causing the murder'.[16] Thus the court was able to preserve the symmetry of the adult assault cases and the child abuse cases, but only at the cost of distinguishing direct child abuse from passive dehydration and nutrition.

It would of course be possible to avoid the asymmetry between active and passive child abuse by revising the rule in cases like *Shockley* to hold that the passive abuse in that case merges with the homicide. That would make for consistent results between adult assault cases (like *Ireland*) and child abuse cases, as well as between the burglary cases (like *Wilson* and *Sears*) and the assault cases. But an asymmetry would now exist between the

[11] 2 Cal. 3d 180 (1970). [12] *Id.* at 188. [13] 678 P. 2d 886 (1984).
[14] *Id.* at 890. [15] *People v Burton*, 6 Cal. 3d 375 (1971).
[16] 79 Cal. App. 3d 669 (1978).

Shockley-type case and other cases where merger does not normally apply, such as kidnapping[17] or poisoning food, drink or medicine.[18] Normally, kidnapping is both inherently dangerous and independent of any resulting homicide, so that felony murder is available. But one might question the logic of making it harder to prosecute a parent who deliberately fails to feed or otherwise care for her child than the non-violent kidnapper who has no intent of harming the child but nevertheless causes an accidental death. Perhaps more anomalous is the comparison between the parent who assaults his child, with the result that the child dies, and the parent who *poisons* his child, with the same result. The former would now be harder to convict than the latter, because in the first case the predicate felony of assault would merge with the homicide, whereas in the second case the predicate felony of poisoning would not.

The reasoning of the *Smith* case is typical, in that courts tend to take a fairly result-oriented approach to merger. Even *Ireland* cited a largely pragmatic rationale for the doctrine, saying that its application to this case would 'extend[] the operation of that rule "beyond any rational function that it is designed to serve" ', and that it would 'effectively preclude the jury from considering the issue of malice aforethought in all cases wherein homicide has been committed as a result of a felonious assault—a category which includes the great majority of all homicides'.[19] But distinguishing the felonies that merge from those that do not in pragmatic terms obscures any hope one might have of rationalizing the merger doctrine. The question is whether the doctrine has an analytical core that would rationalize the various cases. Few courts have conducted any kind of search for a theoretical core of this sort. Among the few that have, several approaches have been proposed to resolve hard cases. The most prevalent of these is one already mentioned, namely that the predicate felony must be based on an 'independent felonious purpose' from the killing.[20] At first glance, the test may seem promising. Assault merges with the homicide, for example, because the purpose of assault is to harm the victim, and it is this intent that produces the victim's death. On the other hand, where the defendant's purpose is armed robbery, the death is entirely beside the point of the defendant's activity. Arguably, moreover, the test can also capture the distinction between active and passive child abuse. In active child abuse, where the predicate felony normally merges, the defendant's felonious purpose is to harm the child, and the death is the culmination of that purpose. But where the defendant passively fails to feed the child, or takes insufficient care against environmental or other hazards, the defendant's purpose is ancillary to the resulting homicide.

[17] *People v Kelso*, 64 Cal. App. 3d 538, 542 (1976).

[18] *People v Mattison*, 4 Cal. 3d 177 (1971).

[19] *Ireland*, 70 Cal. 2d. at 539.

[20] *People v Burton*, 6 Cal. 3d 375 (1971).

The independent felonious purpose test, however, is not as successful as it might seem. First, notice that the distinction between active and passive child abuse does not in fact receive much support from that test. After all, passive child abuse can be entirely purposeful. Moreover, the test even runs into difficulty as restricted to active child abuse. Courts have sometimes denied merger in these cases on the ground that the parent's purpose was to discipline the child, not to abuse him or her. But presumably that is very often the case in child abuse cases, and it would be exceedingly odd to make it *easier* to prosecute the same acts of child abuse when the parents have a punitive, rather than a sadistic, purpose. The independent felonious purpose test is not even entirely compelling as applied to assault. A defendant who intends to harm his victim by beating him up very likely does not have the purpose of inflicting sufficient harm on him to kill him. And if this is so, then how can this test maintain that the felonious purpose in this case—which involves wounding—is not independent of the homicide, where the intention normally required for murder is an intent to kill (or knowledge of or extreme indifference to the possibility of killing)? From the defendant's standpoint, the killing is once again entirely 'beside the point', just as the death of the victim is beside the point of armed robbery.

A second test that has appeared in some of the cases is called the 'same act doctrine', according to which the predicate felony merges with the homicide if it was 'the same act' that was clearly dangerous to human life and which caused the death of the victim. This is the best of the established tests for merger.

The problem with the same act doctrine, however, is that it is unattended by any accompanying theory of the crucial underlying concept of an 'act'. The result is that the cases articulating the same act doctrine do not give it a terribly consistent formulation. Thus in *Garrett v State*,[21] the defendant pulled a gun on a clerk in a store in order to scare the latter during an altercation. The gun accidentally discharged, and the clerk was killed. The Texas Court of Criminal Appeals held that the crime of aggravated assault—based on the act of brandishing a weapon—could not supply the predicate felony for felony murder, as the aggravated assault and the act which caused the homicide were one and the same.[22] But in *Murphy v State*,[23] the court rejected the same act doctrine, under circumstances one would have thought equally suited to the theory. In that case, the defendant set a dwelling on fire in order to collect on the insurance, with the unintended result that someone inside the house was killed. The defendant argued, under *Garrett*, that the act—starting a fire—was the 'exact same act alleged to have been clearly dangerous to human life', and which caused

[21] 573 S.W. 2d 543 (Tex. Crim. App. [Panel Op.] 1978).
[22] *Id.* at 545–6.
[23] 665 S.W. 2d 116 (Tex. Crim. App. 1983).

the death of the victim.[24] The court, however, said that the act of arson and the resulting homicide were 'not one and the same', but it offered no basis for its holding.[25] If *brandishing a gun* is identical to the killing in *Garrett*, then it seems probable that *starting a fire* is identical to the killing in *Murphy*. But until we have a clearer conception of the meaning of 'act', and we have a clearer conception of how to distinguish acts from one another, we will not be able to make sense of a test like the same act test.

Notice, moreover, that the same act test contains an important ambiguity. Consider once again the scenario described in *Garrett*, where the defendant went into a store and held up the clerk, but let us assume this time that the defendant did this in order to demand the money from the cash register, rather than as part of an altercation. On the basis of the act of brandishing a gun, let us imagine the defendant is charged with armed robbery, rather than aggravated assault. If, as before, the gun goes off, will we be prepared to say that the predicate felony of armed robbery merges with the homicide? That would fly in the face of the standard approach to merger, as armed robbery is always the classic example of a crime that does not merge. But here the robbery charge would be based on the same underlying act used to establish aggravated assault in the actual case. And clearly aggravated assault merges with the homicide if anything does. Thus the 'same act' test requires an important piece of clarification: is it the underlying act itself that is used to test for merger, or something like a paradigm act normally used as the basis for charging a crime of a certain sort?

A third approach (not quite a 'test') is to appeal as much as possible to legislative judgment. There are two forms this approach takes—the first is found in common law jurisdictions, and the second in jurisdictions where felony murder is established by statute. In the former, where the *mens rea* for murder is established by statute and the felony murder provision is common law, the argument would run like this.[26] The legislature has established an intent requirement for various crimes, and these legislative judgments would be obscured if courts failed to apply the merger doctrine in various instances. This is supposed to supply the rationale for treating assault as merging with the felony: since every murder, or nearly every murder, contains an assault within it, the legislature's specified *mens rea* for murder would be entirely subverted if assault did not merge, and no meaning could be established for that segment of the relevant penal code establishing an intent or knowledge requirement for murder. On

[24] *Id.* at 119.
[25] *Id.*
[26] California provides the best example of such a scheme, where the murder provision requires a *mens rea* of 'malice aforethought' and no mention is made of convicting for murder in the absence of *mens rea*, as would be the case in a felony murder prosecution.

this rationale, it is acceptable to treat predicate felonies such as armed robbery or kidnapping as sufficiently separate from the resulting homicide, because there will still be murder cases left to give effect to any intent requirement if homicides resulting from these crimes are prosecuted without intent.[27]

This worry about legislative deference, however, seems to be selective and unjustified. Notice that if murder requires intent to kill, knowledge of killing, or extreme indifference to the prospect of killing, then *any* time a murder conviction is won on felony murder grounds the statutory provision for murder will have been obviated. If the legislature did not specifically exempt certain kinds of murder from its mental state requirements, the legislature's express provisions have been ignored. On the other hand, once one accepts that the legislatively established murder provision can be ignored to the extent of allowing *any* felony murder prosecution, there is no reason to object to any particular prosecution that ignores the established *mens rea* for murder. Thus it is hard to see how the worry about legislative deference would allow some felony murder prosecutions and eliminate others.

The second appeal to legislative deference appears in jurisdictions where the felony murder rule is established by statute, rather than common law. Here the argument is to treat the statutory list of predicate felonies as preempting the question of merger, and simply assume that any predicate felony on the list does not merge with the homicide, no matter what the underlying facts. In *People v Miller*, for example, the New York Court of Appeals took this approach to the predicate felony of burglary.[28] The facts were roughly the same as those of the *Sears* case. The court rejected the California approach, arguing that the fact that the New York Legislature had included burglary on the list of predicate felonies meant that burglary did not merge. This, it said, reflected a legislative judgement that 'persons within domiciles are in greater peril from those entering the domicile with criminal intent, than persons on the street who are being subjected to the same criminal intent'.[29] The New York Legislature, however, had not specifically addressed the question of merger, and there is no particular reason to suppose that they had attended to the difference

[27] A good example of this type of approach is *People v Watters*, where the court applied this doctrine to the misdemeanor–manslaughter doctrine, the misdemeanor version of the felony murder rule, 212 Cal. Rpt. 71 (1985). The court held that the *Ireland* rule 'simply has no room to operate', *id.*, in the misdemeanor-manslaughter situation, on the grounds that manslaughter itself is killing without malice, and the mental state for that crime is adequately established by whatever mental state is required for the misdemeanor. Thus if recklessness was required to prove child endangerment, that mental state must be adequate to establish the manslaughter charge as well. In other words, there is no worry about obviating a legislative decision to require intent.

[28] 297 N.E. 2d 85 (1973).

[29] *Id.* at 86.

between a defendant who breaks into the victim's dwelling in order to attack him and a defendant who attacks his victim on the latter's front steps.

Now the *Miller* court may have been right to think that attacks in dwellings pose a special danger that out-of-doors attacks do not. But presumably there would have been a more straightforward way for the legislature to increase the deterrent pressure on such defendants, which is to augment the penalties for indoor homicides over and above those for other kinds of homicides. And meanwhile, it would have made more sense for the court to read the New York statute as including burglary among the predicate felonies *except in those instances in which the burglary merges with the resulting homicide*, and then search for a test that will tell us when this is so. In other words, whether a predicate felony merges with the homicide should depend on the act in virtue of which the defendant satisfies the predicate offense definition. The better test is act-by-act rather than felony-by-felony. For this reason, statutory jurisdictions should not be in a substantially different position from common law jurisdictions where the question of merger is concerned.

Finally, in view of the difficulties with the various approaches to the merger doctrine, several jurisdictions have decided to proceed without any merger doctrine whatsoever. One problem with such jurisdiction however, is that any unintentional killing can be prosecuted as felony murder if the killing occurred in the course of a purposeful assault.[30] Moreover, what would be the result if the defendant has a valid provocation defense that would reduce his conviction from murder to manslaughter? Since prosecutors can take any *intentional* killing and prosecute it on the basis of felony murder instead of purpose or knowledge, they could eliminate any opportunity for defendants to claim provocation. Moreover, the absence of merger would affect even the ordinary kind of manslaughter case, the kind predicated on a *mens rea* of recklessness. A large number of these cases would get bumped up to murder, as long as these reckless killings involved brandishing a weapon or other form of assault.

Thus none of the prevailing approaches to merger appears to provide a principled basis for the doctrine, and eliminating the doctrine altogether does not appear to constitute an improvement. Let us therefore wipe the slate clean and see whether we can provide an alternative account of the logic behind the doctrine of merger.

[30] But arguably this would not lead to objectionable results across the board, since it would merely result in homicide convictions for defendants who intend to inflict grievous bodily injury, with the result that the victim dies. In the wake of the 1957 Homicide Act in Britain, this became the established rule. And thus the absence of merger would arguably introduce into American jurisdictions the British interpretation of malice aforethought.

3. The Redescriptive Test

Before considering what role the merger rule ought to play, let us re-examine the purpose of the doctrine itself. One of the most common rationales offered for felony murder is the advantage it affords the state in meeting its deterrence goals. The deterrence argument has been widely criticized, on the ground that the homicide in felony murder prosecutions is unintentional, and that it is not possible to deter unintentional acts.[31] This criticism, however, misses its mark. The deterrence argument in favor of the felony murder rule is quite legitimate: One way to further deter burglary, robbery, rape, etc., is to add punishment for the unintended homicides that result from these acts to the punishment for the acts themselves.

The problem is not so much that there are no deterrence benefits to punishing felony murder, but that achieving these benefits in this way is arbitrary. For if the legislature wanted to increase penalties for the underlying predicate felony, it could always do so directly, and with greater precision, by simply increasing the penalties for those felonies. A better deterrence argument sometimes offered is that the felony murder rule encourages those committing property and other non-violent offenses to commit their crimes carefully, in order to maximize the chances that no lives are accidentally lost. But this rationale suffers from the same defect as the previous one, just in more sophisticated guise. For if we wish to increase penalties for non-violent felonies that are not committed carefully, it would be better to do so directly, rather than focusing exclusively on that subset of sloppily committed felonies that actually result in death. Thus although the felony murder rule does indeed enhance deterrence, it does so in a highly ad hoc fashion, one that a rational legislature would presumably want to eschew.

A better explanation for the felony murder rule looks to the moral foundations of the doctrine. As Jim Gordley has so eloquently documented in exploring the history of transferred intent doctrines, canon law had traditionally regarded a person as responsible for all the bad effects of his intentional wrongdoing.[32] The philosopher Elizabeth Anscombe explains this doctrine as the rule that 'a man is responsible for the bad consequences of his bad actions, but gets no credit for the good ones; and contrariwise is not responsible for the bad consequences of good actions'.[33] Any other view, she thinks, is not compatible with the Christian (and anti-consequentialist)

[31] See Roth and Sundby, above n. 4.

[32] James Gordley, 'Responsibility in Crime, Tort, and Contract for the Unforeseeable Consequences of an Intentional Wrong: A Once and Future Rule?', in Peter Cane and Jane Stapleton (eds.), *The Law of Obligations: Essays in Celebration of John Fleming* (Oxford: Oxford University Press, 1998), 175.

[33] G E M Anscombe, 'Modern Moral Philosophy', in her *Ethics, Religion and Politics* (Oxford: Blackwell, 1981), vol. III: Collected Papers, 35–6.

teaching that some actions are, in their nature, wrong, and may not be performed for any reason having to do with the balance of consequences. She points out that if a person were to receive 'credit' for the good consequences of his bad actions, a bad act could be rendered permissible by assessing the balance of *its* consequences. And this is what she takes a non-consequentialist Christian ethics to be denying. On the other hand, a person who performs a bad action has nothing to shield him from the bad consequences he brings about. Unlike the person whose act is good, he can offer no justification for his behavior, and thus he is responsible for whatever occurs as a result of what he does.

The doctrine of felony murder is a descendant of this Catholic doctrine, albeit one that presents a sharply limited version of the rule. It does not hold a defendant who commits an illegal act responsible for any inadvertent harm that occurs as a result of his wrongdoing, but instead restricts the reach of the doctrine to cases where the bad consequence is someone's death. It also limits the reach of the doctrine by restricting the relevant acts to illegal acts that are felonies (and in some jurisdictions to those that are inherently dangerous). Despite these alterations of the original deontological doctrine, the felony murder rule is of a piece with this non-consequentialist teaching, and cannot be explained in functionalist terms.

Let us now turn to the topic of merger. At base, the felony murder doctrine says that when the defendant does one forbidden thing (meeting certain specifications), and in the course of so doing he does *another* forbidden thing (meeting certain other specifications) it is not necessary for him to have had any awareness of the latter for him to be guilty of a crime for having done it. That is, the second activity need not have involved a second intentional wrong for the defendant to be responsible for it as a separate offense. At a minimum, this suggests something rather fundamental about the structure of felony murder: there must have been two *separate* things the defendant did. The further specifications, of course, are that the first thing must be a felony (and the right kind of felony, whatever we require) and the second thing must be a killing. From the above formulation, we can infer the central idea behind the doctrine of merger: a potential predicate felony merges with the homicide when the defendant's performing that activity just *is* his killing of the victim. In other words, it is an analytically necessary part of felony murder that there be, at a minimum, two separate things the defendant is doing: one that counts as a felony that is not a killing, and another that is a killing. Merger takes place when instead of two activities, we have only one.

Now it might be tempting to think that any time there is a predicate felony like 'armed robbery', 'burglary', or 'child abuse', there must be a second act or activity which is separate from the act which is the killing. For on the face of it, the acts required to commit a burglary are different from the acts involved in killing. But the problem is that it is often possible that the same act or course of conduct gives rise to more than one criminal charge. And it would seem to follow that where we have two separate chargeable crimes—such as burglary and murder—we still know nothing about whether the defendant was in fact engaged in more than one activity. For if the offense definition for burglary requires that the defendant 'enter a building', it is possible that the defendant actually killed by, or in, performing that very act. Alternatively, the defendant might have satisfied the *actus reus* called for in the offense definition for burglary first, and then performed some second act that produced the victim's death. We thus require a test that will look past the charges to the underlying behavior of the defendant, and figure out whether, in committing several crimes, the defendant in fact was doing only one thing or was doing more than one thing.

Let us begin by interpreting the merger doctrine as requiring that the defendant perform two separate *acts*. We will then need to know what precisely is meant by the notion of an act. The standard philosophical account of this question says that if Harold fires a gun, for example, then *firing the gun* is an act just in case there is some description of it under which Harold did it intentionally. And Harold can be said to have done something intentionally just in case there was something he wanted in doing it and he believed that doing that thing would conduce to give him what he wanted. Since Harold fired the gun in order to warn Frank that he meant business, there was something he wanted in firing the gun and he believed that firing it would help him secure it. The event of Harold's firing the gun is thus intentional under a description like 'Harold's issuing a warning', and the event which is Harold's firing the gun is an act in its own right.

Suppose, then, we understand the requirement that there be a predicate felony and a killing as meaning that there must have been a separate act, in the above sense, for each. The question in each case of merger would be whether the killing was attributable to a person as a separate act, or whether it was simply *another way of talking about* an act he had already performed. The answer to this question is discovered by applying what I shall call the 'redescriptive' test: if the act in virtue of which the defendant satisfies the offense definition for the predicate felony can itself be redescribed in terms of the resulting death, we have only one act under two different descriptions. If, on the other hand, the act cannot be redescribed in terms of the victim's death, but the defendant did in fact cause the victim's death by performing some act, then the act whereby the defendant satisfies the predicate felony and the act whereby he caused the victim's death are separate. In the first case, the predicate felony should merge with the homicide, and felony murder would be unavailable. In the second case, as long as the second act causing death was performed in the same course of conduct or criminal transaction as the non-homicidal felony, the two acts do not merge and the first can supply the predicate for the second, homicidal act.

This test would produce fairly intuitive results for a range of cases. In general, burglary would tend to provide a basis for a felony murder charge, since most killings do not take place merely by the defendant entering or remaining in a building. But assault, in general, would not, as a killing that takes place in the course of an assault is usually straightforwardly caused by that assault, and thus the assault and the killing are one and the same act under different descriptions. Similarly, armed robbery would tend not to merge, whereas felony child abuse (as it is assaultive in nature) usually will. Other crimes, such as arson, can presumably go either way, but if the killing takes place as a direct result of the setting of the fire, in all likelihood the arson and the homicide will merge, and felony murder should not be available.

There is, however, a problem with the redescriptive test we must now address, namely that the test appears to be over-inclusive. For according to the standard action theoretic account, an action can *always* be redescribed in terms of its consequences. If Harry moves his finger, with the consequence that the trigger of the gun he is holding moves, we can redescribe Harry's act of moving his finger as 'pulling the trigger'. And if a further consequence of his action (of moving his finger) is that the gun he is holding fires, we can once again redescribe his action (of moving his finger) as 'firing a gun'. The standard account (as most clearly articulated by the philosopher Donald Davidson) says that the same is true for all the consequences of a person's action.[34] If one of the consequences of Harry's moving his finger is that Frank dies, we can redescribe Harry's action as *killing Frank*. The redescription holds whether or not he intended to kill Frank or even knew that by moving his finger, he would cause Frank's death. Since something is an action just in case there is some description under which it was someone's doing something intentionally, then as long as Harry moved his finger intentionally, and as long as his so moving caused Frank's death, killing Frank is an action Harry performed, under one of its many descriptions.

The problem, then, is that it looks as though by this test, *every* predicate felony will merge with its resulting homicide, since the defendant must have caused the victim's death, and so will have produced the death as a consequence, if felony murder is even a possibility.[35] Felony murder, therefore, will never be available, and it looks as though the redescriptive test will have eliminated the felony murder doctrine altogether. Consider, for example, the redescriptive test as applied to the predicate felony of robbery. In the Model Penal Code, robbery is defined, among other things, as 'threaten[ing] another with . . . serious bodily injury' in the course of committing a theft.[36]

[34] Donald Davidson, *Essays on Actions and Events* (Oxford: Oxford University Press, 1980).

[35] As long, that is, as there is some description under which the defendant's action was intentional. This will hold whenever we have conduct we would ordinarily call *voluntary*, meaning that the defendant is not having an epileptic seizure or experiencing some other condition that produces the movement uncontrollably.

[36] MPC § 222.1(1)(b).

Suppose I hold up a liquor store. I point a gun at a cashier, and demand she hand over all the money in the cash register, threatening to shoot her if she does not comply. Just at that moment my gun accidentally discharges, and the cashier is killed. It would appear that my act of threatening the clerk had as one of its consequences that the gun discharged and the clerk was killed. Thus threatening the clerk with a gun can be redescribed as 'killing' and the predicate felony would merge with the homicide.[37] As long as there is causation between the defendant's felonious act and the homicide, the redescription should hold and it looks as though under this test the offense would merge. But a killing during an armed robbery is the classic case of felony murder.

The over-expansive result of the redescriptive test lies not with the formal structure of the test itself, but with the standard action-theoretic approach to redescription. In particular, orthodox action theory maintains that an act can be redescribed in terms of *all* of its consequences. But there seems reason to suspect that *sometimes* an act cannot be described in terms of its consequences. Consider the following case. A stabs B, with the result that B is seriously wounded and must be rushed to the hospital. While in the hospital, C, a malicious interloper, disguises himself as a surgeon and intentionally operates badly on B, with the result that B dies. B's dying is among the consequences of A's stabbing B. But did A kill B? I do not think he did. That is, in this case it does not seem right to redescribe A's act of stabbing as killing, in the same way that we might describe that action as 'wounding', 'causing pain', etc. Why does the redescription from consequence to act in this case not carry over? One response is suggested by the criminal lawyer's standard approach to such cases, which is to say that C's act 'breaks the chain of causation' between A's act and B's death. In general, lawyers say, the free, voluntary acts of another human being break the chain of causation. A is responsible for his own acts alone. He is not responsible for the voluntary acts of other people.

It is true that if A did not cause B's death, A could not have killed B, so that we could readily explain this case if the lawyers are right that intervening voluntary acts break the chain of causation. But I do not think the lawyers are right. For surely B's death is among the *consequences* of A's act. And what is a consequence of an act but an event or state that is caused by it? Indeed, to see that there is causation here, one has only to note that A's act was a necessary (but not sufficient) condition of B's death. And necessary conditions are always causes in some sense, even though there are cases in which it appears that something can be a cause of something else without its

[37] Of course, whether this is so might depend on exactly why the gun discharged. If it discharged because of some intentional movement of mine, however unintentional the gun's firing, then it is easy to see that the threatening of the clerk caused the gun to discharge which in turn caused the death of the clerk. If, on the other hand, the gun discharged as the result of a twitch or epileptic seizure on my part, then arguably it was not my commission of the felony that *caused* the victim's death, as the twitch functions as an intervening cause.

being a necessary condition for it (as in cases of overdetermination). So I doubt we should abandon the idea that A's stabbing is a cause of B's death, even though there is an intervening voluntary act that separates A's act from B's death. The lawyers are right that *something* is going on in this case that vitiates the connection between redescription and consequence. But we must perhaps restrict ourselves to saying that in some cases, a person's causal connection to an event does not suffice to establish a relation of agency between him and it. That is, there are cases in which A stabbed B, causing his death, but in which A did not kill B, since A's act cannot be redescribed in terms of B's death.

Philosophers might at this point attempt to elucidate the situation by drawing a distinction between A's being *a* cause of B's death and A's being *the* cause of B's death. In the former case, A is only one among many causal factors that leads to B's death, whereas in the latter case, A's participation is singled out as having a more significant role than most other factors that contributed to the result. But the distinction between *a* cause and *the* cause is not any more fundamental than the distinction between 'causing a death' and 'killing'. Indeed, the latter is more comprehensive and hence arguably more salient, given that something's being *a* cause, rather than *the* cause, is only one of the ways that 'causing' a death might fail to be a killing. So we are still left with the observation that not every causing of death counts as a killing, most notably in those cases where there is an intervening voluntary act of another human being.

It is important to see that not every intervening voluntary act 'breaks the redescriptive chain'. For suppose now that A stabs B, once again with the result that B is rushed to the hospital. This time, however, C performs a perfectly reasonable operation on B, which unfortunately causes (or is a cause of) B's death. (B has a complication due to the surgery which is not in any way C's fault.) In this case, it seems sensible to say that the redescription goes through: A's act of stabbing B is killing B, in view of the fact that *someone's* performing a high risk operation on B was a consequence of A's stabbing B that could reasonably have been expected. Thus stabbing B can be killing B, despite the fact that the stabbing was not sufficient, taken by itself, to cause B's death. There are, of course, grey area cases in between the two stabbing cases we considered. What if C's intervention is negligent, rather than either intentional or wholly accidental? Is A's act sufficiently implicated in B's death to say that A killed B in this case? Criminal lawyers are divided. Without resolving these in-between cases, however, the point remains that in some instances the intervening cause seems too insignificant for the redescription to succeed. In such a case, it would appear that the fact that A caused B's death is not a sufficient basis for thinking that A killed B.

Are there other cases where causing death is not a killing, other than those involving intervening voluntary acts of other agents? Another example would be a standard case of wayward causation: A shoots at B and misses, but the bullet takes an unlikely trajectory into a herd of wild boar, who in turn stampede B and kill him. Did A kill B? Possibly, although arguably not, despite the fact that A's act was a necessary condition for B's death. Once again, we might say that although A caused B's death, we cannot redescribe A's contribution to the situation as killing B, given the unlikely and unanticipated way in which this result came about. Further, there are cases of attenuated causation. Thus, for example, conceiving a child will eventually result in the child's death (hopefully when the child is a very old adult), but it surely is not killing him or her. Similarly, firing an employee may cause his children to starve. But it is not itself *starving the children*. Finally, although more controversially, there are cases of overdetermination, such as the three defendants and the classic hiker in the desert example. The first defendant poisons the water in the hiker's canteen; the second replaces the (poisoned) water with sand; the third puts a hole in the bottom of the canteen so that the contents drain out. It seems fair to say that each defendant 'caused' the hiker's death, namely that although each defendant 'killed' the hiker, none can be treated as having caused his death.[38]

Is there anything general we can say about when a person's act can be redescribed in terms of one of its consequences and when it cannot? This is not an easy task, and it is unlikely to be a matter that can be settled on the present occasion. There is, however, a common characteristic with the cases where redescription fails: these all appear to be cases involving some unusual intervention occurred, namely some occurrence that does not seem to come along in the ordinary course of events.[39] The intentional wrongful conduct of an interloper belongs in this category (even if it is wrongdoing that is to be expected), for A is surely absolved of responsibility for *killing* B in the case in which C maliciously performs a wrongful operation, even if A thought such officious intermeddling likely. The intentional, wrongful acts of another are like a freak occurrence, in that the original defendant is entitled to assume they will not occur. The same can be said for the herd of wild boar and cases of attenuated causation: there is no reason to suppose that shooting in the direction of a potential victim will result in stampede that will kill someone, or that firing an employee will result in his children starving. And, holding the specific causal chain fixed by which death occurred, there is no reason to suppose that putting a hole in someone's canteen will result in his dying at the hands of a person who poisons the water or replaces it with sand, and the same can be said from the standpoint of each defendant. So we might say that the unexpected or normatively

[38] This is perhaps controversial. I can imagine someone arguing just the opposite, namely that although each hiker contributed causally to the result, none can be treated as the killer in this case.

[39] The proposal is not perfect, since the couple that conceives a child should surely not be thought to have killed the child in doing so. But arguably the act of conceiving a child could not be *killing* that child, since surely it is not possible to kill someone who does not yet exist. So this is perhaps a special case.

deviant nature of the relation between act and consequence in these cases is what ultimately breaks the redescriptive chain.[40]

Once we allow for the possibility that some causal consequences fail to generate redescriptions, the redescriptive test for merger fares better. Where I assault someone by punching him in the nose, my act of punching can be redescribed as 'killing', and merger will apply. But arguably, where I threaten the clerk with death if she does not hand over the money, it is only in an attenuated sense that my threat causes the death of the clerk. It is true that *but for* the threat, the clerk would not have died. But death results from my threatening the clerk via a fairly circuitous trajectory, similar to the shooting that causes the herd of wild boar to stampede. If this is correct, then the act of threatening cannot be redescribed in terms of the death and it can therefore serve as the predicate felony for the homicide. Let us consider how the revised test handles several other difficult cases.

Suppose a defendant kidnaps a child from her backyard, and, after some elapse of time, he has a car accident with the child in the car and she dies. Does the kidnapping provide the predicate felony for the homicide? Or should the kidnapping and the homicide be thought to merge? Unlawfully removing a person from her home does not carry death with it as among the ordinary consequences of the act. Indeed, being killed in a car accident is still, fortunately, a relatively rare event. Once again, the relation between the defendant's act of driving the victim away from her home and the defendant's killing of the victim is attenuated—at least as attenuated as the relationship between threatening the clerk and the clerk's death. Thus there is a basis for thinking that the kidnapping does not merge and felony murder should be available.

Moreover, in the kidnapping case there is a further point to notice. The removal of the victim from her home has already occurred once the defendant kills the victim. There is thus an independent reason to think that the act whereby the defendant commits the predicate felony of kidnapping is not the same act whereby he kills the victim, since those two acts are significantly separated in time and place. The 'redescriptive break' in this case is created by the defendant's own later voluntary act; his later self is like the officious intermeddler in the hospital who performs the wrongful operation relative to his earlier self! Notice that the causation requirement for felony murder is satisfied in such a case, even though the act whereby the defendant commits the predicate felony is not itself the cause of the victim's death. While the defendant cannot be prosecuted for felony murder if he

[40] The above account squares with the treatment offered by Hart and Honoré in their *Causation in the Law* for when an intervening cause breaks the chain of causation. Hart and Honoré suggest that the causal chain is broken when the intervening act is either the wrongful act of another competent agent or the intervening factor is an abnormal event or 'coincidence': *Causation in the Law* (2nd ed., Oxford: Oxford University Press, 1989), 68 ff. For the reasons I have offered above, however, it seems to me more helpful to speak of redescription than of causation.

did not cause the victim's death, he need not have caused it *by* committing the felonious act itself. Indeed, notice that the defendant would be liable for the victim's death if the car accident occurred while he was trying to return the victim to her home, having had a change of heart. It is thus sufficient for liability that the act that caused the victim's death occurred in the course of the commission of the predicate felony. It need not be the case that the act that is the basis for finding the defendant guilty of the predicate felony is itself the cause of the death.

What about the more difficult, in-between cases with which we began? Consider the felony child abuse cases. If an adult uses extreme physical force against a child, with the result that the child dies, there is every reason to think that the redescriptive test succeeds: The act of violence whereby the adult harms the child is also an act of killing. The predicate felony of abuse thus merges with the homicide. Notice that it should make no difference on this account what the adult's purpose was in attacking the child. If the adult engages in a physical assault of a child for the purpose of disciplining a child, the act is causally no different from an assault undertaken for a different purpose. Since redescription travels along causal lines, the defendant's purposes are not relevant to settling the question of merger. Moreover, the exceptions to redescription based on causation, namely unusual events, coincidences, and voluntary intervening acts, do not themselves vary depending on the defendant's purposes. So it makes sense to reject the 'purpose test' we considered above. Furthermore, the same must be said of the child abuse cases where the parent allows the child to starve or freeze to death: in such cases, the failure to feed a child produces the consequence that the child dies. And since it is a natural consequence of failing to feed a child (however unintentional) that the child will die, the redescription from 'failing to feed' to 'killing' cannot be blocked by unusual or coincidental circumstances and the child abuse will merge with the homicide.

Another close case was that in which the defendant breaks into a dwelling with the purpose of assaulting someone inside. Should the burglary be thought to supply the predicate felony for the homicide? The question is whether the relevant act identified in that prohibition—'entering a dwelling with intent to commit a crime therein'—can be reasonably redescribed as killing. While courts have been murky on this point and the matter has remained subject to much doubt, the redescriptive test would appear to be unambiguous: entering a dwelling, even when the purpose is to bring about a later killing, cannot itself be redescribed as killing. Why not? Once again, the defendant's own later voluntary act (of attacking, assaulting, or killing) breaks the redescriptive chain from entering a dwelling to the victim's death. The defendant did not cause himself to kill the victim by entering the dwelling. It would follow that the burglary in this case can supply the predicate felony for the homicide and felony murder applies. Notice once again that the defendant's *purpose* in entering the dwelling is irrelevant. And this has the benefit of rationalizing the cases that deal with this type of fact pattern, since it seemed arbitary to distinguish the defendant who breaks into a house in order to assault someone from the defendant who breaks into the house to steal some jewelry and ends up killing someone in the process.[41]

Notice, further, that once we have the redescriptive test in place, we can entirely dispense with the inherently dangerous requirement, as well as with a series of rather byzantine requirements that courts also sometimes impose for making sure there is an adequate causal connection between the predicate felony and the killing. There should be no objection to allowing lesser felonies to serve as the predicate if those felonies satisfy the other requirements for felony murder prosecutions. The felonies we should exclude from the class of predicate felonies are those where the predicate felony is so closely linked to the victim's death that we cannot identify the defendant as engaging in two separate wrongful acts. This has nothing to do with the dangerousness of the predicate felony. Indeed, if anything, the dangerous felonies will be the ones that more directly give rise to the victim's death, and so more easily support merger. Thus the imposition of an inherently dangerous requirement tends to get matters backwards. Moreover, it need not be the case that the predicate felony is the cause of the killing—even in the loose sense of cause that lawyers employ when they articulate the notion of 'proximate cause'. For it should be sufficient if the killing takes places roughly 'in the course' of the commission of the predicate felony, given that a defendant's own later act breaks the chain of causation in any event.

Before closing this section, we must address two features of the proposed redescriptive test that will undoubtedly strike some as peculiar. First, a certain paradigmatic case for felony murder will now be a case in which the felony merges with the homicide. For example, suppose the defendant engages in a crime like arson with the result that he causes the death of an occupant of the structure he burns. In many jurisdictions, both common law and statutory, the arson would supply the predicate felony for the homicide and the offense would not merge. This would be the result, for example, under the purpose-based test, assuming that the defendant's purpose is the destruction of property and not the loss of human life. Thus in the *Murphy*

[41] The exception to this might be a case in which the very opening of the window engaged in as the first step of entering the victim's dwelling somehow triggers the victim's death, because, say, it trips a spring gun which malfunctions and kills the victim. But if the tripping of the spring gun was a highly unusual event that intervened between the defendant's act and the victim's death, the redescriptive chain is once again broken and the predicate felony would not merge.

case we considered earlier, there would be reason to think that the court was wrong to reject the argument for merger taken from *Garrett*. Under a newly clarified 'same act' test, the arson in this case would merge with the homicide and could not serve as the predicate felony for a felony murder prosecution.

Or consider a California case, *People v Billa*,[42] where the defendant participated in a scheme with two co-conspirators to defraud an insurance company by burning a truck. In the course of setting the fire, one of the co-conspirators was fatally burned. The court rejected the defendant's argument that the arson should merge with the homicide, citing *Burton* and the independent felonious purpose test: 'the merger rule is limited in application to situations in which the purpose of inflicting violent injury is the single purpose or single course of conduct in which the perpetrator engages'.[43] Under the redescriptive analysis, however, the defendant's argument in *Billa* would have been correct: the act of setting the truck on fire is easily describable as killing under these circumstances, given that there was nothing freakish about the causal route from setting the fire to the burning and subsequent death of the victim. The redescriptive test will thus usually produce the result that arson merges with the homicide, even though arson is not an 'assaultive' offense.

This may seem a counterintuitive result, particularly in cases like *Murphy* and *Billa* where the motive for the offense is economic. But setting a building or a truck on fire is a highly dangerous activity, one that may very well lead to a loss of human life in the ordinary course of events. And this is so regardless of the defendant's specific purpose in setting the fire. Thus it seems reasonable to think that in most cases arson will be analyzable in the same way that assault is, and that the predicate felony will merge with the homicide. And once again this shows the tension between the usual inherently dangerous requirement for predicate felonies and the merger rule: since the felonies most likely to merge are felonies involving dangerous activities (such as assault and arson), we will end up eliminating felony murder altogether if we maintain both requirements at once. As we have found a basis for making sense of the merger doctrine, and the inherently dangerous rule continues to seem ad hoc, we should eliminate the inherently dangerous rule in favor of the revised merger rule I have presented.

A second counterintuitive feature of the redescriptive test is also worth emphasizing. Unlike the approach of most courts to merger, the redescriptive test will produce different results for a given predicate felony depending on the act in virtue of which the defendant satisfies the offense definition. In

[42] 102 Cal. App. 4th 822 (2002).
[43] *Id.* at 834.

nearly all cases of assault, the predicate felony will merge, because the assaultive act in virtue of which the defendant satisfies the offense definition is the same act that quite naturally gives rise to the victim's death. But crimes like arson, burglary, poisoning, kidnapping, and child abuse may vary, depending on the underlying facts. Thus a defendant who is found to commit burglary because he *remains* in a building for the purpose of committing an assault, where the assault results in the victim's death, will probably not be chargeable with felony murder, since the act in virtue of which he commits burglary is the same as the act in virtue of which he causes the death of the victim. But a person who actually hoists a window open and enters from the street for the purpose of committing an assault will probably be chargeable with felony murder, since his act—entering a building with intent to commit a crime—is itself separate from the later act in virtue of which the defendant causes the death of the victim. The difference may seem a fine one, but it is not arbitrary: the defendant in the first case satisfies the offense definition for burglary by killing the victim, whereas the defendant in the second case must do something *else* in order to be guilty of the burglary, other than kill the victim.

Finally, there is an important objection to this account we should consider, which we might call the 'double assault' case. Suppose the defendant punches the victim in the nose, and after a brief interval, he does so again. The victim unexpectedly dies from the second blow. Could we say that the first assault is the predicate felony for the killing, and thus bootstrap the assault into murder without having to prove that the defendant intended to kill the victim? All the requirements seem to be present: there are two separate acts, and the defendant's later voluntary act breaks the redescriptive chain. However, if this is so, will it not be the case that nearly all assault cases resulting in homicide can be treated as cases of felony-murder? How often, after all, does the defendant actually kill the victim with a single act?

Dealing with the double assault case will force us to accept a slight modification of the redescriptive test, for it does not seem acceptable to say that a first assault out of two can serve as the predicate felony for a homicide. Where there are two acts of the defendant's of the same type, followed in quick succession by one another, we should regard the defendant as engaged in a single activity and treat the merger requirement for felony murder as not met. That is, in the double assault case, if the blows are in sufficiently quick succession, it makes sense to think of the defendant as engaged in one activity (viz., attacking the victim), and to treat these as one act for purposes of the redescriptive test. Then we can say that it was the defendant's attack that killed the victim, that the attack can be redescribed as killing, and the test for merger is met.

4. Other Applications of the Redescriptive Test

The problem of merger may seem an obscure one in the jurisprudence of criminal law. But once the problem is understood as a question about whether the defendant has performed one act or two, it can be easily shown to belong to a family of problems that turn on this same question. And just as the action-theoretic foundation of the doctrine of merger has been obscured by judicial decisions on the topic of felony murder, so the action theoretic foundations of these corresponding problems in the criminal law have also been missed.

In the area of double jeopardy doctrine, for example, courts have repeatedly focused on the criminal charges to which defendants are subject in deciding whether the defendant is subject to multiple prosecutions for the 'same offense'. And the prevailing test, as established in *Blockburger*, is whether each of two offenses with which the defendant has been charged contains an element that the other offense does not contain. If so, the offenses are thought to pass double jeopardy scrutiny and otherwise not. But this conception of double jeopardy law has led to an odd result, namely that what is supposed to be a constitutional protection against state infringement on personal liberty is in fact itself subject to, and determined by, the very state law it is supposed to protect individuals against. For whether a person can be punished twice for the same conduct depends after *Blockburger* entirely on the definition the state chooses to use in criminalizing the conduct. A state is thus free to prosecute a defendant multiple times for the same conduct, as long as it invents crimes with non-overlapping elements to define the relevant offenses. As I have argued elsewhere, whether a prosecution violates the double jeopardy provision should depend instead on whether the defendant is being prosecuted twice for the *same underlying act or set of acts*.[44] The redescriptive test will tell us when two acts are the same and when they are different in this context as well.

Indeed, consider the relation between our problem of merger and a typical problem of double jeopardy that arises in the felony murder context. Courts have long been uncertain whether a defendant may be punished *both* for the predicate felony and for the murder in a case in which a defendant is convicted of felony murder. May a defendant, for example, be punished separately for armed robbery and for murder if the defendant kills in the course of committing a robbery? The more common answer is that this would violate the Double Jeopardy Clause, on the ground that the elements of the predicate felony are contained within the crime of felony murder, and that the *Blockburger* requirement that each offense contain an element the other does not contain is not satisfied. But courts

[44] See Claire Finkelstein, 'Positivism about the Notion of An Offense' (2000) 88 *California Law Review* 335.

have not been consistent about this approach. Some, for example, say that the predicate felony can be punished separately if it appears that the legislature intended that result.[45] They thus allow successive punishment for robbery and felony murder based on robbery. Insofar as the question of merger in felony murder and the question of double jeopardy should both turn on an analysis of the underlying acts the defendant committed, however, these problems will admit of a common solution: any case where the predicate felony is distinct from the act that caused the victim's death is both a case in which felony murder can be prosecuted *and* a case in which punishment for both the predicate felony and the murder would not be duplicative. For the question in the double jeopardy area should be whether the defendant is being punished more than once *for the same set of criminally prohibited acts*, not whether the legislature has happened to slice up the definition of the offenses for those acts in a sufficiently fine-grained way that the same acts make the defendant guilty of different offenses.

The redescriptive test should also help solve a family of problems that have arisen under the common law doctrine of what is also called 'merger'. May a defendant be tried and punished both for a conspiracy to commit a crime and for the crime itself? For an attempt to commit a crime and the crime itself? For soliciting an offense and for the offense itself? For attempting an offense and for soliciting or conspiring to commit it? That there should be a common law doctrine of merger makes perfect sense if our analysis is act rather than offense-based. A defendant should not be punished for two offenses if the defendant's commission of those offenses depends entirely upon the defendant's performance of the same act or set of acts. The results of the redescriptive test would be consistent with our intuitions. Conspiracy usually requires the defendant to have done something over and above the thing he must have done in order to be guilty of the substantive offense itself, so a prosecution for conspiracy can coexist with a prosecution for the substantive offense. But this is not so where attempt is concerned, and usually not where solicitation is concerned either. On an act-based analysis, however, double jeopardy and merger should produce the same results.

A more far-flung application of the redescriptive test is found in relation to the thorny problem of whether contrived involuntariness should count for purposes of establishing the involuntary act defense. The question is whether a person who arranges, for example, that he kill his wife under hypnotic suggestion can be thought of as having killed her at all, given that he does so in a state that would normally be exonerating as involuntary. As I have argued elsewhere,[46] the problem requires us to decide whether the

[45] *Todd v Alaska*, 917 P.2d 674 (1996).

[46] See Claire Finkelstein, 'Involuntary Crimes, Voluntarily Committed', in S Shute and A P Simester (eds.), *Criminal Law Theory: Doctrines of the General Part* (Oxford: Oxford University Press, 2002), 143.

act of going to the hypnotist can itself be redescribed as *killing*, since a man cannot be prosecuted for a death if he did not himself perform the killing (or arrange for the killing to be performed by another voluntary agent). If the hypnotic state is a sufficiently unusual intervening event, the redescription will not go through and the man does not kill his wife when he goes to a hypnotist. But if the intervening event is sufficiently ordinary, the redescription will work and the man kills his wife in going to the hypnotist.[47]

It is difficult to know in these obscure cases how precisely the redescriptive test is to be applied. Is the person, like *Decina*, who drives knowing he is subject to epileptic seizures guilty of manslaughter, when he has an epileptic seizure behind the wheel and kills several children?[48] That would depend on whether his driving, knowing he is subject to epileptic seizures, is itself redescribable as 'killing the children'. And *that* will depend on whether the intervening event of his seizure is sufficiently unusual that it breaks the 'redescriptive chain' from driving to killing. Does sleepwalking Mrs. Cogdon kill her daughter 'voluntarily' when she brings an axe down on her head in the middle of the night?[49] That depends on whether the act of going to sleep, knowing she is subject to sleepwalking, can itself be redescribed as killing her daughter. The redescriptive test at least provides a clear framework for answering the foregoing questions. Unlike in the cases we have been considering in connection with merger and felony murder, however, it is particularly difficult to determine whether the redescription holds where voluntariness is concerned. In this regard, however, the difficulty applying the redescriptive test matches the underlying difficulty of the legal question, and so the lack of clear results is not surprising. What is needed in all of these doctrines is a clearer understanding of the notion of an act and the role that acts play in judgments of criminal responsibility. While the analysis I have provided here will not solve all of the problems associated with the various doctrines related to the notion of an act, it should at least go some distance towards improving our understanding of how an act-based analysis can function in the criminal law.

[47] It may seem curious to suggest that a man can kill his wife at time t_1, when at t_1 the wife is still alive. Do we not have to wait until the time at which the wife is really dead to say that her husband *killed* her? And does it not follow from that that the man in question cannot have killed his wife at t_1? The answer is that it does not follow—from the fact that we may not know at t_1 that a man has killed his wife, it does not follow that he has not killed her at that time, despite the fact that she is still alive. At some later time, t_2, we can look back at t_1 and say, 'that is the moment at which he killed her', despite the fact that we did not know at that time that that is what he had done. For a more thorough discussion of the difficulties here, see Judith Thomson, 'The Time of a Killing' (1971) 68 *Journal of Philosophy* 115.

[48] See *People v Decina*, 138 N.E. 2d 799 (1956).

[49] See Finkelstein, above n. 46, at 143.

Index

Note: Names are not indexed if they appear only in footnote citations